19/72

THE HISTORICAL STUDY OF AFRICAN RELIGION

Published under the Auspices of
the African Studies Center
University of California, Los Angeles

The Historical Study of African Religion

edited by

T. O. RANGER
Professor of History, University of California, Los Angeles

and

I. N. KIMAMBO
Professor of History, University of Dar es Salaam

UNIVERSITY OF CALIFORNIA PRESS
BERKELEY AND LOS ANGELES   1972

University of California Press
Berkeley and Los Angeles, California

ISBN: 0-520-02206-8
Library of Congress Catalog Card Number: 76-186104

© T. O. Ranger and Isaria Kimambo 1972
First published 1972

Printed in Great Britain

Preface

This book springs from the Dar es Salaam conference on the historical study of African religious systems which took place in June 1970. It does not, however, constitute the proceedings of that conference. Some admirable papers have been omitted and some panel discussions have not been reproduced. The conference was originally planned to deal with the religious history of all sub-Saharan Africa. But in practice there were fewer papers dealing with West Africa than with East and Central Africa and it was generally agreed that no publication emerging from the conference could hope to do justice to the history of West African religious systems. Thus this book, long as it is, reproduces only those conference papers dealing with the religious history of East and Central Africa.

The editors of this book have many people to thank. The conference itself was generously supported by the University of Dar es Salaam and by the African Studies Centre of the University of California, Los Angeles. It was financed by a grant from the Ford Foundation through the UCLA Committee on International and Comparative Studies. Many people worked hard to organise it and to run it and we owe especial thanks to Mrs Thelma Albuquerque, Dr John Iliffe and Dr Israel Katoke of the University of Dar es Salaam. The Conference meetings themselves were the most open, candid and charitable of academic occasions and we extend once more our greetings and our gratitude to all those who took part in them. Finally, we owe a very great deal to Miss Jocelyn Murray, who was an indefatigable conference secretary and who has been the sub-editor of this book.

T. O. RANGER
I. N. KIMAMBO

Contents

vii

CONTENTS

viii

List of Maps

Introduction

The Dar es Salaam conference on the historical study of African religion was consciously taking part in an artificial, even a distorting enterprise. It separated the topic of African religion from the topics of African politics, economics and social institutions. And it separated the topic of African 'traditional' religion from those of African Islam and Christianity.

Obviously there are profound senses in which such separations cannot and should not be made. Thus in February 1971 a group of Africanists who agreed that 'the study of religion in African societies, far too often neglected, is absolutely essential to the understanding of the dynamics of African societies', nevertheless went on to criticise the organisational assumptions of the Dar conference. They pointed out that it was dangerous to isolate the 'religious' from the secular 'because of the difficulty of defining religion in a society where there may be no direct translation of the English word "religion" '. They asserted that 'it seemed pointless to exclude Islam and Christianity simply because their historical origins were elsewhere . . . Christianity and Islam in Africa are African religions because African societies define themselves as practitioners of those religions.'[1]

With these propositions the editors of this book agree. There *is* no satisfactory definition of religion which allows us to separate it from political or economic or social life; nor can it be maintained seriously that Islam and Christianity have not become African religions in the fullest sense. It was no part of our intention as conference organisers to stimulate the emergence of a distinct discipline of African religious history, nor to circumscribe the study of African religious phenomena. But at the same time we believed that this artificial exercise was a necessary one and that the distortions which it might produce were less dangerous than the distortions which might continue unless it was undertaken.

African historical study has arisen and developed at a time when a holistic approach to historiography is the ideal. It is easy—and justified—for African historians to congratulate themselves on having avoided a division into sub-disciplines of African constitutional, intellectual, economic, social, political history. It is easy, also, for African historians to congratulate themselves on the inter-disciplinary character of their work and on their readiness to draw upon the insights of anthropology and linguistics and political science.

African historiography appears more open and more inclusive than many longer established branches of the discipline. And yet at the same time African historical studies have been narrow in their focus. Essentially they have been political studies—studies of the rise of state systems, or of the response of *polities* to European intrusion, or of colonial administrative systems, or of African nationalism. Concentration on topics like these was inevitable given the circumstances out of which African historical studies grew and given the nature of the source material, for much oral traditional evidence has turned out to be as preoccupied with the institution and development of administrative bureaucracies as are the colonial archives themselves. Not only was this concentration inevitable—it was also desirable. It has produced work of major importance and it has provided us with a skeletal outline for African history.

Still, it will be readily agreed that if it is impossible to abstract *religious* history from political or economic or social history without distortion, so it should also be impossible to abstract *political* history without a similar distortion. Yet this has all too often happened. At the worst we have had histories which appear to have been written on the assumption that only political institutions and external trade relationships changed in pre-colonial Africa, and that it is possible to discuss religious or social concepts and structures in terms of some eternal and unchanging 'world view' of the peoples under study. Even the most sensitive historians have tended either to rely too heavily on anthropological insights, which for all their richness and penetration have rarely been historical in intention, or else to assume that any religious changes that did take place occurred as the result of political change and political need.

It seemed desirable, then, to emphasise the possibility of historical study of the so-called 'traditional' African religious systems, not in order that this might be carried on as a separate activity, but in order that it might be re-integrated with African historiography as a whole.

A similar emphasis seemed necessary in the field of African Religious Studies, from which many of the conference participants were drawn. Of course, no one could accuse the various Departments of Religious Studies in Africa of having neglected the study of African 'traditional' religion. The recent work, *African Religions and Philosophy* by Professor John Mbiti, for example, is enough in itself to refute such an accusation. Yet from a historian's point of view some of the work on African religion which has emerged from the context of African Religious Studies has been alarming. Professor Mbiti himself is at pains to tell us that in a strict sense African religions have no histories – no founders, no missionaries, no converts, no prophets, no martyrs. More than this—the philosophical systems of African religions are a-historical, even anti-historical, based as they are upon a view of time which makes any historical view of the world impossible

The need to demonstrate the *possibility* of African religious history emerges even more clearly from Dr Parrinder's recent survey, *Religion in Africa*. The book has been generally well received; it makes an attempt precisely to avoid the separate treatment of 'traditional' religion, of Islam and of Christianity. But this attempt is undercut by Parrinder's renunciation of the possibility of a historical approach to African 'traditional' religion. He gives us an almost exclusively narrative history of Islam and Christianity, hardly pausing to analyse them in their various African forms, but his treatment of African 'traditional' religion is purely descriptive and in the idiom of a timeless ethnographic present. Thus his book cannot help reinforcing the distorting impression of the dynamic 'historic' religions of Islam and Christianity confronting passive traditional cosmologies.[3]

Parrinder's book has provoked Professor B. A. Ogot to an eloquent programmatic statement. Ogot is inclined to see the argument of 'the difficulty—nay, the impossibility of reconstructing a history of the traditional religion' as merely another form of 'the old excuse employed for a long time by Western scholars to deny the existence and authenticity of African history'. He continues: 'African traditional religions are, after all, an aspect of African societies, and a very significant aspect at that . . . If it is possible, as Parrinder admits, to write an economic or a political history of a pre-literate society, why can one not write a religious history of that same society?'[4]

The Dar es Salaam conference was an attempt to respond to Ogot's challenge. In the case studies which follow the reader will find founders and proselytisers and converts and prophets; the missionologists will find at least an inkling of the possibility of exploring the 'salvation history' of Africa as well as of Europe. For the purposes of this attempt we separated out African 'traditional' religion from Islam and Christianity precisely because at one level it is all too easy to treat *them* historically.[5]

Of course, as will be seen, we did not exclude them altogether; some of the studies in this book deal with their interaction with 'traditional' religious ideas and structures. And of course we hope for treatments of the religious history of Africa which are illumined by a full consciousness of the historicity of the whole range of African beliefs and practices.

The bulk of this book consists of a series of specific studies which demonstrate what can be achieved if historical questions are asked about religious ideas and institutions in African societies. The authors of these case studies would be the first to urge that they represent initial rather than definitive attempts to answer such questions. We believe, however, that they do demonstrate the potential of this approach. Moreover, in their range of interests and sources they represent accurately the growing points of historical inquiry into East and Central African religious history.

We have grouped the studies into Parts two to six each representing a major theme or cluster of themes. We wish to give a brief introductory summary on each, and also on the methodological papers which precede them.

PART ONE: METHODS FOR THE RECONSTRUCTION OF EARLY RELIGIOUS HISTORY

The case studies in this book all have something in common which distinguishes them from nineteenth-century historical speculations about African religion. Nineteenth century speculations were mainly concerned with what happened at the very beginnings; with the emergence of religion as such. By definition they could never really be historical because they could never really have historical rather than inductive evidence. The case studies in this book are concerned with a confessedly late stage of the religious history of Africa. None of them attempt to go back beyond their evidential sources and their evidential sources are all either oral traditional or archival. Thus although this Introduction, and the papers themselves to a lesser degree, indulge in much speculation and raise questions which cannot be settled on the evidence, it is important to stress that a fundamental aspect of the new interest in African religious history is the determination that it should be evidentially based at least as thoroughly

3

as historical studies of pre-colonial African political systems have been. No doubt that is why five of the ten case studies deal with events which have taken place in the last hundred years and which are illuminated by very extensive archival as well as oral evidence.[6]

But the conference did not wish merely to shy away from the past errors of study of African religion. It did not wish merely to abandon the prospect of some sort of reconstruction of African religious history in the period before either oral or archival sources are available. For this reason, although there are no case studies in this book which attempt such a reconstruction, the conference was able to discuss the possibility of it through the presentation of three remarkable papers on method. These papers set out to examine ways in which other types of evidence could legitimately be used for the reconstruction of African religious history, while at the same time stressing the ways in which they should *not* be used. The papers by Michael Gilsenan on the interpretation and use of myth, by Merrick Posnansky on the deductions on religious history that can legitimately be based on archaeology, and by Christopher Ehret on the techniques by which historical linguistics can illumine the development and spread of religious ideas, really speak for themselves.

But although we do not feel that they require much introductory commentary we do not wish in any way to give the impression that we regard them as less significant than the case study papers. In fact work along the same sort of lines as the case studies is already actively under way. If there is to be a further break-through in the field of African religious history it will come through the rigorous application of these and other methods for the recovery of developments beyond the reach of oral and archival evidence. We very much hope that some readers of this book will be inspired by these papers to equip themselves to carry out the kind of research which is needed.

PART TWO: CULTS OF KINGSHIP

The one topic in East and Central African religious history which *has* found its way into a good deal of historical writing is the idea of 'divine kingship' and of 'Sudanic monarchy'. It will be remembered that it has been argued that there was an essential similarity in the institutions of royal states over very wide areas of sub-Saharan Africa; that this essential similarity is seen most clearly in the common or identical religious institutions of these monarchies; and that these religious and monarchical institutions diffused westwards and southwards from the eastern Sudan and adjacent areas.[7]

It is no longer necessary seriously to contest this view, nor its classification of state systems on the basis of religious institutions alone. Several writers have argued cogently that even where cultic similarities exist, differences in bureau-cratic recruitment or in succession mechanisms produce state systems of widely different kinds. But in addition Professor Jan Vansina and others have demon-strated that there are striking differences in the *religious* structures of different Central African state systems and differences which arise not only from the contrasting patterns of belief and practice outside the central royal cult but also from the contrasting conceptual and organisational patterns of royal cults themselves. Yet the discrediting of the idea of the Sudanic state and of the diffusion from a single region of cults of kingship has left the whole important topic of these royal cults in something of a void.[8]

Two of the case studies presented to the Dar conference concerned themselves with this problem. Though dealing with specific cases they raised questions of wider significance. Thus Dr Matthew Schoffeleers' paper throws much light on the problem of the origin of a number of the royal cults of Central Africa even although it is concerned with only one of them, the M'Bona cult of the Lower Shire Valley of Malawi. In his earlier work Schoffeleers has made clear that the symbolic apparatus of the M'Bona cult is in many ways strikingly similar to that of the cult centres of Dzivaguru in north-eastern Rhodesia, or of Mwari in south-western Rhodesia, or of other such centres in Mozambique and the Transvaal. It seems plain that on one level a common symbolic 'system' exists in this wide area. The question is how these similarities are to be explained.[9]

At first sight they can be explained relatively easily in terms of the spread of a certain kind of kingship or chiefship. These cults were for centuries royal cults, associated with the notion of the spiritual power of the dead kings, to whom sacrifices were made at the cult centres. Thus the M'Bona cult has been for centuries the 'official' cult of the Lundu 'kings'; the Dzivaguru cult was one of the key religious institutions of the Mwene Mutapa empire and linked with the system of spirit mediumship for the incarnation of dead monarchs; the Mwari cult gave spiritual support to the Rozvi empire. In none of them was the presiding spiritual figure held to be the spirit of a dead king but rather the High God himself, as in the case of Mwari, or of his prophetic spokesmen, as in the case of M'Bona. But in all the theology of the High God and of his powers of creativity and fertility was combined with the theology of kingship and of the essential role that the kings, dead and alive, played in maintaining the health of the land. Closely associated with kingship as they were it has sometimes been suggested that these cults and the symbols and rites and ideas which characterise them were brought into the Central African area by the migrating groups who imposed or developed kingship there.[10]

Schoffeleers' paper throws serious doubts on this explanation. Admittedly it shows that the influence of the M'Bona cult spread into new areas as these were conquered by the Lundu kings, who in this way undoubtedly diffused the symbols and myths of the cult. But obviously this was a secondary diffusion, having nothing to do with the cultic similarities existing over a much wider area. And Schoffeleers shows that *in origin* the M'Bona cult long preceded the Lundu monarchy or, indeed, monarchy of any kind.

He shows that once we get behind the 'establishment' Lundu tradition of the cult and its origins, it is possible to find layers of other traditions which associate the M'Bona cult with the systems which existed in the Lower Shire Valley before the Lundu state. He shows that the cult was associated with the rule of the chiefs of the Phiri clan who preceded Lundu; he shows that the cult existed among the Mang'anja peoples of that area before the emergence of kingship or chiefship; he shows, indeed, that it existed even before the movement of the Mang'anja peoples themselves into the Lower Shire Valley. In origin, then, the M'Bona cult was not a cult of kingship. It *became* a royal cult through submission to the power of the successive Phiri rulers and only then did sacrifice to the spirits of dead kings and chiefs come to take a central place in its ritual. The essential similarities between the cult and centres elsewhere in Central Africa concern such things as the symbolic lay-out of the cult headquarters, the balance of symbols of earth and sky, and so on, rather than such things as the mode of associating kingship with the cult. (Indeed there were important differences in the ways that the spirits of dead kings and chiefs were assimilated into the cults of M'Bona, Dzivaguru and Mwari.) And these essential similarities appear to date from a very early period, before the development of monarchy.

This approach seems likely to prove fruitful not only for the history of the M'Bona cult but for the religious history of Rhodesia and Mozambique also. It seems highly probable that there also the great royal cults emerged as the result of the imposition of control by kings over pre-existing High God or prophetic centres. There is a marked similarity between the founding myth of the Lundu version of M'Bona and the founding myth of the Mwene Mutapa version of Dzivaguru. In both the king is shown in contest with a prophet figure of marvellous powers; in both the prophet is killed on the orders of the king; in both the king is shown as establishing a shrine to the spirit of the prophet after his death. Schoffeleers demonstrates that what happened in the Malawian case was that the first Lundu king was in contest with the priests of the long existing M'Bona cult centre rather than with 'M'Bona' himself, and that so far from initiating a shrine he took over political control of the already established cult. It seems very probable that the Mwene Mutapa was similarly in contest with an established priesthood and that through this victory the cult of Dzivaguru *became* a royal cult.

The High God, Mwari, cannot be killed by kings. In the case of the oracular cult of Mwari the processes of imposition of royal control were probably more comparable to those that Schoffeleers describes for the dominance established by the Chewa rulers over the High God centres of Malawi. But it seems most likely that the Mwari cult developed in south western Rhodesia rather than being carried from Kilimanjaro or lake Tanganyika by migrating groups, as has been suggested by scholars. And it seems most likely that the influence of the cult preceded the rise of Rozvi kingship.

Such an interpretation leaves us with a number of questions. If the spread of 'divine monarchy' did not produce symbolic similarity over a wide area, what did? If these 'royal cults' were created by the capture of pre-existing cult centres, what did that process involve in both political and religious terms?

Schoffeleers' paper does not address itself to the first of these questions, though it throws much light on the second. But one of the other papers presented to the conference does help us to conceptualise the situation in Central Africa before the rise of the monarchies. Gilbert Gwassa's paper deals with the early twentieth century. But it deals with an area, the southern Tanzanian area, in which widely influential cult centres of fertility exist but where monarchical structures have not developed. Mr Gwassa discusses the operation of the various centres of the Bokero or Kolelo cult at which priestly mediums attend the shrines of divinities who are held capable of giving rain and fertility and success. He shows that they attracted clients over quite wide areas despite the lack of centralised political institutions. These cult centres were in no senses 'royal', though they were associated with particular clans. It seems reasonable to hazard that they originated with early agricultural settlement and owed their common symbolism both to the common concerns and beliefs of agricultural peoples and to the complex patterns of movement and interaction which characterised the agricultural opening up of the southern Tanzanian region. Analogies over such wide areas of time and space are dangerous but perhaps the fact of the extensive influence of the Kolelo cult centres may help us to think back to the pre-Lundu cult of M'Bona. We may guess that the M'Bona cult enjoyed similarly wide influence before the rise of the Phiri kingdoms and that the spread of the cult's reputation under Lundu was probably a reinforcement or a redirection rather than an innovation.

Nothing could be further from the purpose of Dr Schoffeleers' paper, however, nor from the purpose of this book as a whole, than to suggest that the most important thing about the M'Bona cult and its fellow cult systems was an unchanging continuity from the period of early agricultural settlement. Schoffeleers' paper is essentially about change, about the modifications and developments which occurred within one cult as the result of its exposure to a whole series of pressures from different interests over the centuries.

The most obvious changes described by Schoffeleers are organisational ones. There is no need to reiterate them here. But what is particularly interesting from the point of view of African religious history is the suggestion which emerges that such organisational changes could be accompanied, in a sense had to be accompanied, by mythical and symbolic changes as well. The take-over of cults by kings involved, of course, the development of a royal theology. But perhaps it also helped to stress religious themes of wider significance. The myth of M'Bona or of Dzivaguru as the martyr, the Rwandan myths of the ruler who 'redeems' through defeat and death which Dr Gilsenan discusses in his paper, obviously have theological as well as political implications. In a similar way Dr Martinus Daneel has recently suggested that the long history of the Mwari cult's involvement with succeeding political systems in south western Rhodesia has had important consequences for its constantly developing theology.[11]

And if politics could have an impact on theology, so also could theology on politics. When kings took over cults the results were by no means uniform. Sometimes the succeeding kings were very much in control of the cult system; sometimes the officers of the cult retained considerable independence of initiative. These and other differences were no doubt mainly accounted for by the overall balance within the state between the king and his aristocracy, between intrusive groups and original inhabitants, between clan heads and royal lineages, and by the particular political history of individual kingdoms. But it seems that we should also look at the role of particular features of cultic ideas and structures.

At one extreme there are instances in which existing cultic systems are inappropriate to the needs of new or intrusive monarchies so that royal cults have to be built up separately from them. One example of this is given in the second paper in this section, Dr Mutumba Mainga's paper on the religious history of Barotseland. The Lozi kings seem to have built up their elaborate royal cult system of grave mounds dedicated to the dead kings through by-passing rather than taking over the old rites addressed to Nyambe, the High God. The resultant royal cult seems to have been much more wholly linked to the Lozi monarchy than the Mwari cult was linked to the Rozvi empire. The priests of the royal graves certainly could speak with the authority of the dead kings in ways which restricted the freedom of action of the living monarch, but there was not the same co-existence within the cult of a theology of an active High God and the theology of royal spiritual responsibility and power.

Another rather different example emerges from Dr Mainga's paper. The Lozi royal cult had given support to the Lozi monarchy but precisely because it was so closely fitted to the needs of the Lozi kingdom it did not offer much to the Kololo invaders. Of course, this was mainly a matter of the great differences in social, economic and political organisation which made the Kololo kingdom a different type of monarchy. But associated with these differences was the unacceptibility to the Kololo of the image of kingship and of its spiritual responsibilities which the Lozi royal cult embodied. So the Kololo made no attempt to take over the cult.

A third example, different yet again, concerns the invasion of south-western Rhodesia by the Ndebele. The Ndebele kingdom was even more obviously a different type of monarchy and the Ndebele kings did not attempt to take over the Mwari cult in the same way that the Mutapa took over Dzivaguru. But the Mwari cult was different from the cult of the Lozi kings. It was never merely the royal cult of the Rozvi empire but always also the oracular cult of Mwari, the High God. If it could not be used to define the spiritual power of Mzilikazi and Lobengula, it could not be ignored as the Kololo ignored the priests of the Lozi grave mounds. The Ndebele kings had to come to some kind of terms with the Mwari cult and to build it somehow into their system.[12]

Moreover, where kings *did* take over cult systems and made them the basis of their own rites of kingship, there were significant differences in the resulting 'mix'. We may mention only one point here among many. Schoffeleers remarks that the priests and the medium of M'Bona have different potentialities and play different roles. The priests are generally responsive to political realities. Generally, too, they control the medium and the interpretation of his messages. But in the last resort the medium represents the power of the spirit that bloweth where it listeth and can stand out as critic of the political system. This observation reminds us that it is important to ask whether royal cults embody mediumship or not—the Lozi royal cult apparently did not do so, for example—and if mediumship is present to ask what have been the mechanisms for its control.

This observation reminds us also that if in many instances cults *became* royal cults it would be most misleading to suppose that thereafter they remained merely royal cults or that they were always subservient to the monarchy. Even after the rise of the Lundu monarchy the M'Bona cult was much more than merely the Lundu royal cult, and it had to survive, after all, the collapse of Lundu's power. In the same way the Mwari cult and the Dzivaguru observances had to survive the collapse of the imperial systems of the Rozvi and the Mwene Mutapa. Before these collapses there had been considerable tension between 'church' and 'state'. Some of this tension was theological. The Mwari cult or the Dzivaguru cult or the M'Bona cult continued to be appealed to by people living outside the boundaries of the secular state systems with which

8

they were allied. The development of the theology of monarchy, of the idea that the fertility of the land and the health of its people *depended* upon the living king and his dead ancestors, never completely replaced the idea that health and fertility were the province of the High God, or of the divinities, or of prophetic intermediaries to whom direct approach could be made or rather an approach through attendant priests and mediums. Mwari could not be bound to his alliance with the Rozvi kings and in the last resort could repudiate them.

PART THREE: THE INTERACTION OF RELIGIOUS AND POLITICAL INNOVATION

To raise these questions about royal cults, of course, is merely the beginning of inquiry into the relationship between religious and political change in East and Central Africa. Kings and chiefs were concerned with their relation to a whole series of other religious phenomena and so also were the leaders of the many East and Central African societies that were not monarchical.

The two papers grouped in this third section gave the conference an unusual opportunity to probe further into the general question of the interaction of religious and political innovation. The papers were presented by Professor B. A. Ogot and by Professor I. N. Kimambo, in collaboration with Cuthbert Omari. Professor Ogot and Professor Kimambo had both carried out research on the political history of East African peoples which was based entirely, or almost entirely, on oral traditional evidence. Before the conference met, and indeed before it was conceived, they had published the results of this research. And in their books they had presented a particular approach to religion as a factor in political history; an approach based firmly on the emphases of their oral informants.[13]

The essence of this approach comes out of a passage from Ogot's review of Parrinder. It had been his experience, wrote Ogot, 'that the traditional religions have histories which are closely interwoven with the social and political organisations of the different African societies', and that 'as the latter changed, new religious ideas were either produced from within or borrowed from without to deal with the new situation'. The approach, in short, attributed the initiative for change to political need; the history of religion was essentially a study of political or social problem solving.[14]

Professor Kimambo adopted this approach in his book on the political history of Upare in north eastern Tanzania. He was primarily concerned there with the problem of holding together growing numbers of people once the immediate ties of family and clan had ceased to be adequate. In his fifth chapter, for example, he describes the development of 'the southern state system' of Wabwambo in Upare. A good deal of his description deals with religious innovation, with the successive religious or ritual forms that were developed as different ways of holding people together. Initiation rites were not 'a suitable instrument of centralisation' as numbers grew; the emergence of the python shrine at Zimbwe, said to have been established by one of the ruling line, did serve for a while to 'bring together all the Wabwambo for religious worship', but this was not effective for very long because other python shrines soon developed

9

in the regions. 'The problem of designing a ritual which could unite the whole group' remained unsolved. Professor Kimambo goes on to discuss the 'invention' of the idea of the representative clan god, 'prompted by the need for a means of uniting groups moving into a new area'. Finally he describes the successful innovation by king Nguta of the *cha-njeku* ritual, which was envisaged from the start 'as a state ritual in which every member could participate'. This rite emphasised not kinship but territoriality and involved the progression of a sacred bull around the boundaries of the Wabwambo state. 'Nguta had actually succeeded in getting a ritual which was able to unite the Wabwambo state . . . As the population increased and expanded new methods of maintaining unity had to be found. These methods were found in . . . religious institutions.'[15]

Now, participants in the conference accepted that this sort of approach had many merits. It was faithful to the way in which oral informants themselves saw the interaction of political and religious history. It challenged Dr Parrinder's pessimism by showing that religious history could be linked in a dynamic way to the already accepted possibility of tracing the development of political institutions. And by stressing the development of cultic answers to political problems on the spot in Upare it effectively challenged the idea of the importation into the area of 'Sudanic' or any other ready-packaged cosmologies. But it was also felt, and by none more keenly than by Professor Ogot and Professor Kimambo, that the approach left certain questions unasked.

In a recent article Professor Robin Horton remarks that cosmological beliefs begin 'as dependent variables of a particular social situation' but can then 'go on to acquire an institutional framework which transforms them into independent variables with their own power to bring about ideological and social change'. It is true that in this passage Horton was commenting particularly upon what happens to religion in Africa with the advent of literacy. But it is obviously extremely important to explore how far this observation holds for pre-literate African religious systems.[16]

The formulations so far quoted from Ogot and Kimambo present religious change as a 'dependent variable of a particular social situation'. What they set out to explore in their papers for the conference was the question of how far African religions acted as 'independent variables'. How far were there rhythms of symbolic and cultic change distinct from the pressures for innovation which were exercised by the felt needs for solutions to political problems? How far did religious forms, however innovated, come to exercise their own shaping influence on 'ideological and social change'?

In seeking to answer these questions for the Padhola and the Pare Professors Ogot and Kimambo were carrying discussion a stage further than in their previous published work. There is no need to summarise here the conclusions which are clearly set out in the papers. But it should perhaps be pointed out that the conference found the idea of the double focus of the political historian and of the student of 'traditional' belief and ritual—dramatised in the case of the Pare paper by its dual authorship by Professor Kimambo and Dr Omari—a notion with exciting potentiality.

PART FOUR: THE HISTORICAL STUDY OF RITES OF TRANSITION AND OF
SPIRIT POSSESSION CULTS

In quantity, though not in quality, this section is unrepresentative of the interest
currently being shown in its topic. Dr Aylward Shorter's paper was the only
one given at the conference which directed itself towards the problem of how to
historicise 'life-crisis' and 'redressive' rituals. Yet this is one of the growth-areas
of historical inquiry into East and Central African religious systems.[17]

This historical interest is very recent. It springs from an increasing concern
to explore the *historical* implications of the sort of subjects which preoccupy
anthropologists and sociologists. Political historians have often discussed central
royal cults and this has sometimes led them to consider a certain type of spirit
possession. For within central royal cults there were often recognised mediums
who played a key role. Such mediums were believed to be possessed by the spirits
of dead kings, or of martyred prophets, or of God Himself. They were few in
number, 'professional' in their dedication to their austere calling and in their
training, and usually controlled by a watchful priesthood or by dominant
secular political authority. But historians have not until recently been interested
in a very different type of spirit possession, the so-called cults of affliction, in
which very large numbers of men and women were held to be possessed by the
spirits of 'alien' men, or of animals or of divinities; in which there was little
control by the religious or secular establishment; and in which the idea of
possession and the reality of the trance state was used to 'cure' diseases and
neuroses by means of initiation into a spirit cult. These 'democratic' spirit
possession cults were thought of as a peripheral phenomenon, neither requiring
nor lending themselves to historical investigation.

In the same sort of way political historians have discussed how the idea of
the age-set was used to build up Zulu military power, but they have not thought
it necessary or possible to discuss the 'life-crisis' rituals of male and female
initiation which exist in many East and Central African societies. It has been
assumed, indeed, that such ceremonies of initiation were of all aspects of society
the least susceptible to change.

This historical neglect, however, has contrasted sharply with intense anthropological and sociological interest. Many anthropologists have described and
analysed the initiation rites of East and Central African societies, and the recent
work of Victor Turner on the notion of 'liminality' has given rise to lively
controversy. An equally lively controversy has arisen around the interpretation
of cults of affliction—and I. M. Lewis' recent account of this controversy has
been a best-seller in Britain. All this—together with the collection of papers on
mediumship and society edited by Middleton and Beattie—is ample evidence
that these are topics of particular significance for recent anthropological
debate.[18]

It can hardly be healthy for so sharp a distinction to exist between topics that
historians feel to be important and topics that anthropoligists feel to be important. This would be reason enough for bold historians to tackle the topics of
initiation rites and of cults of affliction. But more than this. Many of the
anthropologists who have written on these topics are themselves historically
conscious; or at any rate they deal with models of 'process' rather than with

dels of 'function'. Thus in confronting their material the historian is also con-
nting a particular view, or rather set of views, on process in African history.
Dr Shorter's paper is important as a commentary upon the value and the
iitations of the approach of 'process' anthropology. Most of the delegates to
e Dar es Salaam conference agreed with his findings that the historical con-
iousness of most process anthropologists has amounted to a concern with time
a *dimension* rather than to a concern with history as such. That is to say, pro-
ess anthropologists have often been concerned mainly to set up a model which
orks convincingly in the dimension of time, but have not always been con-
erned to inquire whether this is how things have actually developed in this or
hat particular society. Moreover, there is an inevitable tendency in their work
owards the idea of cyclic or repetitive patterns of events. A process is seen as
working itself out over time, as completing itself, and as in turn being succeeded
by a similar process. A historian must necessarily worry away at such a notion
of the African past.[19]

Dr Shorter proclaims in his paper the possibility of making quite specific
historical studies of life crisis rituals and of spirit possession cults. The idea
that there is something particularly unchanging about rituals of initiation, for
example, cannot stand up to his own work in Ukimbu, or to the recently
published work of Mrs Swantz on the Zaramo, or to Professor Kimambo's work
on Upare. An outline of Shorter's and Kimambo's findings can be found in this
book, but we may briefly summarise here what Mrs Swantz has found for
Uzaramo in the hinterland of Dar es Salaam in order to make our point. The
Zaramo today practice a rite of circumcision for boys, called the *Jando*, which
is accompanied by rituals of initiation. So far from being a long-standing and
unchanging ritual, the *Jando* ceremony has spread into Uzaramo during the
present century, superimposing itself on the older initiation forms. 'The *Jando*
rites have spread north along the coastal belt and on both sides of the Luguru
mountains in this century,' writes Mrs Swantz. Its spread in Uzaramo has been
associated with the spread of Islam, but the idea of boys' circumcision as part
of the ritual of initiation predates Islam in the societies of southern Tanzania,
and most of the *Jando* ceremony is drawn from these sources. 'As the *Jando*
institution has spread widely a comparative study of it should be made in order
to analyse its peculiarities in different ethnic groups and geographical locations
. . . This would be worth undertaking from the historical point of view. It
would also shed light on how cultural features are borrowed and how they
change meaning in the course of borrowing.'

Meanwhile Mrs Swantz' study itself gives us a good deal of insight into what
is involved in a change at so apparently fundamental a level as 'tribal' initiation.
'When borrowed,' she writes, 'a rite is bound to lose much of its former content.
It is carried over to a new context on the strength of some familiar aspects of it,
or together with some familiar features. Later, in the new context, it develops
new meanings, which unite it more firmly into the total system. This development can be demonstrated to some degree in the process of diffusion which
integrated the *Jando* rites into the Zaramo social and cultural system.'[20]

Similarly a whole series of historical questions are raised by the data available
to us on cults of 'democratic' spirit possession. To begin with there is the question of their origin and diffusion. Almost without exception informants in those

East and Central African societies where such cults exist claim that they are of relatively recent origin, often of very recent origin. Always they are held to be much more recent than the controlled spirit possession manifested at the heart of the oracular cult of Mwari, or in the Shona spirit mediums of dead kings, or in the dream prophets of the Nandi or the Tiriki. It is possible on the scattered but voluminous existing information—if one is to take it at its face value—to begin to establish areas in which such cults seem to have had a relatively long history and areas where they are much more recent and to begin to identify patterns of diffusion. Thus at present the Shona culture area, the Swahili coast, the inter-lacustrine kingdoms all emerge as possible areas of origin and diffusion.[21]

Then there is the question of why such cults originated and what their function has been at various periods of their history. In most parts of East and Central Africa there is no strong evidence that carries cults of this kind back earlier than the late eighteenth or early nineteenth century, and most of them are attributed to the later nineteenth and earlier twentieth century. Is there a connection, then, between the emergence of 'democratic' spirit possession and the events of the nineteenth century in East and Central Africa?

At the moment we can do no more than hazard guesses but they are interesting enough to show why this topic is important for historians. One guess is that the development of these cults had a broadly political as well as a social significance. In a number of cases informants have lamented the breakdown of *control* exemplified by these cults, whether the control of a king or chief and his officials or the control of the elders. Perhaps the clearest indication of what is meant here comes from Walter Sangree's work on the Tiriki of western Kenya. The Tiriki political system was controlled by the elders. When they settled in their present locality they took over from its earlier inhabitants, the Terik, the idea of the dream prophet. But the prophet was very strictly controlled. He was not able to *interpret* his dreams; that ability was reserved for the elders. Today in Tiriki there is widespread 'democratic' spirit possession, though admittedly it does not take the form of cults of affliction. Today very many people are possessed by the Holy Ghost and the pentecostal prophets interpret their own visions without any reference to the elders, claiming a direct authority from God.[22]

Sangree's fully worked out case study is an example of the influence of Christian ideas. But it can be argued forcefully that the emergence of widespread spirit possession in East and Central African societies had something of the same effect in pre-Christian times and in non-Christian contexts. Matthew Schoffeleers argues, for example, that 'democratic' spirit possession in Malawi began to develop with the breakdown of Chewa political institutions. Before the early nineteenth century mediumship within the High God cult centred at Msinja, or within the M'Bona cult, was restricted to a handful of 'professionals', but as Chewa and Mang'anja political authorities increasingly lost their power to control the situation in the nineteenth century so spirit possession spread. And Aidan Southall tells us that 'there is a universal feeling among the Alur that the realm of the spiritual has got out of hand in modern times, corresponding to the colonial period and their first awareness of the outside world . . . Their concern is great for the fact that manifestations of *Jok* (Spirit) are more diverse, numerous, violent and unregulated, so few of them falling into the properly co-ordinated channels of orthodox expression which were adequate in the past. It seems as though new and hitherto unknown spirits can fall violently on anyone at any time. Formerly the regular, communal worship of chiefs, elders and people was sufficient to maintain harmony between spirit, man and nature.'[23]

Another guess is that the development of spirit possession cults in East and Central Africa was one result of a general 'enlargement of scale' during the nineteenth and twentieth centuries. The possessing spirits were most often 'aliens'. The treatment of a patient most often involved being dressed in whatever clothes were thought 'typical' of a particular alien group, eating typical food, engaging while in a trance in typical behaviour. Obviously these stereotypes of other peoples are of the greatest interest to historians in themselves. They are of even greater interest when their formulation can be connected with a specific historical event. This is the case, for example, with the possession cult observed by Schoffeleers in the Lower Shire valley whose members are held to be possessed by the spirits of the Barwe soldiers who fought against the Portuguese in the Makombe rising of 1917. But in addition to this it can be argued more generally that cults of possession constituted one way of coming to terms with and seeking to comprehend the interaction of peoples which characterised the nineteenth century.[24]

It has been suggested, moreover, that the *organisational* structures of some of the possession cults also relate to the situation of 'enlarged scale'. Some at least of the cults existed over very wide areas and included initiates from many different African groups. It is said, for instance, that Nyamwezi members of the Swezi cult could find hospitality from fellow cult members in most of the regions between Unyamwezi and the coast, and that the spread of Swezi facilitated travel and trade in nineteenth-century Tanzania.[25]

Finally there is the whole question of the relationship of such cults to change. In his studies of Kalabari religion Robin Horton has suggested that the peripheral minor water spirit cults can serve as a vehicle of innovation because of their very peripherality and lack of control by the establishment. It seems interesting to ask whether this West African finding might also apply to East and Central African situations. Mrs Swantz, in her book on the Zaramo, raises the whole question of innovation within the framework of life-crisis rituals and spirit possession cults. She distinguishes between the kind of change that could be digested by the Zaramo and made sense of within their own system of thought, and the kind of 'modernising' change which cannot be digested or assimilated. For her the 'traditional' does not represent a static or unchanging society but a society in which change took place in certain ways. For her the creative individual working through the cults of spirit possession which are so pervasive in Zaramo society was a major agent and above all legitimiser of change. 'The question of an articulate individual in the traditional society is the final point of discussion. It has been shown that borrowing and recreating symbolic forms has required individuals in whom the identification with the symbols has taken place and has become articulate. There has been individual creativity and initiative in the ritual way of life. The charismatic leaders have been the initiators and creators. They have called on the authority of the past generations and of the spirits with whom they have been in contact to make their own innovations acceptable to the rest of the society. Because of this authority, to which a *mganga* is able to refer, an extended spirit cult can function even in changed conditions. The sanctions for innovated practices are acceptable when they come from outside yet from within the experience of the people.'[26]

These then are some of the hypotheses which historians are beginning to test as they examine the life crisis rituals and the spirit possession cults of East and Central Africa.

PART FIVE: THE NINETEENTH-CENTURY CRISIS AND RELIGIOUS SYSTEMS IN EAST AND CENTRAL AFRICA

The fifth section contains three papers which cover a very wide variety of themes. They were grouped together at the conference on the grounds that all of them dealt with religious responses to what was thought of as 'the nineteenth-century crisis', although in reality they deal with successive crises, culminating in the crisis of desperate resistance to colonial rule. Still, there are ways in which it can be argued that all three of the papers, dealing as they do with conversion to Islam, with the evidence on religious change that comes out of the encounter between 'traditional' religion and Christianity, and with the development of the ideology of the Maji Maji revolt, address themselves to a broad common process.

The most stimulating way to do this is to follow the arguments recently presented by Robin Horton. Horton argues that what is happening in tropical Africa over a period which in some cases begins earlier but which in many regions is concentrated into the nineteenth and early twentieth centuries is a movement from the self-sufficient microcosmic society to the wider macrocosmic society, in which individuals had to make contacts with men of different tribes and races. This process, of course, advanced at a different rate for different individuals even within the same society because some remained as cultivators and others moved out as porters or traders or migrant labourers. Horton sees this process as posing a conceptual challenge to what he boldly sets up as a typical traditional religious system. He argues that in the microcosmic society most attention is paid to the activity of the *spirits* while the idea of the High God is relatively undeveloped and there are few mechanisms of access to him. In order to cope with the realities of the macrocosmic society, he argues, the idea of the High God has to be greatly developed, in particular the idea of his moral concern, because only the High God can sanction the codes of conduct required for wider intercourse. But the development of the notion of the power and moral concern of the High God does not necessarily involve conversion to Christianity or Islam. People do not just scrap their religious systems but seek to modify them, and the existence in traditional religious systems of the un-developed notion of the Supreme Being allows for creative innovation. It is true, Horton agrees, that all this is happening at the same time as the coming of Islam and Christianity so that developments that would have happened anyway have been concealed under the idea of 'conversion'. But he argues that Africans took from Islam and Christianity only those aspects of the new religions which met their needs. Moreover, because Africans were essentially concerned to develop a newly effective system of prediction and control they continued to emphasise the connection between religious belief and healing and prophecy against the wish of official Christianity which had abandoned these aspects of spiritual activity. To the African pioneers of a macrocosmic cosmology, healing and prophecy were the work of God himself rather than of any intermediary spirit.[27]

Horton does not offer any example of these processes happening outside the influences of Christianity. But it could be argued that the three papers in this section provide examples for him. This is, indeed, what Professor Edward Alpers argues in the closing sections of his paper on the spread of Islam in southern Tanzania, Mozambique and Malawi. The pioneers of Islam among the Yao, for example, were precisely the men with the greatest experience of the macrocosmic and the greatest 'need' for the notion of Allah as an active moral force. Professor Marcia Wright's paper on the developments in Nyakyusa religion during the later nineteenth century also shows a process of consolidation going on through which one of a number of 'heroic cults' emerges as a rallying point. And in Gilbert Gwassa's account of the creation of the ideology of Maji Maji there comes through in various ways the idea of the newly active involvement of the Supreme Being Himself.

It is valuable to see these papers in so wide a context. As one would expect, though, the case studies in this book and the examples cited in this Introduction provide as many challenges as supports to Horton's thesis. There is the whole argument presented above that cults of affliction—which represented the *multiplication* of the idea of spirit rather than its increasing insignificance in face of the idea of God—were in themselves a response to nineteenth-century 'enlargement of scale'. Perhaps it could be argued, though Horton does not do so, that the development of the idea of the involvement of alien spirits was one way of trying to meet the macrocosmic challenge and that the stress on the active High God was another. In this case the challenge offered by African spirit churches to the cults of affliction could be seen as a clash between two different responses to the macrocosmic; a clash in which the alien possessing spirits are denounced as diabolical by those who rest their trust in God alone and in His Holy Spirit.[28]

Then there is the problem, dismissed by Horton in a footnote, of those societies in which it is clear that there was an active concept of the Supreme Being long before the nineteenth century. Horton in his note cites the religious situations of the Nuer and Dinka as described by Evans-Pritchard and Lienhardt; another example of 'cultures which show considerable development of the cult of the supreme being even in the pre-Christian, pre-Muslim phase' would be the case of the Mwari cult of south-west Rhodesia which has been cited above. Horton says he thinks it 'possible to reconcile such findings with the hypothesis sketched here, on the assumptions that variations in the extent of the pagan cult of the supreme being are correlated with variations in the extent to which the macrocosm impinges on the life of the individual'. It is true that Martinus Daneel, writing of the Mwari cult, asserts that 'Rozvi influence contributed towards the personification of this deity who became less remote through His interest in the political cohesion of His people'. But we need a much closer examination of this hypothesis that the development of the idea of an active God is related to the development of wide political or economic contacts.

In addition to being seen in the context of this, or any other notion, of a general metaphysical crisis the three papers in this section require some individual comment. Each is an important contribution to a key area of religious historiography in East and Central Africa.

Professor Alpers' paper forms part of the new wave of interest in East and Central African Islam. Until recently Islam in eastern Africa had been almost scandalously neglected by historians and as much misunderstood. Thus it was possible for Professor Trimingham, drawing upon his knowledge of West Africa and of north-east Africa, to make a genuinely useful contribution in his *Islam in East Africa* despite the confessedly short time he spent in that area. However, his book will be replaced very rapidly by studies giving a quite different impression of East African Islam. These studies will pay much more attention to the Islam of whole societies in the hinterland and interior than Trimingham does and less attention to the Islam of the coast as the nearest approximation to a classical type of the faith. These studies will not see variations in belief and practice as indices of a more or less 'pure' Islam, but will rather explore them as Professor Alpers does in terms of the dynamics of social and intellectual change. In this re-assessment of East African Islam, which parallels work now going on in West Africa, contributions will be made both by scholars who come at the question as Islamicists rather than as East African-ists—like Professor B. G. Martin, for example—and by scholars who come at the problem as East Africanists rather than as Islamicists, like Professor Alpers himself. Islam in East Africa is too important to be left solely to the Islamicists! And it is especially important that this new interest in East African Islam should be set in the context of the new interest in the history of African religious systems. What Professor Alpers is striving to do—and he would be the first to say that his paper represents only a beginning—is to break out of the Parrinder picture of 'historic' dynamic Islam encountering passive 'traditional' religious systems and to set the encounter rather in the context of the many manifestations of energy and change displayed by African religion in the nineteenth century and before, some of which have been indicated in this Introduction and more of which are described in the case studies.[29]

Professor Marcia Wright's paper is important in two other ways. First, it is important as an indication of the value of missionary records for the recon-struction of African religious history. Of course, missionaries did not fully understand what was going on—indeed, it is clear from Professor Wright's paper that they badly misunderstood what was going on. But they were inter-ested in 'religion', even if they often had rather distorting definitions of it; and they sometimes found themselves in direct encounters with spokesmen for African cults. This was the case in the country of the Nyakyusa at the end of the nineteenth century and Professor Wright is able, as was Simon Charsley in his little book on Nyakyusa political history, to make very effective use of mission records. Missionary history as such may be dead: but missionary records will be found invaluable for the reconstruction of a more complete religious history.[30]

Professor Wright's paper is important, also, because it represents the most direct confrontation in this book between a historian and an anthropologist. Of course there is no point in confrontation as such, and in this case the anthropologist is a very distinguished one, whose work on the Nyakyusa remains invaluable, and whose services to history as well as to anthropology have recently been very impressively displayed. But the fact remains that in the case of the Nyakyusa, as in the case of many other East and Central African peoples, our knowledge depends upon the work of a single scholar, or in this case on the work of a husband and wife, in a way which could hardly be accepted with satisfaction in any developed field of historical research. For between thirty and forty years the Nyakyusa have been pictured by the world as Monica and Godfrey Wilson saw them. The phenomenon of 'rapidisation' is now at work in African studies as elsewhere and no work of African historiography can expect that sort of unchallenged influence. But still the classic anthropological studies hold their sway, and perhaps especially over historians who are properly reluctant to challenge the arcane sister discipline.

So far as religious history especially is concerned challenge is necessary. It can easily be forgotten that all the classical accounts of African religious systems are twentieth-century accounts; accounts made, that is, after the tendencies described by Horton had been for many decades at work. So far from gratefully accepting them and carrying them back reverently into the past, the historian needs to study very carefully the particular historical configurations at the point when the anthropological study was made and also the development and change within the religious system concerned over the decades immediately before.

It is not that such an inquiry is particularly needed for Monica Wilson's work—far from it. But inquiry needs to be made into each and all of the major anthropological studies of East and Central African religion. It so happens that the evidence for religious change in Unyakyusa is particularly good. On the basis of this evidence Professor Wright argues in what we believe to be a convincing way that some of the historical speculations of the Wilsons are misleading.

Gilbert Gwassa's paper is a major contribution to yet another debate, and a very lively one at that. Over the last five years there have been a number of studies of major resistance movements against the imposition of colonial rule in East and Central Africa. Such studies have established very clearly that the ideologies of these movements of resistance were usually religious ideologies, most often developed out of 'traditional' religious beliefs and structures in ways that offered a solution to the problems of morale and of the need for wider unity. The problem now is that this has been so securely established that to say that the major revolts against the whites were powered by 'millenarian' religious ideologies has become more of a truism than a revelation. The idea no longer tells us very much.

What is needed now is a closer examination of these ideologies of revolt. We need, to begin with, to establish the significant differences within the over-all similarity. Professor L. Carl Brown, writing on the Mahdiya movement of the Sudan in Rotberg and Mazrui's *Protest and Power in Black Africa* has put this very clearly. The Mahdiya was a millenarian movement of revolt. But in what context can it most fruitfully be understood? As Brown says, one can make a sort of case for regarding it as typical of Semitic millenarianism as a whole, or as typical of Islamic millenarianism, or as typical of the ideologies of 'third world' uprisings. And as he also says each of these categories is too general to be useful. We need a tighter, more exclusive category. In the case of the Mahdiya, Brown suggests that it can most usefully be regarded as characteristic of what he calls 'fringe' Islam, and he employs this notion to define in a quite precise and illuminating way what *kind* of millenarianism we confront in this movement.[31]

It is fairly easily possible to do the same sort of thing for Christian millenarianism in East and Central Africa and to show what particular church or sect traditions it drew upon. But the difficulty comes when we seek to do the same sort of thing with millenarian ideologies of revolt which are neither Islamic nor Christian. One problem is that so many people have been reluctant to concede that 'traditional' African religious systems had millenarian implications. Professor Mbiti, for example, has stressed that there is no traditional eschatology and argues that one of the reasons why so many African Christians are obsessed with millenarian ideas is precisely that they have nothing in their own tradition to help them live with or control Christian eschatology. Consequently there has been a tendency to suppose that obviously millenarian themes in otherwise 'traditional' ideologies derive from Christian or Islamic influence.[32]

The temptation is to rest content with disputing this point of view. Clearly we *do* need to reiterate the position taken by Louis Brenner in his review of *Protest and Power*. 'Many authors suggest that the concept of "death-rebirth" is of Christian influence, as if this supposed knowledge is enlightening. Of course this observation explains nothing . . . because the theme of death-rebirth, or movement between the land of the living and of the dead, is not limited to Christianity'. But the temptation is to rest upon a demonstration that 'traditional' religion contained within it the dynamic potentialities of millenarianism. What we need to do is to go on to sort out the many different kinds of millenarianism that were possible in the many different kinds of African religions in East and Central Africa, just as Carl Brown has sorted out different tendencies of Islamic millenial belief.[33]

This is a hard task as it stands at the moment. Before we can really undertake it we need much more specific accounts of the various ideologies of revolt and of how they emerged. It is for this reason that Gwassa's paper on the ideology of Maji Maji is so important. It does describe on the basis of first-hand evidence how the Maji Maji ideology was formed, how it was taught and how it was received. And at once the similarities but also the great differences with, say, the ideology of the 1896 risings in Rhodesia begin to emerge.

Work like Gwassa's encourages us to suppose that we can go on to a meaningful classification of ideologies of protest; to begin to understand why some movements are directed externally against the whites and others directed at internal reconstruction; to begin to understand why some traditions of millenarianism are less effective than others in maintaining a revolt once it has begun; to begin to understand why some societies did not have to hand a usable tradition at all.

And once again we come back with these questions to confront Horton's overall argument. It might be argued that some 'traditional' millenarian tendencies were essentially microcosmic—such as the idea which underlay movements of witchcraft eradication. Such movements spread over very large areas and promised at least an earthly millenium but their promise was always interpreted as relevant to the local microcosmic community. Consequently while it might be a logical step for such movements to denounce whites as witches and to urge a rising against them it would be difficult for them to sustain the sort of wider collaboration or confident morale that a macrocosmic rebellion required. On the other hand it could be argued that some ideologies of revolt developed precisely as a response to experience of life in the macrocosm and that they took the form of a great elaboration of the hitherto under-developed notions of the High God and his relationships to men. Protest ideologies which emphasised the immanence of God, stressed his direct commands to revolt and his direct support for those who took arms, and spoke in terms of a millenium in which God would rule a world composed of the living and the returned dead, stood a much better chance of holding a large scale uprising together.[34]

These are exciting ideas but they contain within themselves another problem. There is an increasing tendency to see the great protest movements of the early colonial period not so much as 'proto-nationalist' revolts against whites as instances of a much broader tradition of 'revolutionary' social protest.[35] The question arises, then, of how far their ideologies were indeed new and how far they were repetitive instances of a recurring tendency towards millenial protest. To take one example—though not one which led to violent uprisings against white rule. Many peoples in Zambia were found by missionaries writing in the early twentieth century to possess ideas about the ultimate return to earth of the High God, Lesa, who was to move across the land from east to west gathering up his people and re-uniting them with the returned dead. These ideas undoubtedly found expression in the so-called Mwana Lesa movement of 1925 where they combined with the Watchtower teachings of Tomo Nyirenda to produce a complex and powerful millenial ideology. Now, clearly it could be argued that not only the Mwana Lesa movement but the very 'traditional' ideas on which it was drawing were a response to the experience of the macro-cosm, and that these notions of the return of Lesa had themselves developed relatively recently. Alternatively it could be argued that for a very long time the remoteness of Lesa had been held in balance by the myth of his activist return and that this myth had been employed over the centuries in a sequence of attempts to accommodate to challenge and change. It seems very important to resolve this argument which *mutatis mutandis* might be applied to the case of Kinjikitile, creator of the Maji Maji ideology, as well as to Tomo Nyirenda. At present our evidence is not conclusive in either direction. But work like Gilbert Gwassa's encourages us to hope that these and other questions may be resolved.[36]

PART SIX: INTERACTIONS BETWEEN AFRICAN RELIGION AND
CHRISTIANITY IN THE TWENTIETH CENTURY

In the final section come two papers which can be linked together in something of the same general way as the papers by Alpers, Wright and Gwassa. And just as these allowed us to make some general observations about the importance of the late nineteenth century for the historian of African religion, so the three papers in the final section allow us to make some points about the importance of twentieth-century studies.

There is a tendency, perhaps, to think of the coming of colonialism as bringing the 'traditional' world to an end. It is all too easy to suppose that initiative passed to the adherents of Islam and Christianity and that where 'traditional' religions had once been co-existent with African societies they now dwindled into broken 'rump' religions. But it is in fact most important to carry our historical studies of African religion into the twentieth century.

To begin with it is in the twentieth century that we find by far the most evidence. There is a great deal of material in missionary and administrative records; there are the classical anthropological studies; there is the rich potentiality of oral evidence. Historical studies of African religious change can be much more securely founded in the twentieth century than for any other period.

Then there is the point which has already been made—namely that the great anthropological studies upon which we must all depend were all made in the twentieth century and must be looked at by the historian in their specific context of date as well as of place. Moreover, only by grasping the twentieth-century evidence can the historian 'link up' with the exciting work being done by anthropologists and sociologists on contemporary manifestations of spirit possession cults or witchcraft eradication movements.

And finally as we appreciate more fully the historicity of African religions, their capacity to innovate, their capacity to respond even to the challenge of the macrocosmic, so we come to abandon the idea of African religion today as merely a pathetic survival. We come to realise that we need to know much more than we do about the ways in which African religious ideas have continued to play a considerable role in the recent history of East and Central Africa.

Thus the twentieth century is a rich, perhaps the richest, field for historical inquiry into African religion. All sorts of topics are at hand for inquiry. We need to know what changes have occurred within those African cult systems which have not only survived but continued to exercise considerable influence. We need to know whether religious forms which seem to be fairly recent developments—such as witchcraft eradication movements—have much deeper roots than we suppose and to ask what are their relationships to other African religious forms. We need to seek to obtain biographical material on 'traditional' cult officers, or witchcraft eradicators, in order to balance the wealth of Christian biography. It is true that some anthropologists, particularly French anthropologists, have based studies of African cosmologies on their interviews with an informant from the heart of the 'traditional' religious system, but what we need now is biography as history as well as biography as revelation.

We need to know, moreover, how witchcraft belief has changed or grown or dwindled during the modern period for which we have such extensive records to help us grapple with one of the most elusive topics in African religious history.[37] And we need to know what have been the interactions between African religions and modern African politics.[38]

The case studies throw some light on these questions. But in general it is not so much these questions, important as they are, but another range of twentieth-century questions which are illuminated by the two case studies in this section. They are united by their common concentration on the interaction of Christianity and African religion.

The study of Christianity in East and Central Africa is in a very different state from the study of Islam. Much more has been written and much work of real value has been produced. But in some respects the Christian historiography of the area parallels the Islamic. Until the last decade historical accounts of the spread of Christianity were usually history from on top and were too little concerned with what it was that Africans were asking of Christianity and doing to it within the mission churches as well as within independent church movements and so-called syncretist cults. There was a tendency also, no doubt encouraged by some of the ideas of a now out-moded school of acculturation anthropology, to assume that the only formulations that made practical or spiritual or intellectual sense were 'pure' traditional religion and 'pure' Christianity, with the latter supposed, of course, to make more sense than the former. It has often been assumed, therefore, that syncretist movements were nonsense movements, caught in the vacuum between two systems, and until recently there has been too little concern to ask what sense any or all of these religious formulations made to those who acted within them. Finally, and particularly relevantly to this book, there has been very little idea of the encounter between Christianity and African religion as a historical encounter on *both* sides.

Consequently it is true for Christian historiography, if to a lesser degree than for Islamic historiography, that it is in process of great change. We may make a final reference to Robin Horton's brilliant re-thinking of the phenomenon of conversion at this point since it brings out more sharply than anything else the character of the challenge to the orthodoxies of mission history. What Horton does is to widen out the issue. It is not enough, he implies, to show that African religious belief was a factor at particular points in the Christian history of Africa; to show, as we now can, that the initial reception of Christianity in different African societies depended partly upon the religious situation in those societies as well as upon the political and economic situation; to show the mutual interaction of, shall we say, the missionary churches in western Mashonaland and the Mwari cult, each in subtle ways influencing the other while remaining distinct. Over and above that, so Horton argues, we must see the total process of conversion and of the diffusion of Christianity as a phase in a specifically African religious historiography. What was going on, he says, was an attempt to define and to know a Supreme Being and an attempt to erect ways of access to him which would have gone on in any event, even in the historically unimaginable circumstances of the absence of Christianity from the colonial situation. Thus much of what we assume to be the work of Christianity has to be seen quite differently.[39]

Obviously Horton's argument is going to be hotly contested and tested and as we have implied above some of the material in this book can be used to challenge it as well as to support it. But the point here is that whether it stands the test of criticism or not, it succeeds in placing African religious ideas and African religious needs at the centre of the modern religious history of Africa.

The two case studies in this section do not raise or treat such wide-ranging issues. But it can be claimed for both of them that they are examples of the newer way of looking at modern religious history in East and Central Africa rather than the older. The two case studies, Professor Ranger's paper on the adaptation of initiation ceremonies within the Anglican church in Masasi in southern Tanzania and Ian Linden's and Matthew Schoffeleers' paper on the opposition to Catholic missions put up by the *Nyau* societies of Malawi, make in fact a nicely contrasting and yet reinforcing effect. Professor Ranger's paper is about developments *within* a Christian mission church and about the Africans who sponsored and supported these developments; Linden and Schoffeleers' paper is about a remarkable and persistent rejection of mission influence. But both are about African decisions as to how far and in what ways Christianity could be used—or not used. And both are about the ways in which these decisions affected 'traditional' concepts and institutions. Linden and Schoffeleers show that by resisting Christian influence the *Nyau* societies themselves chose to change in certain ways, or at any rate chose courses of action which involved change. Ranger shows how an African clergy and teaching class gained control of and transformed the initiation ceremonies of the Masasi area through the use of their influence within the Christian church and suggests how this affected the character of Christianity in Masasi. Both strive to avoid the trap of regarding either the *Nyau* societies or Masasi initiation rites as unchanging traditional 'givens'; both seek to show that *Nyau* in Malawi and initiation in Masasi had a lively history of their own and to indicate some of the dynamics of their encounter with Christianity.

T. O. RANGER
I. N. KIMAMBO

NOTES

[1] Lucy Quimby, 'Report of a Conference called by Professor Marcia Wright, February 24 1971, to discuss the study of African Religions', typescript.

[2] J. S. Mbiti *African Religions and Philosophy* (London 1969).

[3] Geoffrey Parrinder *Religion in Africa* (London 1969).

[4] Review of Parrinder's *Religion in Africa* by B. A. Ogot in *African Historical Studies* vol. III, no. 1 (1970) pp. 182–3.

[5] Lucy Quimby's report accepts that scholars have tended to treat Islam and Christianity in Africa as 'corruptions of an "ideal true form" found elsewhere' and that this has tended to distort African realities. But, as she argues, 'this tradition of mistreatment need not continue'. She goes on to lay down principles with which we would agree. 'The scholar must shift his focus from the religion as an abstract ideal to the religion as a particular African society defines and practices it . . . to look at religion as a composite of a variety of forms of religious behaviour and beliefs, as believed and acted out by a variety of individuals within the society being studied.'

[6] For an excellent account of the distortions of earlier 'historical' studies of African religions see, E. E. Evans-Pritchard *Theories of Primitive Religion* (Oxford 1965).

[7] R. Oliver and J. D. Fage *A Short History of Africa* (London 1962) chapter 4; R. Oliver (ed.) *The Dawn of African History* (London 1961) chapter 8.

[8] Jan Vansina *Kingdoms of the Savanna. A history of Central African States until European occupation* (Madison 1966).

[9] J. M. Schoffeleers, 'M'Bona. The Guardian Spirit of the Mang'anja', thesis presented for the B.Litt, degree, Oxford 1966. Discussing the common symbolic features Schoffeleers writes that the M'Bona cult is 'but one instance of a widespread institution'.

[10] D. P. Abraham, 'The roles of Chaminuka and the Mhondoro cults in Shona political history' *The Zambesian Past. Studies in Central African History* edited by E. Stokes and R. Brown (Manchester 1966).

[11] M. L. Daneel *The God of the Matopo Hills. An essay on the Mwari Cult in Rhodesia* (The Hague 1970). Daneel writes: 'Mwari is primarily concerned with the fertility of crops and women. His interest in tribal politics only dates from the time when the ruling Rozvi tribe had begun to exploit the cult as a centralized "intelligence service" and as a means of consolidating their own dynastic rule over the surrounding tribes. The political significance of the cult emerged even more clearly when the oracular element within the cult was fully developed in the Matopo hills . . . Christian missionaries of this century were faced with a highly syncretised traditional concept of God. The Mbire God of Fertility had attained additional female and sexual connotations through the influence of the Tonga tribes in the Zambezi basin. Rozvi influence contributed towards the personification of this diety who became less remote through His interest in the political cohesion of His people . . . Mwari could eventually be consulted at His shrines. European presence had temporarily turned Him into a militant God, whereafter He assumed, in addition to His rain-making activities, His present role as champion of traditional law and custom.'

[12] Daneel shows that the Mwari cult retained its Shona character throughout the period of Ndebele supremacy and that control of it remained exclusively in Mbire, Rozvi and Venda hands. He cites the high priest, Simon Chokoto: 'We live among the Ndebele and we speak their language, but the customs we honour and the laws of worship we obey at this place, are those of our Mbire Shoko forefathers. We are Vakaranga! There is not a single Ndebele who holds high office here at Matonjeni'. Daneel *op. cit.* p. 46. On the other hand the influence of the Mwari cult was extensive within the Ndebele state. The Jesuit missionaries even asserted that during the reign of Lobengula the Mwari priests exercised more power over state decisions than the king himself!

[13] B. A. Ogot *History of the Southern Luo, Volume I, Migration and Settlement, 1500–1900* (Nairobi 1967); I. N. Kimambo *A Political History of the Pare of Tanzania, c. 1500–1900* (Nairobi 1969).

[14] Ogot's review of Parrinder *African Historical Studies* vol. III, no. 1 (1970) pp. 182–3.

[15] I. N. Kimambo *op. cit.* chapter 5 'The founding of the southern state system'.

[16] Robin Horton, 'African Conversion' *Africa* vol. XLI, no. 2 (April 1971) p. 95.

[17] Currently Mrs Iris Berger of the University of Wisconsin is writing up her dissertation on the Mandwa spirit cults and their history. Miss Mary Carter of the University of California, Los Angeles, is preparing for doctoral work on the emergence, diffusion and function of spirit possession cults in central and southern Africa. Mr Robert Papstein of U.C.L.A. is preparing to work on the religious history of the Ndembu and in particular will attempt to historicise Victor Turner's work on Ndembu cults of affliction and rites of liminality.

[18] See especially, Victor Turner *The Drums of Affliction. A Study of Religious Processes Among the Ndembu of Zambia* (Oxford 1968); I. M. Lewis *Ecstatic Religion* (London 1971); John Beattie and John Middleton (eds.) *Spirit Mediumship and Society in Africa* (London 1969).

[19] This criticism was developed at greater length in a paper discussed at the Dar es Salaam conference but not reproduced in this book. T. O. Ranger, 'Emerging Themes in the historical study of African religion in East and Central Africa', Dar es Salaam June 1970.

[20] Marja-Liisa Swantz *Ritual and Symbol in transitional Zaramo society* (Uppsala 1970) pp. 165–8.

[21] Beattie and Middleton (eds.) *Spirit Mediumship and Society in Africa* (London 1969); Mary Carter, 'Cults of affliction in Eastern Africa', graduate seminar paper, U.C.L.A. May 1971. Miss Carter argues in this paper that the evidence of recent origin ought not

to be taken at face value and that cults of affliction are—or rather were—more intrinsically connected with other parts of traditional religious systems than is generally allowed.

[22] W. H. Sangree *Age, Prayer and Politics in Tiriki, Kenya* (London 1966).

[23] Aidan Southall, 'Spirit Possession and Mediumship among the Alur' *Spirit Mediumship and Society in Africa.*

[24] Schoffeleers describes the WaBarwe possessing spirits in 'Symbolic and Social Aspects of Spirit Worship among the Mang'anja', unpublished doctoral dissertation, Oxford 1968.

[25] For this argument, see Andrew Roberts, 'Nyamwezi Trade', in Richard Gray and David Birmingham (eds.) *Pre-Colonial African Trade. Essays on Trade in Central and Eastern Africa before 1900* (London 1970); T. O. Ranger, 'The movement of ideas, 1850–1939', in I. N. Kimambo and A. J. Temu (eds.) *A History of Tanzania* (Nairobi 1969).

[26] R. Horton, 'A 100 Years of Change in Kalabari Religion', in John Middleton (ed.) *Black Africa. Its Peoples and Their Cultures Today* (Toronto 1970); 'Types of Spirit Possession in Kalibari Religion', in John Beattie and John Middleton (eds.) *Spirit Mediumship and Society in Africa* (London 1969).

M. L. Swantz *Ritual and Symbol in transitional Zaramo society* (Uppsala 1970), pp. 357–8.

[27] R. Horton, 'African Conversion' *Africa* vol. XLI, no. 2 (April 1971).

[28] Horton's article begins as a review of J. D. Y. Peel's book on the Aladura churches of Nigeria. For East and Central Africa the only work comparable to that done on Aladura by Peel and Turner is M. L. Daneel's massive study of Shona spirit churches. The first of what will be four volumes is, M. L. Daneel *Old and New in Southern Shona Independent Churches* (The Hague 1971). Daneel's work contains fascinating data on concepts of spirit in 'traditional' Shona religion and in the Shona independent churches, and in particular on the responses of the Vapostori and Zionist churches to Shona cults of affliction. For a review of Daneel's book in the light of Horton's article see Madoda Hlatshwayo and T. O. Ranger *African Religious Research* no. 2. African Studies Center, U.C.L.A. (Los Angeles Fall 1971). *African Religious Research* is a bulletin of information on research in progress in the field of African religious history and of reviews of relevant books.

[29] J. Spencer Trimingham *Islam in East Africa* (London 1964). For a statement of view close to those expressed here see Peter Lienhardt, 'Introduction', in P. Lienhard (ed.) *The Medicine Man. Swifa Ya Nguvumali* (Oxford 1966).

[30] S. R. Charsley *The Princes of Nyakyusa* (Nairobi 1969).

[31] L. Carl Brown 'The Sudanese Mahdiya', in R. I. Rotberg and Ali A. Mazrui (eds.) *Protest and Power in Black Africa* (New York 1970).

[32] J. S. Mbiti *African Religions and Philosophy* (London 1969).

[33] Louis Brenner's review of *Protest and Power in Black Africa* in *African Historical Studies* vol. IV, no. 1 (1971).

[34] Mary Douglas argues for a distinction between witchcraft eradication movements and 'millenial movements properly so called' in her *Natural Symbols. Explorations in Cosmology* (London 1970). She asserts that witchcraft eradication movements 'spread as solutions offered to a given community and its members for their particular troubles. They are not formulae for saving the world in general. . . . Although the witch-cleansing movement carries a millenial possibility in its promise to end evil and suffering, it differs radically from the true millenarian movement. It is focused on the problems of small local groups, whereas millenialism has a message for the world.' pp. 121–2.

[35] An example of this approach is an unpublished paper by Edward Steinhart of the University of Texas on 'Anti-colonial resistance and nationalism: the Nyangire Rebellion'. The paper concludes: 'If we look within the protest movements, at leaders and followers alike, we are apt to discover that the impulses which the leaders organise and interpret are profoundly anti-authoritarian and revolutionary rather than anti-foreign and "nationalist".'

[36] For a discussion of these problems see, T. O. Ranger, 'The Mwana Lesa Movement of 1925', Workshop in Religious Research, Chilema, Malawi, August 1971.

[37] For a discussion of the sources available for a reconstruction of the history of witchcraft belief in the twentieth century see *African Religious Research* African Studies Centre, U.C.L.A., no. 1 (Los Angeles Summer 1971).

[38] This important subject is discussed in: F. B. Welbourn *Religion and Politics in Uganda, 1952–62* (Nairobi 1965). Marshall W. Murphree *Christianity and the Shona* (London 1969). Ndabaningi Sithole *Obed Mutezo. The Mudzimu Christian Nationalist* (Nairobi 1971).

[39] Robin Horton, 'African Conversion'.

PART ONE

METHODS FOR THE RECONSTRUCTION OF EARLY RELIGIOUS HISTORY

MERRICK POSNANSKY

Archaeology, Ritual and Religion[1]

INTRODUCTION

The archaeological literature of Africa is well seasoned with conjectures about former religious practices. 'Ritual' objects are described whose functional use defies the imagination of their discoverers. It is the purpose of this paper to appraise the evidence that has been presented to imply religious practice, to examine the relevance of such evaluations to the history of African religious systems and finally to suggest priorities for future archaeological work. It is necessary at the outset, however, to decide what we mean by religion and determine the categories of archaeological evidence that might provide information about otherwise undocumented religious practice.

There seems to be no universally accepted definition of what constitutes religion. A fairly widely accepted aspect of most definitions is that religious belief implies a belief in the supernatural expressed in the form of both animate and abstract forces. A religion also implies, according to Spiro[2] an institution which 'is an attribute of social groups, comprising a component part of their cultural heritage'. Besides being an attribute of social groups, religion is seen as one of several culturally constituted belief systems. It has been stressed by most anthropologists that religion is only one aspect of culture as a whole and one can only hope to understand a particular belief system if one fully understands all the other aspects of the sociocultural life of the society being studied. Nevertheless religion for many societies is one of the most basic aspects of culture which may affect all the other facets of social life, though it is arguable as to which facet influences which. Does a patrilineal society believe in a male god because of its patriarchal head or does the religion dictate the kinship structure?

The material aspects of religion and the actual practices performed are only part of the reflection of the totality of the cultural life of such a society. In seeking to define religion, it is impossible to escape the psychological dimension in which a religious belief is viewed as part of Man's image of the world and of his own position in relation to the other component parts of that world, the landscape, the climate, the plants and the animals. The psychological boundaries of religion are the most difficult to demarcate. In present-day religious systems, the tangible aspects of religion include objects of ritual use, in the sense that they are used in religious observances, certain of the symbols, the places of such observances, and objects which have been 'ritualised' because of the observances with which they are associated. A ritual object is one whose meaning is shared in practice because of a common cultural heritage whereas sacred symbols function to synthesise a people's ethos and are objects which serve as vehicles for conceptions.[3] As such, a ritual object can be a symbol, and an actual ritual is seen as a culturally patterned symbolic action.

The archaeologist has to reconstruct the past from the material culture that survives the passage of time. He is hampered by the fact that, over many parts of Africa, it is largely the inorganic objects of stone, baked clay and metal which resist decay. Archaeology is uneven in its attention to the past. Sites where inorganic objects may survive are chiefly those where man has intimately lived, where he has used and broken his pots, shaped and discarded his stone tools and smelted and wrought his metals. These are not always the places where he has chosen to commune with the supernatural. The political aspects of life are sometimes evidenced from the presence of large public monuments such as earthworks and buildings in stone. Only occasionally can sites of religious practice be identified. Many of these are associated with the burial of the dead.

ARCHAEOLOGY AND STONE AGE RELIGION

It is apparent from the care taken in disposing of the dead that one of Man's earliest concerns was with the mystery of life and death. Systematic burials date back perhaps to 40–30,000 B.C. Unfortunately, unless the burials are obviously under cairns, mounds or in rock-cut chambers, their discovery is more fortuitous than is the case with sites of habitation.

The late Stone Age use of painted gravestones, at such sites as Tzitzikama and Coldstream cave in Cape Province of South Africa, is of particular importance as it clearly associates the art at least at an early period with a rite of passage. The oldest South African painting so far found is a gravestone from a Cape coastal cave dating to 3,200 B.C. Other than demonstrating the association, very little can be said except to underline the significance attached to death. In addition, several of the Tzitzikama and other gravestone burials are liberally covered with ochre, accompanied with grave goods and buried in a foetal position.[4]

Religion has most often been inferred from objects it is *assumed* have a religious significance: from figures of clay, terracotta or metal, assumed to be idols or to feature in ancestor worship and from objects found either associated with the dead or in non-functional situations which, often for want of a better explanation, are termed ritual because it is impossible to reconstruct the actions with which they were once associated. It has at the outset to be admitted that prehistoric culture can rarely be more than partially reconstructed from the surviving material remains. It is difficult to interpret the function of many objects and certain 'ritual' objects probably had a quite practical use. Items of regalia present very definite problems in that very often they have no practical function and can be regarded as part of the ritual of kingship. The differences between objects associated with religious ritual and royal ritual are very few in the same way as the dividing line between religion and other aspects of social life are similarly difficult of definition. Without knowing their context, archaeologists could quite easily misinterpret both sceptres and rosaries. For the purpose of this paper ritual objects are assumed to be those used in rituals while symbols are objects or designs with no such apparent use.

An exception to the apparent dearth of information about the non-material aspects of life is the evidence provided by rock art. Rock art dates from as early as the seventh millennium B.C. in North Africa and the Sahara and the fourth millennium B.C. in Southern Africa. It has been estimated that there are altogether more than a hundred thousand rock pictures in Africa,[5] the greatest numbers of which are situated in the Sahara. The art is abundant only in those areas where suitable rock 'canvases' occur, in the mountains of the central Sahara, the inselbergs of Eastern Africa and the inselbergs and mountains of South Africa. In all the areas where rock art is abundant, later Stone Age settlement is also relatively dense, but there are many areas with numerous later Stone Age material where rock paintings and engravings do not occur. These pictures provide a commentary on various aspects of life, particularly the hunting economy, and represent one of the few approaches available to the religious psychology of Stone Age man. Because they provide one of the few insights possible into the non-material aspects of life they have been abused. Too much speculation about the meaning of individual scenes has been indulged in, while in over-reaction to such colourful speculations, other scholars have denied their importance in reconstructing the spiritual life of the artists.

Leo Frobenius, who visited Southern Africa several times before 1930, tried to see an intimate connection between the rich folk literature of Southern Africa and the rock art. He used the folk tales to interpret the paintings and engravings and in this way was very often guilty of imagining scenes which the paintings hardly substantiate. Even if his speculations are reliable, the results would not assist us very much in reconstructing Bushman or Bantu religion in that the reconstructions are made on the basis of myths and traditions already known from other sources. All that it would indicate is a greater common cultural background of two different groups of people and an antiquity for the myths going back several hundred years. The most significant group of paintings interpreted in this way by Frobenius are those from Rusape in Rhodesia, one of which appears to show a cloud with rain falling, a woman above it, a tree growing on the ground with a disjointed woman by its side and a man raising his hands to the sky. Frobenius interpreted this in the light of a Karanga tale of the sacrifice of a virgin in order to secure rain.[6] If this is accepted, then either the Bushmen who drew the picture knew the Karanga tale, or the paintings were the work of the Vakaranga themselves, a conclusion for which there is so far no possible evidence.

There seems to be unanimity in interpreting several designs from Rhodesia and South Africa as the representation of Mantis, a key figure in Bushman folklore, while several rather crudely drawn, often spotted creatures are interpreted as raincows. Their depiction in lakes or holes in the ground could suggest hippopotami but their unreality reflects their mythical nature. There are many extant tales about rain animals which, coming from water, had the ability to bring water. Though the drawing of such an animal is merely the record of a myth interpreted from nineteenth century survivals of Bushman folklore, the attendant details of such paintings indicates that definite rites were associated with such mythical creatures.[7]

It is certainly possible to see elements of the supernatural in the rock art of Southern Africa. The serpents depicted in several of the Matopos shelters are clearly larger than life size. Paintings from Mtoko in north eastern Rhodesia, described by Goodall,[8] depict, in red and brown ochre, seated and very evidently pregnant women whom she has interpreted as Mother Goddess figures. All of them have two long streams issuing from their abdomens, in several cases picked out in white, more than five times as long as the actual figures, on which smaller less detailed male figures in three instances have been found. The streams would appear to be connected with the female procreative system. The colour differentiation of the streams and the bodies of the women could have a symbolic meaning if Victor Turner's interpretation of the symbolic meaning of colour classification in African ritual has any relevance. Turner has suggested a triad of basic colours: red, black and white. He regards them as representing human products which heighten emotion and sees the source of the products as being 'located in the cosmos or in society'.[9] Among the Ndembu, red signifies blood and thus power, white suggests milk and semen and thus life, and black is death and is thus evil. He has suggested that the association of red ochre and black specularite with prehistoric burials has a symbolic significance. Red ochre is particularly common and could represent an attempt to revive the life force.

The magico-religious significance of this triad of colours may also be used to interpret the Tassili paintings where very often the round headed figures, usually the largest figures in a scene and frequently associated with smaller figures in red, are either painted or outlined in white. But the symbolic interpretation of the colour triad should perhaps not be overstressed. The Stone Age artist had only a limited repertoire of colours at his disposal. Blues and greens, normally obtainable from organic substances, were seldom constant enough to be used or have not withstood the passage of time. In this context, it should be noted that the terracotta figure from Entebbe, Uganda, which is discussed more fully in a later context, also exhibits the same basic colour triad and is certainly a 'ritual' object. If the colours do represent life forces and the 'experiences of social relationships'[10] the semen and milk of procreation, the blood of life and the decay of death, there is every reason why they should retain their significance right up to the present day.

In the rock art of the Sahara there is much that is quite evidently of a religious nature, such as masked figures, large figures in white and the association of such figures with inaccessible locations. The large size, often over two metres tall, of the paintings of impersonalised figures probably has a symbolic meaning and is an expression of an all-powerful presence. The masked figures suggest religious rites in which the masks gave the wearers supernatural powers. In a similar way to Frobenius, Henri Lhote has attempted to interpret many of the Tassili paintings in terms of later Fulani folk tales and has likened the masks to Senoutho ones from the Ivory Coast, but the links are very tenuous. The paintings are possibly five to eight thousand years old and mask resemblances are 'generic' rather than 'specific' in character. It is perhaps wise to conclude, as Lajoux[11] has done, that the significance of the paintings was that among other things they reminded the inhabitants of Tassili of their myths and legends. The beings depicted were 'engendered by the imagination of some visionary, belonged to a sacred repertory, to an iconography whose meaning has now escaped us' . . . Tassili and its rock paintings formed an indissoluble aesthetic, economic, social and religious whole. It is likely that many of the animal scenes had a functional use. The frequency of game and the fertility of livestock held a mystery and it is conceivable that the paintings of the animals helped to resolve that mystery, but it is impossible from present evidence or even ethnographic parallels to support the magico-religious function of the paintings over any of the other many interpretations.

It has been argued by Hampate Ba and Dieterlen [12] that the Tassili paintings actually illustrate the *lotori* initiation rites of the Fulani and accurately reflect their religious and cosmological beliefs. Their detailed interpretation of individual paintings is often very convincing and could indicate the great antiquity of Fulani myths and legends. Serpent-like creatures with animal heads, two-headed cows and solar symbols, all of which indicate a belief in the supernatural, are readily interpreted. A word of caution must, however, be introduced. Some of the symbols, particularly those involving the solar system, have also been interpreted by Lhote as being derived from XXIst dynasty prototypes of ancient Egypt. [13] There is, however, no possible evidence, even tenuous, of contact between the Fulani and ancient Egypt. Interpretations of rock paintings are subjective and different observers will make comparisons to symbols with which they are familiar. Perhaps the significant point is that certain similar themes recur in the art or folklore of different peoples which reflect not culture contact but similar responses to the problems of understanding the supernatural.

As with the deep cave locations of the Upper Palaeolithic rock paintings of Europe, it is obvious that the location of many of the sites, and of the paintings within the sites, had a significance which provides some clue as to the institutionalised nature of Stone Age religion. At Lolui island in Lake Victoria [14] paintings were found on the underside of a capstone and on the flanks of the supporting stones in a natural shelter in an inselberg. Among the supporting stones were several rock gongs, which when played used the shelter itself as a resonating chamber. The association of paintings with rock gongs in their striking natural situation, together with the rock floor of the shelter, polished by generations of dancers, enables the word 'sanctuary' to be applied with little hesitation. Many of the Tassili paintings were executed well above the reach of the shelter's occupants so that they had to look up at what are relatively large figures.

We can then conclude from archaeological evidence alone that in the hunting food-gathering stage of life in Africa some religious beliefs, possibly in the after life, existed by middle Stone Age times (? 30–15,000 B.C.) as evidenced by the red ochre on carefully buried skeletons. By later Stone Age times the evidence of the paintings all over Africa indicates a strong belief in the supernatural, and the colours themselves may have had a symbolic meaning. Scenes both from Southern Africa and Tassili clearly illustrate myths in which supernatural elements occur. The masked figures, dancing scenes and the remoteness of situation of certain paintings allow us to postulate that the religion was institutionalised in the sense of possessing persons who performed rites and involving definite areas where such rites were performed. To speculate on the nature of the rites would on present evidence be too hypothetical but there is the possibility that some of the rites may have been connected with improving the fertility of game, promoting the success of the hunt and procuring rain. A final question to be asked is how much of this religious practice continued into more modern times? If Frobenius is correct, it is probable that some of the folklore of the hunters was passed directly over to the agriculturalist, and that the use of red colouring matter and careful disposal of the dead, often with grave goods, was a further Stone Age legacy, while the symbolism of the basic triad of colours continued its relevance, if it can really be proved that they had a significance for Stone Age foraging peoples. Even though groups were small in number, ritual experts were of significance and this too was to be a continuing feature of social development. It sometimes has been inferred from Childe's theories on the Agricultural revolution[15] that it was only the creation of a surplus food supply that allowed ritual specialists to be maintained by the community. Modern ethnographic parallels would indicate that the ritual specialist in a hunting group would not have been a full time 'priest' but only a member of the band endowed with certain recognised 'religious' attributes. It is certain that many symbols had a significance to the whole group and not just to the specialist and in this sense the religious practice was of a generalised nature.

ARCHAEOLOGY AND IRON AGE RELIGION

Religion is rather more difficult to assess for the many settled societies of Iron Age Africa partly because their social groups were larger, their lives more elaborate and their material culture more varied. With settled communities 'ritual' items, many of which are presumably of little importance, invariably increase. Small clay figurines were made by many peoples. From Tanzania, Hans Cory[16] demonstrated their use as initiation symbols. In Tchad they were common in the Sao culture and many were evidently made by children for amusement but others had a ritual use. Most figurines can be looked at in different lights, but only if they are in a specific archaeological context suggestive of a sanctuary or a place of ritual observance, can the archaeologist safely pronounce them to be of ritual significance. Cattle figurines have been found in both Zambia and Rhodesia, normally in late first millennium A.D. contexts. Very often, as in the Kalomo culture, they are crude in form. Does this crudity indicate a hesitation in making too skilful a rendering for fear of bringing bad luck to an actual cow, an innate inability due to youth, or lack of manual dexterity? Do the figurines suggest that a cattle cult existed, or were the figurines created to promote fertility? We have no direct means of answering such questions; all we can say is that figurines existed.

Of rather more interest, as they cannot be mistaken as play things, are the phalli at Zimbabwe and other Rhodesian sites. Mostly 5–10 cms. long and made of soapstone or clay, they occasionally exhibit female breasts on the body of the object. Unfortunately, no undoubted phalli were found in the 1958 excavations but in the earlier excavations, in the Eastern Enclosure of the Acropolis, Bent[17] found phalli, soapstone birds, and soapstone bowls associated with what he assumed to be an altar. Hall found twenty-five more phalli in the same spot in 1903. Also in a terrace enclosure, Caton-Thompson[18] found a free standing wall of no apparent functional use but with a vent running through it, 13 cm. in diameter, which she suggested may have been used for libations. The phalli are thus found at a site which has ritual significance, in a context with other objects of possible ritual use. Attempts were made in the past, and as recently as 1967 by Bruwer,[19] to link the phalli and the conical towers with a Phoenician religion but there are no exotic finds to support this theory and whatever answer is provided must fit the Rhodesian context.

With the study of the oral traditions of Rhodesia by Abraham and later scholars, it has become customary to explain the significance of the ruins in terms of the Mwari cult. Part of our evidence for the religion of Mwene Mutapa derives from Portuguese sources. The power of the Shona chiefs according to Alpers[20] was based on their control of the religious apparatus necessary for communication with Mwari. One immediate problem is that we too often seek to explain the archaeological findings in terms of the evidence from the oral traditions which refer to a Shona group who were not the original inhabitants of Zimbabwe, and whose most exhaustively studied chieftainship was located on the Zambezi. A feature of the cult was the use by spirit mediums of caves and rockshelters to commune with the spirits. It is significant that a large number of the key Rhodesian sites are situated in the areas where convenient clusters of rocks or rockshelters occur for the practice of such a cult. Evidence, however, cannot be inferred about the Vakaranga and/or Shona and their cult earlier than Zimbabwe period III dated to A.D. 1050–1450 by Summers,[21] though on the basis of imported ceramics Garlake[22] would assign a rather earlier closing date. Yet it is in period II that the first figurines occur. The phalli and soapstone bowls are inferred to have been found in period IV contexts dated to A.D. 1450–1834 by Summers,[23] though to a pre-seventeenth century date by Garlake,[24] but unfortunately none has yet been found in a well-dated situation and these types of objects are not mentioned in the traditions. The soapstone birds may have been a kind of totem of the Rozvi and thus of political or clan, rather than of specifically religious, importance. Walton[25] cites present day analogies of carved birds serving to frighten away the dreaded lightning bird, while the difficulties encountered by several European visitors who tried to remove them emphasises the importance attached to the soapstone birds. Summers[26] regards them as memorials to former chiefs, each one distinguished by its own special designs. Zimbabwe illustrates one of the greatest limitations of archaeological evidence—that the objects which survive do not necessarily provide us with the information we require about religion nor do they necessarily relate to information gleaned from other lines of inquiry. Nevertheless we can safely conclude that the large numbers of phalli, soapstone birds, possible altars, rocks and a rockshelter found at Zimbabwe indicate some religious activity, but we would be unwise on the grounds of the archaeological evidence alone to be more specific.

Other features of Zimbabwe such as the great Enclosure and the barbed copper alloy spearheads have also been interpreted as being of a religious character. It is significant that the more conventionally ritual objects like the phalli are all from the Acropolis. The Great Enclosure was so dug about by early excavators that their more scientific successors have been unable to relate many of the earlier finds to the structures that survive. Both the Enclosure and spears can quite easily be thought of as evidence of chiefly authority, the former denoting the power to command the services of his people for constructing a

35

large 'prestige' public work and the latter as items of regalia. Nothing within the Great Enclosure can be specifically termed religious, in the limited meaning of religion, though in the wider sense everything associated with a chief, who embodies the ethos of his people, is religious. Caton Thompson[27] has suggested that the bulls depicted on the soapstone bowls are evidence of a bull or cattle cult. The bowls have only been found at Zimbabwe but they are separated from the cattle figurines by probably at least 500 years and are not accompanied by any other tangible evidence of a cattle cult. Summers[28] interprets fragments of bowls found in 1958 as a foundation deposit for wall buttresses of later period IV date. Again depending on one's subjective approach, such broken fragments of bowls could be regarded as a form of ritual dedication in which the prior act of breaking also has a religious significance, or purely as incidental 'fill' in the deposit. Other creatures, for example a reptile in the 1958 find, are also shown on the bowls and there is thus no reason to postulate a cattle cult though there is every reason to assume that cattle were significant socially and economically.

At Khami, divination pellets were found in association with a hoard presumed to be that of a chief.[29] The divining pellets have been interpreted as such by comparison with those in use by present-day peoples. Associated spears have been interpreted as ceremonial and representations of the chief's power. Small ivory lions from the same hoard may be connected with a religious belief, perhaps associated with the *mhondoro* spirit mediums, and were once probably part of a staff of office. Such finds demonstrate the loss dealt to Zambezian archaeology by the ravages of the Ancient Ruins Company and other treasure seekers of the turn of the century.

The Mapungubwe burials, the only rich undisturbed burials so far carefully excavated in the general Rhodesian area, were accompanied by a gold mace, a gold plated rhinoceros and other items of regalia. There is no supporting evidence which can allow an interpretation other than that they are the regalia of a chief whose subjects were responsible for the labour of transporting thousands of tons of the earth to the top of Mapungubwe hill. Pottery found associated indicates a broad cultural relationship with material from Zimbabwe period III contexts. In the valley, earlier burials at Bambandyanalo, dated to the eleventh century A.D., were said by their excavator, Gardner,[30] to be 'beast' burials because of the association of cattle bones and thus also indicative of a cattle cult of possible 'Hamitic' origin. Bones of domestic animals are however frequently interred with or left for the dead in many parts of Africa at the present day and numerous instances can be cited of the bones of food animals being associated with Iron Age burials. Fagan[31] has cited several other Iron Age sites in Rhodesia and Zambia, where animal bones have also been found but for which no suggestion of a cult has been made.

If cattle cults existed, there is more likely to be evidence of them from East Africa where the Hima-Tusi peoples of the inter-lacustrine area developed highly organised pastoral societies.[32] Though intensely pastoral, with their music, dance, military organisation, social units and social structure adapted to a pastoral life, they did not practise any of the plastic arts. Iron models of cows formed part of the regalia of the *abakama* of Karagwe at Bweranyange in the Bukoba District of Tanzania but it is probable that these were made in the nineteenth century by a local blacksmith or even by Arabs from the East African Coast.[33] In the same general area are the thousand or more schematic paintings of cattle at Bwanjai and Rukorongo. These serve to emphasise the antiquity of the importance of cattle that is also well known from the Bacwezi tales which tell of a pastoral state over a large part of Western Uganda around A.D. 1400–1500.[34] Further instances of the significance of cattle are the presence in both the regalia of Buganda and Rwanda of metal objects in the shapes of horns. But though a cult or devotion to cattle can be demonstrated, the material evidence is insufficient to infer that the cult was ever more than a cult. Rituals there were, deities also, which from the Bacwezi tales similarly had an excessive love for their cattle but further than this archaeology cannot take us.

From East Africa, there is also further evidence of a ritual nature. In Uganda at Luzira[35] and Entebbe[36] broken terracotta figures have been found. The Entebbe figure bears both male and female sexual organs and has no obvious use and is associated with an unmistakable phallus. Both are dated by their associated pottery to the eighteenth century A.D. Other than pronouncing them ritual no interpretation can be given, though the fact that they are broken and were evidently discarded in a midden deposit prompts the suggestion that they were part of a deliberately destroyed shrine. The same conclusion has been reached[37] for the Luzira material which consists of several fairly naturalistic heads and limbs. A shrine continued to exist at the spot till well into the present century but the actual figurines were broken and found in a series of rubbish pits. They could have been smashed by an early nineteenth century Kabaka engaged in crushing the authority of the custodians of the Balubaale shrines. Also from Uganda are parts of broken bowl bellows, excavated from the Munsa earthwork,[38] which have attached in clay either male or female genitalia, indicating that the draught had to come from both male and female bowls in order to produce iron. The antiquity of shrines can often be gauged by the objects scattered around them such as the pots near the 'Witch Tree' at Mubende in Uganda.[39] The latter indicates that there was a deep rooted belief in the natural strength residing in the spirit represented by the tree. But other than such similar slight indications, evidence of religion is difficult to adduce from the surviving archaeological data.

Circles of standing stones are common in Ethiopia, Senegal and the Gambia though rare in East Africa. Those in the Gambia have been dated to the eighth century A.D.;[40] they occur in definite groups and are associated with monoliths and mounds possibly thrown up over graves. They have been variously related to sun cults and to the megaliths of the second and third millennia B.C. of the Mediterranean and Western Europe. They evidently involved a great deal of labour in their quarrying and erection, a labour for which there is no evident functional purpose. It is, however, extremely easy to mistake the nature of many of the smaller stone circles of Africa. In Kenya, among the Kalenjin-speaking peoples, it is customary for certain groups of elders to have a meeting place away from the settlement, occasionally within a wooded[41] area. A very fine squatting circle or *poret*, consisting of stone uprights against which the elders sat, exists at Tambach. Similar ones are also known from the Southern Sudan. If their use were not known from existing traditions, a religious purpose would have been entertained by the archaeologists.

Heaps of stones, decorated grave-stones and massive tumuli mark pre-historic graves in many parts of Africa. The meaning of some of this activity is understood or can be surmised, as with the more recent Galla graves of Ethiopia, from current ethnographic practice, but it is obvious from the far from random make-up of some of the cairns and mounds that elaborate ritual may have been involved in many of the known burial sites throughout Africa. Does a broken grindstone on a cairn merely mean that it was a stone to hand that was used for building, or could it have been associated with the dead person buried beneath and was broken as a symbolic act of freeing the spirit of either the person or the stone? Could stones foreign to the area have been brought in for a purpose? Again we do not know, but the careful analysis of cairns, both of their contents and structure and a comparative analysis, both on a regional and inter-regional basis, may one day yield data on which sounder speculation can be based.

In West Africa there are firmer grounds for reconstructing rituals connected with the dead. In Tchad many Sao figurines, frequently consisting only of stylized heads and often buried with pots in groups, represent spirit burials as they are unaccompanied by actual skeletal remains. Similarly, in Ghana and Ivory Coast, funerary figurines have been found. At Ahinsan[42] in the forest area of Ghana, excavations have yielded large numbers of terracotta heads and pots decorated with figures in addition to undecorated pots, many of which were found in an upturned position. The site is traditionally reported to be a place revered by seventy-seven villages and the figures perhaps represent the spirits of the dead from at least a number of those villages. Similar figures have been found at many other sites in Ghana and the tradition of making funerary figures still persists in the Kwahu area. The association of an excavated site with living traditions makes it possible to interpret the more poorly documented sites. The Ahinsan finds have been assigned to the seventeenth century and it would appear that the making of such figures is only one of many indications of the elaboration of the cultural life of the forest region following the establishment of the Forest States.[43]

In Nigeria, the plastic arts go back even further in time. The Nok terracottas were certainly being made by 500 B.C.[44] while the more sophisticated art of Ife can be dated to as early as A.D. 900.[45] What does this art tell us about the religion of its makers? Unfortunately, it tells us very little. Many objects have been found but until recently very few have been found in an undisturbed primary context, so that their use is obscure. The Nok terracottas may have served as grave or shrine furniture.[46] Most figures are stray finds and neither their associations nor their context help to suggest the type of ritual, if any, with which they could have been associated. The Ife figures feature in present day festivals. They are often found in sacred groves, and are used for sacrifices or are, if large, themselves shrines. Nevertheless the broken state of many of those in shrines suggests that their present ritual use may be secondary. In 1969 at Lafogido Street in Ife the Director of the Nigerian Antiquities Department, Ekpo Eyo,[47] found a group of pots facing into a rectangular enclosure. On four of the pots were the figures of animals associated with royalty —antelope, elephant, ram and bushpig. Fragments of the bases, on which larger sculptures may have stood, were also located. The terracottas in this case have been interpreted as the 'sacred furnishings' of a tomb or temple. Certain heads with their mouths gagged have been found, indicating the practice of human sacrifice probably for religious purpose. What this purpose was we cannot tell; perhaps the sacrifice was connected with ensuring the strength of the *Onis*, or the sacrificed persons were retainers who had to accompany the *Oni* at his death. Nevertheless the general conclusion to be drawn from the art of Ife is that it is largely commemorative, most often of the royal *Oñis*, but certain elements and traditions link it with the later art of Benin, where the art forms an integral part of the ritual of kingship.

The art of Benin, the most abundant of the figurative art of pre-twentieth century West Africa that has survived, could provide on its own a study of the ritual of kingship. As with Ife and Nok the art has rarely been found in an undisturbed archaeological context. Dating is often difficult and what has survived is largely weighted in favour of the 'bronzes', whereas it is certain that numerous wood carvings also existed. The art expresses 'the symbolism of the ceremonial'[48] associated with the highly centralised position of the *Oba*, whose power lay in the 'traditional mystical values attaching to the sacred institution of kingship'.[49] Like other 'divine' monarchs, he was credited with supernatural powers. He was the embodiment of the spirit and continuity of his people, the living ancestor whose health and power had to be ensured by suitable rituals. The plaques show definite ritual scenes and, in conjunction with oral traditions, are an invaluable source of information on the rituals at the Benin Court. Certain gods, often in the figure of the *Oba*, are represented but curiously the practice of human sacrifice is not a regular feature of the ceremonials depicted, an indication of how inadequate the interpretation of the Benin Court life would be without the aid of the historical traditions.

Various creatures which appear in the art, such as snakes or fish issuing from the nostrils of *Obas*, a feature also found in Ife, have been interpreted as indicative of the great magical strength of the rulers[50] and certainly indicate one of the supernatural aspects of kingship. Other elements of royal divinity are the mud fish legs of Oba Ohe, who in one plaque demonstrates further superhuman attributes by grasping two leopards by their tails. Several of the *Obas* have their hands supported by royal attendants or their feet raised from the ground. Art is not dispersed over a wide area as at Ife which is an indication of the change in religious emphasis between Ife and Benin.

But on the whole, the interpretation of the terracottas and bronzes of Nigeria has been left to the art historians. Very often, interpretations are based on single pieces. It is hoped that in the course of time, as is now happening in the Ife area, art pieces will be found *in situ* so that their original context can be determined. If dated, the development of ideas behind the art can be attempted and inferences about religion perhaps drawn.

It would be possible to catalogue numerous instances of religious interpretations of individual objects from all over Africa, either as objects of ritual use, like metal gongs and bells or like figurines such as the *nomoli* of Sierra Leone;[51] or because of their association with burials, or with the ritualized office of chief or king; or because of their context in a presumed sanctuary. But it would merely be a catalogue of *minutiae* without providing detailed insights into former religious systems. This is one of the major drawbacks of archaeological evidence. On its own it offers few insights into the spiritual life of man yet there is a tendency by historians to invoke archaeological research to validate theories arrived at by other lines of inquiry. A monument is thought of as being of religious significance and thus it is held that an excavation should be conducted to find the evidence, which may then in fact be found in the form of ritual objects. It is the existence of such preconceived ideas of the religious character of sites like Zimbabwe or of the Senegambian stone circles, that have made the acceptance or appreciation of archaeological evidence very difficult.

Before looking to the future, certain general observations can be made about Iron Age religion in Africa. With the coming of agriculture the material culture of man increased, and crafts such as pottery became necessary. The graphic arts of the Stone Age, except in the Sahara, declined while the plastic arts increased. It is tempting to see the figurines of early agricultural societies as evidence of religion but this temptation should be avoided. Ucko,[52] in his study of anthropomorphic figures from Crete, suggested various categories of figures —children's toys; initiation figures; vehicles for sympathetic magic, particularly in connection with childbirth and fertility. Chaplin[53] has added the further category of the representation of a deity or spirit. Except for Rhodesia[54] there has been no exhaustive catalogue of African prehistoric figurines and those that have been described could often be placed in several categories. A further Iron Age development is that graves became more elaborate and grave goods increased in number. Does this suggest a greater cult of the dead or is it merely an indication of the more settled life of the agriculturalist? What, however, is certain is that in settled societies, where the dead are buried in proximity to the living and where the social units are larger, there is a greater awareness and respect for the ancestors. The ancestors are often thought of as the living dead. In many societies they participate in the life of the community. Effigies are erected in their honour and in some societies the incumbent ruler symbolises the spirit of the dead founder. But in saying this we are overstepping the bounds of archaeological evidence and it is perhaps in the availability of other lines of evidence, oral traditions and the study of the ethnographic present, that our understanding of the later Iron Age is greater than that of the preceding Stone Age. But though we can utilise parallel studies, very often the confusion as to what constitutes a religious, as opposed to a secular, system is confounded, particularly when dealing with the rituals surrounding sacral rulers. A further development of the Iron Age was the establishment of shrines, of places dedicated to the performance of religious rituals. Within this category are comprised both natural sanctuaries, which also occurred in the Stone Age, and deliberate man-made enclosures, stone circles or even groves of trees. Unfortunately little attention has been given to many of these sites by the archaeologist since they very often provide very little evidence of occupation.

PRIORITIES FOR FUTURE RESEARCH

Future researches must first and foremost study the well-documented material culture of the present in order to interpret past material culture. In Uganda, the foundation of the Museum in 1908 was as a 'house of fetishes'. Many of the fetishes appear to be ordinary objects, shields, spears, horns, etc. Occasionally they have mysterious appendages but if found in an archaeological context, without their normally perishable appendages, they would not be classed as ritual objects or even as objects which had been ritualised. There is a further need to study exhaustively the regalia of yesterday and to illustrate how many ordinary objects in course of time obtain a ritual significance. In the lacustrine kingdoms, billhooks form part of the regalia of rulers[55] and symbolise the ruler's desire or ability to cultivate the whole land. From such examples it is obvious that the archaeologist can never hope to study adequately even surviving material culture without some insights into traditional ethnographic practice. The study of regalia is particularly important where it includes such evident ceremonial items as twin-headed or multi-bladed spears. Why should certain spears be associated with rain-making? Questions like these may be answered by reference to the traditions and only by asking and answering them can we hope to project our knowledge back into the past to interpret the 'ritual' objects dug up by the archaeologist.

We thus have constantly to infer about the past from the present. But such inferences should not only concern material culture. It has been suggested that certain numbers, such as nine, have a ritual significance. Can we infer from this that a repeated occurrence of nine, such as in the openings of a pot, the decorations on an iron object, the facets of a mace, would have had a similar significance in the past? Certain items are meant to be destroyed and are made of perishable substances; some graves never contain burials. An understanding of the reasons behind such practices is essential if prehistoric broken figurines or presumed cenotaphs are to yield other than descriptive data.

Of the utmost importance and a priority for new research in Africa is an accurate description of modern shrines. In Uganda the type of work attempted by Lukyn Williams,[56] in which he described the contents of each of the Buganda jaw-bone shrines, should be followed up. This is particularly important when it is realised that in most of the kingdom areas of East Africa many of the royal shrines have been destroyed or their contents dispersed in the years of rapid political change from 1959. Numerous shrines contain objects of different ages which can at times be dated and thus may indicate the ultimate age of the shrine or the period of its greatest importance. Other shrines may exhibit building techniques that are foreign to the area in which they are presently situated and thus reveal a 'foreign' element in the religion itself. Shrines normally have a permanency not possessed by habitation settlements and the different features of shrines and the shrines themselves should be mapped to indicate geographical distributions which may indicate similarities between cults previously thought of as unrelated. Though this may perhaps smack of a return to the amorphous culture history of the pre-1945 period, in which scholars like Tor Irstam in his *The King of Ganda*[57] listed highly selected similarities of Kingship over a very wide geographical area, the object is not the selection of certain features thought to be similar, but the totality of description. Shrine contents and furnishings have particular names which may preserve clues as to their original use or reasons for their ritualisation. In the mapping of modern shrine data it is important to distinguish between clan and 'tribal' shrines and to relate the distributions both to the modern and presumed former ecology and also to the present settlement pattern. This is clearly a field for co-operation between historians, anthropologists, archaeologists and linguists. It is also evident from the literature of the contact period of 1890–1910, in particular in East Africa, that many shrines were destroyed. Some of the contents found their way to European museums, a well-documented example being the Kibuuka relics of Buganda[58] which were for half a century in Cambridge. There are thus possibilities of relating museum material to historical documents and studying the oral traditions relating to their removal as well as to studying the present state of the shrines. In Uganda a start has been made to the study of modern shrines by Baya Nabaguzi who is examining the historical significance of *Balubaale* shrines around Lake Victoria.

Though the approaches I have described are not strictly archaeological such work would clearly assist the archaeologists in interpreting the remains of former shrines. In the case of the sites of former shrines, particularly those recently destroyed, if permission can be granted, there would be a value in conducting intensive excavations which might either indicate changes that have recently occurred or elucidate the spatial arrangements of such shrines. An objection that is often posed is the social inaccessibility of modern shrines. This is clearly an inhibiting factor in their study but occasions do occur, which necessitate the abandonment of modern shrines. Recently in Ghana Reverend Father Steemers[59] has made a detailed study of the Krachi shrines in advance of the floodwaters of the Volta lake and described the new shrines immediately after their resettlement. The descriptions by Reverend Father Schoffeleers of shrines in Malawi, discussed elsewhere in this volume, further indicate the potentialities for such research.

One can only conclude with a plea for greater care in interpreting archaeological evidence. Too often cults are assumed on the basis of a few ambiguous figurines, religious practices on the basis of unproven ritual objects. Greater knowledge may be forthcoming from a more comprehensive study of recent ethnographic materials, from detailed analyses of the structure, content and social and economic context of graves and shrines, and also from new discoveries of 'art' objects, like those of Nok, Ife and Benin, in undisturbed archaeological contexts. Nevertheless it is apparent that archaeological data on its own has severe limitations for the historical study of religious systems and it is to be hoped that a greater understanding of present and recent African religious systems will open up fresh approaches.

NOTES

[1] The author acknowledges the generous help of the Wenner-Green Foundation for Anthropological Research, which financed field research in both Uganda and Ghana.

[2] M. E. Spiro, 'Religion: Problems of Definition and Explanation', in M. Banton (ed.) *Anthropological Approaches to the Study of Religion* (London 1966) p. 97.

[3] C. Geertz, 'Religion as a Cultural System', in Banton, *op. cit.* p. 3.

[4] J. D. Clark *The Prehistory of Southern Africa* (London 1959) p. 250.

[5] Burchand Brentjes *African Rock Art* (London 1969) p. 2.

[6] Leo Frobenius *Erythräa* (Leipzig 1931) pp. 204–6.

[7] A. R. Wilcox *The Rock Art of South Africa* (Johannesburg 1963) p. 33.

[8] A. Goodall, 'A distinctive mythical figure appearing in the rock paintings of Southern

Rhodesia', in *Actes du IVᵉ Congrès Panafricain de Préhistoire et de L'étude du Quaternaire* (ed. G. Mortelmans and J. Nenquin) section III, Annales du Musée Royal de L'Afrique Centrale, No. 40 (Tervuren 1962) pp. 399–406.

9 V. W. Turner, 'Colour Classification in Ndembu Ritual', in Banton, *op. cit.* p. 80.

10 *ibid.* p. 81.

11 J. D. Lajoux *The Rock Paintings of Tassili* (London 1963) p. 19.

12 A. Hampate Ba and G. Dieterlen, 'Les fresques d'époque bovidienne du Tassili N'Ajjer et les traditions des Peul: hypotheses d'interprétation' *Journ. Soc. Africanistes* 36, (1966) pp. 141–57.

13 H. Lhote, 'Les peintures parietales d'epoque bovidienne du Tassili: elements sur la magie et la religion' *Journ. Soc. Africanistes* 36 (1966) pp. 7–27.

14 G. Jackson, J. S. Gartlan and M. Posnansky, 'Rock Gongs and Associated Rock Paintings on Lolui Island, Lake Victoria, Uganda: A Preliminary Note' *Man* 1965, no. 31.

15 V. G. Childe *Man Makes Himself* (London 1936).

16 H. Cory *African Figurines* (London 1956).

17 J. T. Bent *The Ruined Cities of Mashonaland* (London 1892) p. 129.

18 G. Caton-Thompson, *The Zimbabwe Culture: Ruins and Reactions* (London 1931) p. 76.

19 A. J. Bruwer *Zimbabwe, Rhodesia's Ancient Greatness* (Johannesburg 1965).

20 E. A. Alpers, 'The Mutapa and Malawi political systems', in T. O. Ranger (ed.) *Aspects of Central African History* (London 1968) p. 6.

21 R. Summers, 'Iron Age Industries of Southern Africa', in W. W. Bishop and J. D. Clark (eds.) *Background to Evolution in Africa* (Chicago 1967) pp. 687–700.

22 P. S. Garlake, 'The value of imported ceramics in the dating and interpretation of the Rhodesian Iron Age' *Journ. Afr. Hist.* IX, (1968) pp. 13–33.

23 Summers *op. cit.* p. 695.

24 Garlake *op. cit.* p. 28.

25 J. Walton, 'Some features of the Monomotapa Culture' in *Proc. Third Pan-African Congress on Prehistory* ed. J. D. Clark (London 1957) pp. 336–38.

26 R. Summers *Zimbabwe, A Rhodesian Mystery* (Cape Town 1963) pp. 70–74.

27 Caton-Thompson *op. cit.* p. 189.

28 Summers *Zimbabwe* p. 265.

29 K. R. Robinson *Khami Ruins* (Cambridge 1959) pp. 108–11.

30 G. A. Gardner *Mapungubwe* vol. II, (Pretoria 1963).

31 B. M. Fagan, 'The Greefswald Sequence: Bambandyanalo and Mapungubwe' *Journ. Afr. Hist.* 5 (1964) p. 346.

32 M. Posnansky, 'Kingship, Archaeology and Historical Myth' *Uganda Journ.* 30 (1966) pp. 1–12.

33 J. H. Speke *Journal of the Discovery of the Source of the Nile* (London 1863) p. 170 in 1922 ed.

34 M. Posnansky, Introduction to second edition *Twilight Tales of the Black Baganda* by Ruth Fisher (1911) (London 1970).

35 E. J. Wayland, M. C. Burkitt and H. J. Braunholtz, 'Archaeological discoveries at Luzira' *Man* (1933) No. 29.

36 M. Posnansky and J. H. Chaplin, 'Terracotta figures from Entebbe, Uganda' *Man*, 3 (1968) pp. 644–50.

37 J. H. Chaplin *The Prehistoric Art of the Lake Victoria Region* unpublished M.A. thesis, Makerere University College, (Kampala 1967).

38 E. C. Lanning, 'Genital Symbols on Smiths' Bellows in Uganda' *Man* (1954) no. 262.

39 E. C. Lanning, 'Excavations at Mubende Hill' *Uganda Journ.* 30 (1966) pp. 153–163.

40 P. O. Beale, 'The Stone Circles of the Gambia and the Senegal' *Tarikh* 2, No. 2 (1968) pp. 1–11.

[41] Posnansky, 'Kingship', p. 7.

[42] D. Calvocoressi, West Africa, C.O.W.A. *Surveys and Bibliographies on Old World Archaeology*, Area 11, no. IV (Boston 1969) p. 7

[43] M. Posnansky, 'Discovering Ghana's Past', Ghana National Museum, public lecture, 1969.

[44] F. Willett *Ife in the History of West African Sculpture* (London 1967).

[45] B. M. Fagan, 'Radiocarbon Dates for sub-Saharan Africa VI' *Journ. Afr. Hist.*, 10 (1969) p. 154.

[46] Willett *op, cit.* p. 115.

[47] Ekpo Eyo, '1969 Excavations at Ile-Ife' *African Arts* III, no. 2 (1970) pp. 44–47.

[48] P. Dark, in W. and B. Forman and P. Dark *Benin Art* (London 1960) p. 13.

[49] *Ibid.*

[50] *Ibid.* p. 53.

[51] J. H. Atherton and Milan Kalous, 'Nomoli' *Journ. Afr. Hist.* 11 (1970) pp. 303–17.

[52] P. J. Ucko, 'The Interpretation of Prehistoric Anthropomorphic Figurines' *Journ. Roy. Anth. Inst.* 92 (1962) pp. 38–54.

[53] Chaplin *op. cit.*

[54] R. Summers, 'Human figures in clay and stone from Southern Rhodesia', *Occasional Papers of the National Museum of Southern Rhodesia* no. 21, (1955).

[55] M. Trowell and K. P. Wachsmann *Tribal Crafts of Uganda* (London 1953) pp. 91–92.

[56] F. Lukyn Williams, unpublished list of contents of Royal shrines of Buganda, Uganda Museum (Kampala 1936).

[57] T. Irstam *The King of Ganda, Studies in the Institution of Sacral Kingship in Africa* (Stockholm 1944).

[58] F. B. Welbourn, 'Kibuuka Comes Home' *Transition* 2, no. 5, (Kampala 1962) pp. 15–17, 20; J. Roscoe, 'Kibuka, the War God of the Baganda' *Man* VII (1907); Merrick Posnansky, 'Kibuuka . . . The War God' *Habari* XXVIII, (Kampala 1963) p. 27.

[59] J. Steemers, 'The material paraphernalia of the traditional religious cults of the Kete Krachi area' unpublished paper, Dept. of Archaeology, University of Ghana 1968.

CHRISTOPHER EHRET

Language Evidence and Religious History

Words are the carriers of ideas, and thus on the history of a people's words can be built a history of their ideas, religious and social. Histories of individual words can yield inferences about histories of particular conceptualisations and elements of belief denoted by the words; and because of the interrelations a people construct between their concepts and because of the semantic influences of words on each other, word-histories studied in systemic contexts can reveal systemic change and development. Lexical histories fall in three categories: on extant evidence a word in a language can be shown either to go back to a speech ancestral to the language, or to derive from other words in the language, or to have been borrowed from some other language.[1] Behind each type of word-history lie different human histories.

Word-reconstruction alone usually allows only modest inferences. Its main usefulness is in establishing historical continuities. If a name used today for a particular kind of spirit, for instance, can be shown to go back, with little or no meaning change, to an earlier language ancestral to the modern one, then the concept denoted by the term can be seen to have been current at least since the period of existence of the ancestral language. That evidence by itself will not, however, define the position of the element in earlier systems of belief, that is, will not testify whether or not its over-all role and significance in thought were the same as at present.

Inferences of broader implication can be made from the derivations of a people's ideational words from other words in their language. The metaphors and allusions hidden in word derivations reflect earlier conceptualisations of belief, and kinds and amounts of change between earlier metaphors and present ones will reveal something of the changes over time in outlooks and beliefs of a people. If, as an entirely hypothetical example, the earlier term for the High God, which could be reconstructed to have been identical with the word meaning 'sky' and 'above' had been replaced by a term for God literally renderable as the 'nourisher' or 'sustainer', then one would have to assume that a considerable, even revolutionary, change towards greater immediacy and personal or communal importance of the High God would have to have occurred in the society, coincident with or preceding the coining of the new term.[2] Or a metaphor might be shown to be very long-retained and thus to reflect an area of conservatism in thought. In social thinking, the metaphor of some modern Kalenjin peoples describing foreigners, whether circumcised or not, as 'uncircumcised'—that is, as identifiable with children in Kalenjin society —probably goes back to their proto-Southern Nilotic ancestors. The metaphor also operated among the other linguistic descendants of the proto-Southern Nilotes, the Dadog of Tanzania, where it caused the Dadog reflex of a proto-

45

Southern Nilotic root to lose its original meaning of 'uncircumcised child' and come to mean just 'slave', that is, 'resident foreigner' lacking the political rights of an adult member of society.[3]

In some cases even portions of the broader system of belief of earlier periods can be discerned in word-derivations. The Akie word for ancestor-spirit is cognate with the proto-Southern Nilotic and proto-Kalenjin words for 'God'.[4] For the meaning change to have taken place, the High God and the ancestor-spirits must have been viewed at the time of the semantic shift as belonging to the same category of existence, as being different not in kind but in scale. The earlier word for 'God' got extended to cover the whole category of powers consisting of the High God and the spirits, then lost its referent to the High God with the Akie adoption of a loan-translation of the Maasai word for 'God'.[5] Explaining the meaning-shift itself should be interesting. Did it reflect an increasing attribution of remoteness to the High God and corresponding emphasising of the ancestor-spirits in early Akie religious thought? Did the Akie adoption of the loan-translation then reflect a later partial return to recognition of the High God, or was it adopted simply to fill a felt semantic gap in terminology? Investigation of other Akie religious word-histories or of ethnographic evidence might help in answering these questions.

While study of word-reconstructions and word-derivations can give evidence on continuity and change in a people's concepts and conceptualisations, study of loanwords and loan-translations can shed light on the interaction of different people's beliefs as a factor in religious and intellectual history. Sometimes a loan from one language to another denotes an outright addition to beliefs. Proto-Kalenjin *mu·sa·mpwa·n, an old borrowing from a Nyanza Bantu language, is a probable example. In Bantu the root meant ancestor-spirit in general, though subcategories of evil and non-evil spirits were recognised by the Nyanza Bantu. It was taken into Kalenjin, however, only in the sense of 'evil spirit', while an older Kalenjin term was maintained for ancestor-spirit in general. The term was presumably borrowed to fill a semantic slot created by the Kalenjin development, under Bantu influence, of a new conceptual distinction in their classification of perceived reality.[6]

Sometimes a loan may denote only reconceptualisation of an older element. Northwestern Pokot tarɔrɔt for 'God' and 'sky', a loan translation of an Eastern Nilotic term for the High God which identified 'God' with 'sky' and 'above', replaced the earlier Southern Nilotic metaphor relating 'God' and 'sun'. The change did not represent addition of a whole new power to the Pokot belief system, only modification of the one power's relationship to other elements of perceived reality.

Sometimes, too, loans in the religious sphere may not reflect either modification or addition to the body of religious ideas, but rather something about the social history of the people involved. Words connoting a number of important religious or magical activities have been borrowed into Maasai from a Kalenjin dialect—to pray (-sai), oath (ɔl-muma), to bewitch (-sakut), witchcraft (ɛ-sɛtan), among others—activities none of which can be suggested to be other than quite old and general among East African peoples, far older than the Kalenjin interactions with the Maasai, which date to the present millenium. Here the loanwords reflect an important social development, the formation of the Maasai people earlier this millenium through the amalgamation of a former Kalenjin-speaking people and an early Maasai-speaking community. The Kalenjin groups adopted the Maasai language but carried over many culture words from their former into their adopted language.[7] That so many of these were basic religion-related terms suggests continuity of religious authorities—diviners and medicine men of various kinds—from the Kalenjin-speaking into the Maasai-speaking period. Elucidating the kinds and directions of change in belief systems consequent on such social developments would, however, require further evidence.

While the study of the history of an individual word can reveal something about the change or spread of an element or aspect of belief, investigation of systemic shifts and influences requires a broader approach. The collation of many individual word-histories can to some extent provide this sort of prospect on the over-all religious or intellectual history of a society. The citation above of Kalenjin religious loanwords in Maasai constitutes a limited example of how collation can be useful.

Tools of still greater potential, though, for penetrating pre-literate religious history, are taxonomies of belief.[8] Investigators have found that some sort of system is always present in human perception of a set of items. The system may not have been consciously articulated, but it can nevertheless be elicited by eliciting the folk taxonomy of terms dealing with the items.[9] The oft-repeated comment by Europeans and European scholars that such-and-such an African people had very vague, inconsistent or sketchy beliefs about the High God or some other aspect of religion reflected not African deficiency but European ethnocentrism. The European had become used to articulating belief in specially developed language to be put down on paper, while the African society articulated its beliefs in its practices. The key to understanding the system of these beliefs was the semantic system underlying the people's religious vocabulary.

Taxonomic study is not a substitute for study of individual word-histories and must be integrated with it. An almost point-for-point correspondence of semantic boundaries in religious taxonomies in two languages spoken near each other is, in view of the large arbitrary element in any religious system, powerful evidence for historical connection between the religious systems reflected in the taxonomies. Yet determining whether this connection is genetic relatedness or borrowing, and dating the connection, depends on knowledge of individual histories of words within the taxonomies and of the linguistic histories of the languages involved. In a people's language their words going back to some earlier ancestor language will indicate continuities or partial continuities in individual items of belief between the earlier ancestral community and their later linguistic descendants. Their word-borrowings will indicate specific instances of outside impact on beliefs. But the over-all assessment of the extent of continuity and of the course of change and also of the impact of external influences levied on belief by competing systems, will depend on comparative taxonomic study.

For example, a number of Kalenjin religion-related words have, as was mentioned, been borrowed into Maasai. Alone, their implication is a modest one, of continuity of religious figures. Some syncretism is of course likely. But what form did it take? Did the Kalenjin-speakers who in shifting to Maasai speech brought the words into the Maasai language adopt, for the greater part, earlier Maasai views, or did they cause the religious beliefs of the amalgam community more nearly to approach their own? The probing of the question would require comparison of the religious taxonomies projected for the Kalenjin- and Maasai-speaking societies of the period preceding interaction, with each other and with the modern Maasai taxonomy. Word-borrowings would be only part of the evidence, because intensive influence will not necessarily cause more than a goodly number of terms to be directly borrowed but, on the other hand, will cause extensive semantic shift among retained terms to bring the influenced system of meanings into greater correspondence with the influencing system.

Although comparative analysis is the most productive tack, it should often be possible to draw significant historical conclusions from internal evidence of a single taxonomy. If, for instance, the study of derivations of some of the words making up a religious taxonomy revealed religious metaphors inconsistent with or unwarranted by modern beliefs inferred from the taxonomy, some earlier systemic shift in religious beliefs would be indicated, and closer analysis of the out-of-date metaphors might help in descrying the directions of change. Also, ambiguities and semantic overlap in a taxonomy would tend to show up where significant changes had occurred in a people's religion and all the elements involved in the changes had not been re-integrated according to the newer pattern.

Because of the close connection of words for ideas and their referents, linguistic study is the most direct course towards recovery of preliterate religious history. But since religious ideas are also symbolized in various kinds of objects and acted upon by individuals in particular social roles, a proper religious history would seek to take ethnographic evidence into account, too. Comparative and distributional study of ethnographic evidence for the purpose of reconstructing history has a wide literature and needs no discussion here. The most important recent work is Jan Vansina's 'The Use of Ethnographic Data as Sources for History'.[10]

Vansina's work is especially valuable because further refinements in word-histories can sometimes be made on the basis of it as well. For a word can be treated as a cultural item, and then its distribution and its variant meanings through a people's territory analysed to reveal its origins and its directions and modes of spread in the history of the society. Vansina has in fact used words as just this kind of historical evidence.[11]

Another productive correlation, for recent centuries at least, can be of linguistic evidence with evidence derived from oral tradition. Traditions vary in their coverage of religious history; although they may disclose institutional changes in religion, they rarely deal—outside of Islamic areas—with subtle changes in systems of belief, the area of investigation especially amenable to lexical methods. Correlations between linguistic and traditional data can also be useful in dating a point in religious history, by reference of the linguistic insight to the dating of the correlatable tradition—an inference of some importance because linguistic and ethnographic data by themselves allow only relative dating.

Opportunities for correlating archeological findings with moments in African religious history should be fewer, but occasionally religious artifacts may be correlatable with artifacts expected on the basis of linguistic or ethnographic reconstruction. In such case, some sort of absolute latest date for the appearance of beliefs connected with the artifact might be suggested by the dating of the artifact. More common will be indirect correlation of broad periods of religious developments with archaeologically attested eras. As different eras of history identified in the linguistic and ethnographic evidence are correlated with, and thus dated by, those witnessed in the archaeological record, the religious developments belonging to those eras will be dated as well.

Conjoined, these various sources of evidence should still allow, if not with the detail of documented periods, the recovery of enough of earlier religious developments to make the endeavour an important extension of the field of African history.

NOTES

[1] The reconstruction of word-histories is dealt with in other works. A source written with African historians' needs in mind is C. Ehret *Southern Nilotic History : Linguistic Approaches to the Study of the Past* (Evanston: Northwestern University Press 1971).

[2] This sort of change would very probably have wider repercussions on the belief system which should show up elsewhere in religious words, and the inference could therefore be checked.

[3] For discussion of this word's history, see Ehret *op. cit.* chapter 2.

[4] Akie *asi·sua·nte·*, pl. *asi·sue·*, 'ancestor-spirit', from proto-Kalenjin and proto-Southern Nilotic **asi·s*, 'God'.

[5] Akie *tɔrɔ·ru·t* means both 'God' and 'heavens' or 'sky' as does Maasai *enk-ai*.

[6] C. Ehret, 'Aspects of Social and Economic Change in the Kavirondo-Elgon Region, c. 500–1500 A.D.', paper presented to the African Studies Association meeting in Montreal, Canada, October 1969. See also Ehret *Southern Nilotic History* appendix E-2.

[7] Ehret *Southern Nilotic History* chapter 9.

[8] The investigator must be wary, of course, that he does not interpose his own conception of the scope of 'belief' in the delimiting of his investigation. Proper defining of such a study will usually require first the eliciting of the broader organisation of knowledge in a society and only then, with that context obtained, permit the identification of religious and religion-related knowledge.

[9] Taxonomic studies, unlike other kinds of word-collection, do not move along quickly. They require very careful work with a major informant and subsequent close checking of the elicited taxonomy with several other speakers of the language to ensure that the student is uncovering the ethnosystem and not an ideosystem.

[10] Jan Vansina, 'The Use of Ethnographic Data as Sources for History in T. O. Ranger (ed.) *Emerging Themes in African History* (Nairobi 1968) pp. 97–124.

[11] Cf. Jan Vansina, 'The Kingdom of the Great Makoko', in Daniel F. McCall, Norman R. Bennett and Jeffrey Butler (eds.) *Western African History* Boston University Papers on Africa, Vol. IV (New York 1969) pp. 20–44.

MICHAEL GILSENAN

Myth and the History of African Religion

INTRODUCTION

> The self-illumination of society through symbols is an integral part of social
> reality . . . its essential part, for through such symbolisation the members
> of a society experience it as more than an accident or convenience; they
> experience it as of their human essence.
>
> Eric Voegelin

Much of contemporary social anthropology is directed towards what the
linguist, Ferdinand de Saussure, designated as *semiology*, a science of 'the life of
signs at the heart of social life'.[1] This is in part no doubt due to the rapid
development of linguistics and communication theory. But it may also be connected to more indigenous influences. Durkheim and Mauss bequeathed to the
discipline a central concern both with systems of classification, and in the
former's most seminal book, *The Elementary Forms of the Religious Life*, with the
dynamics of symbolisation in the social process. Though their work has of
course been subject to considerable criticism and refinement this particular
direction has not been lost, even if for a period it was somewhat neglected in the
more empirically minded writings of the English structural-functionalists under
Radcliffe-Brown's presiding genius. More recently, and again often fertilised
by French thought, studies by scholars such as Edmund Leach on Biblical
myths, V. W. Turner on Ndembu ritual symbolism, W. H. Stanner on aboriginal religion and Godfrey Lienhardt in his superb monograph on *Divinity and
Experience* among the Dinka, have broadened the scope of the inquiry and at
the same time furnished us with a more sophisticated methodology and set of
analytical concepts with which to approach that whole complex of phenomena
which goes under the rubric 'religion'.[2] In step with this development the study
of the religious systems of different societies has once again emerged as a central
interest for anthropologists. This 'revival' has also produced a re-evaluation of
the English intellectualist school of Tylor and Frazer, particularly by Jack
Goody and Robin Horton, who have proposed a rather different theoretical
perspective in which the symbolic function is viewed as a by-product rather
than as the essence of religion.[3]

What these modern writers have in common, and what among these factors
differentiates them from their predecessors, is a negative point of identification:
they pay very little attention to the history of religion. It could of course be
argued of Tylor and Durkheim that neither of them was interested in history
proper so much as in quasi-evolutionary speculation on the origins and development of Religion with a capital 'R' (though this would do less than justice to
Robertson Smith's *The Religion of the Semites*). They did attempt to set forth

a broad evolutionary scheme, characteristically allied with a shift from the supposed ritual-instrumental mode of 'primitive' religion to the ethical mode of the 'higher' or universal religions, and however faulty their methods and conclusions, they were concerned with origins and change. With a few exceptions—Guy Swanson's *The Birth of the Gods* is a leading instance—that emphasis has been very much diminished. This is in part a reaction to the way in which Durkheim and Tylor framed their problems of origins, in part because of the influence of functionalist models in which religion played *par excellence* the role of what Max Gluckman has referred to as an 'all-purpose social glue', in part out of the justifiable suspicion of conjectural history and speculative flights of diffusionist fancy and in part because of the very real empirical difficulties that the history of religions raised for the anthropologist in his chosen area of study.

Sociologists of religion since the work of Weber and Troeltsch have been concerned not only with the large-scale classification and interpretation of systems of symbols and beliefs and their relation to social forms but necessarily with the historical development of religious institutions. Weber himself, writing macro-studies on the religions of China and India, Protestantism and Ancient Judaism as part of an awe-inspiring inquiry into religions and society, specifically focused on the dialectics of religion in society, as well as on charismatic and prophetic types of authority as agents of 'breakthrough'. Anthropologists on the other hand were dealing in the main with preliterate, technologically simple cultures each with its own particular religious system: not 'Dinkaism' but 'the religion of the Dinka'. Empirical access to the history of such religions was, and remains to a large degree, highly variable and uncertain. It must be admitted too that such an avenue of research was not always of great interest to the functionalist and synchronically orientated field-worker. Even in terms of more modern theory one might suggest that both structuralism (exemplified by Lévi-Strauss' writings) and the semantics of symbolism (Turner) raise certain important obstructions to diachronic analysis.

Moreover, on the other side of the scholarly fence those few historians who took the Third World as their subject could only see dubious value in the exotic myths that seemed to give anthropologists such everyday nourishment. By definition myths were (and are) dangerous sources for the historian. And though they were undeniably part of what little material seemed to be to hand and were indeed very much part of the received oral history of these societies, they appeared to raise more problems of interpretation than answers. Beidelman, for example, has shown that a Kaguru mythical narrative includes all kinds of elements from the moral/cosmological to lineage politics. On the one hand he describes the clan legend as 'quite incredible in terms of what little we know of conditions in early East Africa', yet other sections he finds agree quite well with more properly historical accounts of the Arab and German impact.[4] If we add to this the fact that at all its levels myth is subject to different presentations and understandings by different classes of people at different times, small wonder the historian is uncertain about its value as evidence. But this has its advantages. It forces us to consider the question: evidence for what? Myth is a dangerous guide to the factual or chronological record, yet it may be indispensable both to a wider understanding of what 'history' must fundamentally entail in the context of our concern with African religions, and to the kinds of problems with which we must deal. Myth can then even contribute to a redefinition of the discipline and its relation to anthropology.

The first part of this study will sketch out the range of topics involved in the general study of myth. This will lead us into a consideration of the relevance to the history of traditional African religions of the structuralist theory and method, chosen because it is the currently dominant approach in this field of anthropology. Finally I shall attempt to draw out the possibilities and implications of our brief inquiry for the kind of research upon which we are engaged, and to offer some very tentative suggestions for collaboration.

THE EPONYMOUS ANCESTOR

It follows that the first science to be learned should be mythology or the interpretation of fables; for . . . all the histories of the gentiles have their beginnings in fables, which were the first histories of the gentile nations. By such a method the beginnings of the sciences as well as of the nations are to be discovered . . . they had their beginnings in the public needs or utilities of the peoples and . . . were later perfected as acute individuals applied their reflection to them. This is the proper starting-point for universal history, which all scholars say is defective in its beginnings.

Giambattista Vico[5] (d. 1744)

It may seem slightly perverse to begin a paper which does not aim to survey different theories of myth with a brief look at a man who in his own age was an isolated figure and whose importance for the study of human society has only recently begun to be appreciated in our disciplines.[6] I do so because we shall find in Vico's almost visionary universal history most of the major ideas which remain thematic for our own approaches to the study of myth. He speaks indeed with great immediacy to the whole subject of the relationship between anthropology and history and has thus the widest relevance to our discussion here.

There is space only to touch on what Isaiah Berlin has described as Vico's 'transforming vision, one of the greatest discoveries in the history of thought',[7] his insight into knowledge in the broadest sense as a social process, a constant becoming that can be analysed by a New Science which will throw light both on the future that is hidden *from* men and their consciousness which is hidden *in* them.[8] Berlin translates Vico's 'philology' as 'anthropological historicism' which will serve as an adequate general label for the *Nuovo Scienza*. To an historical and cultural understanding of this social process of knowing the study of myth was fundamental; fundamental because it was at the root of man's primitive world-view, and accessible to scientific inquiry because, and here he opposed Descartes, like mathematics it is *made* by man and is therefore *true* (*verum*) for him.

Far from being irrelevant superstition to be swept aside (as it commonly was by Enlightenment thinkers), or viewed only in the rather restricted sense of a Malinowskian charter for social institutions, myth was for him a *key* to the understanding of man in his social nature, his intellect, his imagination, his signs and metaphors, his cultural world, his laws and governments and his historical evolution. Myths were vehicles of explanation (rather in the neo-Tylorian sense) but beyond that of perception and apprehension of the cosmos and the social universe. He saw the 'fables' and 'allegories' in short as an essential part of the ever-changing ways in which men create and are created by society.

Myth and fable, says Vico, formed a whole mode of consciousness which in our rationalist scientific age we could only grasp with great difficulty, though this effort and this kind of knowing were at the core of his New Science. In the first stage man thought poetically and formed the first categories and systems of classification through imagination and the unconscious projection of their own sensory experience:

> the first founders of humanity applied themselves to sensory topics, by which they brought together those properties or qualities of relations of individuals and species which were so to speak concrete, and from these created their poetic genera (para. 495). Thus the mythologies . . . must have been the proper language of the fables; the fables being imaginative class-concepts, as we have shown, the mythologies must have been the allegories corresponding to them (403). The first men . . . not being able to form intelligible class-concepts of things, had a natural need to create poetic characters, that is, imaginative class-concepts or universals, by reducing to them as to certain models or ideal portraits all the particular species which resembled them (209).

Religion for Vico grows out of the 'poetic' understanding of early man in whose condition

> the nature of the human mind leads it to attribute its own nature to the effect, and . . . they pictured the sky to themselves as a great animated body, which in that aspect they called Jove (377) . . . In this fashion the first theological poets created the first divine fable . . . that of Jove, king and father of men and gods, in the act of hurling the lightning bolt . . . and to all of the universe that came within their scope, to all its parts, they assigned the being of animate substance . . . They believed that Jove commanded by signs, that such signs were real words, . . . the science of this language the gentiles universally believed to be divination . . . (379).

He observes that men form an idea of what is farthest by what is near at hand. This leads him to a very general proposition about the nature of change in forms and modes of understanding. Having commented on the use of the human body-senses as a source of metaphor referring to inanimate things he goes on to oppose 'rational metaphyiscs', claiming that: 'man becomes all things by *not* (my emphasis) understanding them, . . . for when man understands he extends his mind and takes in the things, but when he does not understand he makes the things out of himself and becomes them by transforming himself into them' (405). *Man*, to adapt Lévi-Strauss' famous phrase, is 'good to think'.

Myths then are ways of comprehending events and phenomena, allegories which can and must be interpreted by the scientific historian as he draws out the grand pattern of *corsi e ricorsi*; and they are moreover records and reflections of major stages in the evolution of human society and of the conflict between human groups (for example his interpretations of the myths of Tantalus and Cadmus, 583 and 679; see Appendix). But Vico recognises that myths are problematic as a historical source. He sees the necessity of investigating critically the event-sequence and genealogies that pseudo-historical myths present in the light of external evidence of chronology, the succession of dynasties and other historical data, and for internal evidence of anachronisms, contradictions, the role of personages known or reliably presumed to be legendary or metaphorical and so forth (see Appendix for his scathing treatment of the myth of Orpheus, para 79). The celebrated *tour de force* of Book Three of the *New Science*, 'Discovery of the True Homer', is particularly significant because of its emphasis on the changes which occur in myths over time. As he quaintly remarks: '. . . they were later misappropriated, then altered, subsequently became improbable, after that obscure, then scandalous and finally incredible' (814). Vico's approach to myth thus anchors it very firmly in the historical process which it both reflects and interprets. And as myth is in these respects multi-dimensional so also must be any analysis which aims to be scientifically critical.

We have already seen even in so brief an excursion into Vico's grand scheme for a universal history the emergence of a series of still vital themes and ideas: of the sociopsychological nature of religion, the 'sympathetic principle', the process of the formation of categories and types and levels of consciousness and social knowledge, the move from a subjective to an objective (and objectifying) understanding and the attempt to produce a science of history and a philological method which could be turned to the study of myth among other subjects. It is important to add to this one final point. Like many other thinkers of his and succeeding times Vico believed in the existence of certain 'mental universals', ideas and notions and mental processes that were part of the natural order and shared by all men (a common rationalist theme). This guided him to the belief that a basic dictionary of these universals could be constituted by means of the New Science.

> There must in the nature of human things be a mental language common to all nations, which uniformly grasps the substance of things feasible in human social life, and expresses it with as many diverse modifications as the same things may have diverse aspects (161). But . . . there shines the . . . light of a truth beyond all question: that the world of civil society has certainly been made by men, and that its principles are therefore to be found within the modification of our own human mind (331).

We might then claim for Vico what Lichtheim has termed the 'Hegelian insight': that the problem of history is the problem of consciousness. This is not to say that he presents a fully coherent philosophical theory, nor is it to ignore his emphasis on political and economic transformations and conflicts. His stress on the beginnings of men's knowledge in the senses (374), their projections of this subjective self into the cosmos, and the significance of the imagination both in its historical role and for the historian's understanding of his subject is balanced by his tracing of the rise of agriculture and civilisation, of cities and forms of writing, and the evolution of and opposition between social groups and classes. Yet the concern with the 'creative mind' seems to me to be predominant, and I shall use Vico's own words on this topic as a link with the work of the most influential of contemporary mythographers:

> From these first men . . . all the philosophers and philologians have begun their investigations of the wisdom of the ancient gentiles, and they should have begun with metaphysics, which seeks its proofs not in the external world but within *the modifications of the mind of him who meditates it.* (374; my emphasis)

MYTH, HISTORY AND STRUCTURALISM

> These masterful images because complete
> Grew in pure mind, but out of what began?
>
> W. B. Yeats

The previous section dealt with Vico not only because of his intrinsic importance for our subject but in order to use him as a filter through which the writing of Claude Lévi-Strauss can be viewed, and vice versa. Looking at each 'through' the other may suggest new insights into the range and implications, the problems and potentialities, with which the study of myth confronts us. It need hardly be said that there are great differences between them, though in a sense these differences are either mutually correcting or complementary. Central to both, however, is a concern with the operations of the 'creative mind' (perhaps the best translation for Lévi-Strauss' term *esprit*) and with man as *homo significans.*

Lévi Strauss' thought takes its place within the general framework of structuralism, a wider body of theory and method derived ultimately from a school of linguistics but important also in psychology and literary criticism. A brief reference to his use of the concept 'structure' and the analytic and methodological principles with which he works is therefore necessary before we come to a discussion of his approaches to myth and its significance for history and the historian.

Lévi-Strauss makes an explicit distinction between his use of 'structure' and that of the dominant figure of the functionalist/comparativist school in British social anthropology, Radcliffe-Brown. The latter saw structure as something existing 'on the ground' in time. He used it 'to denote this network of actually existing social relations of the particular primitive society under study', and held that 'existing social relations are the concrete reality which should interest the researcher'.[9] Lévi-Strauss on the other hand states quite bluntly that 'structure' has 'nothing to do with empirical reality but with models built up after it';[10] social relations are only the raw materials out of which the anthropologist builds his theory. He is talking then initially in terms much closer to Evans-Pritchard's remark that the ethnographer 'seeks to reveal the patterns which, once established, enable him to see it as a whole, as a set of interrelated abstractions', though Lévi-Strauss pursues his theoretical inquiry much further into the nature of analytical constructs. He sets up four basic conditions which a model must fulfill to be properly called a structure: (1) it must have the characteristics of a system (no element can be changed without it being changed in all its elements); (2) it must be possible to order 'a series of transformations resulting in a group of models of the same type', thus transcending the limits of a specific case; (3) the first two propositions make it possible to predict how a model will react if one or more of the elements are submitted to certain modifications (the basis for a distinction between observation and experimentation); and (4) the model must be constituted so as to make intelligible all the known facts.[11] We shall see how important this last point is for analysis of myths.

Two final points need to be made. First, that 'conscious models' (often what we would call norms but applicable presumably to native interpretations of myth and to Durkheimian 'collective representations' in general) are *not* explanatory in nature—indeed if anything they obstruct scientific explanation—but are intended to perpetuate the phenomena under study. And second, that we must differentiate between mechanical models in which the elements are 'on the same scale as the phenomena themselves', and *statistical* models in which the scale is different (he uses marriage laws in primitive and our own societies respectively as illustrations).[12]

This is stated with admirable clarity and a good deal more theoretical rigor than anthropologists normally employ, but there are difficulties which should be noted because they bear on our discussion. One is a certain vagueness about the term 'scale', a concept as potentially significant as Durkheim's equally suggestive but amorphous 'density' in *The Division of Labour*. Though it appears to be crucial for the *type* of model, mechanical or statistical, anthropological or historical, which can be constructed, it is not precisely defined. More fundamentally, ambiguity still surrounds the relationship of the model to the data from which it is derived and by reference to which it is in some sense tested. As the linguist André Martinet has noted, 'there is quite a difference between a model which is valid only in so far as it accounts for the relevant features of a given reality in their reciprocal relations, and a model which claims to be independent of the latter'.[13]

Lévi-Strauss' concern with patterns of relations and general laws received its first major demonstrations in *Les Structures Elémentaires de la Parenté* (1949) in which he examined different levels of exchange (principally of women) and communication and the structures of kinship in simple societies. Of more relevance here, however, is the series of studies which began with *Le Totémisme aujourd'hui* (1962), in which he returned to a classic Durkheimian theme of classification but moving towards the rules for sets of relations rather than origins, continued with *La Pensée Sauvage* (1962), and further developed into the three volumes of *Mythologies*, *Le Cru et le Cuit* (1964), *Du miel aux cendres* (1966) and *l'Origine des Manières de Table* (1968).

As I have mentioned above the theoretical jumping-off point for his study of totemism and myth has been structural linguistics, particularly as exemplified in the work of Roman Jakobson who has examined the structure of binary opposites which underlie language. Behind the apparently infinite diversity of spoken languages Jakobson finds (and there is a principle of economy of explanation here) a limited set of oppositions, twelve in number 'among which each language makes its phonematic choice.[14] Again, describing his own method Lévi-Strauss quotes Jakobson and Halle and indicates a characteristic of his analysis of myth: 'The supposed multiplicity of features proves to be largely illusory . . . The same laws of implication underlie the languages of the world both in their static and dynamic aspects.'[15] In addition to these structuralist premises there are two principles derived from de Saussure which are of great significance for Lévi-Strauss' theory. One is of the arbitrary nature of linguistic signs, which he uses to attack the Jungian notion of the mythological archetype. The other is the distinction between *langue* (language) and *parole* (speech). The former term pertains to the synchronic and the latter to the diachronic dimension.[16] Now it is true that in a later essay he moves to reduce the divergence between these two levels (Saussure had already indicated the complementary nature of the two different perspectives).[17] Nonetheless, it is possible to trace out in Lévi-Strauss' thinking two sets or series of terms which distinguish, where indeed they do not oppose, History and Anthropology. I shall list them in the following simple manner:

parole	*langue*
non-reversible time	reversible time
diachrony	synchrony
syntagmatics	paradigmatics
concrete	abstract
event	structure
social relations	social structure
'real' object	'reconstituted' object
history (in a double sense)	anthropology

Despite the fact that Lévi-Strauss' observations on the relationship of history and anthropology are widely scattered through his writings and by no means always consistent, it is clear that he postulates multi-levelled distinctions between the one, anchored in specificity and chronological linear time, and the other, in abstractions and synchronic relations.[18] History appears usually to be a kind of preliminary inquiry, like rigorous ethnographic fieldwork, but to be denied that deeper intelligibility to which structuralism leads.

> Thus, anthropology cannot remain indifferent to historical processes and to the most highly conscious expression of social phenomena. But if the anthropologist brings to them the same scrupulous attention as the historian, it is in order to eliminate . . . all that they owe to the historical process and to conscious thought. His goal is to grasp, beyond the conscious and always shifting images which men hold, the complete range of unconscious possibilities.[19]

For a scholar who claims an intellectual debt to Marxism to treat the historical process as being of the same level as conscious thought is a peculiar confusion, and precisely a view of history that Marxism has sought to transcend. This dehistoricising of the concept of structure is part of a significant development whereby the 'total social fact' of Mauss becomes more and more the total theoretical construct; Durkheim's *collective conscience* yields to a universal logic of the mind; *men* are absorbed into *Man* (a very eighteenth-century trait!). And as a complement to this progression *kinship*, embedded in the 'lived-in order' (Lévi-Strauss' phrase) and seen in terms of exchange and communication, is succeeded by *totemism*, more of the order of pensée yet at the same time linked to relations between social groups and social taxonomics. Finally this in turn is followed by *myth* at the third stage. And why by myth? Because it is in myth that the 'code-breaker' is most free from the distortions and contingencies of history and the social process and can most easily examine the free play of the logic of the mind (presumably in some inherent universal sense though this is ambiguous). Being *least* encumbered by constraints, myth is *most* significant for the central concern of anthropology: 'la récherche des contraintes mentales.'[20] It is in this sense 'the most fundamental form of inauthenticity' because unattached to social relations and social knowledge.[21] It pertains to the mind or *esprit* in what one might call its purest form, and shows it to be of the nature of 'a thing among things', determined by discoverable laws in all its activities.[22]

The body of rules governing the production of myths can be elucidated and in a series of ordered transformations they can be revealed to be mutually convertible—the ultimate form of cultural translation. But this is *not* a revelation of 'how men think', for men have no understanding of the systems of interrelations. Rather it is to show how myths operate in men's minds *without their being aware of it.*[23]

We reach in myth a third code order: that generated by the search for 'la traductibilité réciproque de plusieurs mythes.' The myths themselves are founded on codes of the second order. Lévi-Strauss puts forward the master key at the third order. Now this latter seems to be at once (*a*) the construct in and of the mind of the structuralist; (*b*) at the same time somehow inherent in the dialectical interplay of the myths themselves; and moreover (*c*) transcends in a manner of almost infinite extension the actual limits of historical, linguistic and social contact and communication between societies that yet *unconsciously* obey this tertiary code. Since history has been firmly pushed aside—its explanations of myth being contingent and largely *ad hoc*[24]—no criteria appear to remain for judging the limits or boundaries, whether logical or 'real', of this interminable extension. In such a situation without check the anthropologist's mind is as free of constraint as myth itself. When, furthermore, myth and music are compared particularly in respect of their relation to time, which goes beyond that of both *langue* (non-reversible) and *parole* (reversible) into a specific pattern of timelessness (perhaps nonchrony!) one is denied yet another dimension in which some questioning, test and evaluation of the argument might be conducted.[25] Nor is it enough to say grandly that in showing the existence of the all-transcendent myth-sets bound neither by space nor time one is presenting ethnographers, historians and archaeologists with a problem,[26] when the terms of the discussion in which one presents it make any 'solution' inadmissible or downright impossible.

This question of criteria both for delimiting the unit of analysis and for determining the validity of any proposed explanation brings us to Lévi-Strauss' method. Since the Durkheimian *conscience*, linked to a basic social referent, has been thrown out and Lévi-Strauss has agreed with F. G. Lounsbury that there is no correlation between categories of thought on the one hand and 'behaviour' on the other,[27] how are we to approach so elusive yet so vital a phenomenon as myth? The methodology is clearly set out and can be presented very briefly as a set of principles.

First of all he opposes elaborate typologies of myth (myths of creation, historical myths and so forth). Questions of definition are therefore of relatively minor concern. Folk tales, legends, fables and pseudo-histories are alike proper subjects for the cryptographer.[28] Most important, the analysis must be exhaustive in two senses: *all versions* of the myth must be taken into account in a multidimensional frame of reference,[29] though in talking of 'the myth' it must be realised that 'l'unité du mythe n'est que tendancielle et projective, elle ne reflète jamais un état ou un moment du mythe';[30] and second, the deciphering must comprehend *all details* of the myth while at the same time preserving the principle of economy of explanation.[31] *Any* myth or any version of the myth can be used as the jumping-off point and can be followed through its endlessly spiralling series of transformations, inversions and variations (the premise on which *Le Cru et le Cuit* is based). Control of the experiment is maintained by the structuralist demand for the total fact and the total interpretation of the fact. Only in this way, in Lévi-Strauss' view, can it avoid the *ad hoc* quality of the historical method which can always press plausibility and logic into service. In the identification of the basic units, the mythemes, the only way we can check ourselves is by the operation of the aforementioned mythographic Occam's razor, the use of the 'unity of the solution; and ability to reconstruct the whole from a fragment, as well as later stages from previous ones.'[32] We should attempt then to isolate not only relations, but bundles of sets of relations which can be created quite out of diachronic sequence. We are to read the orchestral score *vertically* not horizontally.

We have already seen that the definition of the total fact raises major difficulties, despite the fact that Lévi-Strauss' programme is more rigorously worked out in terms of theory and method than is the case with any other anthropologist that I know of. The difficulties become more obvious as we proceed further to actual practice.

The inquiry centres on a fundamental opposition of Nature and Culture. The categories out of which the myth universe is constructed are derived from the realm of nature which furnishes a natural taxonomy; it provides the raw material for a pattern of structural homology of natural and social system (the conceptual scheme of group relations) manifested in so-called 'totemism'. Nature is a tool of and a pattern for thought. In myth the available material is expanded to the human senses:

> En second lieu, ces codes sont du même type: ils utilisent des oppositions entre des qualités sensibles, promues ainsi à une véritable existence logique. En troisième lieu, et puisque l'homme possède cinq sens, les codes fondamentaux sont au nombre de cinq, montrant ainsi que toutes les possibilités empiriques sont systématiquement inventoriées et mises à contribution.[33]

All these codes present a series of relations and transformations in the form of the progressive mediation of oppositions. In terms of meaning, exploration should take us beyond the variations in the semantic significance of elements (the reason for the non-admissibility of an explanation based on archetypal symbols). It also presumably, for Lévi-Strauss, denies the possibility of universal systems of colour symbolism in which V. W. Turner has a fundamental interest, because the principle of the arbitrary character of signs undercuts much of Turner's theoretical framework.

Now the nature and origin or ground of these oppositions is as ambiguous as the status of the structuralist's tertiary code.[34] Given a binary bias and its somewhat inflexible limitation of choice it is possible, as Burridge has shown, to derive several sets of oppositions and it will not be clear at what level they are situated and whence they are drawn.[35] Rather as with a brilliant literary critic, one is left wondering whether the poet really said or intended that or whether there is any way of validating the analysis or of going beyond the subjective, semi-intuitional stage, or whether indeed the question should or even can be asked.

The mediation of oppositions relates fundamentally to the resolution of a problem or problems. This is basically what myth is all about: 'since the purpose of myth is to provide a logical model capable of overcoming a contradiction (an impossible achievement if, as it happens, the contradiction is real) . . .'[36] The solution may also be offered as a kind of mirror or inverted image of the social pattern actually present to the consciousness of the natives. Sometimes the problem is at the most general level:

> Comme un crépuscule des dieux, par conséquent, les mythes décrivent cet effondrement inéluctable: depuis un âge d'or où la nature était docile à l'homme et prodigue envers lui, en passant par un âge d'airain où l'homme disposait des idées claires et des oppositions bien tranchées par le moyen desquelles il pouvait encore maîtriser le milieu, jusqu'à un état d'indistinction ténébreuse où rien ne peut être incontestablement possédé et moins encore conservé, parce que tous les êtres et les choses sont mêlés.[37]

At others it is more immediately socially specific, as an example from a very different setting and a different author shows:

> . . . the Biblical story of the succession of Solomon to the throne of Israel is a myth which 'mediates' a major contradiction. The Old Testament as a whole asserts that the Jewish political title to the land of Palestine is a direct gift from God . . . the Jews should be a people of pure blood and pure religion . . . But interwoven with this theological dogma there is . . . a tradition which represents the population of ancient Palestine as a mixture of many peoples over whom the Jews have asserted political dominance by right of conquest. The Jews and their 'foreign' neighbours intermarry freely . . . the reader is persuaded that the second of these descriptions, which is morally bad, exemplifies the first description, which is morally good.[38]

One of the troublesome issues this approach raises is that the problem is frequently deduced from what is presumed to be an answer. At what level, social, cultural or logical (or combinations of these) is the problem to be located and is it as unconscious as the tertiary code for those people who must in some sense be held to think through and live it out? In his examination of the Oedipus myth (his main foray into the 'non-primitive' world) Lévi-Strauss suggests that the story deals with a problem that the culture itself creates: it is believed that mankind is autochthenous yet humans are born from the union of two; not from one.[39] But it may be more generally existential in a 'universal' sense concerning man's ultimate condition. Here we come to antinomies of Life and

Death, Order and Chaos, Man and Woman. And in Leach's analysis we are dealing with a problem of legitimacy, endogamy and political relations.

This question of levels is neatly encapsulated in a recent debate over the myths surrounding the Cwezi (on whom more below). Taking the polarity of right and left hand as central Needham relates a 'problem' in the ethnography of the Nyoro to a general inquiry into symbolic classification and symbolic reversal which he explains as based on a set of pairs of opposites.[40] In this framework the myth or traditional history of the ruling Bito dynasty is interpreted as reflecting a fundamental opposition between categories, in this case Order and Disorder, rather than as Malinowskian sources of legitimacy. Beattie on the other hand argues that the myth of Bito resolves a different level of problem closer to that put forward by Leach for the story of Solomon.[41] The first Bito king, Rukidi, comes from north of the Nile and is represented as uncouth, black, savage and thus inauspiciously 'contradictory' of the Bacwezi he replaces. They are white, identified with gods, civilisation and auspiciousness. In the legend, despite this polarity, Rukidi is made the patrilineal grandson or great-grandson of the former Cwezi king. To Needham this fictive descent rules out the 'myth as charter' argument because it gives the Bito a 'sinister' descent; rather the myth describes a transition from Nature to Culture. For Beattie on the other hand the descent fiction gives the reigning dynasty some authoritative claim to their position:

> It is these uncouth foreigners' very unsuitability to take over the ancient kingdom, so dramatically symbolised in the story of Rukidi, that provides the structural rationale for the myth of his royal origin. According to the myth he is accepted, even welcomed, as the new ruler after the Bacwezi's departure . . . That the myth should serve a social function is perfectly compatible with the fact that it symbolises . . . a complementary opposition between the auspicious and the inauspicious. It is precisely because the Rukidi story brings together . . . these opposite qualities that it serves so admirably to resolve a contradiction in Banyoro's conception of their own history, and to validate the intrusive Bito dynasty's right to rule.[42]

These levels are not necessarily irreconcilable but they are a source of analytical confusion. The criteria for the validation of interpretation and definition of the problem area are obviously not as clear as they initially appeared in Lévi-Strauss' scheme. Needham regards the argument of legitimacy from legendary genealogical incorporation as invalid. Beattie claims his colleague's table of dyadic opposites to be (*a*) a confusion of 'given' or 'natural' (right/left, man/woman) with 'cultural' (cook/brew); (*b*) not present in 'Bunyoro thought' (a major point of ambiguity in both his and the structuralist arguments is the precise meaning of a phrase such as this); and (*c*) a mis-statement on some key relations alleged around the poles auspicious/inauspicious.

Let us return to Leach's interesting discussion of the Solomon story, which will serve appropriately as a kind of mediating term between tertiary code and social function explanation. In this instance *chronology is incorporated as part of the structural significance of the myth* and the principle of exhaustiveness is followed in dealing with the whole of the text, '*regardless of the varying historical origins of its component parts*' (author's emphasis).[43] He explains the myth in terms of a dramatic structure that develops two parallel themes—sex relations and political relations. Like all good analysis this 'makes sense' of a large body of confusing and inchoate data and lays bare some of the foundations of the selective historical memory of a particular people at a particular period. Moreover the transformations of the myth are sought within a field bounded by time, space and cultural unity. Unlike Lévi-Strauss' pursuit of the dialectics of a disembodied *esprit* transcending the social and cultural, Leach gives us some purchase on the setting within and of which the myth delivers its message, and therefore the greater possibility of critique and 'disproof'.

Some doubts however persist. Leach says that the aim of his essay is 'to demonstrate the creation of a myth as the precipitate of the development of an historical tradition'.[44] The intention is of the greatest importance since it emphasises the *process* of the unfolding of the myth through time, linked to the historical specificity of a given society. But there is in fact little in the way of any discussion of the historical development within which the myth crystallised. In the light of the stated intention of the inquiry should not the mythographer at least hint at the historical situation as a changing process and the praxis of Palestinian Jewry in the third century B.C. (as Max Weber tried to do in detail in his *Ancient Judaism*)? Can the creation of a myth be elucidated without such a treatment, or at least a sketch for it? What are the levels of the relation of myth development to historical change? Is the myth much less at the unconscious level than Lévi-Strauss supposes and is it subject to quite conscious 'ideological' manipulations by a specific interest group, the canon lawyers? Is not the continuing problem, theoretical and empirical, of the relationship of structure and event slightly obscured by the notion of precipitate, which is suggestive but may involve the idea that myth has an essentially epiphenomenal nature? And if this is the case, might not the problems be drawn out by historical analysis without resort to the 'elegance' of the structural approach? In the light of these questions Leach's final remarks seem a trifle cavalier:

> Robert H. Pfeiffer is a modern orthodox Biblical historian of the first rank, and he analyses at length precisely the same story of the succession of Solomon as I have done. He uses a simpler, more straightforward procedure and he finds in the story nothing more exciting than a prosaic account of actual historical events . . . If literalists prefer it that way, I am happy to leave it at that.[45]

The difficulties that arise in the analysis of structure and event are compounded in Lévi-Strauss' thought by a critical ambivalence that surrounds both 'external' reference and content. With regard to the former, myth is seen as the most fundamental form of inauthenticity, the least constrained and most free of all processes of the *esprit*. This has the valuable result of warning against a single-minded reduction of myth to a 'reflection' or 'expression' or 'refraction' of the anthropologist's idea of what constitutes a pattern of social relations. But in addition he very properly stresses the multi-dimensional interdependence of myth and its social frame:

> mais cette solidarité ne résulte pas dans des rapports rigides, imposant des adjustments automatiques entre les niveaux. Il s'agit plutôt de contraintes

à long terme, dans les limites desquelles le système mythologique peut, en quelque sorte, dialoguer avec lui-même et s'approfondir dialectiquement: c'est-à-dire commenter toujours, mais parfois sous forme de plaidoyer ou de dénégation, ses modalités plus directes d'insertion dans le réel.[46]

And he suggests too a series of checks on different levels of myths (of origin, migration and village tales, all among the Pueblo), despite previous warnings against this kind of procedure, by relating them to social, economic and technical activity.[47] Unfortunately, too often these relations remain unexplored, as does the relation of the myths to the belief systems and shared apprehensions of the life-world. The other constituent elements of this worldview, cosmological, ritual and religious, are not invoked. That his approach can be immensely fertile is shown by Lévi-Strauss' own analysis of the *Geste d'Asdiwal*, but in the main ethnographic references seem to be almost interludes in the complex flow of his reasoning.[48] We learn little of the systems of symbolisations which in all societies inform and are informed by myths. The drive to universality ends in its own brand of material reductionism and leads to the functioning of that 'object' the human mind which obeys its particular laws.[49] This may *ultimately* be true and demonstrable, but it is a huge and perhaps not even very useful leap for the anthropologist infant to take at this stage. Meanwhile there is a real danger that the union of knowing and being-in-the-world, to use the phenomenologists' phrase, will be totally dissolved.

The structuralist perspective can certainly be defended; it is a matter of calculating the profits and losses in completeness of interpretation. In his essay on the legitimacy of Solomon Leach gives one kind of answer to our question, evidence for what?

> ... whereas a theologian can find in the Old Testament texts a mystical message which has hermeneutic import for the whole of humanity, my own analysis reveals only a patterning of arguments about endogamy and exogamy, legitimacy and illegitimacy as operative in the thought processes of Palestinian Jews of the third century B.C.[50]

This directs us *through* the cultural tradition of the 'sacred history' or myth to some of the structural underpinnings of the society. In so doing it reveals a pattern that eludes more conventional modes of analysis and indicates problems that are as central to history as to anthropology. But it is at the same time too restricted, too one-dimensional. Max Weber's studies of religion (curiously ignored by anthropologists) and the central place that the 'content' and ethic of myth and religion play in his discussion of economic and social patterns of societies of very different types show that too much is being sacrificed and too limited a field is being staked out. This is a major point because we *have* now to deal with societies in which often large-scale religious movements are emerging across tribal, social and cultural boundaries as part of extremely complex patterns of social change. To turn away from the moral, ideological and symbolic and to sternly avert the eyes from these levels of meaning in myth is to woefully impoverish our whole subject and our capacity to translate others' lifeworlds into our own.

Structure itself occurs in the process of becoming.

Emile Durkheim

We have seen some of the difficulties and problems that structuralism raises in the study of myth and we have also touched on its theoretical and methodological strengths. I have invoked Leach as a mediating figure, but there is perhaps another who is of even more relevance to the purposes of this conference and who attempts to employ the structural approach to myth to shed light on historical processes. Luc de Heusch's fascinating series of studies on the Kingdom of Rwanda demonstrates the possibilities for a genuine synthesis of historical and anthropological method, as opposed to merely eclectic borrowing.[51]

Most of the facts are already fairly well known so I shall here present only a brief sketch of the background.[52] Rwanda is one of the more densely populated areas of Africa and until the civil war that began in 1959 it was socially, politically and economically dominated by a pastoral Tutsi aristocracy which ruled over the vast majority of peasant Hutu (de Heusch gives figures of 10% and 85% of the population respectively). He suggests that the Tutsi are of Nilotic origin, unlike the broad mass of the population which is Bantu. The state was erected on what Maquet calls a 'premise of hierarchy'. De Heusch goes so far as to describe it as a caste society, marked by rigorous endogamy and the structuring of Tutsi-Hutu relations within a highly asymmetric framework of clientship. Under the guise of exchange of services the Hutu were in fact bound in servitude, condemned to sustain their 'feudal' lords in parasitic superiority. This system of power was preserved and even reinforced under Belgian occupation.

The central political institution was the sacred kingship. The king on succession took his place as one of a stereotypical series of roles, herder, warrior and so on, which followed in cycles one after the other. With the Queen Mother he magically controlled the rhythms of nature, and when he lost his strength and grew old he had to take poison at the hands of the *Biru*, who served him as priests, councillors and guardians of the esoteric traditions. De Heusch considers that the full panoply of sacred power developed as a religious complement to the growth of the State, rather than being an archaic phenomenon.[53] This would mean a fairly recent evolution, since the great age of Tutsi military expansionism was from the mid-eighteenth to the end of the nineteenth century. It would also, if I read de Heusch correctly, correlate significantly with a period of intense competition for power both at the centre and in the 'provinces'. The division of agriculturalists and herders was formalised in the creation of chiefs of the herds and chiefs of the earth charged with handling the problems of distribution of land use that were probably exacerbated by the population density. The kings attempted to play off the powerful lineage heads and thus maintain court control and centralised power against the constant fissile tendencies. This internal structural strain led to a kind of Mameluke system whereby each ruler on his succession formed a new corps of 'Janisseries' bound directly to him as an autonomous military unit.

The social system was thus characterised by a series of oppositions, even contradictions, and this opposition is carried over into the cult of Ryangombe. The latter is the myth-king of the *kubandwa*. Together with his followers, the *Imandwa* ancestor hero figures, he is the centre of what de Heusch terms a *'religion initiatique de salut'*, that attempts to transcend through myth and ritual the structural principles of Rwanda society. The dying, tragic hero-king offers salvation on earth and after to his initiates, and takes them under his and the *Imandwa*'s mystical protection. On each of four planes, alliance and kinship, relations between the sexes, socio-economic stratification and the level of kingship de Heusch sees a mystical *'contestation'*, a negation of social reality. Ryangombe offers a theodicy of suffering and a promise of salvation founded on a *refusal* of the premise of hierarchy and subordination. Though Tutsi themselves belong to the cult, de Heusch interprets it as an attempt to transcend the alienation of an insupportable socio-economic order. Others have viewed it differently: Maquet as essentially unificatory, an expression of *consensus*, and Claudine Vidal as the ritually performed *subjection* of all the castes to royalty which must be founded in sacredness as the only guarantee of order against non-sense.[54] *But these arguments need not be mutually exclusive.* It is the characteristic of myth and of religious systems in general to bear many meanings, to be multivocal and to answer to a wide range of human concerns and interests. What is crucial is that one would expect these distinct 'elective affinities' of the myth for different strata of Rwanda society to be worked out in praxis and in ideology/worldview.[55] Indeed the different interpretations of and selections from an essentially common body of myth within a society or cult are historically quite critical. For it is on these selections and interpretations that men act, legitimate action and bestow authority, and grasp their social meaning in relation to other men. (That these interpretations may of course be ideological in nature is not at issue.)

De Heusch carries out three operations essential for the historical study of myth and for answering the question, evidence for what? First, he relates it to the wider religious system. There men are only safe from the unpredictable and often maleficent acts of the ancestors if they call on the assistance of *Imana*, the beneficent but distant High God. In the *kubandwa* cult sickness or possession is a sign of grace (if that is not too dangerous a word) and the occasion of the incorporation of the initiate into a new mystical family; those aiding him are strangers (Cwezi); the ancestors themselves are differentiated by their membership or otherwise in the cult; and *Imana* plays no part, for the saviourking is the agent of deliverance. Second, he links the new relations of men with the sacred to *different levels* of opposition within Rwanda society. Third, he explores the logic of myth transformation *à la* Lévi-Strauss but with historical reference and in a complex series of patterns which he traces through the limits of the old Cwezi empire of six hundred years ago. By carefully following the transformations of the myth in all its versions through a defined area and in the context of historical knowledge he is able to show the dialectic of myth and event and the subtle interplay of the religious and political systems. Myth then not only reveals the variations of a society's conception of itself, its structure and its history, but can be tentatively used to suggest fruitful hypotheses to the historian.

What de Heusch's analysis attempts to capture is that elusive process of the changes in myth over space and time and he does this by 'controlling the experiment' more strictly than Lévi-Strauss feels compelled to do. He takes account of the levels of the myth and the distinction between minor and structural variations, which is of considerable importance for our problems of method. In this way he is able to incorporate the diachronic dimension. This is all the more essential because, unlike Lévi-Strauss, he is dealing with a society which evolved through contradictions and extreme social differentials and intense struggles for power. This demands an attention to praxis if myth is to be shown as a part of the social process. So that if myth furnishes an 'everywhen', a mystical timeless context for apprehension of all human and natural life, it is also constantly in a state of becoming or re-creation, generated by men in their specific socio-historical context:

> Mythopoeic thought is probably a *continuous* function of aboriginal mentality, especially of the more gifted and imaginative minds which are not few. The notion of a time when myths were, or ceased to be, invented is probably a schematic figment.[56]

Myth suggests possibilities that, in conditions of profound disjunction of the moral and social orders, may become demands, to be acted on by men in large groups mobilised at the call of a revitalising prophecy that appeals to the myth as a coming-to-be and not only as time past. In cults of salvation myth themes are realised in the most immediate sense in action destined to transform the 'everywhen' into the 'here and now', and if the old traditions no longer answer to the imperatives of new circumstances, as is often the case for example in the Cargo Cults, new myths are adopted and transformed almost overnight at the summons of a Prophet, the instrument of a new call to realise the myth, to actualise it in relations between men. All religious phenomena are in tension between the eternal and the mutable, and by a paradox must be the latter if they are to remain the former.

De Heusch's work suggests that one significant field of collaboration between anthropologists and historians should be in carefully delimited areas which could be defined according to multiple criteria, linguistic, historical, population movements and fluctuations of political relations, institutional complexes such as that of the sacred kingship, and so forth. The study of myth would of course be only one topic, and fruitful generalisations would depend on more refined conceptualisations for the analysis of demographic material, ecological and technological variables, social organisation and belief systems. Sufficient material already exists for the Nilotic peoples (Nuer, Dinka, Shilluk, Anuak) and the Interlacustrine area for combined studies of this nature.

My remark about refined analysis in other related subjects implies too that the historian examining myth in a given context must be prepared to look outside geographical limits to writings on Mediaeval Europe, Cargo Cults in Oceania, ritual in Highland Burma, and so on. Furthermore, on specific topics such as the use of genealogies as evidence, the methods of anthropological investigation which has examined genealogies in many areas as social rather than necessarily historical truths (in the narrow sense) can be of special relevance. Studies of the telescoping of lineages and the levels of descent at which such operations are likely to occur in a given type of kinship and social system, for example, can assist the historian in the sifting of such material.[57] For geneal-ogies, like other myths, are part of peoples' conceptions of their own history and of their moral and social universes. The relationships between these concep-tions (and changes in them) to the social processes require an understanding of the key underlying structural problems which they seek to resolve.

On the other hand, it seems to me that only if we anthropologists go beyond our present state of lip service to history into actually thinking historically can we be saved from the kind of intellectual Indian rope trick that our theory all too often becomes. We have reached a point where a considered rejection of present inherited Western divisions of intellectual labour is in order. The study of myth and of traditional African religions may hopefully force us, in short, to a radical redefinition of our two disciplines.

APPENDIX

The following is intended to serve as an illustration of Vico's analysis and interpretation of myth. The first example of the fable of Cadmus, shows his analysis of myth as historical allegory, the second, the myth of Orpheus, demon-strates his critical method.

Paragraph 679   The Myth of Cadmus

This whole divine and heroic history of the theological poets was only too unhappily described for us in the fable of Cadmus. For first he slays the great serpent (clears the earth of the great ancient forest). Then he sows the teeth (a fine metaphor, as noted above, for his ploughing the first fields of the world with curved pieces of hard wood, which, before the use of iron was discovered, must have served as the teeth of the first ploughs, and teeth they continued to be called). He throws a heavy stone (the hard earth which the clients or *famuli* wished to plough for themselves, as above explained). From the furrows armed men spring forth (in the heroic contest over the first agrarian law aforemen-tioned, the heroes come forth from their estates to assert their lordship of them, and unite in arms against the plebs, and they fight not among themselves but with the clients that have revolted against them; the furrows signifying the orders in which they unite and thereby give form and stability to the first cities on the basis of arms, as is all set forth above). And Cadmus is changed into a serpent (signifying the origin of the authority of the aristocratic senates, for which the ancient Latins would have used the phrase *Cadmus fundus factus est*, and the Greeks said Cadmus was changed into Draco, the dragon that wrote the laws in blood). All of which is what we above promised to make clear: that the fable of Cadmus contained several centuries of poetic history, and is a grand example of the inarticulateness with which the still infant world labored to express itself, which is one of the seven great sources of the difficulty of the fables which we shall later enumerate. So easy it was for Cadmus to leave a written record of this history in the vulgar characters which he brought to the Greeks from Phoenicia! And Desiderius Erasmus, with a thousand absurdities unworthy of the learned man who was called the Christian Varro, will have it that [the fable] contains the story of the invention of letters by Cadmus. Thus the illustrious history of such a great benefit to the nations as the invention of letters, which must have made itself known far and wide, is concealed by Cadmus from the human race in Greece under the veil of this fable, which remained obscure down to the time of Erasmus, in order to keep hidden from the vulgar such a great invention of vulgar wisdom that from the vulgar these letters received the name of vulgar letters!

Paragraph 79   The Myth of Orpheus

This Orpheus, who reduces the wild beasts of Greece to humanity, is evidently a vast den of a thousand monsters. He comes from Thrace, a country of fierce warriors [*Marti*, Marses], not of humane philosophers, for the Thracians were through all later time so barbarous that Androtion the philosopher removed Orpheus from the number of sages simply because he had been born in Thrace. And [yet] in her beginnings he came forth so skilled in the Greek language that he composed in it verses of marvellous poetry, with which he tamed the barbarians through their ears; for though already organised in nations they were not restrained by their eyes from setting fire to cities full of marvels. And he finds the Greeks still wild beasts [though] Deucalion a thousand years before had taught them piety by his reverence and fear of divine justice. On Mount Parnassus, in front of the temple raised to divine justice (which was later the dwelling of the Muses and Apollo, the god and the arts of humanity), Deucalion with Pyrrha his wife, both with veiled heads (that is, with the modesty of human cohabitation, meaning marriage), seize the stones that lie before their feet (that is, the stupid brutes of former savage times) and make them into men by throwing them over their shoulders (that is, by the discipline of household economy in the state of families). Helen too, seven hundred years before, had brought [the Greeks] together by means of language and sown the three dialects among them by means of his three sons. And the house of Inachus could show that it had founded its kingdom three centuries before and had continued the royal successions through that period. Finally comes Orpheus to teach the Greeks humanity; and, from the savage condition in which he finds it, he brings Greece into such splendor as a nation that he is a companion of Jason on the naval enterprise of the Golden Fleece (naval enterprises and navigation being the last discoveries of peoples), and he is accompanied on this expedition by Castor and Pollux, the brothers of Helen, for whose sake the famous Trojan war was fought. So in the life of one man so many civil things are accomplished, for which the extent of a thousand years would hardly suffice! Such a monstrosity of Greek chronology in the person of Orpheus is like the other two we have observed above: one in Assyrian history in the person of Zoroaster, and another in Egyptian history in the two Hermeses. It was perhaps because of all this that Cicero in his *On the Nature of the Gods* suspected that such a person as Orpheus never existed in the world.

NOTES

[1] C. Lévi-Strauss *The Scope of Anthropology* (London 1967) p. 16.

[2] E. R. Leach *Genesis as Myth, and Other Essays* (London 1969); V. W. Turner *The Forest of Symbols* (Ithaca, New York 1967); W. H. Stanner *On Aboriginal Religion* (Sydney, n.d.); Godfrey Lienhardt *Divinity and Experience: The Religion of the Dinka* (Oxford 1961).

[3] Robin Horton, 'A definition of religion and its uses' *JRAI* vol. 90, pt. 2, (1960); Robin Horton, 'Neo Tylorianism: Sound Sense or Sinister Prejudice?' *Man* vol. 3, no. 4, (December 1968); J. Goody, 'Religion and Ritual: The Definitional Problem' *British Journal of Sociology* (June 1961).

[4] T. O. Beidelman, 'Myth, Legend and Oral History: A Kaguru Traditional Text' *Anthropos* 65, (1970) pp. 74–97.

[5] Giambattista Vico *The New Science* translated by Bergin and Fisch (Ithaca, New York 1948) para. 51. All references are to paragraph numbers.

[6] For a survey of different interpretations of myth see Percy Cohen, 'Theories of Myth' *Man* vol. 4, no. 3, (September 1969) pp. 337–53.

[7] Isaiah Berlin, 'A Note on Vico's Concept of Knowledge' *New York Review of Books* (24 April 1969) pp. 23–26.

[8] The reader is also referred to articles by E. R. Leach and David Bidney in: G. Tagliacozzo and Hayden White *Giambattista Vico: A Symposium* (Berkeley and Los Angeles 1969).

[9] A. R. Radcliffe-Brown *Structure and Function in Primitive Society* (New York 1952).

[10] C. Lévi-Strauss *Structural Anthropology* (New York 1963) p. 279.

[11] C. Lévi-Strauss *Structural Anthropology* pp. 279–80.

[12] *Ibid.* p. 283.

[13] André Martinet, 'Structure and Language', in Jacques Ehrmann (ed.) *Structuralism* (New York 1970) p. 4. The reader is also referred to Michael Lane (ed.) *Structuralism: A Reader* (London 1970) and to E. Nelson and Tanya Hayes (eds.) *Claude Lévi-Strauss: The Anthropologist as Hero* (Cambridge, Mass. 1970).

[14] R. Jakobson *Essais de linguistique générale* (Paris, 1963) p. 105, cited in Luc de Heusch, 'Vers un mythe-logique?' *Critique* 219–20 (August-September 1965) p. 691.

[15] R. Jakobson and M. Halle *The Fundamentals of Language* (The Hague 1956) cited in Lévi-Strauss *Structural Anthropology* p. 83.

[16] Lévi-Strauss *The Scope of Anthropology* pp. 28–9.

[17] See F. de Saussure *Course in General Linguistics* (New York 1966) pp. 87–8.

[18] See G. Parain, 'Structuralisme et Histoire' *La Pensée* no. 135 (October 1967) pp. 38–52 for a useful gathering together of Lévi-Strauss' views on history and anthropology.

[19] Lévi-Strauss *Structural Anthropology* p. 23. Also see *The Savage Mind* (London 1966) chapter 9, for his debate with Sartre.

[20] C. Lévi-Strauss *Le Cru et le Cuit* (Paris 1964) p. 18.

[21] G. Charbonnier *Conversations with Claude Lévi-Strauss* (London 1969) p. 55.

[22] C. Lévi-Strauss *Le Cru et le Cuit* p. 18.

[23] *Ibid.* pp. 19–20.

[24] *Ibid.* p. 156.

[25] *Ibid.* pp. 23–24; *Structural Anthropology* p. 209.

[26] As Lévi-Strauss does in *Le Cru et le Cuit* p. 16.

[27] Lévi-Strauss *Structural Anthropology* p. 72.

[28] Lévi-Strauss *Le Cru et le Cuit* p. 12.

[29] Lévi-Strauss *Structural Anthropology* pp. 216–17.

[30] Lévi-Strauss *Le Cru et le Cuit* p. 13.

[31] *Ibid.* p. 155.

[32] Lévi-Strauss *Structural Anthropology* p. 211.

[33] Lévi-Strauss *Le Cru et le Cuit* p. 172.

[34] See also N. Yalman, 'The Raw: The Cooked: Nature: Culture—Observations on *Le Cru et le Cuit*', in Leach (ed.) *The Structural Study of Myth and Totemism* (London 1967).

[35] K. O. L. Burridge, 'Lévi-Strauss and Myth', in Leach *ibid.*

[36] C. Lévi-Strauss *Structural Anthropology* p. 226.

[37] C. Lévi-Strauss *Du Miel aux Cendres* (Paris 1966) p. 221.

[38] Leach, 'The Legitimacy of Solomon', in *Genesis as Myth* p. 31.

[39] Lévi-Strauss *Structural Anthropology* p. 216.

[40] R. Needham, 'Right and Left Hand in Nyoro Symbolic Classification' *Africa* vol. XXXVII, no. 4 (October 1967) pp. 425–52.

[41] J. Beattie, 'Aspects of Nyoro Symbolism' *Africa* vol. XXXVIII, no. 4 (October 1968) pp. 413–42.

[42] *Ibid.* pp. 431 and 433.

[43] Leach, 'The Legitimacy of Solomon', in *Genesis as Myth* p. 80.

[44] *Ibid.* p. 27.

[45] *Ibid.* p. 83. But compare this with the quotation on p. 40, below.

[46] Lévi-Strauss *Le Cru et le Cuit* p. 338.

[47] *Ibid.* p. 339.

[48] Reprinted in English in Leach *The Structural Study of Myth and Totemism*; See also *The Savage Mind* p. 248.

[49] cf. Engels: '. . . it is self-evident that the products of the human brain, being in the last analysis also products of nature, do not contradict the rest of nature's interconnections but are in correspondence with them.' *Anti-Dühring* (Moscow 1962) p. 55. Quoted in N. M. Geras, 'Lévi-Strauss and Philosophy' in *Journal of the British Society for Phenomenology* vol. 1, no. 3 (October 1970) p. 55, a critique of Lévi-Strauss' theory that is particularly relevant to our discussion of structuralism and history.

[50] Leach, 'The Legitimacy of Solomon' in *Genesis as Myth* p. 26.

[51] See Luc de Heusch *Le Rwanda et lacivilisation interlacustre* (Brussels 1966); 'Mythe et société féodale: le culte du kubandwa dans le Rwanda traditionnel' *Archives de sociologie des réligions* vol. 9, no. 18 (July–December 1964); 'Nationalisme et Lutte des classes au Rwanda', in Willy Frolich (ed.) *Afrika in wandel seiner Gesellschaftsformen* (Leiden 1964) pp. 96–108.

[52] The reader is referred to an essay by Elizabeth Hopkins, 'The Nyabingi Cult of South-western Uganda', in Robert I. Rothberg and Ali Mazrui (eds.) *Protest and Power in Black Africa* (Oxford 1970) pp. 258–336.

[53] De Heusch *Le Rwanda . . .* p. 127.

[54] J. J. Maquet, 'The Kingdom of Rwanda', in D. Forde (ed.) *African Worlds* (Oxford 1954) p. 171; Claudine Vidal, 'Anthropologie et Histoire: le cas du Rwanda' *Cahiers Internationaux de Sociologie* vol. XLIII, (July–December 1967) pp. 151–3.

[55] For the concept of elective affinity see Max Weber's essay, 'The Social Psychology of the World Religions', in H. H. Gerth and C. Wright Mills *From Max Weber* (New York 1958) pp. 267–301.

[56] Stanner *On Aboriginal Religion* p. 237.

[57] By way of example the reader is referred to E. L. Peters, 'The Proliferation of Segments in the Lineage of the Bedouin of Cyrenaica' *Journal of the Royal Anthropological Institute* 89 (1959) pp. 29–53.

PART TWO

CULTS OF KINGSHIP

MATTHEW SCHOFFELEERS

The History and Political Role of the M'Bona Cult among the Mang'anja

With its history of six centuries of Maravi control, the M'Bona shrine at Khulubvi is one of Malawi's most ancient.[1] It was once the heart of a cult that made its influence felt throughout the vast territory bounded in the south by the lower reaches of the Zambezi, in the east by the Indian Ocean, in the north by the Shire Highlands, and in the west by the ancient trade route to Tete. The extent of its influence may be compared with the Mwari, Chaminuka and Dzivaguru cults south of the Zambezi and, in the northern and western sections of the Maravi confederation, with the cults of Chauta and Chisumphi There is a fundamental similarity between these different cults, not only in the vast extent of their influence, but in their ideologies and external organisation and in their relationships with the socio-political structures of the societies in which they flourished. These similarities would suggest that some treatment of this complex of cults as a whole would be fruitful at a future date.

M'Bona cult assumes such prominence today in that it seems to have been maintained virtually intact; its main shrine and network of subsidiary shrines, its officialdom and elaborate rituals that regularly demand the co-operation of traditional religious and political authorities, have been preserved. Furthermore, the survival of the cult is matched by a considerable body of oral traditions that is constantly added to and modified to accommodate recent events.[2]

In this paper the history of the cult is presented as a case study of the manipulation of a religious institution by a variety of interest groups. The nature of a religious institution is taken here to include both its official character as shrine, functionaries and rituals and its non-official character as a body of informal history, myth and rumour in the population at large. Similarly the wider population must be considered as an interest group in itself alongside secular and religious authorities, if the political aspects of the cult are to be seen in the correct perspective.

The M'Bona cult has been for centuries characteristic of the Mang'anja, a society of hoe cultivators, who are ethnically a sub-group of the Maravi, and who occupy southern Malawi and the adjoining districts of Mozambique. Before the Yao, Lomwe and Sena migrations which began around 1850 and only recently slowed down, the territory of the Mang'anja extended throughout the Lower and Middle Shire and included the western part of the Shire Highlands. Only in the Lower Shire Valley, though, do the Mang'anja today constitute a sizeable group maintaining political power and controlling village headman-ships. In 1966 the Lower Shire area, comprising the two administrative districts of Nsanje and Chikwawa, numbered 127,000 Mang'anja as against 131,000

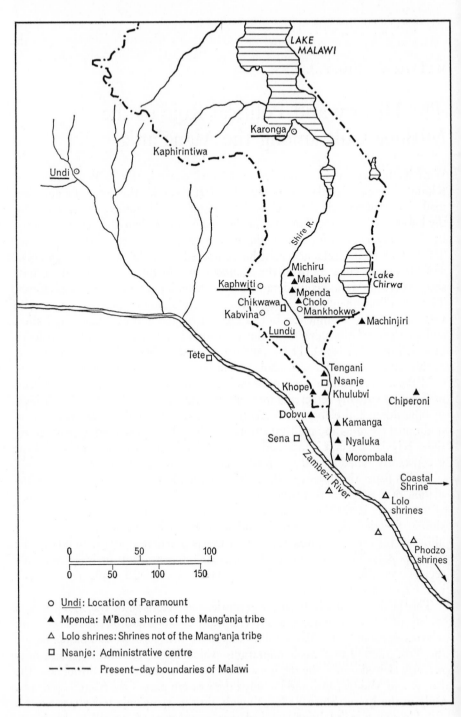

Expansion of the M'Bona Cult

foreigners, derived mainly from the Sena and Lomwe migrations.[3] In the Nsanje district, which has been severely affected by Sena migration, the Mang'anja only represent some 34% of the total population. Despite this the Mang'anja control all the existing chieftaincies in the Nsanje district. In the Chikwawa district, however, half of the eight chieftaincies are held by the descendants of Livingstone's Kololo servants, who took advantage of the depredations wreaked upon the Mang'anja in the second half of the nineteenth century by famine and Portuguese slaving forays to assume power.

Before these nineteenth-century incursions of Portuguese slavers, Kololo, Sena and Lomwe, the Shire Valley had been Mang'anja territory for many centuries. But it is important for the history of the M'Bona cult to realise that the Mang'anja themselves had once been intruders. Before the fourteenth century the Shire Valley seems to have been inhabited by the so-called Kafula peoples, of whom little is known but from whom a number of surviving customs and institutions probably derive. By the fourteenth century, however, the Valley had been entered by migrant groups moving south out of what is today the Central Region of Malawi. These migrant peoples are called in the oral traditions by the name Chipeta. They are held to have been the founders of the Mang'anja populations in the Valley, although the name Mang'anja and the political institutions which were for so long characteristic of the Mang'anja people developed later.

These political institutions largely sprang from the coming of the Phiri chiefs. At some point in the fourteenth century rulers of the Phiri clan imposed themselves over the peoples of the Central Province and also over the Chipeta–Mang'anja. Originally there was a hierarchical relationship of seniority among the various Phiri chiefs. Kalonga was the most senior; next came Undi, under whom in turn were a number of tributary chiefs, the most important of whom for our analysis was Chief Kaphwiti. Kaphwiti himself was senior to other Phiri chiefs, the most important of whom for the future was Chief Lundu.

Mang'anja political history was for a long time made up of the shifts of power within this Phiri hierarchy. First Undi broke away from the supremacy of Kalonga and bestowed upon the Kaphwiti chiefs who had followed him in this secession the control of the Lower Shire Valley area. Then, at some time in the sixteenth century, the Lundu chiefly line broke away from the authority of the Kaphwitis. The heart of the new power of the Lundus, which became very extensive, was in the Lower Shire Valley. Gradually the Mang'anja peoples of the valley were integrated into the Lundu paramountcy through the operations of its political and religious institutions.

All Mang'anja chiefs within the boundaries of the Lundu paramountcy regard themselves to this day as perpetual kinsmen of Lundu. This system of perpetual kinship is based on traditions that the first Lundu divided his kingdom among his matrilineal kinsmen. The resultant net-work of relationships provided for an overall political structure which traditionally consisted of a loose confederation of chiefdoms each of which enjoyed a large measure of political autonomy. Despite this absence of a strongly centralised power, individual chiefdoms were seldom able to assert complete independence from the larger structure, a notable exception being that of Lundu himself.

Another important integrative factor was provided by the religious system.

The Mang'anja make a fundamental distinction between what are termed 'spirits of the land' and 'spirits of the household', the former being invoked for the well-being of the country and the population as a whole, the latter by individuals and lineage sections. Thus, for instance, territorial spirits are invoked at times of drought, epidemic diseases, wars and similar calamities.[4]

There are further differences between the two categories of spirits which are of consequence to this study. One of these is that the veneration of domestic spirits is only for a limited duration, whereas that of the territorial spirits may continue indefinitely; another that domestic spirits can only be invoked by their own kinsmen or those delegated by them. The status of territorial spirits can only be accorded to deceased royals, either those who have been chiefs during their lifetime or royal kinsmen of great fame. So the politically integrative function of territorial cults rests fundamentally on their control by a royal house. This held true also of the shrines consecrated to the High God, of which there existed at least two in ancient Malawi, since God, there as elsewhere, was always invoked in conjunction with the deceased members of the controlling royal lineage.

Not all royal cults are of equal importance, each one's sphere of influence as a rule being co-extensive with that of the royal lineage to which it belongs. Theoretically therefore, and to a large extent also in actual practice, the hierarchy of the territorial cults reduplicates that of the chiefdoms. This is further stressed by the fact that the official mediums attached to these cults recognise among themselves a system of perpetual kin-relationships similar to that pertaining between the chiefs.

There is little doubt that in terms of spheres of influence M'Bona's cult has been, and still is, the most important among the Mang'anja. This is only to be expected since it was the official cult of the Lundu paramountcy. Its strong links with the Lundu dynasty are demonstrated on the one hand by its absence in those Mang'anja areas over which Lundu never held sway, and on the other by the rise of separatist movements in chiefdoms which in the course of time refused to recognise Lundu's overlordship.

From all initial indications the M'Bona cult seems to have originated at this determining point in the history of the Lower Shire Valley, when the Chipeta had become Mang'anja and when the Lundu paramountcy had emerged as the summit of a complex system of political relationships. From all initial indications, indeed, the cult seems to have had as its primary function the expression and preservation of this Mang'anja cultural and political system. In short the M'Bona cult appears to be associated with the Lundu rulers in something of the same way that scholars have associated the oracular cult of Mwari with the Rozvi empire and its ancestral Shona state systems.

A dominant layer of oral tradition supports this interpretation. Thus the late Group Village Headman, Mbeta, from Nsanje, asserted that M'Bona came soon after the arrival of the 'Agoa' (Goanese), whom he described as a 'kind of Portuguese from India', which would place the original M'Bona in the latter half of the sixteenth century. Moreover, as we shall see, a strong layer of tradition connects the killing of M'Bona with the Lundu chiefs, and there is no doubt of the prominent role which these chiefs played in the ritual structure of the cult.

One of the interesting results of historical inquiry into the cult, however, is that other evidence is revealed which challenges such an interpretation. This evidence, which by extension suggests interesting questions about the Mwari cult and other 'imperial' cult systems, shows that the figure of M'Bona, or rather of successive representations of M'Bona, played a key role in all three of the main stages of the Mang'anja order: in the Chipeta migrations to the Lower Shire Valley and in the advent of the Phiri rulers under Kaphwiti as well as in the rise of the Lundu paramountcy.

The historical evidence suggests, further, that an M'Bona cult, though not necessarily or even probably in the same form throughout, has existed in the Shire Valley since before the time of the Chipeta entry into the area; that it was taken over by the Chipeta from the Kafula; and that it was subsequently taken over by each succeeding African ruler of the Shire Valley Mang'anja. In the course of this long history the image of M'Bona appears to have changed, at one time being that of a chief and migration leader, at another time that of a prophet, at yet another that of a martyr or saving victim. The site of the chief M'Bona shrine changed. So also did the ceremonies and structures of the cult as it developed in association with increasingly elaborate paramount chieftainships. It is a remarkable story of continuity and yet change. Above all it is a story of manipulation of an ancient and deeply rooted cult by successive and varying interests.

A 'primary' layer of Mang'anja traditions suggests that the M'Bona shrine was taken over by the Chipeta migrants from the former Kafula inhabitants. In the same way the traditions of the Chewa of the Central Province suggest that they too took over their great shrine at Kaphirintiwa, at which the High God Chauta was worshipped, from the Kafula.[5] It seems that other important Maravi shrines also mark sites of earlier Kafula settlements. It seems, finally, that the *Nyau* society and certain forms of spirit possession may also have been inherited from the Kafula.

But the earliest events in which M'Bona is now remembered to have been involved are the Chipeta migrations themselves. At this 'secondary' level of Mang'anja tradition M'Bona is depicted as a chief who established himself and his followers near the present Nsanje.[6] To commemorate the occasion he is said to have carved his tribal tattoos on some rocks in the hills west of Nsanje, which are still known locally as the 'Chipeta tattoos', *Nembo za Chipeta*. His fame was so great, so this level of tradition runs, that after his death he became the principal guardian spirit of the area and a shrine was dedicated to him at Khope Hill near these tattoo marks.

This level of tradition mentions two areas in the present Central Province as M'Bona's birthplace, Kaphirintiwa in the centre of early Chewa country and Ncheu in the south. The former tradition is highly significant. Kaphirintiwa was the major Chewa shrine in the Dzalanyama Hills, which was acknowledged by all the Chewa sub-tribes. M'Bona's supposed origin from the Kaphirintiwa shrine in this 'secondary' or Chipeta level of Mang'anja tradition can be taken as an early acceptance of the supremacy of the Chewa cult, no doubt corresponding to the early political supremacy of Kalonga. This supremacy is underlined by the fact that worship at Kaphirintiwa was directed to the High God while most other shrines, including M'Bona's, were dedicated to deceased chiefs or famous royal personages. Kaphirintiwa was the only shrine to possess a sacred drum as its central cult object, this drum being the main symbol of the High God. In short, what seems to have happened at this stage was the taking over of the Kafula shrines by both the Chewa and the Chipeta-Mang'anja. The shrine at Kaphirintiwa continued to enjoy a recognised supremacy, but the M'Bona shrine at Khope Hill, now controlled by the Chipeta, was widely influential in the Shire Valley.

Yet a third layer of Mang'anja tradition links the M'Bona cult with the establishment of the Phiri chiefs over the Chipeta-Mang'anja. This layer of tradition describes how Chief Kaphwiti, following Undi in the break with Kalonga, arrived in Chipeta country. The story runs that M'Bona was accused of sorcery by Kaphwiti's enemies on the grounds that he had withheld the rain. His accusers demanded that he undergo the poison ordeal. M'Bona refused, saying the ordeal was unjust and that he himself had been given supernatural powers by God through which he could infallibly detect witches and sorcerers. As a result M'Bona, followed by Kaphwiti and his people, was forced to flee to the south. Kaphwiti settled at Khumbo on the Wamkurumadzi river and came to control all the region south to the Zambezi. M'Bona was put in charge of the Chipeta shrine at Khope in the Nsanje Hills.[7]

Reduced to its essentials this story links a refusal to undergo the poison ordeal with the break between Kalonga and the followers of Undi and Kaphwiti. The episode only becomes meaningful if we suppose that Kalonga had been forced into a widespread administration of the *mwabvi* ordeal. It would seem, then, that the Phiri invaders were already suffering serious internal dissensions by the time they reached the area of Lake Malawi. There can be little doubt that the Kalonga did prove the more powerful as both Kaphwiti and Undi were forced to leave.

Such a crisis among the Phiri invaders would provide the occasion for the appearance of prophetic figures proposing alternative methods of witchcraft eradication and opposing the abuse of the poison ordeal. While little is known about the origin of such prophets, in M'Bona's case at least there is evidence that an official medium attached to the Kaphwiti chiefdom took on this role to lead what must have been a semi-political movement of protest.[8]

As Undi and Kaphwiti established themselves in the west and the south so they re-modelled the shrines at Kaphirintiwa and Khope Hill. Undi moved the Kaphirintiwa shrine twelve miles south-east to Msinja. At the same time a predominantly Phiri officialdom was set up around the new shrine, considerably checking the political power of the cult leader, Makewana, the 'Wife of the Spirit'. This conclusion is supported by Ntara's important statement that before the advent of the Phiri the Chewa had no other chiefs but these 'spirit wives'.[9] The leading new Phiri official, Kamundi, was known as 'Makewana's husband' and 'Python', epithets which associated him directly with the Deity and emphasised his supremacy over Makewana. It seems that Kaphwiti carried out a similar reconstruction. A Phiri official, whom this third layer of tradition identifies as M'Bona, was appointed as chief official over the old Chipeta shrine at Khope Hill, which was significantly renamed Malawi.

A fourth series of traditions associates M'Bona with the Lundu kingdom which developed in the sixteenth century from a chiefdom subject to Kaphwiti. Again the stories are cast in the form of a conflict, this time between M'Bona and Lundu, followed by accusations of rain-withholding. The poison ordeal is not mentioned in these stories. Instead Lundu resorts to open violence and has M'Bona murdered. According to this dominant level of tradition, M'Bona was captured on Malawi Hill and killed at Ndione on the edge of the Dinde marsh some six miles due east. After his death his head was severed from his body and buried separately at Khulubvi, which lies midway between these two places. Shortly afterwards, M'Bona's medium made it known to Lundu that a shrine should be built at this spot in honour of M'Bona.

The gist of these traditions seems to be that Lundu killed an official, probably the leading functionary of M'Bona's shrine on Malawi Hill, and had the shrine moved to the plains below. This removal of the shrine may have been more than incidental. A similar event took place when the first Undi moved the Kaphirin-tiwa High God shrine to Msinja. In both cases the chiefs concerned had made themselves independent of a traditional paramount and established more tightly controlled political organisations. The establishment of a new shrine centre within a short distance of the old one may well have been a move to assert their independence—and their supremacy over the cults—without completely severing their links with the past. At the same time the greater accessibility of the new shrines and their more elaborate organisation seems to reflect their closer links with the new political authorities and the increasing political influence of the shrines themselves as centres of expanding state systems.

But though this layer of tradition is a dramatisation of Lundu's restructuring of the cult, the story of 'M'Bona's' death has a high degree of historic prob-ability. The period during which the Lundu paramountcy emerged was marked by an atmosphere of violence. Its foundation was marked not only by revolt against the Kaphwiti overlordship but also by an usurpation of the Lundu title by a representative of the junior Lundu line. This man, whose name is variously given as Chauma or Sakhonja, had the legally elected chief drawn from the senior line, who held the hereditary title of Mankhokwe, murdered. He next established his headquarters on the west bank of the Shire, thus driving a wedge between the northern and southern parts of the Kaphwiti kingdom. His main intention seems to have been to obtain control of the river traffic with Sena and he faced the task of bringing the southern chiefs to recognise his over-lordship. To achieve this he must have been able to command considerable military power.

There are two indications that this was indeed the case. The first is the fact that Lundu at one time posed such a threat to the Portuguese that they had to join forces with Kalonga Muzura in 1622 in order to defeat him. Similarly it has become increasingly probable that the notorious Zimba raiders, who began their rampages some forty years earlier, were controlled by Lundu.[10] In short there are strong indications that the period of Lundu's rise to power was marked by pronounced violence which lasted for about half a century and that the killings of Mankhokwe and 'M'Bona' form part of this pattern.

In conclusion it may be said that the four levels of tradition concerning M'Bona have now been merged into one single tradition, which runs together several different individuals acting over a period of at least two centuries. The fourth, Lundu, version of the tradition is the frankest of the four. Where the

79

Chipeta version and the Kaphwiti version conceal the taking-over and remodelling of the pre-existing cult, each claiming the original M'Bona for its own, the Lundu version deals openly enough with the clash between Lundu and the M'Bona cult officer which preceded Lundu's take-over of the cult.

Once that take-over had been completed, however, the influence of the M'Bona cult from its new base at Khulubvi began to expand as Lundu's power itself expanded. Most of the chiefdoms of the Lundu paramountcy appear to have had a M'Bona shrine; specific information has so far been obtained of shrines at Michiru, Malabvi, Machinjiri, Mpenda, Cholo and Chiperoni in the highlands, and Lundu, Tengani, Kamanga, Nyaluka, Morombala and Dobvu in the Lower Shire Valley, the latter four being located in Mozambique territory. Further down the Zambezi, Junod reported M'Bona worship at Marromeu, south of the delta, among the Phodzo hippo hunters. He called M'Bona 'the god of the river', which he understood in animistic terms as applying to the Zambezi. The local population set apart one woman as a wife for M'Bona in each of their clans. When the river was in flood, gifts were presented to these women in order to appease the angry spirit. Junod was further told that this practice was found all along the banks of the Zambezi.[11]

Schebesta, who was in the lower Zambezi during the first World War, recorded the existence of the M'Bona cult in areas along the north bank that he visited. He was also able to establish that the inhabitants recognised Khulubvi as the great mother shrine. It had such a fame among them that regular pilgrimages were made to it. Price corroborates this from Maganja da Costa, about half way between Quelimane and Antonio Enes, on the east coast.[12]

These examples from outside the Lower Shire Valley suggest that such shrines had spread throughout the area once held by the Lundu paramounts, and that Khulubvi ought indeed to be considered as the religious centre of their kingdom. The cult seems to have been adopted even by some peoples living outside the boundaries of the Lundu kingdom, such as the Phodzo of the Zambezi delta. Here it should be remarked that both the Lolo peoples who lived within and the Phodzo who lived outside the historical Lundu boundaries traditionally had highly segmentary political systems, which did not come anywhere near even the relatively low degree of centralisation of the Mang'anja. This may partly account for the utter lack of resistance on the side of the Lolo against the Lundu regime over a period of nearly two centuries. It may also explain the obvious popularity which the M'Bona cult seems to have enjoyed among them. From the scarce information at hand it appears that in those regions there was an acute awareness and recognition of the central position of the Khulubvi shrine. It would be in line with the usual pattern known from the shrines of Malawi if such recognition reached its climax at times of drought when they observed the custom of sending delegations with gifts to Khulubvi. In more practical terms, it is probable that the M'Bona cult provided the Lolo as well as the Phodzo with a more powerful religious means to counteract general adversities than they formerly had at their disposal. This may therefore have been the basis on which the cult exercised its politically integrative function. From the reports by Schebesta and Junod it appears that the Phodzo and the Lolo were able to organise the cult locally; this involved the establishment of cult leaders and more or less regular contacts with Khulubvi. The persistence of this organisation until well into the present century seems to provide proof of its vitality and popular appeal.

From this it does not follow, however, that the cult could fully integrate the conquered Lolo into the Mang'anja political system. The Lolo were never allowed to participate in the cult to the degree the Mang'anja were. To this day foreigners are not allowed to participate actively in the ceremonies at Khulubvi. Furthermore, only Mang'anja chiefs were allowed to maintain permanent representatives there. Such representatives as were allowed settled in the neighbourhood of the shrine, and the most important among them were given the status of village headmen under the name of their own chief. Finally, since M'Bona's history is essentially that of the Mang'anja people in general and of the Lundu paramountcy in particular, the Lolo were unable to identify themselves entirely with it. The result was that the M'Bona cult, while binding the Lolo to the Mang'anja, emphasised the political superiority of the latter. This only accentuated an already existing situation, for the Lolo of the seventeenth century thought of themselves as inferior to the more highly organised people surrounding them.[13]

While on the whole the M'Bona cult must be regarded as a key integrative factor in the political organisation of the Lundu paramountcy, it remains true, nevertheless, that it could also be employed to express dissent. A review of the history of the Cholo M'Bona shrine highlights this point.

There is no doubt that this particular shrine is the most important after Khulubvi. It is located on a small plateau some 3,000 feet above sea-level, overlooking the Shire Valley with Khulubvi about sixty-four miles to the south. Local traditions state that it was founded by the first Lundu, the original Mankhokwe, at the time of his settlement under Kaphwiti. Changata, a well-known rain-caller of the Banda clan, was put in charge, a position which his descendents hold to this day. The Cholo shrine was thus founded before Khulubvi, and it is to be regarded as an off-shoot of the M'Bona shrine established by Kaphwiti on Malawi Hill. This is also indirectly confirmed by a local body of myths in which the episode of M'Bona's killing by Lundu does not occur.

The shrine lost much of its religious and political importance after the Mankhokwes had been deposed. However, the Lundu paramounts never took the step of appropriating it, perhaps for fear of resistance. Instead, they established a rival shrine at the place of the present Mpenda village some eight miles to the west of the Cholo shrine.

Towards the close of the eighteenth century considerable changes took place in the distribution of power in the Lower Shire Valley. On the north bank of the Zambezi the Portuguese prazos had grown considerably in numbers and size. The estate holders functioned more or less as independent chiefs and were on occasion able to command thousands of retainers, known as Chikunda, who began to pose a serious threat to the chiefdoms to the north. Chiefs whose territories bounded the prazos had either to defend themselves or perish. Tengani, who controlled the Shire immediately above the prazos, had a standing army which controlled the river banks.[14] The then Mankhokwe, who had managed to free himself from Lundu's overlordship and regain his former territory, was threatened by the Chikunda. But little help could be expected from Lundu who now found himself threatened by his former vassal. Mankhokwe had organised his territory adroitly enough in the space of half a century to be thinking in terms of expansion. One of the consequences of Mankhokwe's resurgence was that the Cholo shrine was revived and given such a conspicuous place in the politics of Mankhokwe's chiefdom that Rowley compared it to some kind of theocracy. Each village had its headman; over certain districts was a superior chief and over all the land was the Rundo (i.e. Lundu Mankhokwe), and over the Rundo was a supposed spirit named Bona, who made his abode on top of a mountain called Choro (Cholo), and to whom the Rundo resorted for counsel in times of trouble and distress.[15] The text goes on to describe that counsel was in fact sought from M'Bona's 'wife', a woman set apart for his worship, and who, unlike her counterpart at Khulubvi, also acted as the spirit's medium.

It should be noted here that not only were there two rival shrines in the two rival chiefdoms, but that the shrines were part of one and the same cult which was being manipulated to back up claims as well as counterclaims. However, Lundu Mankhokwe could not get round the fact that Khulubvi had built up a much wider influence than Cholo, and that, if ever he wanted to supplant the Lundu paramounts, the Khulubvi shrine must be brought under his control. The political situation around the middle of the nineteenth century brought him very close to the realisation of his dream.

The rise of the *prazos* and the consequent loss of control over Bororo resulted in Lundu's territory being reduced to less than its pre-Zimba size. By the mid-nineteenth century the Lundus had dwindled to such insignificance that none of the members of the Livingstone and U.M.C.A. expeditions seem to have been aware of their existence. Instead, mention is made of two paramounts, Tengani and Mankhokwe, who respectively ruled the area below and above the Ruo-Shire confluence.[16]

There existed a second power block, at first unnoticed by the English, which was Kaphwiti's chiefdom. Here, much the same situation prevailed as in Lundu's territory. Kaphwiti, who lived at Chirala on the opposite bank from Chikwawa, had become a mere shadow of his name. Instead, two strongmen ruled his country in the persons of Chibisa and Kabvina.[17] Both men controlled strategic points on the Tete trade route: the Shire ford at Chikwawa and Mikolongo village some thirty miles west to Chikwawa which was a fixed caravan halt.

The attitudes of the two blocks towards the Portuguese could not have been more different. Whereas Tengani and Mankhokwe had armed themselves to the teeth to keep the slavers out, both Chibisa and Kabvina allowed trading and slaving parties from whom they exacted dues.[18] It was into this situation that Livingstone marched in January 1859. He had some trouble in being allowed through Tengani's barricade, and his party was subjected to continual abuse from the river banks. Neither was there much love lost between the English and Mankhokwe.[19] Their hostile relationships were further aggravated by Livingstone's friendship with Chibisa who, under the guise of providing the expedition with guides and porters, was in fact using them to lay claim to every part of Mankhokwe's highlands area.[20] Although there was little response to Chibisa's advances at the time, neither were they forgotten. Two years later they sent for Chibisa's celebrated war tail to help them out.[21]

Unfortunately, this particular instance of disregard for Mankhokwe's position coincided with another case of white intrusion into this territory, *viz.* the founding of the U.M.C.A. mission at Magomero in 1861. The missionaries' stay at Magomero did not last long, however; they were forced to leave during the following year. On returning to Chikwawa they decided to see Mankhokwe about a more suitable site on Mt Cholo. Stewart and Waller, two members of their party, were dispatched to see the chief, but were not immediately admitted, as Mankhokwe had visitors from Khulubvi who were there requesting a new wife for M'Bona. Normally, it would have been the duty of Lundu to provide such a woman, but in view of Lundu's deplorable state of health and the apparent inertia of his counsellors, the Khulubvi delegates turned to Mankhokwe. The latter was most willing to oblige in order to gain the sympathy of the Khulubvi officials and their possible support against Lundu. An additional reason for Mankhokwe's eagerness may have been his desire to counteract rumours which blamed the current drought on his previous neglect of his ritual functions.[22]

The messengers from Khulubvi had on their side serious reasons for their mission. There had been a severe drought over the past year, which according to Rowley had decimated the population and severely reduced their resistance to the Portuguese slavers. The Mang'anja of the Valley were virtually on the verge of extinction. M'Bona's medium had announced that these calamities had befallen the tribe because of their neglect of his shrine which for some time had been without a 'spirit wife'. If one was not provided soon worse was going to happen.

The U.M.C.A. missionaries, who were spending the night outside Mankhokwe's village, were woken up, as Stewart describes it, 'by a tremendous hubbub in the village', as a married woman was dragged from her home to become M'Bona's wife. The cries of joy mingled with the wailings of her husband and children, and the next morning she was taken to Khulubvi to continue the age-old line of spirit wives.

Mankhokwe now found time to listen to his visitors who, after having stated their case, were allowed to look for a site on Cholo Mountain. In view of Mankhokwe's earlier distrust of Europeans and his former request to Chibisa to drive them out of his country,[23] his permission to let them live on Cholo was something of a *volte-face*. Two reasons may have accounted for this.

Livingstone's Kololo servants had been left behind at Chibisa's because of insubordination, and had begun opening new gardens and raiding the surrounding areas for wives and labourers. Their raids led to innumerable complaints from the neighbouring headmen, and there was a general feeling that at the first available occasion the Kololo would try to seize power. Although the U.M.C.A. missionaries tried to keep aloof from these conflicts, they were generally accused of siding with the Kololo, a rumour which the Kololo did nothing to contradict. The move to Cholo was therefore seen by the missionaries as a way of publicly dissociating themselves from this band of robbers. As this would isolate the Kololo, Mankhokwe may have welcomed this move.

Another reason may have been that Mankhokwe deliberately wanted the missionaries to get into difficulties that he knew would arise, difficulties which

might hasten their departure from the country. When the missionary recon-
naisance party moved up the slopes of Cholo, they met with such fierce resistance from the officials of the shrine supported by the local population that they
had to drop their plans. Nothing could persuade the inhabitants, not even a
solemn guarantee given by Mankhokwe, to allow the missionaries to settle on
the sacred hill.[24] Dispirited, the missionaries went back to Chibisa's where
some of them died after showing signs of dementia, an illness ascribed by the
population to M'Bona's vengeance.[25]

Meanwhile, the *prazo* owner and notorious slaver, Paul Mariano, alias
Matekenya, assisted by some relatives, had managed to break Tengani's resistance in the south and began to carry off whatever remained of able-bodied
people. There was nothing Livingstone could do as the slavers had the tacit
consent if not the active support of some of the Portuguese officials. Mt Morambala, which for more than two centuries had been a prosperous place within
easy reach of the Sena trade, became deserted. Those who were not captured
fled, and some of the chiefs such as Nachikadza and Kamanga took refuge in
Tengani's area leaving the M'Bona shrine on Morambala unattended. Their
security at Tengani's, however, was short-lived. Mariano, who for years had
been held at bay by Tengani's formidable warriors, was finally able to push
into the country, one of his aims being M'Bona's village at Khulubvi which
had been hit less hard by the famine on account of its marsh gardens at Dinde.
The village and the shrine were destroyed. Any inhabitants who had not escaped to the hills were enslaved, and foodstores and valuables carried away.
This event took place between August 1862, when the new wife for M'Bona
had been elected, and May 1863, when Kirk found the village destroyed.[26]

It is instructive to compare the traditional accounts of the destruction of
the Khulubvi shrine with those of the repulsion of the U.M.C.A. missionaries
at Cholo. Whereas the missionary episode has been preserved essentially
correctly apart from a few embellishments, the story of the destruction, the
famine which preceded it and the slaving forays which followed it, have been
changed beyond recognition into a resounding victory for M'Bona and his
followers. According to these traditions Matekenya had massed an army of
Chikunda retainers on the opposite bank of the Shire ready to attack the shrine,
but M'Bona sent a drought which brought the enemy to the brink of starvation
and made Matekenya sue for peace. A cracked china cup and two wooden egg
cups still kept at the shrine are said to have been given by Matekenya among
other gifts when he made his peace with M'Bona.[27] As can be seen from the
account, the Chikunda raids are still mentioned but as having been unsuccessful. The place of the drought has been changed in the time sequence and it is
being made to work against the invader in favour of the Mang'anja. Finally,
Matekenya's coming to the shrine is depicted as that of a supplicant and not
of a destroyer. Memories of the destruction linger in private accounts, but the
official tradition never admits it.

The U.M.C.A., ironically enough, found refuge later at M'Bona's deserted
sanctum at Mt Morambala, where they were left in peace and could daily watch
large canoes laden with slaves heading for the Zambezi and the sea. Soon
Livingstone was to leave, and the last check on the ambitions of the Kololo
was removed.

Given the free hand they had wanted the Kololo brought the southern part of the west bank under their control in a series of quick moves, thus cutting short Mankhokwe's plans for expansion. After some years of brave but unsuccessful resistance Mankhokwe, too, lost his chiefdom and had to take refuge with one of the predecessors of the present Chief Mabuka in Mlanje. Many years later, when peace was finally restored, the Mankhokwes came back and settled on the west bank a few miles away from their rival Lundu who had not fared much better. They were now physically severed from their shrine by the Shire and its marsh lands, with the Kololo chiefdom of Makwira on the opposite bank. The Cholo shrine once again dwindled to insignificance and is now little more than an ancestral shrine of the Changata chiefs.

A few years later the High God shrine of Msinja was to be sacked under similar circumstances by the Portuguese slave raiders Mala and Chipapi with their Chikunda men.[28] There, as with Khulubvi, the raiders had been attracted by rumours of enormous quantities of ivory which were said to be kept by the officials. But from this juncture the histories of the two shrines, which had run a parallel course for many centuries, were to become completely different. Khulubvi was revived with its complete organisation after a short interlude, but at Msinja only a small spirit house was built after many years and put in charge of a woman, while its officialdom remained scattered over a wide area. The main cause for this seems to have been the long period of Ngoni raids which prevented any rapid restoration of the Msinja shrine and which, on the other hand, resulted in its officials accepting headmanships elsewhere. The keepers of the cult drum had also set up a rival shrine. In addition to this, Undi's authority which might have reconciled the factions was effectively checked by the establishment of international boundaries in 1892.

The definition of these boundaries also had its effects on the Khulubvi shrine. The British promised protection to the Mang'anja chiefs if they paid taxes. Tengani, who after the death of Lundu and Kaphwiti had become the senior Mang'anja chief, agreed to this arrangement and by so doing was able to save his own chieftainship and have that of Mlolo restored.[29] The Lundu chieftaincy was not revived, the members of the royal family, on bad terms with the British, having gone to Chiromo. Instead, Ngabu, one of Lundu's subchiefs, was raised to the status of a full chief and given those parts of Lundu's chiefdom which had not fallen to one of the Kololo.

Having thus taken advantage of the Europeans to secure their positions, Tengani and his fellow chiefs now set out to check the demands made by these foreigners. Tax collectors were refused access to the Khulubvi area, and no amount of pressure could bring the inhabitants to comply with the law.[30] On the other hand, the officials were not loath to approach the successive District Commissioners for contributions in cash or in kind whenever a major ritual was to be performed.

The beginnings of the colonial period brought another threat to the cult in the form of the Christian missions. In 1900 the South African General Mission established itself at nearby Lulwe. This strongly evangelical mission vigorously pursued the task of Christianisation, this meaning primarily the establishment of prayer centres and village schools. Since each building required the permission of chiefs and headmen there were frequent dealings with such officials

85

who, though unwilling to be converted themselves, gladly consented to their sons being taught the rudiments of literacy and the Bible. The resulting generation of youngsters entering school in the first quarter of the century was to have a profound influence on the cult in more ways than one. The most notable of these pupils was the future Chief Molin Tengani. An excellent school record meant that he was chosen for further training as an evangelist, a role he fulfilled brilliantly until called to the Chieftaincy in 1934.[31] Molin Tengani was an enlightened but stern ruler who in time became a staunch supporter of European rule and finally of the doomed Federation of Rhodesia and Nyasaland. He stood squarely behind the agricultural reforms which were rejected by the population. The Tenganis had become the main authorities of the Khulubvi shrine after the demise of the Lundus, but Molin made it clear after his accession that as a Christian he dissociated himself from it, and he further discouraged any attempts at performing the rites. Consequently, the influence of the cult dwindled to a serious extent, and the shrine remained without a spirit wife until 1949 when a severe drought revived it again in the teeth of continued opposition.

In 1921, before Molin Tengani's accession, the Catholic Mission had established itself as Nsanje and without delay set itself to opposing the S.A.G.M. Rival schools were set up all over the district and countless conflicts ensued in which the headmen and the local population were increasingly involved. The result was that, although there was a plethora of schools, few of them maintained a sufficient standard, and most of them were short-lived.[32] The Seventh Day Adventists, who had arrived before the Catholics, had ensconced themselves at Chief Mlolo's and confined their activities to a few well-run schools in the northern part of the district.

Both in the Catholic and the S.A.G.M. camp there were many defections, and some of these lapsed Christians became officials of the cult. The present Malemia and Ngabu belonged to the S.A.G.M., and the medium Chambote was once a Catholic. During the drought of 1949, which initiated the revival of the cult, and the period of profoundly anti-European sentiments generated by the federal issue in the following years, many educated Christians were driven to change their attitude to traditional religion. They became quiet if not active supporters of Khulubvi against Tengani and the European officialdom.

The teachings of Christianity, however, had their influence on the M'Bona traditions. The relative social unimportance of physical fatherhood, which had been reflected in the M'Bona myths, was positively converted into a tradition in which M'Bona was born of a virgin. The stories of M'Bona's rain-making power and the rivalries of his relatives became repatterned along the Cain and Abel theme. M'Bona was made to let food rain from heaven, and finally, Khulubvi, where his skull was buried, became Calvary, 'the place of the skull'.

In all these stories an explicit comparison is made with Christ, and the phrase 'black Jesus' (*Yesu Wakuda*) is often heard. This has resulted in the widely held idea that God had two sons, a white one called Jesus and a black one called M'Bona. These two are supposed each to have their own section of the world to look after: Jesus for the whites and M'Bona for the blacks. And each saviour can only be approached by his respective section of the community. The office of Chilamwa, who was traditionally an usher, has now evolved into that of a preacher dressed in black to contrast with the Catholic missionaries nearby, a striking instance of this duality.[33] Still, however great the Christian influence, it has remained restricted to the myth rather than to the cult, to the outer fringes of supporters rather than to the inner core of officials, and to the educated rather than to the non-educated. As a result, the cult as opposed to the myth is considerably less syncretistic. The pressure of Christianity and education, however, increase irrevocably, and it is to be expected that the cult itself will become more and more affected.

The defining of international boundaries, which divided British and Portuguese territories, also led to considerable waves of immigrants who came to look either for work or for security. While the Lomwe fitted in quite well with the Mang'anja because of their similar social systems, this was not the case with the Sena. The Sena are a mixture of people from different ethnic groups south of the Zambezi who are patrilineal and virilocal in contrast to the Mang'anja.[34]

There were various reasons for the Mang'anja to welcome these invaders. Coming in small separate groups, they posed no direct threat to the Mang'anja political structure, and no group insisted on having its own headman.[35] Many villages had yet to regain their pre-1864 size, and their headmen were glad to settle strangers in their area, thereby greatly adding to their status. Finally, the newcomers brought with them refined skills in woodwork and smithery unknown to the Mang'anja. Although intermarriage took place freely with a consequent rapid change in the social system, the lineages of the headmen kept aloof and maintained the traditional system. The greatest change in village structure was the appearance of large numbers of unrelated people. Under the traditional system the headman of the village was normally the head of its senior lineage and also related to the junior lineages. Non-related persons were incorporated into the autochthonous lineages by a putative relationship with a deceased member.[36] If there was no real blood or affinal relationship between a headman and his subjects, at least the pretence was there. This system changed completely with the advent of the Sena. Both their different social system and their great numbers did not allow for the application of this principle, and kin loyalty changed to political loyalty. The size of the villages increased enormously; the Mang'anja headmen rose in status, and the concept of their authority became more bureaucratic.

While all this was welcomed, the headmen needed to define their identity against those foreigners who had come to be thought of as belonging to a lower social class. They preserved their identity by maintaining matriliny, language and history, and by avoiding intermarriage. The headmen had two channels for co-operation: their meetings with the chiefs, all of whom had remained Mang'anja, and on a separate level, their meetings at the M'Bona shrine. It goes without saying that many headmen were of mixed blood although these did everything to pass themselves as Mang'anja. This was of little consequence to the chiefs, who could not depose a headman officially recognised by the Administration. Here, the cult of M'Bona acted as a powerful corrective. There was and is an absolute prohibition on non-Mang'anja entering the shrine or participating in the rituals. Although this prohibition is sometimes cautiously manipulated, Mang'anja self-awareness is as a rule so great that they will carefully scrutinise any new headman, and if he is considered non-Mang'anja ban him from participation. The fundamental political organisation is therefore preserved to a great extent within the cult.[37]

The drought of 1949 and subsequent famine which had initiated an intense revival of the cult also moved the agricultural department to intensify their efforts at soil conservation and increased food production. Agricultural supervisors were appointed and the co-operation of the chiefs obtained to make the scheme a success. One definite specification was that gardens had to be ridged and ridging completed by the following October. This system was entirely alien to the population of the Lower Shire Valley who had traditionally used mound cultivation in combination with the slash-and-burn method, and when there were no more woods to be burned had taken to a system of shallow cultivation. The more sophisticated among the population argued that the method of ridging was superfluous from the point of view of soil conservation since there was little danger of the soil being carried away on flat land, and that it was also illogical as regards increased production since ridged gardens tended to dry out more quickly than others. The less sophisticated argued that the new methods were against the ways of the ancestors, and that their application would end in disaster. They were supported by the medium at Khulubvi, who prophesied that the drought would continue if the ridging was done. Rumours circulated; Lundu was said to have received a messenger from M'Bona in the form of a baboon who told him that a new wife was needed for M'Bona. Some fishermen at Chiromo had reportedly dragged up from the Shire an iron box in which they found a little man who limped when he tried to walk. Upon inquiry he said that he was sent by M'Bona, that his limp was caused by the ridges, and that he had come to implore Tengani and others not to implement the regulations. Law and opposition to it crystallised in the persons of Tengani and the medium Chambote. Obstinate villagers were arrested; others complied in a half-hearted way.

Attention now became focused on the issue of federation. Once more Tengani sided with the Europeans and became known as one of the staunchest supporters of federation in the country. The general unrest led to the declaration of the state of emergency in 1959, and one of the first persons to be arrested was the Khulubvi medium who was locked up in Chiromo prison. The day after his arrest he became seriously ill and had to be taken to Nsanje hospital. He himself describes his sickness and subsequent early release as being due to M'Bona who did not allow him to come under the authority of Europeans.

Some time after the general election of 1961 Molin Tengani was sent into retirement and succeeded by Stonken Tengani whose appointment roused great expectations among the Khulubvi officials. The circumstances of independence combined to give the cult a new thrust. The harsh agricultural policy was abolished and a period of peace set in.

A final case of the erection of a rival shrine, this time of a clear-cut separatist nature, occurred in 1967 at Tengani's court, although it must be said that the issues at stake were primarily non-political. The present Tengani had, at the time of his accession, expressed his willingness to co-operate with the Khulubvi officials. This meant among other things that he would be called upon to fulfill certain ritual functions whenever the Khulubvi shrine had to be ceremonially rebuilt. There is an ancient belief that no Tengani could fulfill this function more than once. After the first occasion one of his sons would die, and after the second Tengani himself would die. This belief, which is very strong in the area, had led a number of Tenganis in the past to flee across the Shire, and it led the present Tengani to decline politely the first invitation which came to him. At the second invitation he decided to break his links with Khulubvi, stating that he was not satisfied with the way the shrine was run. Tengani's separatist move, however, was to be more than compensated by the restoration of the Lundu paramountcy on 5th July, 1969, at which occasion all the Khulubvi officials were present. Again, Evans Lundu, the new paramount, promised them full co-operation and expressly stipulated that no foreigners should be allowed to visit the shrine unless with his specific permission.

There were still a few more issues in which the cult became involved, one of which was that of cattle. It has become customary for people in the higher income bracket to invest their money in cattle. These are a general nuisance when they move their grazing grounds to the river banks where people have their marsh gardens. The gardens are soon destroyed, and it becomes generally impossible to open up new ones. People's complaints were finally taken on by the medium, who prophesied that all the cattle had to be removed from the district, but his admonitions went unheeded since even some of the officials were cattle keepers.

CONCLUSION

It appears that the nature and degree of the political involvement of the M'Bona cult may be studied on three distinct levels according to the interest groups confronting each other, the issues involved in such confrontations, and the ways used to manipulate the cult.

Among the interest groups there have been three ethnic units employing the cult for their own purposes. The Chipeta-Mang'anja invaders drove out the Kafula and sealed their take-over of the country by the appropriation of their shrine. When the Mang'anja conquered the Makua-Lomwe peoples two centuries later, they bound them to themselves by allowing them to establish subsidiary shrines under the aegis of Khulubvi. Subsequent ethnic confrontations involved foreign invaders in the persons of the Portuguese slavers, Sena immigrants, colonial administrators and missionaries. The Mang'anja continued to define their identity vis-à-vis the Sena in terms of the M'Bona cult by refusing them ritual functions. In their confrontations with the European powers of the government and missions, which were also frequently articulated in terms of the cult, the Mang'anja were able to join with the Sena.

In the course of the Mang'anja history two foreign political elite groups have appeared. The first of these were the Phiri who appropriated, renamed and re-organized the existing M'Bona shrine to make it the main religious centre of the Kaphwiti kingdom. The second group were the Kololo whose attempt at subjugating the Mang'anja territory was largely unsuccessful, due mainly to their small numbers and to foreign interference. However, one contributing factor seems to have been their failure to seize leadership of the M'Bona cult as they had done with the *Nyau* societies. The chief reason for their failure was mainly a geographic one since the Khulubvi area at the time of their expansion was more or less under the control of the *prazos*, while at a later stage Tengani was able to assure himself of British support against the Kololo.

The cult also played a conspicuous role in the rivalries between the royal lineages of Mankhokwe and Lundu on one hand and those of Kaphwiti and Lundu on the other. From the political viewpoint it must be considered a mistake on Lundu's part to have failed to appropriate the Mankhokwe shrine on Cholo in the same way as he did Kaphwiti's shrine on Malawi Hill. There, the killing of M'Bona and the consequent foundation of Khulubvi established his ownership in a way that was never again to be challenged. His half-hearted dealings with the Cholo shrine, however, left intact an institution which in due time was going to be employed against him. Mankhokwe ultimately failed to seize control of Khulubvi and thereby establish a firm claim to the paramountcy for much the same reasons as the Kololo, but his position was much stronger as he already enjoyed the support of its officials.

The cult officials themselves, occupying a pivotal position, played of necessity a number of different roles. There is first their relationship with the political establishment which is marked by a high degree of interdependence. An attitude of loyalty to the paramount has been a constant feature of the cult officialdom. This may be inferred from the fact that Lundu had to kill one or more of the leading officials of Kaphwiti's shrine. A more telling example, however, is the faithfulness with which the Khulubvi officials have been reiterating the rights of the Lundus at a time when they seemed doomed to lasting obscurity. No doubt, this loyalty was not wholly disinterested, but it was none the less marked.

The ritual positions at Khulubvi have stayed hereditary within certain lineages. This raises the question whether officials were ever able to pose a threat to the secular rulers. Here, we may recall their dogged resistance against Chief Molin Tengani and their refusal to acknowledge headmen and chiefs of mixed blood. It remains doubtful, however, whether they have ever been able to pose a serious challenge to the position of the paramount. For this, their own position is too precarious. There are a dozen or so officials, each with his own responsibility and each with the backing of his own lineage, relatives and villagers. No one can take a decision with regard to cult or shrine without the approval of the others, and no one can assume primacy without upsetting the structure. At least in its present organisation it would appear that the diffusion of power throughout a rather large group acts as a positive check against any usurper. Nevertheless the officials as a group are able to act as a focus of resistance against unpopular persons or policies.

A further interest group, and one of very recent origin, are the traditional agriculturalists in their resistance against the cattle owners. In this case the focus of resistance has been the medium rather than the officials, and it may be seen as an instance of resistance against a socio-economic rather than an ethno-political group. The medium occupies a pivotal position all by himself. Unhampered by loyalty to one specific group he is able to speak out on a great number of issues involving a wide variety of persons, groups and institutions. While the roles of secular and religious authorities with regard to the cult may be said to be primarily of a structural nature, the medium seems more concerned with the contingencies which threaten the structure as a whole.

In conclusion to this section it can be safely said that the cult does not allow for exclusive interest groups, and that it may be employed by or against one and the same group. In terms of size these groups range from the relatively small ones of the cult officials and established chiefs to medium-sized ones representing an ethnic group or the population of a district, to large-sized ones representing for instance the entire Lundu kingdom or the entire African population.

The issues involved in the various confrontations are equally different. With regard to external politics the cult has been used to consolidate conquests and integrate partially or entirely conquered peoples such as the Chipeta-Mang'anja and the Makua-Lomwe. For internal politics it served as a key integrative factor, alongside the perpetual kinship system, in uniting the political elite and the general population within the Lundu kingdom. More rarely, and only if there were enough supporting factors, was it also used to express dissatisfaction with and independence from the political establishment. In the sphere of modern as opposed to tribal politics the cult has locally been a potent focus of nationalist tendencies and activities. Outside the sphere of direct politics it has played a role in people's efforts to preserve traditional agricultural methods against the introduction of garden ridging and the proliferation of cattle, and their traditional religion against the encroachment of the Christian missions.

Finally to be considered is the behaviour of the various interest groups. Appropriation, relocation and renaming of the main shrine occurred whenever a new group took over political control of the Mang'anja area. Only in traditions concerning the wars against the Kafula and the murder of M'Bona are there any indications that violence was used. During the Lundu period, when the Mang'anja had conquered the Bororo, they were able to strengthen their position quite peacefully by establishing or allowing the Lolo to establish numerous subsidiary shrines such as were also widespread within the traditional territory of the Mang'anja. The difference between these and the Lolo ones, however, was that the Mang'anja were allowed a far greater degree of participation in the cult. They protected themselves to a certain extent against an overdose of foreign influence by allowing Mang'anja alone to represent their chiefs at the shrine, take ritual positions and assist at the ceremonies.

The ceremonies themselves, which we have not been able to discuss in this paper, and the events which occasioned them were also potent integrative factors. Thus, for instance, the procession of a new wife for M'Bona slowly winding its way through the valley from the paramount's court to the Khulubvi shrine, a distance of some ninety miles, symbolized in a very marked way the unity of Lundu's heartland. The rain sacrifices and the occasional rebuilding of the shrine required the participation and co-operation of all the Mang'anja chiefs. Dissent with the paramount or with the cult officials could be expressed by establishing or reviving a rival shrine. The population which has no direct authority over the organisation of the cult has been able to feel itself unified more directly through the body of M'Bona's myths. Its feelings have been expressed by adaptations of the myth and by rumours in the contexts of the myth itself.

It should perhaps be finally emphasised that the failure of the cult to unite the Mang'anja against the invaders of the nineteenth century is directly attributable to the concurrence of a natural disaster, undermining the cult leadership, and severe attacks from a number of different quarters. This failure should not however be allowed to blur the vital political role played by the cult in integrating the Mang'anja people in every phase of their history from the fourteenth century to the present day, in times of expansion as well as decline. The M'Bona cult, both in its institutional and prophetic roles, in myth, ritual and officialdom, has been the embodiment of Mang'anja identity, society and aspirations for over six centuries. The strength and persistence of this cult may perhaps be explained by its ability to express and articulate the interests of the varied social groups that have played their part in the history of the Mang'anja. The success of the cult, then, as a religious institution, should be measured not in terms of its participation in violent confrontations but precisely in its ability to channel such confrontations and maintain relative harmony throughout the main phases of Mang'anja history.

NOTES

[1] Marari is here used as an ethnic, Malawi as a geographic designation.
[2] I am indebted to the Nuffield Foundation, London, for financing the fieldwork on which this study is based, and to Dr I. Linden, University of Malawi, for critically reading the early drafts.
[3] These figures are estimates based on the percentages of Mang'anja and non-Mang'anja in thirteen sample groups.
[4] This and other features of Mang'anja religion are more fully described in J. M. Schoffeleers, 'Symbolic and Social Aspects of Spirit Worship among the Mang'anja', doctoral dissertation, Oxford 1968.
[5] S. J. Ntara *Mbiri ya Achewa* (Limbe 1965) p. 61.
[6] *The Handbook of Nyasaland* 2nd edition (London 1910) p. 65; 3rd edition (London 1922) pp. 32, 73–4. The version given in the 1910 edition was obtained from Tengani; that in the 1922 edition from the cult officials, Ngabu and Chiphwembe.
[7] This story is remembered both by the Mang'anja and the Chewa, from whom Ntara collected it. Chewa informants insist, however, that Kaphwiti's flight came before Undi's own break with Kalonga, while Mang'anja informants are equally insistent that Undi stands as their great ancestor, the first king, senior to Kaphwiti, and that Kaphwiti broke away from Kalonga as a tributary to Undi. See Ntara *op. cit*, p. 22. A statement supporting the Mang'anja interpretation was recorded by Livingstone. See *A Narrative of an Expedition to the Zambezi and its Tributaries, and of the Discovery of Lakes Shirwa and Nyassa, 1858–1864* (London 1865) p. 198.
[8] The ordeal episode in the M'Bona story seems to point to very early occurrence of witchcraft-eradication movements in the Lake Malawi area. If historically verifiable, this would lend a new dimension to the current discussion of these movements which continues to view them in the context of colonial and post-colonial government and as an expression of conflict between traditionalist and progressive forces. Cf. R. G. Willis, 'Introduction' *Witchcraft and Healing* (Edinburgh 1969) pp. 8–9.
[9] Ntara, *op. cit.* p. 15. A similar statement was made by the present Makewana of Msinja in an interview with the author in October 1969. The movement of the shrine to Msinja is described by Ntara, p. 13, and by W. H. J. Rangeley, 'Makewana the Mother of all People' *The Nyasaland Journal* vol. V, no. 2 (1950) pp. 32–3.

[10] The date of Lundu's defeat is given in G. Schurhammer, 'Die Entdeckung des Njassa-Sees' *Stimmen der Zeit* (1920) p. 349. Evidence that Lundu controlled the Zimba is provided by E. A. Alpers, 'The Mutapa and Malawi Political Systems' in T. O. Ranger (ed.) *Aspects of Central African History* (London 1968) p. 21. Dr Alpers' theory appears to be corroborated by some Mang'anja traditions which mention a certain Tundu as a kinsman of Lundu and M'Bona and as the ancestor of the Zimba. This Tundu is known as the spirit of destruction, and a sacrifice was made to him at Khulubvi in May 1967, when birds ravaged the rice fields. It is quite possible that he is to be identified with the rebel Tondo whom the Portuguese sought to castigate in 1599.

[11] P. Ph. Junod, 'Notes on the Ethnographical Situation in Portuguese East Africa' *Bantu Studies*, vol. VIII, no. 3 (1936) pp. 309-10.

[12] P. Schebesta, 'Religioese Anschauungen der Asena—Mulungu und seine Verehrung' *Bibliotheca Africana* vol. III, no. 1 (1929) p. 5; T. Price, 'The Meaning of Mang'anja' *The Nyasaland Journal* vol. XIV, no. 1 (1963) p. 75.

[13] Manuel Barreto, 1667, in G. Theal *Records of South-Eastern Africa* (London 1898-1903) vol. III, p. 480.

[14] Livingstone *op. cit.* pp. 75, 76, 81, 96.

[15] H. Rowley *The Story of the Universities' Mission to Central Africa* (London 1866) pp. 151, 266.

[16] Rowley *op. cit.* p. 89.

[17] Kabvina was the most important sub-chief of Kaphwiti and a member of the royal lineage; his alliance with Chibisa is mentioned *inter alia* by Rowley *op. cit.* p. 132. Chibisa, although the best documented Mang'anja chief in the Livingstone and U.M.C.A. records, remains a rather shadowy figure. Mang'anja traditions mention him as a 'younger brother' of Kabvina, who maintained a stronghold at Doa opposite Tete and another at Chikwawa. He was shot in early 1863 by a certain Terera or Mello.

[18] For the attitude of Tengani and Mankhokwe towards the Portuguese, *cf.* Livingstone *op. cit.* pp. 76, 96; for the alliance of Chibisa with the Portuguese *cf.* Livingstone in J. P. R. Wallis (ed.) *The Zambezi Expedition of Dr. Livingstone* (London 1956) p. 188 (6th August 1861).

[19] Livingstone *op. cit.* p. 108.

[20] H. P. Wilson, 'David Livingstone: Some Reminiscences' *The Nyasaland Journal* vol. XII, no. 2 (1959) pp. 16, 20-1.

[21] O. Chadwick *Mackenzie's Grave* (London 1959) p. 44.

[22] Rowley *op. cit.* p. 130.

[23] Livingstone in Wallis *op. cit.* p. 188 (1st August 1861).

[24] Rowley *op. cit.* pp. 400-1.

[25] The fate of the U.M.C.A. has been excellently described in Chadwick *op. cit.* In October 1966 an old man at Ngabu told me a story of some missionaries who once tried to visit M'Bona's shrine. Although they were forbidden this, they nevertheless insisted and finally managed to enter the sacred grounds. The results were horrifying. After they had returned to their mission, some went mad and roamed the villages 'like people possessed' before finding their death. The old man's story could only have been an account of what happened to the U.M.C.A., circulating among the population for over a century as another proof of M'Bona's power.

[26] R. Foskett, (ed.) *The Zambezi Journal and Letters of Dr. John Kirk, 1858-1863* (London 1965) p. 521.

[27] Wooden egg cups are locally used for drinking strong liquor.

[28] Information obtained from the Msinja officials, October 1969.

[29] Interview with the late Chief Molin Tengani, November 1966.

[30] The issue of tax exemption still leads to occasional tussles with officials of the Administration. A partial solution has been found by exempting the four male officials living in the

immediate neighbourhood of the shrine. The sons of tax-paying age, however, are not exempted, and have to live outside the Khulubvi area.

[31] Details of Tengani's life are from a manuscript written by one of his sons.

[32] Diary, Catholic Mission, Nsanje.

[33] Information provided by the cult officials. In actual practice Chilamwa's ritual dress does not differ from that of the others.

[34] Sena is a collective name locally used to indicate immigrants of foreign stock such as Chikunda, Dzowa, Manyika, Mwenye, Nyungwe, Phodzo, Tonga and Zimba.

[35] An exception is to be made for the aristocratic Mwenye families who claim descent from the Sena Muslims and generally insist on having their own headman. Their number, however, is very small.

[36] E. W. Chafulumira *Mbiri ya Amang'anja* (Zomba 1948) p. 4.

[37] It is common among the officials to express their dissatisfaction with people of their own number or others in authority by stating that they are 'Tonga'.

MUTUMBA MAINGA

A History of Lozi Religion to the End of the Nineteenth Century

Today the Lozi occupy the Western Province, formerly Barotse Province, in the south-west corner of Zambia, adjoining south-east Angola. The basis of Lozi religion is threefold: first there is Nyambe or Mulimu, that is, God, or the Supreme Being. Next to him in importance and power come the spirits of the ancestors, first the royal, then the non-royal, both known as *balimu*. Last come the *miluti*—the shadows or spirits.[1]

The apparent consistency and uniformity in Lozi beliefs concerning the Universe, the after-life and the supernatural may at first seem to make it difficult, if not unnecessary, to reconstruct a religious history. Religions in many societies, however, comprise attempts to influence by prayer and manipulation the supernatural forces which are believed to control the achievement of the different goals of the society as a whole, and of the individuals of which it is composed. Of necessity the nature and character of religion is influenced by the needs of society at given times and therefore by its history. A history of religion then becomes possible to reconstruct because religion has had constantly to adapt itself to meet new developments in society and, in the case of the Lozi, particularly to the development of the structure of the state.

Attempts to analyse practices in Lozi traditional religion recently revealed the existence of three almost separate forms, or 'denominations'.

THE NYAMBE CULT

In one form Nyambe—God—appears predominant and all prayers and requests are addressed to him directly. Nyambe is recognised as the Creator and Origin of all things. He is esteemed superior to all spirits. A number of Lozi proverbs present Nyambe as 'omniscient' and 'omnipotent'.[2] He controls the Universe and lives and fortunes of mankind. When making plans for the future it is the usual practice to add '*Mulimu ha lata*'—'God willing'—or '*Ku ziba Mulimu*'—'Only God knows'. Nyambe's ability to punish is illustrated in the myth of Kamunu, the first man, whom Nyambe punished for killing and eating other animal species. Whenever Kamunu killed an animal Nyambe deprived him of one of his own possessions, first his pot, then his dog. Finally Kamunu brought death to mankind when Nyambe deprived him of his son.[3]

Nyambe is said to have lived formerly on earth with his wife Nasilele but later to have been compelled by man's aggressive nature and intelligence in imitating him to flee to heaven. After his ascension to heaven the

95

sun came to be regarded as the symbol of Nyambe and prayers to him were always made at sunrise. There is no evidence of the existence of special priests for Nyambe. The oldest member, whether man or woman, usually officiated on behalf of the family or village. An altar of white sand or a *katala*—a wooden structure—on which a bowl of water or any other offering was placed was always constructed on the eastern outskirts of the village. Nyambe, it appears, was worshipped on special occasions only, and in times of crisis, which included sowing and harvest times, war, drought, sickness and death.

THE ROYAL GRAVES AND THE ANCESTOR CULT

The second form in Lozi traditional religion centres on the institution of the royal graves, where prayers and sacrifices are directed to the spirits of the ancestor kings, as distinct from Nyambe.

At the heart of the Lozi state is the institution of kingship and the royal cult. The Lozi king came to be recognised as the head of the socio-economic and administrative structure of the whole state. The Lozi hold that all members of the royal family have divine ancestry through their descent from Mbuyu, daughter of Nyambe. This divine ancestry endows an individual with *mali a silena*—royalty—and makes him eligible for the kingship if his descent is through the male line. In addition to this, the office of kingship came to have its own immense prestige. Once chosen, the king was elevated above all others by a number of ceremonies and rituals. At the time of his installation a prince goes through a series of purification rites.[4] Once these rituals are performed and the prince is invested with the insignia of power and presented to the public, he suddenly becomes surrounded by mystery and ritualism. His public appearances are restricted and he can communicate with people only through an intermediary. The king's elevation is demonstrated further through the use of figurative language when referring to his person and the objects of his household.[5] Thus, the assumption of his office puts the king in a special class above ordinary human beings.

The special position of the king continues even after his death. It is believed that at his death he becomes even more powerful than during his human life. For he can, in his new form, influence the fate of individuals and of the nation as a whole. Thus the king, on his death, is buried at a site previously chosen by him. The site is guarded by a number of people chosen to come with their families to build a village and live near the grave. Among the villagers, at the royal grave, is a special official known as *Nomboti*,[6] whose duty is to look after the actual grave, to attend to the needs of the departed king and to perform the task of an intermediary between him and the people. *Nomboti* is supposed to have special powers to communicate with the dead king. He presents offerings to him from individuals seeking special favours of his spirit, whether it be for good luck in hunting, or good health. He also performs official sacrifices on behalf of the nation which are offered by the reigning king. In case of natural disasters such as drought, famine or war, the reigning king produces a sacrifice in the form of an ox, or whatever is deemed necessary, and this is presented to *Nomboti* who, after the animal is slaughtered, takes the suitable parts and presents them to the spirit on the *limbwata*—an opening at the grave through which the dead king is supposed to receive offerings. *Nomboti* implores the spirit to intervene on behalf of the nation. After this communication he goes to report to the king either at the capital or wherever the king may be waiting for the reply from the spirit.

The dead kings, through their *Linomboti*, also have an important role in the policy making of the country. If an important decision has to be made, the spirits are consulted in a similar pattern to that described above. Their verdict guides the nation or, to be precise, the reigning king and his immediate advisers. The dead spirits are also consulted for guidance based on decisions taken under comparable circumstances earlier in Lozi history.[7]

At the election of a new king the candidate has to be presented and accepted by his predecessors. This is done partly at the time of installation, when some special rites are performed at the graves of the ancestress Mbuyu at Makono, and of the first king Mboo.[8] After the installation the new ruler goes on a tour of all the grave sites in the country, making sacrifices and seeking the approval and blessings of all his predecessors.[9]

The death of a king is symbolically presented as the death of the whole nation, in that all fires are put out. Fire is the source of life. It gives warmth. Food is cooked on it. It gives light in darkness. New fire is lit ceremonially by the new king. Then all the inhabitants relight their fires, supposedly from the original flame. The nation is, as it were, resurrected at the time of a new succession.

The *balimu*, or spirits of non-royal ancestors, have for the surviving members of their families a role comparable to that of the royal ancestors for the nation as a whole. Libations and prayers are made to the spirits of dead ancestors in times of family crisis. Their blessings and good will are sought for good health, prosperity, success in hunting, etc. When neglected, the ancestor spirits can cause illness to individuals or can bring bad luck.

The spirits, then, whether they be royal or common, are, like Nyambe, accredited with powers to influence and shape the fate of humanity.

SORCERY, WITHCRAFT AND MAGIC

Sorcery, witchcraft and magic may be described as a denial, rather than as a form, of religion. In the study of Lozi religion and religious practice sorcery, witchcraft and magic are, however, included because there is clearly a level at which belief in these exists or existed to the near exclusion of both the Nyambe and ancestor spirit cults. Their function is basically the same, that is to provide man with the ability to exercise direct control over his fate.

The Lozi claim to have borrowed most of the practices relating to sorcery, witchcraft and magic from the Luvale, Mbunda and related people.[10] C. N. M. White, writing on Luvale beliefs and rituals, contrasts their belief in Kalunga, the Supreme Being who plays no part even in the most important puberty rituals, with the content of beliefs in medicine and doctors which 'in many of their facets are plainly reflected as in the other parts of the total corpus of Luvale beliefs'.[11]

Throughout the approach of the Luvale to their whole corpus of beliefs, and to the actions and rituals relevant to it, White continues to point out, emphasis lies far more on the aspect of manipulation.[12] He found no equivalent in Luvale religion to the concept of 'the sacred', and any rituals performed followed strict formulae not because they were 'sacred' but rather essential and inescapable in order to manipulate and influence hidden forces. Kalunga provides a justification for certain phenomena and a basis for some explanations of causation. But he does not relate to the social and political structure of the living in the way in which Nyambe, or the spirits of the ancestor kings, did among the Lozi. The Luvale have no communal rituals associated with chieftainship. They do not regard their rulers as divine and their graves are not sites of public sacrifice. According to White, neither Kalunga nor the spirits of the ancestors appear in any Luvale proverb as the source of the moral code. The moral code has been worked out pragmatically to ensure the cohesion of society without being attributed to supernatural forces.[13]

The Lozi, like the Luvale and the Mbunda, believe in witchcraft and sorcery as explanations which account for instances of illness, death or misfortune. Both the sorcerer and the witch are seen as operating within ordinary human relations rather than in the realm of the super-natural.[14] The sorcerer is believed to have special knowledge, particularly of magic, which enables him to manipulate matter so as to cause injury.[15] Both sorcerers and witches can be detected by diviners, who through the use of medicines and counter-magic can cleanse witches and protect society and individuals from sorcery and witchcraft. Divination also provides a means to predict the future and ascertain causes of sickness, death or other natural and human disasters.

THE CO-EXISTENCE OF RELIGIOUS FORMS

The three separate forms or 'denominations' of religion identified above operate simultaneously in contemporary Lozi society. A single occurrence can be celebrated simultaneously, through three separate rituals, each with a character and order of its own. The occurrence of drought is a good example. In the Nyambe cult it appears that there were regular prayers for rain at the time of sowing, which was always in September, just before the rains were due. The people in a village or district assembled, bringing with them seeds of different types, hoes and axes. It appears that formerly there were fields set aside, *masimu a Nasilele*—'fields of Nasilele'—(Nyambe's wife).[16] The assembled people proceeded to dig in the *simu ya Nasilele* (singular form) and planted the seeds while singing and praying that Nyambe should send rain to make Nasilele's seeds germinate. As time passed, perhaps because of the increasing demand for land, the tradition of reserving special fields for Nasilele was abandoned and instead waste land was used.[17]

In the cult of the royal graves, the ruling king offered prayers and sacrifice in times of drought to the royal ancestor spirits on behalf of the nation. The sacrifice always consisted of cattle, which had to be black. Black signified dark rain clouds. The animal was given to the *Nomboti*, who presented it to the dead king at the grave. Then it was slaughtered. Certain parts were removed, specially prepared and offered at the *limbwata*. The rest of the meat was cooked and eaten publicly by the assembled people. They were led by the *Nomboti* who in song and prayer requested the ancestor spirit to send rain to his people.[18]

A ritual of this nature was performed only by groups in the areas affected by drought. Therefore the prayers would be made only to the spirits of the kings buried in the area. National rituals were performed in all regions on occasions which were of general significance, such as war.

Apart from prayers to Nyambe and the ancestor spirits, there is yet a third alternative for avoiding drought. This is through resort to medicine-men or rain-doctors. The medicine-man is approached by the people to change the forces of nature. It is believed that the rain-doctor can make rain fall through the use of the appropriate combination of magic and medicine. He usually worked secretly, shut up in a hut, while people remained outside, singing and dancing or waiting anxiously for the first signs of rain.[19]

Numerous other examples can be given to illustrate the different types of ritual in the Nyambe cult, the royal ancestor cult and medicine and magic. But how does one account for the co-existence of three such separate forms of religious practice? A study of Lozi traditional religion and its history, as of any other traditional religion, necessitates a thorough understanding of Lozi society and history.

AN ATTEMPTED RECONSTRUCTION OF LOZI RELIGIOUS HISTORY

The first clue to the answer seems to lie in the composition of Lozi society. The name Lozi describes a number of sub-tribal groups which were brought together and to some extent turned into a homogeneous cultural and political entity by a highly centralised administration. Lozi tradition and available evidence suggest at least three successive waves of migration into Bulozi, the last of which comprised the founders of the present Lozi dynasty. The new rulers appear to have incorporated two earlier distinct groups which have been identified both regionally and linguistically.[20] One was in the northern part of Bulozi. Their descendants are still identifiable and appear to be concentrated in Kalabo District. Their languages have close affinity to Siluyana, the present Lozi court language.[21] The second group was in the south. Today their descendants seem to be concentrated in Sesheke, while their languages have close affinity to the Tonga languages of the Southern Province of Zambia.[22] In addition to these founder groups, at the height of the Lozi state's power the Lozi influence extended to the Kafue River in the east, to the Mashi or Chobe River in the south, the Kwito River in the west, and the Zambezi–Kasai watershed in the north.[23] The co-existence of multiple forms of religion and religious practice could therefore have resulted from the coming together of several different groups. But a further explanation can be obtained from the growth and historical changes within the Lozi state. As already seen religion is never static. In certain instances it is possible to identify special forces which made for change in religion.

Earlier in this paper an examination of Nyambe's character revealed him as the Creator, the Origin of all things, while in a number of Lozi proverbs he is presented as omniscient. But a close examination of the myth of Kamunu and Nyambe reveals some limitations in Nyambe's power and character. For instance he was *surprised* by man's ability to imitate him, and he came to *fear* man until he finally *fled* to heaven from him. Equally significant, Nyambe had

99

to resort to diviners in his efforts to find a suitable place of refuge out of Kamunu's reach.[24] For his ascent to heaven, Nyambe not only had to consult his official diviner, but ultimately had to rely on the spider to provide him with a web. It would appear, then, that of necessity man had sometimes to rely on forces other than Nyambe. Thus it is possible to see how the Lozi, while admitting that Nyambe and the spirit ancestors exercise separate influence, still consider them of complementary significance.[25]

On the other hand there is evidence to suggest that the Nyambe cult was originally predominant among the earlier inhabitants of Bulozi, particularly in Kalabo. It was evidently supplemented by the religious practices of later immigrants, the founders of the kingship, who established the institution of the royal graves.

The centre of the Nyambe cult appears to have been in the present Kalabo District. This fact is suggested by the existence at Liumba in Kalabo, of *Lilunda la Nyambe*—the hill of Nyambe—where Nyambe and his wife Nasilele are supposed to have dwelt during their stay on earth. Close to *Lilundu la Nyambe* is a small lake where the *Baoli*, or Queens, of Nyambe used to carry out their toilet.[26] In the same vicinity, it is said, are the remains of a huge hearth where Nyambe boiled his great pot, *Nyunguluyela Matanda*.[27] Finally, there is in the same area a huge *muzauli* tree from the top of which Nyambe is said to have ascended to heaven on the spider's web[28]. If the Nyambe cult originated in Kalabo it ultimately spread all over Bulozi, since groups even in the extreme south, such as the Mbukushu, today have beliefs and myths of Nyambe.

Perhaps owing to the high degree of decentralisation in the pre-Lozi state period, the cult of Nyambe lacked coherence. It seems clear that its influence was eroded during the period of the Lozi state. *Lilundu la Nyambe* is pointed out by some local groups, who speak of the awe in which it was held by previous generations.[29] The limited knowledge in Bulozi concerning the existence and location of places like it suggests that if it was a great religious centre, it ceased to be recognised as such a long time back. Alternatively, if it was recognised as an important centre by the early inhabitants of Bulozi or Kalabo, the later immigrants, the rulers, did not so recognise it.

There is no evidence to suggest that the earlier inhabitants of Bulozi had an ancestor spirit cult, comparable to that of the ancestor king cult, although the idea of an afterlife is present in the myth of Nyambe and Kamunu.[30] The transition from the pre-Lozi state to the founding of the present dynasty is presented in Lozi tradition through a second set of myths of origin and creation in which Nyambe is still the Creator, but where the place of the generic man is taken by the founders of the Lozi dynasty.[31] Religion here has an important political function. The founding of the Lozi state is not only explained, but given the prestige of a divinely ordained event.

The origin of the institution of the royal graves is traced back in Lozi tradition to Mboo (first king) whose spirit is said to have shifted from the place in which he was buried at Ikatulamwa to a place of his own choice at Imwambo.[32] But the first reference and full account of ceremonial sacrifice to the ancestor spirits on royal graves does not appear until the reign of Ngombala (sixth king).[33] Over a period of time, it would seem that the new rulers built up the royal cult and generally created around themselves a sacred myth.

The institution of the royal graves and the royal cult were both greatly undermined during the first half of the nineteenth century, while the second half of the century saw a struggle to re-establish them by Lubosi Lewanika.[34] There were, from quite an early stage of the development of the Lozi state, inherent weaknesses within its internal structure, which contributed to its collapse in the first half of the nineteenth century. Despite the exalted position of the king, administration became more complex as the territorial area of the Lozi state increased. As a result of increased centralisation under a single king, the ambitious and able 'royal' had no outlet for his ambitions, except to succeed the king, either after his death, or through a successful conspiracy. In theory, as already seen, all male members of the royal family of direct descent from the ancestress Mbuyu were eligible for the kingship. Every time a new succession took place there was a crisis within the royal family. On the other hand, when such a crisis occurred, the senior *indunas* and the aristocracy generally were in a position of great power. Their support became essential for successful candidature. Thus the balance between king and bureaucracy, which an active and able monarch could always maintain to his advantage, was upset at regular intervals.

In addition to these problems, centralisation in Bulozi had to reckon with a degree of regional and factional difference. In the first place, there was the division between the Luyana groups in the north, who also happened to dominate the central government, and the Tonga groups in the south. The Tonga groups did not hesitate to seize any opportunity which promised to undermine the Luyana authority, or to reverse the political roles of the two groups. Whenever the central kingship showed signs of weakness at least a section of the Tonga group in the south would rebel and seek to re-establish some sort of autonomy. Similarly, as was to become clear during the nineteenth century, they did not hesitate to ally themselves with an outside group which offered them a chance to defy Luyana authority.

The second cause of rivalry arose from the existence of dual kingships covering Namuso, the northern part of the plain, and Lwambi, the southern part (Lealui and Nalolo divisions today). This division went back to the time of Mboo (first king) and his brother Mwanambinyi. Traditions about Mwanambinyi[35] seem to point to his having broken from the Lozi parent group following disputes within the royal dynasty. Mwanambinyi nearly succeeded in establishing an independent kingdom in the present Senanga area, which, although eventually crushed and brought back under central control, developed into a genuine rival centre of Lozi power. During the reign of Ngombala, the sixth king, the southern kingship was re-established to care for the southern half of the kingdom. Although ultimate control and power was vested in the northern ruler, the southern groups sometimes tended to identify themselves with the southern kingship, while the southern ruler himself now and then showed aspirations towards either full autonomy or control of the central kingship. The result was a number of civil wars between Namuso and Lwambi.[36] The final blow came in about 1840, when Bulozi was invaded by the Kololo,[37] a people from the south and originally of Sotho stock. The Lozi, undermined by the problems analysed above, and torn in a civil war at the time of the invasion, failed to put up effective resistance. They were not only defeated, but they split into three groups, two of which went outside Bulozi into exile, to Nyengo and to Lukwakwa on the Kabompo.[38]

The social and political uprooting of the Lozi in the middle of the nineteenth century came to have far-reaching consequences on the history of their religion. Their going into exile meant a physical separation from the royal grave sites, which were scattered all over the Plain. This separation was so critical that it is reported that on one occasion the group in exile at Nyengo secretly visited the royal grave site at Ikatulamwa.[39]

Thus the Lozi, forced into closer physical contact with the Luvale and Mbunda groups, and denied access to their centres of worship, were exposed to and came to accept new religious practices. Medicine, magic and divination became predominant factors in a society which previously had placed itself largely at the mercy of supernatural forces.

But it would be misleading to attribute the use of medicine, magic and divination to the accident of exile, as it affected the Lozi in the nineteenth century. As already seen, Nyambe is said to have relied on diviners. In the same myth of Nyambe and Kamunu it is said that Nyambe banished Kamunu. But Kamunu returned after a year's absence, carrying a fighting club and a pot of medicine, both of which he had acquired during his banishment from God.[40] The early military victories of the Lozi under Mboo (the first king), are attributed to magic and medicine,[41] while Mwanambinyi, Mboo's brother, is remembered in tradition as the miracle maker, who had in his employment the most powerful medicine-men of his time.[42] Finally, the first association between the Lozi and the Mbunda/Luvale medicine-men is traced back to a period before the Kololo invasion, during Mulambwa's reign.[43] According to Mbunda traditions it was the desire to acquire powerful medicines and magic that prompted Mulambwa (the tenth king) to invite Mwene Muundu, the first of the Mbunda immigrants, into Bulozi.[44] To Mulambwa and his successors, stable kingship could be assured through the employment of medicine-men and magic.[45] The Czech traveller, Dr Emil Holub, recorded in 1875 that

> in Sipopa's employment there were ... two old wizen-looking magicians or doctors ... who exercised almost supreme control over state affairs ... That there had not been a revolt long ago against Sipopa's tyranny was mainly attributed to the belief that he had those in his secret council who could divine any plot beforehand and frustrate any stratagem that could be devised, and even when his despotism grew so great that the life of the highest in the kingdom was not safe for a day, not a man could be found to lift an assegai against him.[46]

Later, in accounting for Sipopa's fall from power, Holub observed that a 'certain charm which he had publicly exhibited and proclaimed infallible failed to produce its proper effect'.[47] Despite Sipopa's fall his successors continued to employ Mbunda doctors. During the 1880s Lubosi Lewanika found the Mbunda witch-finders and diviners a handy political weapon to rid himself of suspected rivals. The missionary Adolphe Jalla, on his arrival in Bulozi in September 1889, commented on the extent to which witch-finding was being employed: 'Accusations of witchcraft were the order of the day. It was the surest way of disposing of those of whom one was jealous or whom one hated.'[48] Jalla also reported that Lewanika had boasted to him, saying, 'The divining bones—*litaula*—point out whom I want.'[49]

It was not surprising at all that the Mbunda doctors and diviners opposed Lewanika's accepting missionaries and British protection. It is said that the divining bones stopped Lewanika from receiving Coillard on his first visit in 1876 by giving non-committal predictions.[50] Later they blamed national disasters such as drought, locusts and even smallpox on the new religion and on the white men who brought it: 'either our Gods are angry or the white man's God is bringing evil upon you. Better have nothing to do with them.'[51]

Lewanika soon discovered that the weapon of divination could be effectively used against him. In February 1887 one of his trusted young advisers was accused of being a witch and was put through the test of *mwati*, the poison ordeal, and the boiling water test. 'The unfortunate chief was soon struggling with death amidst insults and curses.'[52] A few months later, in May, Lewanika returned from a hunt to find the floor of his house sprinkled with blood.[53] Suspiciously enough, when Lewanika turned to the diviners their tests failed to detect the man responsible.

The first direct confrontation between Lewanika and the Mbunda doctors came in December 1892, when the divining bones made Lewanika their victim. The missionary Coillard received a desperate message from the king.

'Know,' he said, 'that the Mambunda, the initiated, the Masters of the Secret Art, have been consulting the divining bones . . . Well, it is I, myself, whom the bones have seized upon and denounced. They accuse me of having brought the curse of small-pox to the nation and of preventing the rain from falling.'[54]

As a result of the medicine-men turning against him, Lewanika began to work actively to undermine their position. In 1892 when he was accused by the divining bones, Lewanika's position was not strong enough for him to take decisive action. But by February 1897 he was able to arrest two medicine-men and break up their instruments. He then declared that 'where witchcraft was concerned it was the accuser not the accused who was to be punished'.[55] From this date the diviners' political influence was eclipsed though they retain some social significance to this day.

The establishment of the first Christian missions in Bulozi in 1885-6 introduced a new element into the religious and social thought of the Lozi. Like so many who 'brought the Gospel' to Africa, François Coillard and his fellow members of the Paris Missionary Society (representing the French Reformed Church) saw the whole of traditional Lozi religion as paganism and inevitably opposed to the establishment of Christianity. Coillard took Lewanika's fight against witchcraft and divination as a sign of his approaching conversion: 'God has inclined his heart towards the gospel.'[56] But Lewanika, although willing for his own short-term advantage to ally himself with the missionaries, did not fail to see that for his person and his office the strongest security lay in the old Lozi traditional structure. The old Lozi kingship cult and the royal ancestor spirit cult provided a supernatural basis for Lewanika which placed his person and office above ordinary men and public scrutiny. In addition to this a faction of his trusted supporters was opposed to Christianity. There was even a formal declaration by these *indunas* that Lewanika would forfeit his throne if he were converted to Christianity.[57] When one of Lewanika's wives was converted the *indunas* remonstrated that their prior consent should have been obtained.[58] The missionaries recognised the force they had to contend with, and they labelled this faction the 'Pagan Conservative Party'. The *indunas*, like the Mbunda medicine-men, feared the new religion and the Europeans because both would clearly reduce the king's dependence on them. In addition to this, however, the 'Pagan Conservative Party' were pure traditionalists bent on seeing a revival of Lozi institutions in their former splendour. Over the issue of British protection they had declared in 1888 to Lewanika, 'We serve you because you are king and sovereign, but if you become the *mutanga*—slave—the subject of a master and a foreigner, that is humiliation the Barotse will never accept.'[59] Lewanika, therefore, though embracing and encouraging missionary technical instructions never became a full convert and refused to be baptised.[60]

Under Lewanika, indeed, the tradition of divine kingship was revived and brought to the fore. One of the *indunas* in December 1894 explained to Jalla the basis of Lewanika's authority and honour:

> Our king is the son of the divinity, a God himself. This is the reason behind all the honour paid to him. This is the reason people lower themselves before him and before all that belongs to him.[61]

Lewanika gave new strength to the institution of the royal graves and formed a particularly strong alliance with the royal grave keepers.[62] He chose Ngalama (fifth king) who was buried in Kwandu, for his special protector, and his seventeen wives were assigned as priestesses to the various tombs.[63]

Despite the missionary presence, Christianity was to make little headway in the period before the establishment of effective British administration. In October 1900 Coillard wrote in despair that *borena* (kingship) and its patronage 'does far less for the Gospel than people suppose, while everywhere its hostility creates immense difficulties'.[64]

The Missionary Conference at Sesheke in July 1902 similarly admitted, 'Perhaps the greatest obstacle which we meet in our work is the wonderful fascination of the power which the king and the chiefs of different degree still wield.'[65]

The initial approach of the missionaries was to superimpose not only religion but also Western culture and institutions over and above traditional structures. They failed to understand the strength or nature of the religious feeling that underpinned these structures. Later they despaired of action in isolation and came to look to the coming of the colonial administration to bring about the required change.[66] The missionaries might have been advised to attempt to place Western Christianity in a meaningful historical and cultural relationship with the traditional cultural and religious mores of the Lozi. Something vital might have sprung from this. Instead we have the declining old plant of the traditional religion of the villages and the equally declining plant of the 'new' religion of the mission stations whose roots have only in a few cases reached right down to the springs of Lozi religious feeling.

NOTES

[1] For a brief analysis see V. W. Turner *The Lozi Peoples of North Western Rhodesia* (London 1952) pp. 48–53.

[2] Interview with *Induna* Lingulunde Inyama, Libonda *Kuta* on May 19, 1970; with Prince Kufunduka Mubukwanu Liatitima, Mwandi *Kuta*.

[3] A. Jalla *Litaba za Sicaba sa Ma-Lozi* (Capetown 1921 reprinted 1959) p. 2.

[4] Installation rites are kept very secret, but I have been given some accounts by court officials.

[5] Interview with *Mulena Mukwae* Nakatindi, Mwandi, in June 1968. Princess Nakatindi is the daughter of Yeta III and granddaughter of Lubosi Lewanika.

[6] Interview with Liyamine Ndate Sitali, Mulumbo Village (site of Yeta III's grave), in October 1968; with *Induna* Lingulunde Inyama, Libonda *Kuta*, who officiates at Mboanjikana Akatoka's grave.

[7] *Linomboti* are sometimes invited to the *kuta* to join in or advise in deliberations.

[8] The installation rituals to the southern kingship at Nalolo are sometimes performed at Kwandu, the grave of Ngombala (sixth king), who in Lozi tradition is credited with the founding of the southern chieftaincy.

[9] The missionary Coillard's first encounter with Lewanika was in 1886 while Lewanika was going round on a similar ceremony following his return to power after the 1884–5 rebellion. See F. Coillard *On the Threshold of Central Africa* (London 1897) pp. 216–18.

[10] C. M. N. White *Elements in Luvale Beliefs and Rituals* Rhodes–Livingstone Paper no. 32 (Manchester 1961) p. 35.

[11] *Ibid*. p. 67.

[12] *Ibid*. p. 29.

[13] *Ibid*. p. 42.

[14] *Ibid*. p. 40; interview with *Mwene Muundu* Muyamba, Luutwi *Kuta* on 22 May, 1970; and with Nyambe Ikacana, Silinyi Village, on 17 May, 1970.

[15] Mr Nyambe Ikacana told a story of two witches who caused 'false' haemorrhage that even baffled doctors at Yuka Hospital.

[16] Interview with Makuyuya Kapao, Nakonga Village, on 15 May, 1970; with Ndate Namakau Mukungu Kambangala, Nasikena Village, on 15 May, 1970; and with *Induna* Lingulunde Inyama, Libonda *Kuta*, on 19 May, 1970.

[17] Interview with *Induna* Lingulunde Inyama, Libonda *Kuta*; see Turner *op. cit.* p. 49.

[18] Interview with *Induna* Lingulunde Inyama, Libonda *Kuta*.

[19] Interview with *Mwene Muundu* Muyamba, Luutwi *Kuta*, an Mbunda chief who claims to have formerly trained as a medicine-man.

[20] Jalla *op. cit.* p. 8 (see also the translation, 'History, traditions and legends of the Barotse Nation', CO Africa No. 1179, p. 4); M. Mainga, 'The Origin of the Lozi: Some Oral Traditions' in E. Stokes and R. Brown *The Zambesian Past* (Manchester 1965) pp. 238–47; see also M. Mainga, 'A History of the Lozi People to 1900', London Ph.D. thesis, 1969, a revised version of which is being published by Longmans.

[21] G. Fortune, 'A Note on the Languages of Barotseland' *Proceedings of the Conference on the History of Central African Peoples*, Rhodes–Livingstone Institute (Lusaka 1963); M. Mainga, 'History', p. 96.

[22] E. Jacottet *Études sur les langues du Haut Zambèze* (Paris 1896).

[23] M. Mainga, 'History', p. 330.

[24] When consulting a diviner, it is customary to refer to the fact that divination originated from Nyambe, thus making the diviner's decision unchallengeable.

[25] Interview with *Induna* Lingulunde Inyama, Libonda *Kuta*.

[26] Both *Lilundu la Nyambe* and the lake were pointed out to me and subsequently visited by me on 17 May, 1970, while in Kalabo on a research trip. The main informant on this

subject was Pastor S. Sharpa, of Kandiana Village, at present pastor at Liumba Mission (Seventh Day Adventists).

27 It is said that before Nyambe ascended to Heaven he decided to test the intelligence of the various animal species. He put the *Nyunguluyela Matanda* filled with water on a big fire and then asked each animal species in turn to try and take the pot off the fire. They all failed except man and his family who succeeded in taking the pot off by first putting out the fire by pouring water on it. Nyambe then warned the animals to beware of Man.

28 The *mazauli* tree was mentioned to me but not seen by me. Account from Pastor S. Sharpa, Liumba Mission.

29 Interview with Pastor S. Sharpa, 17 May, 1970.

30 It is said that everything that Kamunu lost and saw broken or dead was later seen intact or alive in Nyambe's household. Jalla *Litaba* p. 2.

31 Sikota Akufuna, 'Makalelo a Bulena bwa Selozi' (The Origin of the Lozi Kingship), typed manuscript, 1959; Jalla, 'History', p. 4.

32 Jalla *Litaba* p. 10.

33 Collated traditions of the Lealui *indunas*.

34 M. Mainga, 'History', pp. 307–8.

35 *Ibid.*, pp. 120–2; interview with Kumoyo Akende, Nalutunda Nalilowa Village; and with *Induna Kakene* Siangu Mubita, Lianyi Village. The title of *Kakene* has a history which goes back to the first Ngambela of Mwanambinyi, the first *Kakene*.

36 M. Mainga, 'History', p. 186.

37 The exact date of the Kololo invasion of Bulozi is not known. For a detailed discussion see C. M. N. White, 'The Ethno-History of the Upper Zambezi' *African Studies* vol. 21, no. 1 (1962) p. 26; Edwin W. Smith, 'Sibitwane and the Makololo' *AS*, vol. 15, no. 2 (1956) pp. 49–74.

38 M. Mainga, 'History', pp. 198–9.

39 G. C. R. Clay, 'Barotseland between 1801 and 1864', *Proceedings of the Conference on the History of Central African Peoples*, Rhodes–Livingstone Institute (Lusaka 1963) p. 13.

It is interesting to contrast the attitude of the Kololo towards Lozi religious institutions with that of other conquering groups. The Ndebele, for example, took care to propitiate the priests of Mwari after the overthrow of the Rozvi Empire, sending tribute to them, giving them a place at national ceremonies, and consulting them over the succession. In other instances, invading dynasties took over an existing royal cult, inventing genealogies to conceal the true relationship, and burying their own dead kings in accordance with the prescriptions of the royal cult. The Kololo did none of these things. They made no gifts to the royal grave keepers and accorded them no role in their system. Indeed, it seems likely that the graves were deserted and their keepers in exile throughout Kololo rule. And certainly on Sebitwane's death no effort was made to assimilate the dead king into the Lozi royal cult. He was buried in the Kololo manner, in great contrast to Lozi custom. 'The burial of a Bechuana chief,' wrote Livingstone about Sebitwane's death, 'takes place in his cattle pen, and all the cattle are driven for an hour or two around and over his grave, so that it may be quite obliterated.' (David Livingstone *Missionary Travels and Researches in South Africa* London 1857 p. 90).

40 Jalla *Litaba* p. 1.

41 Sikota Akufuna *op. cit.*; Jalla *Litaba* p. 9.

42 Information from Ndate Muyunda Wamunungo, Silele Village; see Jalla *Litaba* pp. 15–16.

43 Y. W. Mupata *Mulambwa Santulu u amuhela bo Mwene* (Mulambwa Santulu welcomes the Mbunda chiefs) (London 1958).

44 Interview with *Mwene Muundu* Muyamba, Luutwi *Kuta*.

45 One of the well-known traditions about Mulambwa is that he had himself cut up and stewed with medicines and was then resurrected to rise to great power as a ruler of the Lozi.

[46] Dr Emil Holub *Seven Years in South Africa* (London 2 vols. 1881) vol. 2 p. 241.

[47] *Ibid.*

[48] A. Jalla *Lewanika, roi des Barotsi* (Geneva 1902) p. 7.

[49] *Ibid.*

[50] D. F. Ellenberger *History of the Basuto, Ancient and Modern*, translated by J. C. Macgregor (London 1912) p. 325.

[51] *News from Barotsiland* no. 4, April 1899.

[52] F. Coillard *On the Threshold* pp. 282–3.

[53] *Ibid.* p. 287.

[54] *Ibid.* p. 494.

[55] A. and Emma Jalla *Pionniers parmi les ma-Rotse* (Florence 1903) p. 300.

[56] Coillard *On the Threshold* p. 376.

[57] *News from Barotsiland*, no. 5, August 1899.

[58] Jalla *Pionniers* p. 154.

[59] Coillard *On the Threshold* p. 331.

[60] Coillard to Boegner, 5 August, 1888 (Paris Mission Archives); *News from Barotsiland* no. 13, September 1901.

[61] Jalla *Lewanika*. See also Coillard *On the Threshold* p. 329. He referred to Lewanika as the 'personification of Divine Right' as early as 1888.

[62] Interview with Mrs Ma Joane Lumba Zaza, Mule Village, 2 January, 1963.

The missionary Coillard was compelled to offer a piece of white cloth for sacrifice before he could meet Lewanika who was on tour of the royal graves in 1886. See Coillard *On the Threshold* p. 216.

[63] Jalla *Lewanika* p. 12.

[64] Coillard to M. Bianquis, October 1900 (Paris Mission Archives).

[65] *News from Barotsiland* no. 17 (December 1902) p. 14.

[66] *News from Barotsiland* no. 9, July 1900.

PART THREE

THE INTERACTION OF RELIGIOUS AND POLITICAL INNOVATION

I. N. KIMAMBO and C.K. OMARI

The Development of Religious Thought and Centres among the Pare

INTRODUCTION

The aim of this paper is to look at the development of Pare religious thought and worshipping centres from two points of view. The first is to view religious centres as places where people communicated with the supernatural Being (God) in a group form. The second view is to look at these religious centres as a means of mobilising society. Evidently in a traditional society the two views are very much interrelated and it is somewhat artificial to try to separate them. Yet historically this kind of analysis may be useful since it is the theological content which transcends the time limit and provides the mythical basis on which the society is united. On the other hand, it is possible to view historically how the needs for social, political or economic mobilisation may be connected with the development of religious ideas. The analysis attempted in this paper is limited to the development of Pare society in the pre-colonial era.

The Pare (or Asu) are a Bantu-speaking people living in north-eastern Tanzania. Although they are mainly agriculturists, a limited amount of herding is practised, especially on the lowlands. According to a recent survey[1] the Pare consist of some sixty-five patrilineal clans with segments (or lineages) scattered all over the country, on a patrilocal basis. The preliminary results of the 1967 Census indicate that the Pare numbered 149,635.

It is clear that the segmentary nature of Pare kin groupings has been dictated by the hilly nature of their country. Covering about 3,050 square miles, the Pare country consists of a range of mountains divided into three sections. The South Pare range borders the Usambaras while the North Pare one slopes into the lowlands of the Chagga country. In the middle there is a smaller range usually referred to as Middle Pare. The physical features of this country—with separate ridges, slopes and plateaux—have therefore posed a continuous problem of how groups settling in different areas could remain united. The religious ideas examined in this paper do explain how mobilisation has always been attempted as an ideal in the face of the practical necessity to segment.

Pare traditions indicate that their various clan heroes came into the country in small groups and from various directions. The largest numbers are those claiming to have come from the Taita Hills in the east and the Nguru Mountains in the south. Yet there are several other groups who claim connections with the Maasai steppe in the west, Kilimanjaro in the north and Usambara in the south. Their stories of migration are complicated. But it is significant to note that most of these groups agree that the Pare country was already inhabited

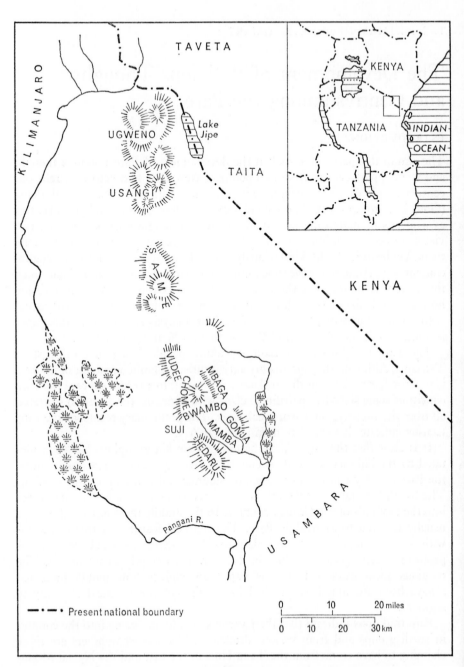

Upare

by other people: by groups known as *Vimbiji* or *Sivira* and by the *Vasi* who were hunting-gathering people. The main task of the newcomers, however, is said to have consisted of clearing the country of a more settled people known as the 'Wagalla'. The stories of how the so-called 'Wagalla' were overcome and driven out are complicated, and may relate to a mythical acknowledgement that this region had been inhabited by Bantu-speaking people for a long time, as the archaeological work of the staff of the British Institute of History and Archaeology is beginning to indicate.[2]

THE BASIC FEATURES OF PARE RELIGIOUS THOUGHT

It is within the conception of this long mythical past that the basic features of Pare religious thought have to be understood. These centre on two concepts: the idea of a creator (*Kiumbi*) who created the ancestors and all the things they needed, and the position of these ancestors as mediators between God (the creator) and the living members of society.

The creation story relates that this *Kiumbi* had his dwelling place beyond the sky. But once upon a time he used to have fellowship with people regularly. Unfortunately people disobeyed him by eating the eggs which he had ordered them not to eat. This they did because they were cheated by a person known as *Kiriamagi*. As a result God withdrew himself to a far up abode. This left the people alone without their former fellowship with God, although he sometimes visited them.[3] People attempted to build a tower so as to reach God's place and thus attain the former fellowship with him. But the higher they built the farther God's place receded. Eventually God punished the people with a severe famine, during which all the people died except two youths—a boy and a girl. All the people on earth descend from this pair. Since then man's fellowship with God has been remote and communication with him has to be sought through the ancestors who are closer to him than the living members of the society.

It is, however, difficult to envisage how this universal view of God's fellowship with men can be placed on the historical plane of the Pare themselves. Mystically, of course, the story has the benefit of demonstrating the unity or oneness of any community, whether big or small. The Pare claim that when they arrived in their country they had both concepts of God and of the ancestors. At the beginning the individual families which migrated to the area had to use their houses as centres of worship. Occasionally, they could worship the *Kiumbi* directly by going outside the house and spitting either saliva or beer towards the sun while saying prayers appropriate to their needs. But more regularly they would offer the beer at the central pole of the house addressing their prayers to the *Kiumbi* through the ancestors. The idea of 'ancestor worship' has often been misinterpreted. In the case of the Pare it is clear from the prayers said to the ancestors that the ultimate recipient of the offering is intended to be God himself. For such prayers, after mentioning the chain of ancestors, always end with *Kiumbi* who created all things, asking him to grant the needs of the community. In this sense the ancestors, as members of the community, participate in the worship as intermediaries since, as its senior members, they are supposed to be closer to God.

Clearly the development of religious centres on the Pare Mountains has been influenced by the need to attain and maintain fellowship with the God who, supposedly, had receded far away from men, while at the same time preserving the unity of the worshipping community. Yet the worshipping community has never been static. Even if we accept the simplified idea of a single family migrating to a new area and becoming the nucleus of a new community, we can also see how soon this family would find itself expanding. The idea of worship in a single house might continue as a family affair, but for the extending community such a centre would soon prove to be too limited in space. As pointed out earlier, religious ideas have always governed the other activities of traditional societies. Thus as the people were developing socially, economically and politically, religious centres came into being as a reflection of these developments. Similarly, the idea of intervention by the ancestors of the area from which the immigrants came gave way to the more lively memories of the founding ancestors in the new area.

The religious centres which developed on the Pare Mountains varied considerably in size and the scale of participation. Family worshipping services in the house undoubtedly continued, but centres catering for larger groups (such as lineages, clans and sometimes even a whole chiefdom) were established. Two important religious developments can be identified from this multiplication of worshipping centres. Both hinged on the need to maintain fellowship with God. The first one consisted of the attempts by various Pare communities to bring God nearer to the worshipping community so that there could be a direct fellowship. This was done by making representative figurines known as *Mrungu wa Gu* (God who lives upstairs) for the whole kin group. The second was that of establishing shrines in which both the living and the dead members of the community could participate.

The concept of a representative God seems to have developed in South Pare and had hardly reached North Pare in the early years of the present century. It involved the making of two figurines, male and female, whose ingredients symbolised the various aspects of human life. These figurines were then put in a pot and stored upstairs in the house of the senior member of the clan. The *Mrungu wa Gu*, therefore, represented the God who had moved far away from his creatures, and when individual members of the clan had problems they had the assurance of speaking to God directly through the elder in whose house the representative figurines were kept. It is clear that the corporate ownership of *Mrungu wa Gu* is more than a theological accident (as we shall see later) since in the various other shrines established in the Pare country it was not uncommon to have prayers directed to God himself if divination showed that this was the proper procedure. And, in fact, even offerings to ancestors always ended with a direct supplication to God.

Turning now to the idea of shrines or worshipping centres outside the house we have to remind ourselves of the importance of the original place where the founder of the group settled. Most shrines (*mpungi*) are situated in such places. The location of these centres varies from place to place. Some are marked by a 'sacred' tree which has almost acquired a totemic value for that particular clan. The baobab tree is the most common example. The usual claim is that the first ancestor brought such a tree with him and planted it at his first settlement as a 'sacred' sign for the founded community. In most cases, however, the *mpungi* consists of a small ritual forest at the original settlement.

The importance of the *mpungi* is that all members of the corporate kin group participated in the gathering. Goats, sheep and even oxen were sacrificed and offered to ancestors together with some beer. Prayers were said to the ancestors mentioning them by names, according to the memory of the officiating elder. Thus, in effect, all members, living and dead, were participating in the ritual which ended with offerings and prayers to God himself as we have already mentioned.

In connection with the *mpungi* worshipping centre, and strengthening the idea of the presence of the ancestors, there developed the concept of the 'ancestors' village' in which their skulls were kept and could be seen in their order of seniority. The ancestors' skulls were kept as near as possible to the *mpungi* but in a protected place, usually in a cave. Although services at the *mpungi* were always connected with the ancestors, the actual seeing and paying reverence to the ancestors was done at least annually during the ceremony of 'cleaning the ancestors' village'. It was during such a ceremony that the names recited in different rituals were realistically connected with the skulls of the ancestors which symbolised their spiritual presence, and this effectively reminded the living members of their common history.

There existed other religious centres bearing various names, but they all worked under the *mpungi* concept. They consisted of sacred groves of varying sizes according to the size of the community intended to participate in them. The *zimbwe* shrine of Bwambo and the *ngaghe* of Gonja are examples. The extreme expansion of this concept is that of *mshitu* (the initiation forest) which often covers a large area of land.

Pare religious ideas of worship have therefore developed around two main purposes: to have communal worship and to honour their ancestors. The religious worshipping centres became places where communication between God (who had withdrawn from men) and the people was made possible. By means of prayers, supplications and offerings, people were able to establish their broken relationship with God (supernatural powers) in a corporate form. Whether in *Mrungu wa Gu* ritual or at other religious centres, the gap in fellowship between God and men was sealed or narrowed. Thus, these religious worshipping centres became places where God's revelation and omnipresence were experienced.

Secondly, the religious worshipping centres became historical symbols reminding people of their past. In some cases an important event within a clan or lineage has warranted the establishment of a religious centre, often bearing the hero's name. Thus whenever people met together for worship they were reminded of their past of which they were participants through the loins of their parents. In this way their past was brought to life; the clan or lineage's name was popularised among the members; and the people themselves felt united as one group with a common purpose.

RELIGIOUS CENTRES AND THE MOBILISATION OF SOCIETY[4]

We have already pointed out that in Pare traditional society it is impossible to place the sacred and the secular in separate compartments. Consequently the religious centres mentioned above had many functions, besides acting as worshipping places. In fact there are examples indicating that religious thoughts were often developed as a means of solving certain prominent social, economic or political problems, the solution of which required mobilisation of the members of that particular society. Such problems may involve defence, prevention of droughts and famines, maintenance of irrigation channels, regulation of marketing systems, etc. What makes the Pare religious centres particularly interesting is that it is possible to relate their scale of mobilisation with the historical growth and expansion of the societies concerned. Roughly, four scales of mobilisation can be identified: (1) the unity of the extending family, (2) the unity of segmented but related kin groups, (3) the unity of several kin groups in the same geographical area, and (4) the unity of a larger political entity.

1. The Unity of the Extending Family.

From the point of view of the community, the basic religious centre is the *mpungi*, the shrine of the corporate group—a clan or a lineage. Whether existing under a 'totemic' tree or in a ritual 'forest', the concept of its origin and development was always the same: it marked the sacredness of the place where the founding hero of the group first settled. It is therefore clear that such a centre was formed after the sense of community had developed. Although the connection with the founding ancestor may seem to make the religious function predominant, behind it was the need to keep the community united. The trend on the Pare Mountains can be summarised as follows. At first a family forms a settlement in an area. As the members of the family increase (in two or three generations) it becomes difficult to keep them united under the rituals of a household. The original settlement begins to gain superiority as a common place of origin, i.e. it becomes a shrine (*mpungi*) symbolising the unity of the group. It becomes their 'sacred' meeting place and during their meeting they are able to solve their social, political and economic problems as a corporate group.

Ideally things would have remained smoother if a community had been able to remain at this scale. But, as we pointed out earlier, societies are never static. As they grow in size they also encounter new problems the solutions of which need new ideas and new efforts. The Bwambo community of South Pare is a good example to mention here. Moving into South Pare (probably from North Pare) about fifteen generations ago, they settled on the fertile flat plateau of the South Pare range near the Shengena peak. They formed their own community under the clan name of Bwambo. Other people who had settled there before them were adopted into the clan and became full members. Within three generations, the community had expanded over a wide area of the plateau, almost from the east to the west of the range. Then the idea of uniting such a large group under the kinship concept began to fail.

The Bwambo example was an exceptional one. The geographical condition of the Bwambo plateau made travel to one centre possible for longer than most other groups on the Pare Mountains. For in a mountainous country like Upare, the growth of community and its expansion to another region (ridge, slope or plateau) was often followed by segmentation. New segments of the community were formed with their new *mpungi*, although continuing to revere the founding hero. These new segments were in fact becoming new lineages of the original clan. Thus, *mpungi*, the basic religious centre on the Pare Mountains, has been a uniting factor within the lineage, but since there has been no limitation on the possibility of forming such centres, it has also been a dividing factor. Multiplication of *mpungi* has made segmentation possible within the same religious concept.

2. *The Unity of Segmented Kin Groups.*

Multiplication of *mpungi* might give a limited solution to the problems of a segmentary society, but it would be unlikely to satisfy the need for keeping the expanding community united in order to strengthen its political and economic position. Again the Bwambo community of South Pare serves as a good example. When several *mpungi* had been formed in the different parts of the Bwambo country, different religious ideas were employed to bring the various lineages together. It will suffice here to mention the two important ones: the *Mrungu wa Gu* and the shrine known as *zimbwe*. It is impossible to determine exactly when the idea of *Mrungu wa Gu*, as representative God (already mentioned), started in the Pare country. Dr Steven Feierman, who has conducted a thorough study of the Shambaa, has identified a similar kind of institution in that society.[5] It is therefore possible that the religious ideas connected with these figurines spread to the Pare Mountains from Usambara. What is important here is that Bwambo traditions indicate that between the tenth and eighth generations back the problem of unity was a prominent one. *Mrungu wa Gu* was adopted during this period when several lineages had been formed and, some say, some members had even settled in Usambara. The idea was to have one representative God kept in the house of the elder at Bwambo and this God would be consulted by all the Bwambo who had expanded over the whole plateau, and even those who had gone to Usambara.

This may have worked for a while. But the *Mrungu wa Gu* ritual was even more limited, in terms of bringing groups of people together, than the *mpungi*. First of all its rituals were held in a house, and therefore consultation had to be limited to individual families coming from all over Bwambo country at different times. There was no sense of social occasion in which all the Bwambo came together. Secondly, the idea of multiplying shrines had already offered a solution to problems of this kind. Why not make separate *Mrungu wa Gu* for each lineage? This was in fact done and, in order to preserve the oneness of the whole group, each separate *Mrungu wa Gu* had to be made by taking a portion of the contents of the original one. The idea of mobilisation partly failed, although the recognition of the seniority of the original figurine remained as a symbol of unity. The ritual appeal of this institution, however, seems to have been very popular. All clans and lineages in South Pare seem to have adopted it, and by the end of the nineteenth century it was also penetrating the North Pare section.

The *zimbwe* shrine may have been more successful. It is said to have been started by one of the famous Bwambo ritual leaders known as Mabeku about ten generations ago. It consisted of a grove in which a big python (*itara*) was kept and a ritual shrub known as *ore* grew around it. The evolution of *itara* and *ore* as ritual symbols for the Bwambo community may be beyond historical memory. But we know that all the Bwambo members were supposed to congregate annually at this shrine; they sacrificed animals and consumed them on the spot. A more important historical symbol is that Mabeku is also said to have established a military shrine near the *zimbwe* and this was known as *ndambi*. In fact this consisted of no more than a stone around which young people congregated and ritualistically sharpened their war weapons.

Both the *zimbwe* and the *ndambi* shrines indicate the kind of problems the Bwambo community was facing between the tenth and eighth generations back. Other powerful groups were establishing themselves: the Mjema group was becoming a threat on the eastern side while the Nkeni group was threatening on the southern side. The *zimbwe* shrine, however, never provided a lasting solution. Like the *mpungi*, Bwambo groups learned to duplicate the shrine by taking the *ore* shrub and growing it in another place, thus forming some kind of miniature shrine which could relieve them of the need to make annual trips to Malumbi where the *zimbwe* shrine was. Although this idea of *itasio* (shrine) around a python grove has remained exclusively a Bwambo institution, similar worshipping centres attempting to transcend the boundaries of a single lineage have been tried by various clans. The best example is the grass (*ngaghe*) shrine of the various Gonja lineages which became the focal point for their members.

3. The Unity of Several Kin Groups in the same Geographical Area.

As we have already seen, ritual centres modelled on the idea of mobilising kin groupings had severe limitations in meeting the situations of expanding scale. Territorial expansion of human settlement is unlikely to be limited to a single kin group. The Bwambo solution of adopting everybody into the clan also met its limitations. The Bwambo example again illustrates how religious centres can be used to achieve unity within an expanding scale. It was about eight generations ago when their famous leader known as Nguta decided that the union of the Bwambo country ought to be defined on a territorial rather than on a kinship basis. He organised a state ritual in which every member living within the territory, whether Bwambo in kinship or not, could participate. This ritual came to be known as the *njeku ya isanga* (the state bull) and the final shrine where the ritual bull (*njeku*) was sacrificed came to be known as *cha-njeku*.

The ritual of the state bull consisted of taking the ritual bull around the boundaries of the territory claimed by the group. For the Bwambo it meant going round the whole southern plateau and thus increasing the conflict with the other political groups that had been formed. But in terms of mobilisation it gave a chance for every person within that territory to participate in the ritual during the procession and identify himself as a member of this territorial community regardless of his kinship affiliation. In the end the bull was sacrificed at the central shrine, which was in effect recognised as the political centre, and every section of the country obtained either meat or stomach contents (*mafumba*) to take to their area as a sign of unity, prosperity and peace for the whole territory.

At least for a couple of generations Nguta's solution had given the Bwambo country a unity which it had failed to obtain on kinship lines. The break up of the Bwambo chiefdom near the end of the eighteenth century and further fragmentation in the nineteenth century were caused more by pressure of other groups from different directions and the rise of new ritual ideas able to challenge those of the Bwambo community itself. But, as far as the state bull ritual was concerned, this was a positive contribution to all Pare groups claiming territory. Every chief had to perform this ritual at least once during his reign. Even single clans which held territory as corporate property also adopted this ritual.

Some other regional rituals were important in strengthening the solidarity of the people living in a geographical area. Some of these were based on names of certain 'deified' heroes, such as Kivia, Mwevo, Chegho and Mnduwambele. Although the formation of such centres can be identified with certain crises within a chiefdom or a ruling group, the fame these centres acquired made them 'universal sanctuaries' for anybody coming to the area, even foreigners. Most of them were situated in the boundary districts where a foreigner coming in had to have something offered to the shrine of the hero of the area before he could safely enter the territory. Such ideas were important in controlling the population of a territory, even as far away from the mountains as Lake Jipe. Yet with new ideas of long distance trade invading the country, such ideas were no longer enough to keep out invaders.

4. The Unity of a Larger Political Entity.

With the development of state rituals based on territorial definition, many Pare groups were able to constitute themselves into separate political entities. There are, however, two other ritual ideas which, under powerful leaders, became useful tools of political centralisation. The first was that of rain-making which was more prominent in South Pare, and the second was that of initiation rites (*mshitu*) which were more powerful in North Pare.

Rain-making rituals were a part of many religious functions which took place at the *mpungi* of various sizes. But the establishment of rain-making as a kingly institution seems to have begun with the arrival of four rain-making clans, at various periods, in the South Pare region. These were the Mjema, the Nkeni, the Mhero and the Mbaga groups. Although their rain-making rituals were different, they had one thing in common: they established rain-making shrines in which these rituals were carried out. Together with rain-making, these groups also combined ritualistic ideas aimed at protecting the well-being of the society, preventing diseases, warding off vermin, etc. Such religious ideas were of great impact in society since they promised to guarantee the economic prosperity of the society concerned and, therefore, all these groups gained political powers with support far beyond their kin groups.

In many cases the political entities established by these groups remained small chiefdoms. But in the case of the Mbaga, we have an example of how these new ideas were used to expand Mbaga political influence. Rain-making shrines were different from the other shrines in that they could not be duplicated. An expansion from the original area in Mbaga resulted in the formation of a new political entity, with a rain-making ruler, but whose ritual facilities had to be replenished from time to time by visiting the rain-making shrine in Mbaga. Through this process, the Mbaga political system expanded to Kizungo in Middle Pare and Usangi in North Pare in the latter half of the eighteenth century.

The expansion of the rain-making chieftainship to North Pare became the main point of conflict in the North Pare political system whose centralisation had depended on the exploitation of a different kind of ritual institution—the *mshitu* (initiation rite). This was one of the rites of passage through which a boy became an adult. Normally all Pare clans owned their own *mshitu* (initiation forest) in which these rituals were conducted. In South Pare most of these rituals tended to last for no more than a week. In North Pare, however, a system of centralisation had started since about the sixteenth century, under the famous ruler known as Mranga. Through this system *mshitu* became a much longer training programme in the ritual forest lasting for as long as six months. Starting from Ugweno the Suya ruling group under Mranga gradually centralised the control of the *mshitu* rituals until the whole of the North Pare plateau came under what came to be known as the 'Gweno mshitu'. This institution became a powerful centralising weapon, not only because it was controlled by the ruling group, but also because its rituals were of such sacred nature that no initiated member of the society was supposed to disobey them. It was in this well organised society that the rain-making chieftainship of Mbaga intruded and found a seat in Usangi where the Gweno organisation had not been under strong Suya supervision. The conflict between these two ritual bases of organising society remained in North Pare well into the colonial era.

CONCLUSION

In this paper we have tried to examine the development of the concept of community worship in Pare society. We have seen how the Pare themselves have a remote view of creation of society and of human beings by a supernatural being who maintained close fellowship with his creatures until they disobeyed him. As a result of their disobedience men were punished and only a pair was left to regenerate mankind. At the same time God moved away from the rebellious creatures and, from the point of view of the Pare, all the efforts made throughout their history in creating religious centres has been an attempt to regain the lost fellowship. It is in this framework that the idea of 'ancestor worship' has to be understood. On the other hand, all these religious centres have been the social and political rallying points for these societies as they tried to solve their various problems. As the scale of mobilisation changed, so did the scale of such centres. In a way, the 'two points of view' of Pare religious thoughts must historically appear to be complementary. It is difficult to appreciate the ritual centred pattern of life at all levels of Pare organisation without the theological understanding. Similarly, it is difficult to try to separate what was religious and what was secular in the development of Pare society without distorting the whole picture.

NOTES

[1] I. N. Kimambo *A Political History of the Pare of Tanzania, c. 1500–1900* (Nairobi 1969).

[2] The work of R. Soper has already appeared in *Azania* II; and the results of further work in the region by the Institute are awaited. The general impression gathered so far is that the whole region between Kwale, Pare and Kilimanjaro may have been inhabited by Bantu-speaking people as early as the third century A.D.

[3] A full account of the Asu religious system can be seen in C. K. Omari, 'God and Worship in Asu Traditional Society', Ph.D. Thesis University of East Africa 1970.

[4] Further information on this section can be obtained in Kimambo *A Political History of the Pare*.

[5] Personal communication. Dr Feierman's Ph.D. thesis on Shambaa history has already been submitted to Northwestern University, Evanston, Illinois; and we understand he is now preparing a D.Phil. thesis in anthropology on the same people for Oxford University.

BETHWELL A. OGOT

On the Making of a Sanctuary: Being some thoughts on the History of Religion in Padhola

Let them make me a sanctuary, that I may dwell among them.
(Exodus, XXV, 8)

In his discussion of the interrelationship of secular history and religion, Arnold Toynbee advanced the hypothesis that

> Man begins by worshipping Nature; when he ceases to worship Nature, he is left with a spiritual vacuum which he is impelled to fill; and he is then confronted with the choice of substituting for the worship of Nature either a worship of himself or an approach to Absolute Reality through the worship of God or quest for Brahma or for Nirvana.[1]

He was putting forward this hypothesis as an alternative explanation to Father Schmidt's theory which, he admits, on the basis of existing evidence we can neither adopt nor reject, that 'the worship of God which has been brought in the field by the latterday higher religions is a revival, not an innovation, and is, in fact, a revival of the earliest religion of Mankind.'[2] Without discussing the broader question raised by Toynbee as to whether the Padhola were originally Nature worshippers before they turned to God for succour, I wish to argue in this paper that for the last five hundred years or so, when the Padhola have existed as an historical entity, they have worshipped only one God. The monotheism introduced by the latter-day higher religions such as Christianity and Islam in the area therefore represented neither a revival, nor an innovation, but an attempted merger of the differently derived concepts of God. I hope to show further that Padhola religion has been influenced in significant ways by four major events:

(*a*) Their migration from the North of Uganda to their present home around Tororo in Eastern Uganda.
(*b*) The permanent settlement in, and the terrain of, their new home.
(*c*) The breakdown of social structures as a result of increased internal and external pressures during the last three decades of the nineteenth century.
(*d*) The introduction of European rule and Christianity at the beginning of this century.

The Padhola who number about 125,000[3] are among the smallest groups of the River-Lake Nilotes.[4] Their earliest settlement in Eastern Uganda dates back to the middle of the sixteenth century.[5]

Padhola religion cannot be understood except in the context of the Nilotic Vision of Reality, which, as I have explained elsewhere, is embraced in their

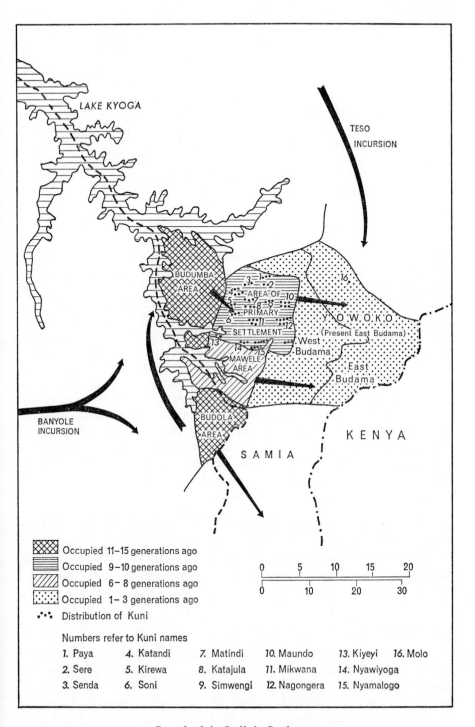

Growth of the Padhola Settlements

concept of *Jok*,[6] which provides a metaphysical theory about the 'Creator–Created' relationship. The religions of the River-Lake Nilotes are therefore all monotheistic, and as Thomas and Scott observed several years ago, their Supreme Being, *Jok*, is 'regarded with a reverence which appears almost Semitic in spirit. Although he is recognised in his different manifestations—a development not unusual even in more highly intellectual religions—*this does not detract from his fundamental oneness*'. (My italics [7]).

In the case of the Padhola and the Kenya Luo, the use of the name 'Jok' to mean 'God' has to a large extent been superseded by 'Were' and 'Nyasaye' respectively, for reasons which I have discussed elsewhere.[8] But the important point to stress at this stage is that these two groups subscribe to the general metaphysics of the Nilotes and hence their religious ideas can only be understood when considered against that wider background.

PADHOLA RELIGION

The Padhola's conception of God (*Were*) is that of a white, merciful and good Being. To them there is only one Supreme Being who manifests himself in different ways. As *God of the Courtyard*, (*Were Madiodipo*), for instance, He looks after the family and the home; and as *God of the Wilderness*, (*Were Othim*), He watches over men while they are out hunting or fighting or on a journey. And their reverence for the name 'Were' is like that of the Jews for the name 'Yahweh'. They never speak the name: instead they always call Him '*Jamalo*' (the Man from above).

It is *Jamalo* who created the universe. He first created the sky and the earth; and then created in the sky all the animals and fishes and sent two of each kind to the earth. Then He created a boy and sent him to the earth. Later on He sent him a little girl, who became his wife. At that time the earth was very fertile and brought forth everything in abundance. Peace and harmony reigned everywhere. In those days man ate his food uncooked because *Were* had not yet sent him fire. Man asked for fire and *Were* sent fire tied to the tail of a dog. And this marked the beginning of settled life.

The Padhola do not see *Were* in a human shape—He is like wind—and hence they do not attempt to depict Him in sculpture or painting. But in traditional society it was customary for each village to erect a little spirit hut, a kind of tabernacle, a sanctuary where the *God of the Courtyard* (*Were Madiodipo*) was worshipped and offerings to Him placed. Any animals for sacrifice had to be white or of light colour.

LIFE HEREAFTER

An important aspect of Padhola religion is their belief in the life hereafter. They hold that when a man dies, he only discards the body (which they liken to a garment) but the spirit (*tipo*) goes up to *Were*. They further believe that a dead man can return to his people in an invisible form to communicate his wishes to the living. For example, if a man died unmarried his spirit could even demand his share of the dowry. If his death had been due to foul play, the man could take revenge on his enemies. They believe that people who die unjustly first state their case before God and if the guilt of the murderers is proved, avenging spirits together with the spirit of the deceased are dispatched back to earth to punish the guilty. But a man who merits his death, say through stealing, adultery or any other shameful deed, has no avenging rights.

The Padhola believe, too, that a dead man's spirit moves about like wind—intangible and invisible—and appears to whomsoever it wants in dreams. Only the spirits of evil men are denied this privilege; and to the Padhola, as to other Nilotes, such spirits which are excommunicated from the community are believed to be 'completely dead'.

The good spirits or what H. D. F. Kitto has termed the 'unseen partners in the social group',[9] played an important role in the religious life of the Padhola. They were supposed to possess more *jok* power than their living brothers and sisters, and hence they were more powerful and nearer *Were*. Unlike *Were* who is impersonal, the spirits were closer to men and were involved in their everyday life. And since they operated upon man's environment with a view to harnessing all the forces in favour of their particular social groups, the spirits were tied up with the cycle of nature—sowing, harvest, birth, death, etc., and were preoccupied with the problem of ensuring fertility for men, animals and crops. *Were*, on the other hand, was not circumscribed by any natural cycles: He acted directly in human life and could not be regarded as a member of any social group.

ALL-PERVADING CHARACTER OF PADHOLA RELIGION

Padhola religion pervaded the whole of existence. Every aspect of life and every important occasion had its appropriate religious ceremonial. And the principle act of worship was the sacrifice, which was offered on all religious occasions.

Before a family could sow *kal* (eleusine), for example, a special religious ceremony had to be performed. The owner of the home (the father) took a little lump of earth, made a little hole in it with his finger, and filled it with grain. Then every member of the family spat into the hole, after which the lump of earth was taken to the field together with an egg for the spirits in order to secure a good harvest.

At harvest time, the father would fetch the first grain from the field. This was threshed, roasted, ground and cooked. Then the father put it in the *God of the Courtyard's* hut, and while the whole family sat in a circle, the father took a piece of *kuon* (bread) broke it, mixed it with the liver of chicken, divided it up into small pieces, and then threw the pieces towards the four corners of the globe invoking *Were Madiodipo* saying,

Take this, eat it, and may you protect us from our enemies.

After this prayer, the food was eaten and the harvest was picked and gathered in.

EFFECT OF MIGRATION ON PADHOLA RELIGION

What I have so far described may be regarded as representing Padhola religion prior to their migration southwards. During this major movement which lasted from about 1500 to 1850, each clan organised its own migration, tackled its own problems in the wilderness and fought its own enemies. No spirit huts could be erected for the *God of the Courtyard*, for the clan was permanently on the move. The security and survival of the clan became a much more serious problem than it was either before or after the migration. Hence, each of the nineteen Padhola clans of Luo origin had between one and three *kunu* (plural *kuni*) or guardian spirits which travelled with it and guided it during the hazardous journey to Padhola. Each *kunu* had a sanctuary, a shrine where members of the clan went to ask for succour from the dumb spirit. (All *kuni* were supposed to be dumb, as they themselves could not communicate with human beings except through *Were*). As the clans moved, different sites were designated as holy, and therefore as the new sanctuaries of the clan *kuni*. When the clans reached West Budama (the present home of the Padhola), the *kuni* are thought to have taken up residence in stones, trees or hills near or within the primary area of settlement of the clans.[10]

DEVELOPMENT OF PADHOLA RELIGION IN WEST BUDAMA

The first Padhola settlers, some nine small clans, arrived in West Budama between ten and eleven generations ago, and settled in the *Lul* (forest) area of the present county. They looked upon this land as a kind of Promised Land, which *Were* had reserved for them. Unlike other Nilotic peoples, their first settlement marked the end of their migration. They no longer looked for new and better homes, and for the next eight generations they merely expanded into territories which they had already claimed as theirs.[11]

The Padhola's almost religious attitude towards the area of primary settlement was reflected in their ritual and belief. And just as it was in the Exodus that the Israelites came to know their God, Yahweh, who had delivered them from Egypt and made them his people, so it was during the migration that the Padhola really came to know *Were* through his servants *Kuni*. When, therefore, they reached their Canaan in Eastern Uganda, permanent sanctuaries had to be established for the guardian spirits.

The ecology of the area to a large extent determined the location of the clan shrines. As Professor Southall has pointed out, 'the *mvule* trees which dot the whole country and the rocky outcrops, consisting of tangled heaps of huge fantastically shaped monoliths, which crown many of the low hills', are among the major ecological features which provide the basis for significant sociological interpretations. 'Nearly all these rocks,' he continues, 'are regarded as shrines requiring some ritual attention, while large *mvule* trees are often adopted as shrines by local clan sections.'[12]

All the shrines were located in the area of primary settlement. Splinter groups that later moved away from the 'holy' area to acquire land in other parts of Padhola territory, had to go back to the clan shrines for communal worship.

The practice of locating shrines in prominent physical features, which may be a survival of the original Nature worship, is common in history. In Greek mythology we are familiar with Mt Olympus as the home of gods. Similarly in the history of Israel, mountains (for example Mt Sinai) or high places were favourite places for the worship of the gods.

The problem with this kind of religious practice is that it tends to encourage social divisions. All the clans operated as self-sufficient theocracies, which vaguely shared in the worship of *Were*. And since the Padhola being a small group settled in an area surrounded by non-Luo peoples, the clan *kuni* later proved inadequate to unite the Padhola in the face of internal and external challenges which faced the tribe in the nineteenth century.

THE EMERGENCE OF A CENTRAL CULT, BURA, *c.* 1870

Up to about 1870, the clan had formed the largest social, religious and political unit among the Padhola. Each clan had a council of elders, a clan leader and a *Kunu* or shrine. But between 1760 and 1840, different Padhola clans, for want of land in the area of primary settlement, started to plant their colonies in the upper section of the *Mawele* region. By about 1870, the Padhola were settling in the *Yo Woko* area. In both of these regions of secondary settlement, the average size of the clan was between 80 and 500 people. And it was into these areas with tiny clan organisations that several non-Luo groups migrated. It was therefore becoming difficult, if not impossible, for the traditional pattern of life, including traditional religion, to be practised in this frontier area.

Moreover, the age-old conflict between the Padhola and the Banyole (called 'Omwa' by the Padhola) over the possession of the area bounded by the villages of Nyawiyoga, Kiyeyi, Budaka, Senda and Paya was renewed in a more intensified manner between 1860 and 1880. Furthermore between 1840 and 1880 both *Mawele* and *Yo Woko* were invaded by Iteso settlers and, in 1882, Padhola territory was attacked by a combined army of the Baganda and Basoga led by a Muganda war-leader, Seruti. It looked as if all the Padhola's neighbours were conspiring to enslave or exterminate them. Internally, there was a breakdown of social structures due to economic pressures. It was therefore evident that new institutions which could meet the needs of the Padhola people were needed. It is in this context that the emergence of the cult of *Bura* at this time must be discussed.

According to Padhola tradition,[13] this cult originated from Bugwere, where it is known as *Nyakiriga*. It was introduced into Padhola by a certain man called Akure, the son of Mbwekes, a war captive of the Nyapolo clan. He is supposed to have been initiated into the mysteries of the cult by his maternal uncles in Bugwere. But why did they decide to apply the name 'bura' to the cult?

The origin of the name 'bura' is not clear; but the Padhola are unanimous that it is not a Padhola word. Crazzolara has asserted that 'the name Bura or Vura must have been a great and famous name'.[14] Today it carries different connotations in different areas in Acholi, Alur and Madi districts. In some areas, it applies to clan groups, while in others it is applied to larger tribal or kingship groups.

But the term *bura*, according to Crazzolara, had an esoteric meaning in many societies.[15] For example, among the Acholi clan of Patiko, the residence of the *Rwot* (chief) was simply called *bura*, while among the Pari *bura* means 'royal dignity'. Crazzolara further tells us that, 'In former times *bura* meant, in Atyak (Acholi), the same as *Kagore*, i.e. the place of assembly or assembly itself. Like the old German *Dingstaff*, it was the sitting of the people's court.[16] This is similar to the meaning of *bura* in *Dholuo* spoken in the Nyanza Province of Kenya, where it means a meeting or a conference or a court case. It has recently been suggested by Taban lo Liyong, who is an Acholi, that the word *bura* is of Bari origin.[17]

Whatever may be the origin of the term, the important fact is that the *bura* cult became a new focus of Padhola unity. Akure's father Mbwekes, though a foreigner, gradually emerged as an accepted war-leader in the Nyapolo clan, his leadership being based largely on rain-making and powers of divination.[18] Although his son Akure inherited his divination powers, he was not a warrior like his father. And it is suggested that it was in order to strengthen his weak position that he imported the *bura* cult from Bugwere.

He established a shrine for *bura* at Nyawiyoga, a rock in the *Lul* area. But when Majanga son of Kinara, Akure's herdboy, took over as the chief priest of *bura*, he built a special shrine at Tewo in Maundo forest, and the place soon became a focal point for the whole tribe.

There are many conflicting accounts, most of them involving supernatural powers, as to how the changeover took place. Professor Southall's summary of the sequence of events is in broad agreement with my own findings. He writes:

> Then a series of supernatural events ensued which resulted in Akure relapsing into obscurity and Majanga emerging as undisputed leader of the tribe. Accounts of these supernatural events are infinite in variation and elaboration. All stress that he became the medium or mouthpiece of the spirit *Bura*. This gave him unrivalled powers of divination and prophecy to which all Padhola deferred unquestioningly. He is supposed to have disappeared for a week or more. When he was found, people asked him where he had been. He replied that he could not show them until they brought chickens and beer flour. Then he took them and showed them a new shrine of *Bura* at Tewo, which is a striking rock outcrop. Previously *Bura* had lived at Nyawiyoga, another spectacular rock. After this others were possessed by *Bura* from time to time, that is to say, they became ill and their illness was diagnosed by the diviners in these terms. They then had to carry out sacrifices to *Bura* to be healed and so themselves became minor mediums of *Bura* and lieutenants of Majanga, like him receiving gifts from clients but on a smaller scale and within more restricted localities. All had their shrines at *Bura's* rock Tewo.[19]

The use of religion to hold an empire, kingdom, state or society together is not unknown in history. The common religion of the Greeks, for example, was revealed in the existence of shrines, like those of Zeus at Olympus and Apollo at Delphi, where, as C. M. Bowra had said, 'Greeks from all parts joined in sacrifices and games and forgot local differences in a consciousness of Hellenic unity.'[20] We should also note that in the history of the Israelites, the *Nebiim* (Plural of *nebi*), usually translated into English as 'prophets', appeared at the time of the Philistine oppression and during the period of the divided monarchy. Their activities were associated with *national shrines*. The Padhola were therefore not acting in any different way from other societies in accepting a central shrine.

To the Padhola *Bura* was a special kind of *jwok* (spirit) through whom *Were* spoke to them. He was consulted on all important occasions by the menfolk only, since women were not allowed at the shrine. As they approached the shrine, the clients cried out to the shrine-keeper (*Jakur-Pecho*), who by tradition must be a member of the J'Amor clan,

'We are coming, we are coming,
Tell the master we are coming.'

They would then remove all clothes and cover themselves up with leaves. The offerings brought were of traditional foodstuffs such as finger millet beer, bulls and chickens. Banana or maize beer was not permitted.

DESCRIPTION OF THE BURA SHRINE

In my book, *History of the Southern Luo* Volume I, I have included a diagram showing the positions of ritual objects at the *Bura* Shrine, without any explanation.[21] Here I shall attempt a brief description of the shrine.

The shrine which is located in Maundo forest is about three miles from Nagongera in the direction of Paya. From the main road the site is about a mile into the forest. Dominating the site is a huge rock, which is slightly tilted forward. A huge dome rises on it to a height of about 25 feet. At the foot of this rock is a huge cavity into which the sacrificial beer is poured before it is drunk. High up on the walls are chicken feathers stuck in different positions. Each feather is supposed to represent a chicken killed at the shrine.

To the right of the rock is a collection of head rings made of grass (*thache*, singular *thach*) which are used for carrying beer pots to *Bura*. Far out on the right is a tall *mvule* tree, at the foot of which fowl feathers are deposited. Close to the tree is a flat slab of stone which marks the spot where skulls of slaughtered animals are heaped. On both sides of the shrine are about twenty six huts, one for each clan, and a special one for Majanga.

To the left of the shrine are:

(*a*) a small hollow rock called *Were Jaradada* or 'God the Scooper'; and
(*b*) Odora's pot into which every client has to pour some beer. Between the pot and the animal skulls is a fire over which meat is roasted, a fire which must never be extinguished.

As a diviner, a war-leader and the chief priest of *Bura*, Majanga gradually emerged as the undisputed leader of the Padhola. The clans were welded together into strong political as well as fighting units under his over-all command; and he ruled autocratically. And in the wars with the Banyole and the Iteso at the end of the last century at which the Padhola were usually victorious, large acquisitions of territory, stock and women were made.[22] It was under Majanga, for example, that the Padhola conquered Senda, Soni and Nabyoga from the Banyole.

But the new political organisation which was held together largely through the cult of *Bura* never had time to take root. The Baganda warriors, this time armed with 1,000 guns, and led by the experienced war-leader, Semei Kakungulu, invaded West Budama in 1903, and defeated the forces of Majanga, who was arrested and imprisoned. In the following year, he was released after being bound over to keep the peace. But he did not live to see the establishment of British administration, for he died in 1905. His name still lives among the Padhola as a hero who saved his society at a critical moment. Perhaps the poem, *Bura Leb Bari*, by Taban lo Liyong, may be cited as a fitting epitaph to the leadership of Majanga.

Bura Leb Bari

To the best of my knowledge
'Bura' is a Bari word
Which has spread through the breadth and width
Of the lands of Lwo since encounter with Bari
speakers.

Jo-Padhola had a hero named Majanga.
Whom *Jwok Bura* had elected.

From the lowly position of milking Akure's
avuncular cows
He won enough cows to get a wife.

He was a cowherd, who was no mere cowherd:
Here was a cowmilker whom no angry cow
wants to kick;
Majanga was a husband a little bit beside the herd:
Things were all straight in his home.

A day, Majanga went hunting. Before they left
the home he saw one of his colleagues already
writhing from python attack.
When he informed his friend, people said
Majanga had lost his mind.
One day a girl was wailing to death six
miles away from leopard attack.
People rushed there to see Majanga tell
right again.

Rwot Akure had a big cow possessed of *Jwok Bura*:
Akure's rule lasted when he had that cow
His rule ended when it went to Majanga.

People's respect sought Majanga.
Majanga's stocks increased as Akure's diminished
more and more.
At long last Akure too was ruled by Majanga.
Possessed by *Jwok* Bura, he was feared and
then blessed with obedience.

Through all these he wielded quite an army.
At a go he routed the *Omwa* who had fought
them year after year.
He drove them all to Busoga
Ensuring perpetual peace for all Jo-Padhola.

THE INTRODUCTION OF FOREIGN SANCTUARIES IN WEST BUDAMA

In an essay submitted for the Hancock Memorial Prize at Makerere University College Mr Bernard Onyango, himself a Ja-Padhola, estimated that about 55 per cent of the African population in Bukedi District of Uganda was Christian, a tiny minority professed Islam, and the rest still believed in traditional religion.[23] These estimates, with some minor modifications largely over Muslim figures which are lower, most probably applied to the Padhola section of Bukedi. This means, in effect, that in 1955 about 50% of the Padhola were adherents of foreign religions while the remainder still stuck to traditional religion. But a deeper study of the history of religion in Padhola during the colonial and post-colonial periods shows how misleading such statistics can be. And for the purpose of this discussion, I shall concentrate on two major aspects of the subject.

The first point concerns the manner in which Christianity (which is really the dominant foreign religion in Padhola) was introduced. Kakungulu and his soldiers not only established their military superiority by defeating Padhola soldiers, they also attempted to show the superiority of their religion by first arresting Majanga, the chief Priest of *Bura* and then erecting the new Christian shrines throughout the territory. Hence, to the Padhola, Christianity was a *conquest religion* which symbolized their inferior position.

Most of Kakungulu's agents were avid readers and determined teachers. They were eager to teach the people over whom they ruled, and this greatly facilitated the work of the Church. However, the tendency was for each area to follow the religious denomination of its agents. And since most of the agents were Baganda, the medium of instruction became Luganda. It was regarded as almost ungodly for the Padhola to worship in their own language at the new and foreign sanctuaries!

Initially the Christian converts recruited by the Baganda 'missionaries' were sent to Mbale in Bugisu (if Protestant) and to Budaka in Bugwere (if Catholic) for baptism and simple instruction in Luganda. This pilgrimage for religious education hampered the work of the 'missionaries', for the Padhola converts were often away from their societies for long periods. Some were even sent to far away missionary centres in Buganda. Moreover, each trainee had to be provided with food by his relatives during the journey and while at the mission centre. The result was that only children or relatives of chiefs and well-to-do parents could afford to become Christians.

But in 1913, Father J. Willemen of the Roman Catholic Mission moved from Budaka to open a mission station at Nagongera in Padhola. He ordered that Dhupadhola should be used in all Catholic churches. The wisdom of these two decisions was shown immediately: Padhola Christians did not have to live away from their people for long periods and they could now worship God in their own language. Thousands of them flocked to join the Roman Catholic Church, largely to express their independence of Baganda 'missionaries'. The result is that even today the majority of the Padhola are Catholics.

But the struggle for cultural independence continued in the Protestant Churches, which were still run by the Baganda and where the language used continued to be Luganda.

By the mid-1930s most of the Baganda 'missionaries' had been withdrawn from Padhola. But the language used in Protestant Churches and in administration continued to be Luganda. Also, the Protestant authorities recruited all the clergy from neighbouring tribes in Bukedi District. The Padhola regarded this policy as a conspiracy between the missionaries and the Bantu groups to keep them in subjection. As Onyango has clearly shown, it was this strong feeling among Padhola Christians against outsiders which in 1944 led to the rebellion against the leadership of Erisa L. Masiga, a Musamia pastor, who was then in charge of Padhola. On Christmas Eve in that year, all the doors of Protestant Churches throughout Padhola territory were locked, and orders were sent to all Christians forbidding any form of worship on Christmas day. They could not have chosen a better day to express their disrespect. Masiga was accused of despising the Padhola as ignorant and backward in his sermons. In anger he retorted that the Padhola had not yet produced a clergyman and he was, therefore, in their country in missionary capacity.[24] The Padhola won, and Masiga was removed.

He was succeeded by Asanasiyo N. Malinga, an able Munyuli, who was a good administrator and a good church leader. Eventually, he, too, failed because he was a Munyuli, a member of the traditional enemies of the Padhola. In fact, his appointment had been interpreted by the Padhola as an attempt on the part of the missionaries to support the Banyuli in their age-old fight. Thus Christianity was still identified with the *conquest of the Padhola by other tribes*.

In 1953, Malinga was replaced by Lamu Dakitali, the first Padhola pastor to be appointed. This was regarded as marking Padhola Christians' independence.

DIVISIVENESS OF CHRISTIANITY

The second major aspect of Christianity which has influenced the history of religion in Padhola is its divisiveness. By the time Christianity reached East Africa it was highly intellectualised and conceptualised. Christianity was thus introduced to Padhola as a spiritual concept. To some people this concept was embodied in Roman Catholicism and to others Protestantism represented the *right concept*.

These separate and mutually hostile systems attempted to recruit adherents from a people with its own Vision of Reality, which the missionaries were unable to appreciate. As we have seen, the Padhola religion was local and peculiar to the Padhola; and the priest had to be a particular person of a particular clan. It had no decalogue or record of dogma in a Qur'an or a Bible.

The European missionaries had little difficulty therefore in concluding that the Padhola were a people *without* religion and hence they had a kind of religious *tabula rasa* on which to write the Ten Commandments. This assumption and the resulting approach posed a major conflict which is still unresolved.

The new faith, to the Padhola, was merely restating what they had believed in all along. The belief in one God, a Holy Trinity (*Were, Were Othim, Were Madiodipo*) and the goodness of God were all contained in Padhola religion. Even the concept of the Communion of Saints sounded very much like the Padhola idea of the community of good spirits. As Father Willemen observed.

> Our children like to talk about religion at home and their home people listen eagerly because they love their own religious customs, and some are even very much like our own. Their belief in after-life makes them bring their children for baptism.[25]

And hence the African converts tended to look upon Christianity as just another version of the Vision of Reality. It was probably superior because it was professed by white men and because it was based on a Book. It was certainly a ladder to social, political and economic advancement. For instance, only Christians (and a few Muslims) could become chiefs, and the clerks and inter-preters were recruited from among those who had been to mission schools and were therefore regarded as Christians. Hence, many Padhola became Christians because it paid to be one.

Thousands of children and adults were baptised and confirmed. For instance, it has been recorded that in the month of March in 1953, Mgr John Crief confirmed more than 1,000 adults at Nagongera Mission alone.[26] Marriages were solemnised and many churches (the new shrines) built throughout Pad-hola. Some of the Christians, especially the Protestants, were so keen to make a clean break with the past that a group of them decided, in 1940, to set *Od Bura* (the shrine of *Bura*) on fire.[27]

But all these were merely outward *signs and symbols*. The majority of the Padhola still believed sincerely in their old testament. Many embraced the new faith because, as we have said, it was fashionable as well as economically rewarding. It was also a sign of social status to have a Christian name or to have a church wedding. Unlike the old religion which was all-pervading in the lives of the Padhola, the new faith was more a question of Church-going.

Few joined the new faith because they had decided to obey Christ's command: 'Take up your cross and follow me.' And yet this was one of the most important distinctions between the old and the new religion. According to the new mes-sage, religion was a matter of personal decision: *each individual had to make his own decision to take up his own cross and to follow Christ.* But to the majority of Padhola Christians, religion remains a group activity, and in the event of any conflict between the old and the new testaments, the former always wins. As Onyango has correctly pointed out, a missionary may tell a Padhola convert that polygamy is wrong and so-called ancestor worship unchristian, but

> when the first glow of Grace fades and the newly baptised parent has a dying son in his arms; when no prayer evokes the necessary inward faith in religion and no amount of penicillin seems to herald a recovery, then the temptation to consult the nearest diviner and offer the bull to the dead assumes a form of an ultimatum yielding which, for a time, casts no shadow on the Christian conscience. That is not hypocrisy.[28]

In other words, those Padhola we classify as Christians sincerely observe all the outward Christian signs, but when it comes to making a fundamental personal decision, they all go back to their old testament. And that is why the Padhola have again re-built the shrine of *Bura*, and during certain tribal festivals, both Padhola Christians and non-Christians assemble at the central shrine to re-dedicate themselves for the tasks ahead.[29]

The general spiritual malaise observable in most African societies today is attributable, I think, to the failure to reconcile the old testament in these societies with the new faith by either Christianising the old practices or by Africanising Christ or both.

THE DENOMINATIONAL RIVALRY

In addition to the apparent incompatibility between the old and the new testaments in Padhola religion we have referred to, further confusion has resulted from the fierce rivalry between Protestantism and Roman Catholicism. And while preaching that in Christianity there should be neither Jew nor Gentile, the missionaries, Catholic and Protestants alike, have been forced by the history of Europe to be negative and uncharitable. And as Dr Lampert has observed, 'There is no greater spiritual ruthlessness than the ruthlessness of the meek who know God.'[30] In Padhola, they preach charity and the brotherhood of men and practice hatred in the name of God. Such an attitude is puzzling to the majority of the Padhola to whom religion is not a matter of intellectual discussion or controversy over sacraments or dogma. To them the important aspect of religion is the Vision of Reality it brings to the believer. As Onyango has pointed out, the denominational rivalry has been taken so seriously in Padhola that clans or even families have been irrevocably split. For instance, in 1949 the Catholics in Paya county 'banded together to oppose with arms if necessary the nomination of a Protestant chief to rule over them. Five ringleaders ended in the Protestant jail'.[31] Two years later a Protestant father turned out his promising son who had become a Roman Catholic.[32] The result is that although there are many sanctuaries in Padhola today, most of the people believe that *Were* no longer dwells among them.

NOTES

[1] A. Toynbee *An Historian's Approach to Religion* (London 1956) p. 18.

[2] *Ibid.* Also see Father W. Schmidt *The Origin and Growth of Religion* English translation by H. J. Rose, (London 1921).

[3] Provisional figures, Uganda Census, 1969.

[4] See D. W. Cohen, 'The River-Lake Nilotes from the 15th to 19th Century' in B. A. Ogot and J. A. Kieran (eds.) *Zamani* (Nairobi 1968) chapter 7.

[5] For detailed study of their history, see B. A. Ogot *A History of the Southern Luo, Volume I, 1500-1900* (Nairobi 1967).

[6] B. A. Ogot, 'The Concept of Jok' *African Studies* 20 (1961) pp. 123–30.

[7] H. B. Thomas and R. Scott *Uganda* (London 1935) p. 96.

[8] B. A. Ogot, 'Traditional Religion and the Precolonial History of Africa—The Example of the Padhola' *Uganda Journal* vol. 31, no. 1 (1967) pp. 111–16.

[9] H. D. F. Kitto *The Greeks* (London 1951) p. 195.

[10] See B. A. Ogot *History of the Southern Luo*. Note that the same concept is found in parts of Busoga, where the name of the guardian spirit is *enkuni*. But as David W. Cohen has pointed out, 'The *enkuni* of Busoga is probably related to the Lwoo peoples, and it may have been the Lwoo impact upon Busoga that caused the term to be incorporated in the various Lusoga dialects.' David W. Cohen, 'Early Migrations and Settlements in South Busoga' Seminar Paper, History Department, University College, Nairobi, January 1967.

[11] See Ogot *History of the Southern Luo* pp. 84-5.

[12] A. W. Southall, 'Padhola: Comparative Social Structure', Paper presented at the East African Social Science Conference, Makerere, January 1957, p. 1.

[13] *Padhola Historical Texts* vol. II, pp. 75-9; 135-9 (Oral texts collected by B. A. Ogot, in the possession of the History Department, University of Nairobi).

[14] J. P. Crazzolara *The Lwoo* Part III (Verona 1954) pp. 336-7; 476-7; 506-7; 520-30.

[15] *Ibid.* pp. 337-8.

[16] *Ibid.* p. 338.

[17] See his poem, 'Bura Leb Bari' in his *Lwo Culture from Lolwe to Maal Kaal*, unpublished manuscript in the Cultural Division of the Institute for Development Studies, University College, Nairobi, and reproduced on pp. 130-131 of this book.

[18] Such an acceptance was not uncommon. Oguti, an Atesot, was later adopted by the Padhola, and he and Majanga played a leading role in resisting the Teso invasion.

[19] Southall *op. cit.* p. 14.

[20] C. M. Bowra *The Greek Experience* (London 1957) pp. 13-14.

[21] Ogot *History of the Southern Luo* p. 124.

[22] E. M. Persse *Tribal Notes* Uganda Society Library, Kampala (MS. file of notes on Eastern Ugandan peoples, collected between 1910 and 1920).

[23] B. M. A. Onyango, 'Some Pastoral Problems in the Christianization of Bukedi with special reference to Padhola', 1955, p. 14. [Makerere Institute of Social Research Library, file marked *Religion*; 20, 12/15.] The 1959 official census for Bukedi gives the figures of 32 per cent for Catholics and 28.2 per cent for Protestants.

[24] Onyango *op. cit.* p. 9.

[25] *Report by Father Superior* 25 August, 1918, p. 10, Nagongera Mission Archives.

[26] Onyango, *op. cit.* p. 3.

[27] *Ibid.*

[28] Onyango *op. cit.* p. 3.

[29] See *Uganda Argus* 13 January, 1970.

[30] E. Lampert *Studies in Rebellion* (London 1957) p. 16.

[31] Onyango *op. cit.* p. 4.

[32] *Ibid.*

PART FOUR

THE HISTORICAL STUDY OF RITES OF TRANSITION AND OF SPIRIT POSSESSION CULTS

AYLWARD SHORTER

Symbolism, Ritual and History: an Examination of the work of Victor Turner

INTRODUCTION

Significance is an essential property of being. All beings are signs, expressing to the beholder, either their own nature, or, over and above this, their contingency towards other beings. Thus, the perception of an object having a certain colour, shape and movement tells me that there is smoke; and smoke, in turn, suggests fire. This may be called natural significance. Man is a being that achieves self-knowledge, and this he does by imparting significance to the phenomena of his experience. In the measure in which this significance is given in arbitrary fashion, it may be called 'conventional'; and in the measure in which conventional significance is further founded on natural significance, it may be called symbolic. There are few signs more conventional than the combination of phonemes that make up a word. For example, in the language of the Kimbu of Tanzania the word *mpingu* has the significance of 'bead necklace'. On the other hand, one detects symbolization when, during the girls' puberty rites, the word *mpingu* signifies not only the beads that are sought by women, but also the children desired by them. Signs which veer towards the purely conventional require explanation. Signs that veer towards the symbolic speak for themselves through an existential context and need only to be experienced. Thus, it is the context of female puberty and the expectation of motherhood which provides the clue to the symbol in the case just mentioned. Symbols are, therefore, essentially an appeal to experience, *pensée engagée* (Gusdorf) or 'the science of the concrete' (Lévi-Strauss), depending on a context that is socio-cultural and in some measure historical.[1]

Lévi-Strauss has shown that the symbols of a society have a structure, that they form a set of classifications or a model for thinking and talking about nature and social life. Partly on account of the linguistic analogy which was his starting point and partly because his material consisted in the extensively recorded mythologies of South America, Lévi-Strauss was more interested in literary than in ritual symbolism. Victor Turner has reversed this emphasis, and in doing so has explored more fully the cultural and historical context of symbolism. As a consequence his conclusions have an importance which goes far beyond the cultural frontiers of the Ndembu people of Zambia among whom he carried out his research.[2]

Symbols appeal to experience in society, culture and history, and therefore, it is altogether natural that they should find expression in action, particularly collective action, and action which is a process of greater or lesser duration. Such symbolic action we call ritual. It is a dramatization of ideals, values and expectations, a bridge between the level of ideas and the level of practical daily life. Whereas Lévi-Strauss sees ritual as a 'favoured game' which is a force for social integration[3], Turner stresses the dialectic of ritual, its tensed unity or *Gestalt*, 'whose tension is constituted by ineradicable forces or realities, implacably opposed, and whose nature as a unit is constituted and bounded by the very forces that contend within it'.[4] Whichever view is taken, ritual is of crucial importance for the social process and Turner agrees with Monica Wilson's statement that in the study of rituals lies the key to an understanding of the essential constitution of human societies.[5] Symbolism, and especially ritual symbolism is the means by which a man shares his inmost experiences with other men. Through ritual man is able to express values which are otherwise inexpressible and to experience them as shared.

Turner enumerates four observed structures within ritual: (1) The symbolic structure: ritual is 'an aggregation of symbols', not a key to the understanding of society, but a 'bunch of keys'. (2) The value structure: ritual is the communication of an authoritative message about crucial values and the relationship between values. (3) The telic structure: ritual is purposive—it is a system of ends and means. Often it consists in the manufacture of certain key symbols, and these are designed to have an effect on people, whether or not they are thought to be potent in a non-rational-technical sense, and whether or not there is a religious appeal to ultra-human entities. (4) The role structure: ritual is the product of the interaction of different human actors who represent different social categories. The meaning of a ritual, therefore, cannot be limited to any one of its structures, but is the product of all of them. For example, the meaning transcends the purposes of those who take part, and Turner sees three orders of symbolic reference: (1) The manifest sense, of which the subject is fully conscious and which is related to the explicit aims of the ritual. (2) The latent sense, of which the subject is only marginally aware, but could become fully aware. (3) The hidden sense which is completely unconscious and relates to basic, infantile experiences shared with other human beings. Turner's three orders correspond to Bevan's three classes of symbol; those behind which we can see, those behind which we think we can see, and those behind which we cannot see.[6]

To discover these meanings in ritual, Turner proposes three analytical frames or contexts within which to view the symbol: (1) The exegetical meaning is that ascribed to the symbol by the participants. Here the investigator will recognize the manifest, and possibly the latent sense of the symbol. (2) The operational meaning derives from the manner in which the symbol is used in the whole context of the rite. (3) The positional meaning refers the symbol to the totality of cultural elements and institutions in society. In these last two frames traces of the hidden sense of the symbol will appear alongside the senses already discovered in the first frame.

All of these procedures assist the investigator to crack the cultural code of the rituals he is studying, and it appears that to do this, he must cast his net extremely wide. Analytical concepts such as 'role structure' and 'positional meaning' demand that ritual be placed in its 'field context', and this Turner describes in the language of *Gestalt* psychology. The field context is not simply a network of static social entities, but a process, a configuration of changing and developing elements—in short, a history. Ritual expresses the constant dialectic of this historical process.

RITUAL AND HISTORY—CRITIQUE OF TURNER

To say that Turner sees ritual as an aspect of a historical process is not to say that he is a historian, and it soon becomes evident that the history in which he is interested is history on a very reduced scale, 'micro-history' to use his own term. He is not really interested in the historical origins of a given ritual, in the manipulation of ritual by historical personalities or groups, or in evidence of cross-fertilisation of rites between cultures. Micro-history has a very reduced extension in space and time, and its chief concern is with the lives and relationships of the immediate actors in the ritual drama. Moreover, micro-history exhibits little significant change. This is because Turner's dialectic is not really Hegelian and there is no synthesis at a higher level, transcending both the original thesis and antithesis. Instead it is a series of repeated and balanced oppositions. We discuss below Turner's ideas of communitas and structure. These are modalities of social inferiority and superiority, and according to Turner there is a human 'need' to participate in both modalities at once. This is the foundation for 'a dialectical process with successive phases of structure and communitas'.[7] Ritual provides a continual possibility of synthesis, and there is a repeated ebb and flow between inferiors seeking structural superiority and superiors seeking the freedom of communitas. This processual analysis provides the anthropologist with an excellent methodology for understanding ritual, but it says little to the historian.

In spite of this, the method is not without fruit. It enables Turner to develop a typology with historical implications of which he is at least partly aware. This typology consists in a broad division of ritual into two categories: (1) Redressive Ritual, or Ritual of Affliction and (2) Ritual of Life Crisis. Both these types of ritual are characterised to a greater or lesser degree by a ritual liminality that is accompanied by what Turner calls the experience of 'communitas'. In some cases liminality is so powerful an element that we can speak of a third category, (3) Liminal Ritual. Let us first describe each of these categories briefly.

Redressive Ritual, as its name implies, exists to redress a calamity or an affliction which has brought about a crisis in the affairs of a social group. This may be a natural disaster which affects every member of the group, or it may be a sickness or affliction that has befallen an individual who thereupon becomes the symbol of the tensions within the community. After a lengthy process of divination which reveals what social structures are involved and what the details of the relevant micro-history are, a ritual is performed which is designed to make hidden tensions explicit and to restore the *status quo ante*.

Life Crisis Ritual, on the other hand, is less concerned with society as a whole than with the individual entering a superior ritual and social status. Such ritual introduces the candidate into a specific community, cult-association or category, and the theme of suffering as a means of entry into this category is stressed. Circumcision and puberty rituals, various other forms of initiation, and funerary rituals are of this type.

The idea of liminality, or Liminal Ritual, is a development of Van Gennep's classic concept of the *rite de passage*, which, in a certain measure, applies to all ritual.[8] In the *rite de passage*, there are three phases: separation from a previous status, a threshold or liminal period, and a moment of aggregation or incorporation. It is the liminal period which is all-important. This is a period of instability between two fixed terms, a period of ambiguity, uniformity, passivity, lack of structure and lack of status. It is characterised by the unstructured sense of comity which goes to the root of the individual's being and which gives him a profound sense of oneness with humanity. This is what Turner calls 'communitas'. Communitas is anti-structure in its very essence, and yet paradoxically it serves to emphasise the need for structure. Liminal ritual gives structural inferiors a symbolic structural superiority, and structural superiors aspire to the rediscovery of their humanity through the experience of communitas. This is why people don masks and join secret societies.

Communitas is of three kinds: existential, ideological and normative. Existential communitas is the spasmodic and spontaneous experience, the happening, and this, in its turn, tends to generate imagery and speculation about a utopia. This is the ideological communitas which is a commonplace of western literature. Finally, in societies where structures are more rigid and complex, and where there is greater need for social control, communitas itself is given an enduring, institutionalised form. Examples of this were the religious and mendicant orders of Medieval Europe. In Africa, as Turner notes, there has been less need for institutionalised communitas, since the structures were more communitarian.

Turner observes that redressive ritual is more responsive to social pressures than life-crisis ritual, and he deems it necessary for the student to take the causative importance of historical personalities into account in this type of ritual. However, he believes that the existence of ritual depends on the relative absence of change, and the relative unimportance of historical personalities as causes of change. Ritual is 'quintessential custom', it does not flourish where there is novelty, or in times of change. Nevertheless, there is a homology, not merely between the diachronic liminality of ritual and the synchronic inferiority of marginal groups and categories in political, legal and economic systems, but also between diachronic liminality in ritual and historical eras which are themselves liminal. Liminal periods of history are those characterised by rapid social change and they tend to throw up millenarian or mystical movements possessing a liminal ritual which cut across ethnic and national boundaries. Such movements continue until their original impetus is exhausted or they have been institutionalised. They are, as Turner believes, attempts to slow up the process of change, but they are like so many patches of new cloth on an old garment. In the end they fail. The old social order is passing and its symbols will be replaced by a new social order with, perhaps, symbols from the modern political ideologies or the missionary religions. For Turner, millenarian movements in the liminal periods of history are not a bridge to new forms or levels of ritual symbolism. They are not constructive of the new ritual, although, of course, he recognizes that human beings cannot live without symbolism and ritual, even in the new social order.

Turner reaches this position because of his reluctance to place his study of ritual in a wider historical context. However, I do not think that we need share his pessimism. On the contrary, I believe he has opened the door for historians who wish to look for a continuity of ritual symbolism in periods of rapid change. Also, by his emphasis on ritual as part of a historical process which includes pressure from historical personalities and groups, and still more by his categories of redressive, life-crisis and liminal ritual, I believe he has issued a challenge to historians to go beyond the boundaries of mere micro-history. The remainder of this paper is an attempt to take up this challenge, using examples from the history of Tanzania.

REDRESSIVE RITUAL AND CHIEFSHIP

Rituals of redress are concerned with a crisis in the affairs of a social group, and if one examines the institution of chiefship in the multi-chiefdom societies of western Tanzania, it soon becomes clear that it is very much bound up with ritual of this kind. The chief was not, of course, a merely ritual figure at any period, but what political power he enjoyed depended on his effectiveness in the ritual sphere. The numerous deposition stories show this very clearly. His political credibility depended on his ability to manipulate certain rituals of redress, mainly concerned with rain-making, natural prosperity and the avoidance of, or recovery from disaster. One of the best examples of this is the deposition of Chief Mwachiluwi of the Wungu (Bungu) in about 1770. The Wungu raised no objection to his accession some twenty years earlier. It was only after four years of drought and the total desiccation of Lake Rukwa that they realised that his accession had been irregular and that he must be deposed.[9]

The chief, and by extension the chiefly family, were a kind of catalyst in the society they ruled. They possessed a special charisma which both set them apart from their people, and yet gave them an ultimate relevance to their profoundest needs. Except in the matter of the dynastic principle, they resembled the Judges of the Old Testament who judged Israel and who were essentially deliverers who brought the people redress. Deliverance in western Tanzania had a military aspect as well, even if this was not always the main aspect, as it is in the Book of Judges. The charisma of the Judge consisted in his being raised up by God, out of the blue, so to speak. This was a sign that 'God was with the Judge'.[10] Similarly, in western Tanzania, the charisma of the chief and his dynasty depended on their having come from somewhere else. The chief was the type of charismatic stranger, symbol of a power that was ultra-human. The ideas are well brought out in the song sung at the installation of the Kimbu chief. In this song the chief is the son of a stranger who comes from far away, and this distant origin is likened to the distant heavens from which the chief and his regalia, the conus-shell, take their symbolic origin.

Son of the stranger,
I come from far away,
There, up in the heavens,
The conus-shell came forth,
And the straps of the conus-shell;
Even the eagle was left behind,
When I soared aloft.[11]

The charter for chiefship in western Tanzania is the myth which proclaims a distant origin for the chiefly dynasty, a place of mystical importance, Mount Hanang the source of rain, or Usagara famed for its rain-making. It would be possible, on the basis of these charters, to draw a 'mystical map' of traditional Tanzania, but we would be wrong to conclude that such a map was purely mental. There is ample evidence for the acceptance of foreigners as chiefs, and their acceptance depended as much on ritual superiority as on a superior technical knowledge. Mystical geography is not necessarily a *post factum* justification for the rule of a chiefly dynasty; it is more likely a factor in the original acceptance of that dynasty.

What is true for the acceptance of the chief himself is equally true for the acceptance of the emblems of chiefship. One of the most remarkable facts in the history of East and Central Africa is the very ancient and extremely widespread use of the conus-shell as an emblem of authority. The shell originates on the East African coast, but the further away one goes from the coast the more ritual importance it assumes. Among the Luguru, the shell is the ordinary symbol of the status of an elder, of his integrity and authority, but among the southern Kimbu and the Bungu the shell is the symbol of the chief's especial charisma and is held in such reverence that no one, not even the chief himself (except on the day of his installation) is allowed to set eyes on it. The lengths to which the peoples of the interior went in order to obtain these shells is well known. According to the traditions of the Sumbwa, which are among the earliest references to long distance trade with the coast, conus-shells were the primary lure.[12]

There can be no doubt about the astral—and more particularly, the solar—symbolism of the conus-shell disc. The Kimbu explicitly associate the shell with the sun and sky when they say that 'It comes from the heavens', or that 'It comes from the supreme being in his sun-aspect (*Ilyuva*)'. The Luguru elder swears an oath and points to the sun, at the time of receiving his conus-shell emblem.[13] The whiteness of the shell and the coil design are associated with the supreme being among several peoples, and use of the word 'sun' for the supreme being is extremely widespread in one of the forms: *Rua, Lua, Ijua, Izuva, Yuva, Ilyuva, Lyoba, Zyoba*.

We have seen that military leadership was merely one aspect of a charismatic leadership that was primarily ritual. This was true even at a time when military leadership was of growing importance, as in the latter part of the nineteenth century. Not only did war medicine play an important part in the campaigns of Mkwawa, Mirambo and Nyungu-ya-Mawe, but these leaders needed the foundation of a legitimate ritual chiefship in order to be credible military leaders. Nyungu-ya-Mawe was perhaps, particularly conscious of this. Nyungu knew that the chiefs he conquered would forfeit all ritual respect when they were deprived of effective political power, but he also knew he must guard against the temptation of his appointed deputies, the *vatwale*, to become ritual officers. His successor actually shot a *mutwale* on the spot who claimed the right to make offerings to a deceased chief. Nyungu was virtually claiming to be the only one with any right to ritual power in the countries he conquered. He alone had the charisma of a chief.[14]

Physical possession of the emblems of chiefship could also be used to political advantage. In the second quarter of the nineteenth century when conus-shells were rare in western Tanzania, a Kimbu called Shambwe bought a quantity of them from an Arab trader in exchange for ivory. These he distributed, thereby founding a whole network of client chiefdoms in Ukimbu, Ukonongo, Ugalla and Upimbwe. The creation of Shambwe's hegemony directly depended on his lucky acquisition of these ritual objects, since many of his clients disposed of a greater military force than he did himself.

The role of the chief, therefore, in redressive ritual, as giver of redress, liberator, and—so to speak—'great outsider', sheds light on the acceptance of foreigners as chiefs, whether they were conquerors like Nyungu, or whether they did not dispose of military power at all, which was the case with Shambwe. Military power was, perhaps, relatively unimportant compared to the basic ritual assumptions about chiefship. This view of chiefship also helps to explain why objects of ritual value, like the conus-shell regalia, enjoyed such a wide distribution, and why the need for them had such important political and econo-mic consequences for Tanzania as a whole.

LIFE-CRISIS RITUAL AND ITS POLITICAL MANIPULATION

Rituals of redress dramatise the conflicts and tensions at, and between, different structural levels within society. They aim at resolving a crisis in interpersonal relationships on a micro-historical plane, and at re-establishing unity, security and prosperity. Life-crisis rituals also dramatize social conflicts and tensions, but it is more a question of helping individuals to accept the claims of society as a whole than reconciling the claims of actors who represent different social levels and categories. As Turner describes it, life-crisis ritual provides emotional support for a social structure which is essentially unchanging but which is still relevant. In terms of micro-history, therefore, Turner is right to say that it is less responsive to social pressures and to personalities as factors of causa-tion. However, on the larger plane, life-crisis ritual is subject to such pressures and personalities in so far as these shape the social structure itself and the ritual which expresses the claims of society. The response of the individual is ultimately to submit, and the ritual provides an emotional outlet or catharsis for the con-flict between himself and society. This affords an even greater scope for mani-pulating the rituals to personalities and groups which are structurally superior. One might propose, therefore, a slight modification of Turner's position, and say that it is not so much that the claims of society or the social structure are unchanging, but that they cannot be changed by the individual who undergoes the ritual.

Tanzanian history offers us several examples of the political manipulation of life-crisis rituals. One of these is given to us by Professor Kimambo in his account of the political history of the Pare.[15] The unity and stability of the Gweno state rested on the policy of its rulers in controlling and shaping the initiation rites, known as *ngasu ya mshitu*. Chief Mranga established a council of elders called *Chila ya Mshitu* to supervise the initiation of commoners in all forest camps, and the rites were deliberately lengthened to six months or more. He also introduced the royal friction drum called *kafu* to distinguish the initiation conducted by members of the royal clan from that of commoners who used a drum called *diri*. Through the *kafu mshitu* and the *Chila ya Mshitu* Mranga controlled the whole institution and used it to rid himself of political opponents who disappeared during the initiations and were said to have been swallowed by the *mshitu*.

Eventually, however, the tight control over the ritual, and its exclusiveness backfired on Ugweno. There was no mechanism for admitting new groups of settlers like the Wambaga who were forced to return to southern Pare for initiation. Ultimately, this was a source of conflict between the Wambaga and the other communities of north Pare.

In southern Ukimbu the circumcision of boys and the girls' puberty rituals were closely supervised by the chief and his family. However, in the second half of the nineteenth century circumcision began to be abandoned because of vulnerability to attack from neighbouring peoples when the male population was in the forest camps. The girls' puberty rituals became a family, rather than a community, affair in the first years of the twentieth century due to the general dispersal of the population in a time of greater security. The place of these life-crisis rituals was largely taken by the *uwuxala*.[16] This was a political secret society managed by members of the chief's circle. It was at once focused on the loyalty due to the chief and on the control of the chiefship itself. In short it was a means of revaluing chiefship at a critical moment in its history. The *uwuxala* was extended to include children in both its male and female sections; indeed it began to specialise in the annual initiation of children. It also performed its dances at the funerals and inheritance ceremonies of the initiated, and it could take place anywhere where there was a nucleus of members. The *uwuxala* still performs today and attracts new members, chiefly adults. When people speak about it they use two modern analogies, the school and the political party. In view of the multi-functional character of the school in Tanzania today, it would be truer to say these two are a single analogy and that the *uwuxala* and the modern school are an ancient and a modern expression of a single principle—the political manipulation of life-crisis ritual. It is interesting to see how the Kimbu are able to interpret the modern situation quite accurately by referring to the symbols of the old. This is not quite the same thing as saying that the symbols of the old social order are contributing to the symbolism of the new, but it leads us on to challenge Professor Turner's agnosticism on this particular point in a discussion of liminal ritual.

LIMINAL RITUAL AND MODERN IDEOLOGIES

Because liminality confers on those who experience it a profound sense of oneness with humanity, it tends to transcend ethnic and cultural boundaries. It can do this in one of two ways, either through what Professor Ranger has called 'the movement of ideas' passing like trade goods from hand to hand or from group to group, or it can take the form of a more or less organised social movement.[17] In the first case, there is a cross-fertilisation of ideas and each ethnic group makes its own synthesis. In the second, a group or category of people enlists members from every culture. Although Turner is right to see in liminal ritual a patching of the old cloak, the cross-fertilisation of ideas which it entails must surely have important consequences for the future.

Good examples of the cross-fertilisation of ideas resulting in a local synthesis are those of the Swezi and Migawo spirit possession guilds in Unyamwezi and Ukimbu. The Chwezi-Swezi traditions unite the interlacustrine kingdoms of Uganda, Rwanda, Burundi and north-western Tanzania as well as Buha, Usumbwa, Usukuma, Unyamwezi and Ukimbu.[18] In Unyamwezi the Swezi guild has been influenced by the symbolism and mythology of the Kubandwa in Rwanda-Burundi but its actual techniques owe more to Swahili spirit possession than to the rituals of the interlacustrine area. Cory was of the opinion that the Swahili spirit possession guild (Shetani, Majini, Mapepo, Maswahili) had spread inland and Professor Kimambo cites the view of Dannholz that spirit possession in Pare was of coastal origin.[19] The Migawo ritual of Ukimbu is an even more interesting synthesis of Swezi traditions, Bende cosmology and coastal spirit possession techniques.[20] Swezi and Migawo rituals have all the characteristics of liminal ritual as Turner describes it. They cater for the suffering and disabled and those who are on the margins of society. And yet, such is the power of the weak, the rituals enjoy a privileged place in the ceremonies accompanying the installation and burial of chiefs. The lodges of the guilds themselves imitate local government structure complete with clerks and messengers. These guilds are communities of the suffering which satisfy needs not catered for by organised religion and organised medical services, and they are also meeting grounds for the structurally inferior and the structurally superior. Moreover, through cross-fertilisation a new mystical geography comes into being, analogous to the mystical geography which validates chiefship. It is through this consciousness of an extraneous origin for the ritual, through this acknowledged contact between peoples and this response to a wider environment, that participants in this type of ritual express their oneness with humanity.

In the organised social movement cultural boundaries are transcended by the prophet or emissary who arrives with the message or the ritual technique. Mystical geography is replaced by a real and sustained contact or network of contacts. Well known examples of such movements are the Maji Maji movement or the Mchape movement, and several of the African churches in which glossolalia is usually prominent. To call such movements organised is, perhaps, an overstatement. Professor Ranger calls them 'unorganised and not very articulate'. The point is, as Turner shows, that there is a tension between structure and anti-structure in these movements and that this is a characteristic of liminality. Communitas has to be preserved in a concrete form; it must not disappear in a wider and impersonal organisation.

We come now to the crucial question of how liminal ritual can build a bridge between the ritual symbolism of the old order and the ideologies, political and religious, of the new. Turner, himself, supplies the answer. Quoting Martin Buber's picture of a nation as a community of communities and its people as bound to its representatives through common action and common experience, he writes: 'Buber's phraseology which strikingly recalls that of many African leaders of one-party states, belongs to the perennial speech of communitas, not rejecting the possibility of structure, but conceiving of it merely as an outgrowth of direct and immediate relations between integral individuals.'[21] The institutions of one-party states, therefore, are seen as a means of maintaining communitas. There has often been a tendency among historians and social scientists to scoff at the claims made by politicians that a modern ideology is based upon a traditional African socialism. This is, perhaps, partly because we were unwilling to rise above the micro-historical plane, and because our picture of traditional Africa was that of a society, tribal, isolated and unchanging. With Turner's stimulating ideas about ritual as a starting point, we have been able to indicate that this is a limited picture, and that traditional African ritual demanded and afforded an opening on to a wider environment, an opening which became explicit in liminal ritual. Just as guilds practising liminal rituals reinforced a sense of community in society at large, so do the modern experiments of collective farming, the school as a self-sufficient community, and the National Service or Youth Camp. Politicians who use the language of traditional kinship, life-crisis ritual or even liminal movements such as the Maji Maji rebellion, to introduce these new institutions are not, I submit, guilty of exaggeration.

When we turn to the ideologies of the established religions, we can already discern an attempt to make the continuity between the old and the new orders explicit. Churches have been slower than independent governments to recognise and use traditional ideas and values expressed through symbolism and ritual. They imposed monolithic structures and symbolic models that were prefabricated in Europe, while African ideas and symbols went underground. The missionary experience and especially the experience of living through the political revolution that led to independence, has helped theologians to develop a more positive theology of salvation and a theology of human culture. Coupled with this, there has been a rediscovery of the Christian community and a growing abandonment of juridical attitudes. It was interesting, for example, to hear a Roman Catholic Bishop at a session of the Study Seminar of his Church in Tanzania in 1969, declare that, 'for explaining the sense of the whole life of the Christian community, as well as Church communion, authority, etc., the word *ujamaa* in its wide sense is far better than the legalistic, ecclesiastical term, collegiality (hallowed though the latter term is by the documents of the Second Vatican Council)'.[22]

CONCLUSION

The aim of this paper has been mainly to see in what ways Turner's analysis of African ritual is important for the study of history in Africa. In attempting to do this, we have gone beyond the level of history in which Turner himself is interested for the purpose of his own anthropological study. However, I do not believe that what has been said about the wider historical implications of his analysis is ultimately foreign to Turner's thinking. Indeed, there seems to have been a progress of thought between his discussion of redressive and life-crisis rituals published in the years up to and including 1968, and his scintillating account of liminal ritual published in 1969. A closer attention to liminal ritual has led him to see in the concept of liminality an explanatory model for historical facts very far removed in space and time from the recent history of eastern Africa. We have ventured to suggest that both redressive and life-crisis ritual are similarly capable of extension and offer us wider perspectives than may have been thought possible for the history of pre-colonial Africa.

148

NOTES

[1] G. Gusdorf, *Mythe et Métaphysique* (Paris 1953) p. 20; Claud Lévi-Strauss, *The Savage Mind* (London 1966) pp. 1–33.

[2] V. W. Turner *Lunda Rites and Ceremonies* Rhodes-Livingstone Museum, Occasional Paper No. 10, (Livingstone 1953); 'A Lunda Love Story and its Consequences', *Rhodes-Livingstone Journal* 19, 1955; *Schism and Continuity in an African Society* (Manchester 1957); *Ndembu Divination: its Symbolism and Techniques* Rhodes-Livingstone Paper No. 31, (Manchester 1961); *Chihamba, the White Spirit* Rhodes-Livingstone Paper No. 33, (Manchester 1962); 'Three Symbols of Passage in Ndembu Circumcision Ritual', in Max Gluckman (ed.) *Essays in the Ritual of Social Relations* (Manchester 1962); 'Ritual Symbolism, Morality and Social Structure among the Ndembu', in M. Fortes and G. Dierterlen (eds.) *African Systems of Thought* (Oxford 1965); 'Colour Classification in Ndembu Ritual', in M. Banton, (ed.) *Anthropological Approaches to the Study of Religion* A.S.A. 3, (London 1966); *The Forest of Symbols* (Ithaca, New York 1967); *The Drums of Affliction* (Oxford 1968); *The Ritual Process* (Chicago 1969).

[3] Lévi-Strauss *op. cit.* p. 30.

[4] Turner *The Ritual Process* p. 83.

[5] *Ibid.* p. 6.

[6] E. Bevan *Symbolism and Belief* (London 1938, reissue 1962) pp. 227–8.

[7] Turner *The Ritual Process* p. 203.

[8] A. Van Gennep *The Rites of Passage* (London 1960).

[9] F. G. Finch, 'The Story of the Wawungu' *Tanganyika Notes and Records* No. 52 (1959) pp. 82–92.

[10] Judges ii, 16–19.

[11] A. Shorter, 'Ukimbu and the Kimbu Chiefdoms of Southern Unyamwezi' (Thesis submitted for the degree of D.Phil., Oxford University 1968) p. 261.

[12] Evidence of Mwami Kizozo at Ushirombo, November 2, 1966.

[13] A discussion about the solar symbolism of conus-shell discs is to be found in Shorter *op. cit.* pp. 257–61. I am indebted to various informants about Luguru custom. Chief among them are Rev. P. Mkude, and Rev. C. Vermunt.

[14] Shorter *op. cit.* chapter IX; 'Nyungu-ya-Mawe and the Empire of the Ruga-Rugas' *Journal of African History* IX, 2 (1968), pp. 235–59; 'The Kimbu', in Andrew Roberts (ed.) *Tanzania before 1800* (Nairobi 1968) pp. 109–12.

[15] Isaria N. Kimambo, *A Political History of the Pare of Tanzania, c. 1500–1900* (Nairobi 1969) pp. 47–64, 121.

[16] Shorter, 'Ukimbu and the Kimbu Chiefdoms', pp. 311–21.

[17] T. O. Ranger, 'The Movement of Ideas, 1850–1939', in I. Kimambo and A. Temu (eds.) *A History of Tanzania* (Nairobi 1969) pp. 161–88.

[18] Luc de Heusch *Rwanda et la Civilisation Interlacustre* (Brussels 1966.) This is a very full, historical discussion of the Chwezi traditions.

[19] Kimambo *A Political History of the Pare* p. 189.

[20] A. Shorter, 'The Migawo: Peripheral Spirit Possession and Christian Prejudice' *Anthropos* Vol. 65 (February 1970) pp. 110–26.

[21] Turner *The Ritual Process* p. 143.

[22] Bishop Blomjous quoted in transcript of S.S.Y. Session (Dar es Salaam 1969) (mimeographed).

PART FIVE

THE NINETEENTH CENTURY CRISIS AND RELIGIOUS SYSTEMS IN EAST AND CENTRAL AFRICA

MARCIA WRIGHT

Nyakyusa Cults and Politics in the Later Nineteenth Century

A religious belief, in the form of an heroic tradition dating back more than two hundred years, is common to the people living around the north end of Lake Nyasa. Within this religious zone were to be found in earlier times at least four different cults reflecting a variety of motives and special historical circumstances. The Kinga in the Livingstone Mountains in the east, perhaps the most fervent believers in the heroic tradition, preserved the memory of miracle-working heroes who had been born among them but were later expelled. In order to appease these powerful exiles, the arbiters of prosperity, Kinga priests gathered ritual offerings and moved annually, and in times of emergency, down steep paths into the Nyakyusa valleys to sacrifice at the groves and grottos sacred to the heroes. Whereas the Kinga priests comprised a class distinct from the chiefly lineages of that people, ritual and secular functions were fused in the Nyakyusa princes, who claimed descent from the heroes.[1] This paper, being primarily concerned about the interrelationship of religion and politics among the Nyakyusa, will refer only occasionally to their ritual partners, the Kinga, and will generally ignore the remaining devotees of the heroic tradition, such as the Ngonde and the Kukwe.[2] It will be argued that the heroic tradition among the Nyakyusa was heterodox until the twentieth century, and that the uniformity and hierarchy described in the 1930s was problematic. Such centralisation as did occur ought to be dated from the later nineteenth century.

THE PEOPLE OF RUNGWE

The Nyakyusa live to the north and northwest of Lake Nyasa in an area called Rungwe, surrounded by mountains which afford considerable natural protection and in the nineteenth century served to exclude much of the commerce and warfare that disturbed the surrounding region. Within the area, the lake plain has always supported the densest population of people and cattle. Behind the plain, the uplands are gained by a sharp ascent, in early times made by following one of the several river valleys. The valleys and highland pockets, much like the ridges of Gikuyu country and the vertical divisions of Kilimanjaro, favoured segmentary social and political organisation. Abundant rainfall, rich soils and relatively advanced agricultural techniques allowed each entity to be economically self-contained. The Kinga, masters of iron smelting and working, supplied one of the few lacks and in return they received access to more reliable sources of food than their mountains afforded.

The Nyakyusa and their neighbours in Rungwe became exposed intensively to new political factors in the colonial period, especially as they occupied the home district of the Langenburg District, which approximated to the Mbeya Region of present-day Tanzania.[3] As such, they experienced the continued pressure of colonial administrators for uniformity which, together with other generalising processes, contributed to a blurring of the former political, geographic and ethnic sense of identity. 'Nyakyusa' in a loose sense now means people coming from Rungwe, but before 1900 migratory labour and colonisation had not yet encouraged this generalisation. The peoples of Rungwe had been introverted and almost wholly divided among themselves. The Lugulu and Kukwe of the north never acknowledged a political or ritual relationship with the peoples of the south, even though they shared features of language and culture. A lineage of rulers known to scholars as the 'Nyakyusa proper' lived around Masoko in the middle uplands and on the lake plain. Shifting alliances in the later nineteenth century de-emphasised the original connection of the plains princes with Masoko and saw them move towards a closer relationship with the people of Selya, to the east of Masoko.[4]

Even within a particular division, many discrete polities coexisted, each presided over by a prince. These rulers had a variety of relationships with other princes of their particular lineage and, owing to chronic competition and adversary tactics, with all surrounding princes. That the Nyakyusa proper of the lake plain shared the same lineage did not mitigate their competition, either between divisions in different geographical areas or between generations in a single polity. In these circumstances the usage of 'prince' instead of chief is preferred because it conveys tentativeness and fluidity in the accession to and holding of power.[5] The nature of princely authority was complicated: strong authority rested upon personal ability and prestige enhanced by positive public opinion, on fulfilment of the charismatic promise conveyed by the mystical charter of the lineage, and on performance of ritual functions.

The cults devoted to the founding heroes of princely lineages provided the organisational means of mobilising collective pressure among princes.

THE HEROIC CULTS

Imminent and immanent spiritual forces were honoured by the Nyakyusa. Their divinities were god-like brothers, Nkekete, Kyala, Lwembe and Mbasi, who had come from Ukinga bringing fire, metalworking, new crops and, in some cases, an ability to model cattle in clay and breathe life into them.[6] The first recorded version of the deeds of the original Lwembe, reflecting the perspective of the Kinga, was taken down on 28 January, 1901:

> That the ancestor of the priestly family of Luembe, living southward from Manow, was Kinga, is generally acknowledged here. Never before, however, had I been able to fathom the history of that priestly family so famous among the people. Today I heard the following unbelievable things about them.
>
> The grandfather of the Luembe still living now, so I am told, lived with the Kinga Chief Nkuama (that is in the area of our Tandala Station). Even as a herdboy, he understood secret arts and attracted the attention of the people.[7]

The Kinga explained on this occasion that Lwembe had brought forth a spring of water, turned stones into calves, and, in later life, when no longer able to make cattle, grew grain in the palm of his hand. Gifts were sent by the Kinga to the grove at Lubaga in Selya district commemorating this hero in times of famine and at every planting time. In return for their iron wares, they received seed corn and other food.[8]

The Kinga, it seems, played a significant role in the stability and survival of the Lwembe cult. Perhaps this was so because the harsh, precarious life on the mountain-tops gave frequent reason for prayer and sacrifice. Another interpretation would be that economic conditions changed much more slowly for the Kinga, who continued to rely upon the export of iron wares to the valleys in a time after the Nyakyusa enjoyed a greater diversity of market opportunities. The existence of a special class of priests also made the heroic tradition relatively tenacious and rigid in Ukinga. It must be remarked that the Kinga did not venerate Lwembe alone; the iron hoes typical of their offerings were to be found at cult sites of Mbasi and Kyala as well. The association of Kinga priests with rituals at Lubaga lent considerably to its aura, however, for when these priests descended into the valleys, they created a mood of terrified fascination by beating the sacred drum that demanded to be 'fed' with the blood of a child. Attention to ritual formalism seems to have been another Kinga attribute in evidence at Lubaga in the 1930s.[9] The heroic tradition derived considerable resilience from this tension of different religious needs and ecological factors.

For both the Kinga and the Nyakyusa the heroes were identified with fertility and prosperity. A failure of nature in these respects was taken to be a demonstration of heroic displeasure. The purpose of the demonstration was to extract a compensation for some offence. Confrontation of a similar sort belonged to the Nyakyusa style in purely temporal affairs as well: a prince or individual threatened violence or seized a pawn in order to open the way for a peaceful settlement by arbitration. Where it was a matter of conflict between princes, and should this limited violence fail to bring about a reconciliation, the cults could be invoked. Irregularity of rain, or plague, or some other natural sign, was needed, however, to validate this resort.[10] It does not seem to be valid to claim that the heroic cults operated to impose 'the king's peace', for the cults seem to have required dramatic natural disorder before being activated to mobilise sanctions.[11] But given the correct coincidence of events, the cults doubtless facilitated collective political action on the part of princes subscribing to them.

The Nyakyusa did not dwell upon cosmology and concerned themselves little with creation and the creator in the abstract. Good and evil, on the other hand, were always thought to be active and persuasive. Criminal manipulation of evil through witchcraft or sorcery was believed to be common. Evil spirits could also be released by violation of a taboo or through grudgeholding, in which case disease was visited upon the guilty person. The interplay of good and evil and the use of evil to neutralise evil and make way for the good inherent in nature is a very interesting reflection, on the metaphysical level, of the Nyakyusa style of confrontation.[12] It should be remarked that the bountiful environment of Rungwe probably moulded this essentially optimistic view that countervailing forces were all that well-being required.

Witchcraft was the only thing thoroughly evil in itself. Yet even there, the imagery of good and evil was mixed. Autopsies were frequently performed to determine whether a witch had caused death by sending a python to eat at the belly of the victim.[13] The python in this case would be the agent of the witch, but pythons also operated in positive ways. They were killed to supply an ingredient for the medicine taken by princes and headmen to enhance their spiritual weight or *ifingila*. One of the effects of the medicine, also called *ifingila*, was that leaders who were 'heavy', with pythons in their bellies, could see and fight witches. Finally, in the sacred grove at Lubaga, a python 'licked' a candidate for priesthood whom the hero Lwembe accepted.[14]

While the cults were a particular responsibility of the aristocracy, 'defenders', diviners and medicine men served the commoners' needs for supernatural aid. The opinions of these specialists could become generally known and influenced public opinion. A person judged by a village to be a witch was ostracised and obliged to move away if he did not repent or submit to the *mwafi* ordeal. The accused gained a fresh start in another village because witchcraft was held to be effective only within the confines of one settlement.[15] Diviners and defenders as religious specialists therefore functioned within the same very localised setting.

Princes had responsibilities in a number of religious sectors. As protectors of their villages, they helped to deal with witchcraft. They also conducted ritual in preparation for war and raids, made libations in honour of their ancestors, and contributed to the appeasement of the heroes. The heroic tradition and its cults, for all their limitations, afforded the only framework through which the particularism of the Nyakyusa could be overcome.

THE HISTORY OF THE HEROIC CULTS: THE IDEA OF THE 'DIVINE KINGSHIP' OF LWEMBE

Until recently we owed nearly all of our knowledge of the heroic cults of the Nyakyusa to the work of Godfrey and Monica Wilson, who carried out extensive anthropological field research in Rungwe. The Wilsons were not primarily concerned with historical questions but they did come to certain conclusions about the history of the heroic cults. Briefly, they came to regard the cult of Lwembe at Lubaga as having achieved a spiritual paramountcy over all other cults and as having taken on the character of a 'divine kingship' with a sequence of priest-kings going back many generations. If we examine the nineteenth-century evidence, however, it becomes plain that the concentration of religious attention on the Lwembe at Lubaga occurred only in the mid-1890s. It seems important to re-examine the evidence for the religious history of the Nyakyusa.

Before turning to the other evidence, however, it is instructive to trace, so far as possible, the emergence of the interpretation which caused the Lwembe-ship to be seen as a long-standing 'divine kingship'. Perhaps the best short description of the Nyakyusa religious system ever published is that by Godfrey Wilson, written in 1935 or early 1936. By then the anthropologist had lived for some time in Selya and learned something also of the ritual centres in other parts of Rungwe. He had singled out the groves of Lwembe as the site of the most vigorous continued practice of traditional religion at the cult level:

The chiefs of Lubaga had a far-reaching religious preeminence, but no general political influence at all beyond their own country.[16]

The ritual is esoteric, there is no gathering of the people at the sacrifice, and only chiefs and those with hereditary priesthoods come to it. But, on the other hand, everyone knows when a sacrifice is taking place, and, in spite of the influence of missions, most people in the pagan community believe in its efficacy.[17]

So much was observation. But following this description, Wilson went on to remark: 'Traditionally each chief of the Lubaga was ritually installed into a position somewhat resembling that of Sir James Frazer's 'Divine Kings', into a position hedged with taboos. . . .'[18] The germ of the 'Divine Kingship' thesis was therefore already present before the Wilsons went afield to find a re-enforcing African prototype. There was no incumbent Lwembe to question, since the Lwembeship had fallen vacant in 1913 when the priests at Lubaga were unable to find a prince willing to succeed to the title and office of Lwembe.[19] But in the country of Ngonde, in Malawi, where the people belonged to the same linguistic and cultural family as the Nyakyusa, there was to be found an extant personification of an heroic ancestor, the Kyungu. The Kyunguship was occupied, even though it had obviously been transformed. Not withstanding all the conceivable problems, the analogy was made to fit: 'The Nyakyusa actually possessed in the Lwembes, the hereditary chiefs of Lubaga, a line of spiritual paramounts or high priests, whose religious functions were remarkably similar to those of the Kyungus in Ngonde.'[20]

The Wilsons themselves believed that the later history of the two offices had diverged. The Kyungus of Ngonde, they held, built upon their spiritual authority to become the secularised paramount chiefs of their country, having exercised strict economic control by monopolising the ivory trade. The Lwembes, although their spiritual authority was assumed, had not followed this course, and Godfrey Wilson offered a material explanation for this: 'That they never achieved secular paramountcy at all was mainly because they were poor.'[21]

Clearly some doubtful assumptions were at work here. The spiritual authority of the Lwembes, which in fact probably existed to a limited extent before the 1890s, is assumed for a much earlier period on the basis of observations made in the 1930s. The comparison between the Lwembes and the Kyungus was manifestly too difficult to make for any very hard conclusions to emerge from it. Moreover, in building up the idea of the 'Divine Kingship' of Lwembe Monica Wilson necessarily obscured the existence and function of the other cults and heroes in Nyakyusa tradition. And the cost of maintaining the argument also included the alteration of some primary observations about the Nyakyusa. For example, it was a dictum in the Wilsons' work that rituals ran along lines of kinship. There was a clear contradiction of this rule in regard to communal rituals, however, for while the lineages of Selya princely families remained separate from those of the 'Nyakyusa proper', their ritual centre at Lubaga was acknowledged to be effective for princes in both areas. The solution was to gloss over the geneological divisions and to suggest a genetic relationship among those associated with the Lubaga cult of the Lwembes: 'All the Nyak-yusa proper (*that is those of Selya, the Lake plain and Masoko*), send cattle to sacrifice at Lubaga (the grove of Lwembe).'[22] Summing up the theory in 1959, Monica Wilson stated that Lwembe was the only hero in Nyakyusa country to establish a divine kingship, that all princes of the lower Nyakyusa valley were his descendants, and that all sacrificed to him and recognised the spiritual over-lordship of his heirs.[23]

The archival record throws the gravest doubts upon those anthropological reconstructions. It happens that European missionaries entered the Rungwe area at a time of significant change in the balance of the heroic tradition. They recorded, though certainly not in a fully comprehending way, the events which led to the increase in the influence of the Lwembe. These events, in fact, took the form of a conflict between the heroes Lwembe and Mbasi, through their human representatives, in which Lwembe was victorious and Mbasi was vanquished. It was from this victory, so it seems, that the wide influence of Lwembe dated.

THE CONTEXT FOR A RE-INTERPRETATION OF THE DEVELOPMENT OF THE HEROIC TRADITION

We will examine this conflict in more detail below, but first it is necessary to set it in context. Two main points need to be made. First, the results of Lwembe's victory over Mbasi in the mid-1890s warn us of the difficulties of interpreting oral tradition relating to the cults. Though it is clear that Mbasi had been both quite distinct from Lwembe and had enjoyed his own wide area of influence, as early as 1901 the fusion in the heroic tradition brought about by Lwembe's victory had caused a merging in the minds of some Kinga at least of the identity of the two heroes.[24]

Second, we should not regard the victory of Lwembe over Mbasi as an unprecedented disturbance of the balance within the heroic tradition, a disturbance perhaps provoked by white pressure. It is plain that there had been similar shifts of balance before. Thus a tradition tells us of the killing of Nkekete, the brother of Kyala and Lwembe:

> When Lwembe went down into Selya he found the hill people (BeMwamba) and the people of the plain (Mwakyembe's men) already there. They feared him because he had all things, and they still fear him. He was greater than Nkekete. They cut Nkekete's throat, but they couldn't kill Lwembe.[25]

In another version, Nkekete was killed because he did not have as great spiritual weight as Lwembe. These indications attest to the fact that heroes had been eliminated from the heroic tradition before, though regrettably they give no indication of the historical context. It was the misfortune of Mbasi to have been bested at the beginning of colonial times when the missionaries, for purposes of religious translation, were looking for the local equivalent of Satan. His identity therefore suffered through missionary misapplication as well as through popular adjustment of myth.

Even the failure to find a member of the Lwembe lineage to act as the new representative of Lwembe in 1913, and the continuance of cult observations by the attendant priesthood alone need not be seen as an unprecedented consequence of colonial and Christian pressure on traditional cultic institutions. The nineteenth-century evidence suggests that the cult of Kyala was similarly restructured well before the colonial period. Around the middle of the nineteenth century a new hereditary professional priesthood was founded at PaliKyala, the cult centre on the semi-island Ikombe on the north-east side of the lake. A certain Mwakinyasa, an immigrant Kisi medicine man, was ceded ritual leadership by the local princes, who were supposed to have said: 'Let the ritual come out of our bodies and go to Mwakinyasa'.[26] Kyala had no special heirs in whom to become re-incarnated and his selection of Mwakinyasa as his medium was signalled by the success of Mwakinyasa's medicines in bringing full harvests. It should be noted that the cult of Mbasi in later years was also served by a priest with no prior relationship to the prince-participants. From the description of this priest, Mwanafungubo, it appears that his credentials were not connected with medicines, but with psychic traits appropriate to one susceptible to possession. He was described as of 'grey, sickly colour, thin body, with hollow cheeks and rolling eyes'.[27] In other respects the priests of Kyala and Mbasi were more alike. The seat of Mbasi had once been a lake-side lagoon; waters gurgling in a cave on the shore provided for the oracle through which Mwakinyasa 'spoke with Kyala'. Also, like Mwanafungubo, Mwakinyasa kept wives and cattle in the name of the hero he served.[28]

Viewed from an historical perspective, the Kyala cult appears quite clearly to have been in decline at mid-century and to have owed its revival to a change in leadership. As the Wilsons learned, Mwakinyasa himself was looked back upon in the 1930s as a near-hero, credited with the introduction of new crops.[29] This interesting development shows the strength of the heroic tradition and suggests how particular families of princely heirs may have become candidates for the 'divine kingship', but it begs the historical question of why the new leadership was needed. A possible answer may be that in the earlier nineteenth century princes of the Kyungu line had established themselves in Saku, on the eastern end of the plain in the environs of PaliKyala. These outsiders were then expelled by a Saku-Nyakyusa league, whereupon the Nyakyusa achieved an ascendency and spread at the expense of the Saku.[30] Both the Kyungu and Nyakyusa princes would have continued to refer primarily to heroes other than Kyala, and PaliKyala survived as a territorial shrine. To appease its hero was a contingency measure taken by those who wished to keep in with the local deities while continuing to participate in their own cult. An excellent example of contingency observance in the 1890s was provided by Mwanjenya, the strongest prince of the eastern plain, himself a supporter of Mbasi, who made offerings to Kyala through his nephew.[31] The princes of Saku, according to their own statement, became spiritually incompetent. Kyala survived, therefore, as a popular divinity, enjoying strong support from the Kinga who looked to rituals at PaliKyala as assurance of good rainfall. Under Mwakinyasa's administration, PaliKyala served an eminently multi-tribal constituency including Kisi, Kinga, Saku, and Nyakusa.

The revival of PaliKyala obviously entailed an adaption of the heroic tradition. The cult's constituency was now made up both of princes who sent livestock and commoners who regularly brought grain and beer.[32] Mwakinyasa and his lineal heirs became territorial rainmakers, praying to the hero divinity, rather than acting as mediators of an active anthropomorphic spiritual prince.

The immanence of Kyala faded and his remoteness helps to explain the very good relations between his priests and the Lutheran missionaries. The Berliners adopted 'Kyala' as the vernacular word for God and thereby brought about a further change in the understanding of the concept of Kyala throughout Rungwe. But an essential change in the cult had taken place before missionary intervention.

It is plain, then, that significant changes had regularly taken place within the heroic tradition in correspondence with political developments. In this context we can use the fully documented victory of Lwembe over Mbasi in the mid-1890s to understand more generally the dynamics of cultic change among the Nyakyusa.

FACTORS OF CHANGE, 1886–1900

During the last fifteen years of the nineteenth century, events moved very swiftly for the Nyakyusa. Before 1886, the episode of the insurgent Kyungu princes in Saku had created a lasting sense of enmity against the Ngonde.[33] In the late 1870s the Sangu chief Merere occupied part of the Kukwe country in the north and extended his sphere of influence over Lugulu as well. He did not, however, trespass into Masoko or Selya. The other major power in the region, the Ngoni, passed either through Bundali to the west of the Nyakyusa or marched to their Songea lands by an easterly route.

Any illusion that Unyakyusa would not suffer at the hands of these powers was rudely upset by the combined Sangu-Ngoni expedition of 1886. Aiming to raid the rich herds of the Nyakyusa, the invaders joined up in Ukinga, descended the escarpment via the Madehani Pass, and swept through Selya unopposed, collecting a number of cattle. Moving on to the lake plain, they eventually encountered a force of defenders under Mwamakula which turned the tide.[34] Most cattle were recovered, either immediately or from the retreating enemy. The great war captain of the Sangu, Mwandangara, died in the battle.

Although the Nyakyusa emerged victorious in this defensive action, they were by no means capable of a sustained military or diplomatic effort. Warfare had been and remained an *ad hoc* business and local affairs demanded constant attention.[35] Their solution to the problem of external pressure was to look for an ally or defender to countervail the threat of renewed attacks. Transient contacts with European traders having been friendly, it was to them that the Nyakyusa began to look. Mutual interest became apparent especially when the next incursion came from across the Songwe in the west and was made by groups increasingly at odds with the traders at Karonga. Kanyoli, a headman of the Kamanga, had leagued with one of the Muslim traders who had been attracted in increasing numbers by the ivory trade conducted by the African Lakes Company.[36] Sometime in March 1887, Kanyoli and these Muslims made their foray against the Nyakyusa, Kanyoli expecting to keep the cattle and the Muslims expecting to keep the slaves that would be captured. Mwakyusa, the leading prince of the western Nyakyusa, rallied his people and inflicted a devastating defeat on the invaders. Many of those who survived the battle were drowned in fleeing back across the Songwe. Kanyoli himself was killed and beheaded.[37] It is an interesting reflection of the Nyakyusa propensity to remember events in religious terms that we find this episode narrated in the 1930s as an attack by Kanyoli with an 'Arab or Swahili witch doctor' in his train.[38]

However disguised the terrestrial power struggle remained for most Nyakyusa, it was very much in play in the subsequent conflict between the African Lakes Company and the 'Arabs'. The relations between them deteriorated rapidly and strengthened the need for reciprocal support of the Europeans and the Nyakyusa. The strongest princes of the western, central and eastern plain (Mwakyusa, Mwamakula and Mwankenja respectively) agreed to a pact with the Company whereby either the Nyakyusa or the African Lakes Company would come to the rescue of the other party in case of attack.[39]

Raids and tests of strength multiplied in the second half of 1887. In September, Merere raided into the Songwe Valley, not actually into Unyakusa, but close enough to cause concern. At the end of October or the beginning of November, the 'Arabs' began their siege of Karonga. In December, the Nyakyusa raised this siege and became more and more important in the strategic reckoning of the A.L.C. But shortly after this action Mwamakula, its main leader, died, the victim, so it is said, of his princely rivals: 'Mwamakula died by means of a poisoned mat brought to him by a wife Seba at the instigation of her father Mwaseba (third son of Mwakapesile and father of the present headman Mwandemere).'[40] Mwaseba, in other words, was the brother of Mwankenja, prince of the eastern plain. Whether or not the incident is historical, it illustrates the conflict between the eastern and central divisions that persisted into colonial times and confirms that a broadbased league among the Nyakyusa was feasible only in moments of dire threat.

The strongman who next emerged in the central plain was Mwanjabala, Mwamakula's brother, who assumed a regency during the minority of his sons Mwakalukwa and Mwakalinga. Mwanjabala drove Mwaseba into exile and thereafter attempted to secure his frontiers. The 'Arabs', it was reported, were building a stockade just one day's march to the west of him. To shore up his western flank, he sought the support of the Scottish missionaries and travelled to the Kukwe village of Kararamuka to contact them.[41] In later days, after sustaining serious attacks by the Sangu, the Kukwe claimed that the Nyakyusa victories of 1886–7 had caused them to look south for aid to withdraw them from the Sangu sphere.[42] Deference was not evident, however, in the relations of Kararamuka and Mwanjabala; the Kukwe ruler took offence at Nyakyusa liberties and was certainly unready to forego any local autonomy.[43]

Another example of tension between neighbouring rulers existed on the eastern frontier. There Mwakatungile was embroiled in a standing feud with Monemtera, the Kinga chief who commanded the mountain end of paths into Selya. Monemtera was considered to be the 'friend of Merere' and the disagreement had originated with the seizure of cattle at the time of the Sangu-Ngoni retreat.[44] The obvious strategic element was never, apparently, articulated. Just as the commercial motives for 'Arab' activities were ignored, so the bad relations with Monemtera were interpreted as a protracted personal duel that could not be arbitrated.

For all the evidence of growing external menace, the peoples of Rungwe remained jealously decentralised and unmitigated in their rivalries in the later 1880s. As yet there was no evidence of an apparatus working through the cults to ensure cohesion. The possibility of a new adaptation of the heroic tradition may have been signalled, however, by the movement of the Mbasi priest away from the lake plain and up into the middle Lufilio Valley near where Mwaka-tungile lived.

The alliance with the African Lakes Company continued, meanwhile, and the growing strength of the garrison at Karonga was no doubt appreciated by the plains princes. Protection on their eastern flank was a positive commendation for the trading post set up by the Company on the northeast side of the lake at Rumbira. And being outside of Unyakyusa, in Kisi country, with extremely difficult access by land to the centres of population, the Rumbira post was hardly intrusive. In fact, as the Company and the successive German occupants learned, the asset of safe anchorage for steam vessels was far offset by commercial and political inaccessibility. It was mainly from Karonga that trade spread. By 1890 the Company's African agents began to succeed in stimulating the sale of surplus food grown in Rungwe, making inroads upon the economic self-sufficiency of the area by establishing a consumer market for cotton cloth.[45]

Besides such mild commercial activities, there were continuing, but very tentative, probes by missionaries. Dr Kerr-Cross carried out most of the diplomacy for the Livingstonia Mission; given the uncertainties of missionary strategy and his own rather unevangelical temperament, the impression of European religious purposes could not have been strong.[46] As a diplomat representing the European allies, on the other hand, he gained considerable influence, some of it reflected in the name Koroso which survived on the central plain among the descendents of Mwakalinga.[47]

When the German missionaries arrived in 1891, the Nyakyusa–European entente appeared to be serving its defensive purpose.[48] No further Ngoni raids had taken place and pressure along the Songwe had declined. The Berliners, coming with recommendations from Kerr-Cross and in the company of A.L.C. employees, stepped into the predefined role of Europeans as external defenders. Kumoga, an agent of the Company and subsequently *capitao* for the Berliners, confessed in later years that the missionaries had seemed no different than traders in motive and that he had represented them as identical.[49] Certainly the princes thought they were getting more of the same. Mwaihojo summed up on their behalf when he formally greeted the Berliners and praised them for their cloth and their strength as deterrents to the Ngoni. When several of the younger missionaries demonstrated their firearms they hoped to create an awe which might be turned into recognition of a general and spiritual ascendency.[50] It is highly doubtful, however, if any prince at that time foresaw a European over-rule in any sphere, and this display more probably only satisfied them that their hospitality would be repaid by the conventional services.

To a limited extent, however, the Nyakyusa did look at the newly settled missionaries in the light of their religious values. Alexander Merensky encouraged this by trying hard during his temporary residence to project his personality in terms of personal power. He was at the time a vigorous man in his fifties, with a presence and dignity of the sort associated with *ifingila*. Prince Mwaihojo was especially solicitous in the early days about the good health of the chief missionary.[51] Mwaihojo may have been sensitive on the religious level owing to the fact that he had once been driven by brother princes from his home area and managed to regain status in the middle Lufilio Valley in part because he became the protector of the Mbasi priest, Mwanafungubo.[52]

Settling in Mwaihojo's area, therefore, the missionaries had entered the main area of influence of the Mbasi cult. Their first station at 'Wangemannshöh' was only an hour away from the Mbasi shrine. In their first encounters the missionaries snubbed Mwanafungubo, who seized an early opportunity for revenge. The formulation of his indictment rang true in the heroic tradition: 'It is the whites who hinder the rains. They do not cultivate the land, they do not need you, but they will impoverish you, Konde. Kill the whites with spears. Take their cotton goods.'[53] But the princes did not yet see the whites as so serious a threat and would not execute this penalty. Instead they moderated it to a boycott, aiming to cut off provisions, and even this action ended immediately the rains resumed. Nevertheless, given the high prestige of the Berliners and their continuing role as external defenders, the degree of solidarity achieved in the boycott is a very good indicator of the considerable influence of the Mbasi priest and cult during this small crisis.

Plagues of locusts and of rinderpest in 1892 and 1893 brought on a more protracted period of disorder. The rinderpest was particularly crucial, given the social and economic importance of cattle in Unyakyusa. The dying herds created a general sense of urgency and the heroic tradition appeared very obviously relevant, especially in view of the close connection in myth between the heroes and cattle. Mwanjabala, the key man among central plain princes, at this time became the active champion of traditional religion as represented by the Mbasi cult. Sending a man with the offering of an elephant tusk, he asked Mbasi to resurrect a cow as a sign of good will. On another occasion, Mwanjabala took the missionaries to task for meddling in the affairs of the hero and threatened violence if they did not disengage. And he put pressure on Mwaihojo, as the cult's immediate sponsor, to effect a reconciliation between the Mbasi priest and prince Mwakatungile, who were quarrelling over a woman, Kinjorobo.[54]

Carl Nauhaus, head of the Berlin Mission, was ready enough to withdraw both from direct religious conflict with the heroic tradition and from involvement in complex judicial proceedings over the disputed woman. He attempted instead to get the princes to decide the case collectively. The princes met and decided that the woman should be returned to Mwakatungile. It seemed that the missionaries had successfully set in motion a procedure analogous to that usually activated through an heroic cult, and that the judgement of the princes had resulted in the discomfiture of the Mbasi priest. But appearances were deceptive. Popular opinion maintained that the council of princes was only a facade for the continuing intervention of Nauhaus: 'You kill us, because it lies in your hands to withhold her or return her to Mbasi.'[55] Moreover, upon further investigation it became clear that although the princes had decided the case against the Mbasi priest they had not withdrawn their livestock from the cult centre, where cattle served as a kind of insurance against political isolation. Trying to understand such apparently paradoxical behaviour, Nauhaus discovered that, far from being in any way convinced by the Christian religious message, the majority against the Mbasi priest had been marshalled by the senior priest of the Mwamukinga lineage, who was allegedly jealous that

Mwaihojo, a relative stranger and not a kinsman, rather than he himself, had the advantage of sponsoring the Mbasi cult.[56]

Exploring the matter at its roots, the bridewealth paid for the woman, it was discovered that 'Mbasi' had in fact paid her father. Confronted by this fact, Mwakatungile sought to prop up his shaken position by a resort to casuistry, exploiting Christian teachings. He reportedly declared that the woman's father had 'eaten his cattle', that is, received bridewealth from him, for the following reasons: 'When Mbasi had appeared, he (Mwakatungile) gave him (Mbasi) several cattle, as a sign of recognition of his majesty. These cattle had been given for Kinjorobi. But Mbasi is not God, and therefore has no right to take cattle from any person. Therefore they were still his (Mwakatungile's) property.'[57]

Whatever the residual confusion, the Mbasi priest had in fact moved off soon after the council decided against him. This time he located himself in the vicinity of Lwembe's shrine at Lubaga. That part of Selya had only recently been hit by the rinderpest and again the Berliners could be represented as disturbers of the peace owing to their political miscalculation in buying land from certain inferior authorities. Again missionary meddling and heroic displeasure seemed to coincide. Mustering support among the Selya princes led by Mwai-popo, Mwanafungubo gained the woman again for Mbasi, whom he said would thereafter allow nature to prosper. But this victory was short lived. Once normalcy returned and the imminence of the heroic retribution receded, it was not surprising that such an undignified, not to say excessively anthropomor-phic, representation of the hero made Mwanafungubo vulnerable. Moreover, Mwanafungubo had been operating in the heartland of Lwembe's area and claiming obedience from princes of Lwembe's lineage. Some sort of confronta-tion between the two was inevitable. It took the form of a poison ordeal in which the representatives of Lwembe and Mbasi confronted each other. The Lwembe had kept aloof from factional politics and had been careful not to be drawn into the role of arbitrator. Now he reaped the fruits of this policy. Mwanafungubo was defeated in the ordeal and unmasked as the source of the guttaral sounds in the Mbasi grove through which the oracle was manifest. The lineal descendant of the hero, Lwembe, triumphed over the priest-medium.

The missionaries regarded the downfall of Mwanafungubo as a blow to tradi-tional religion as a whole. In this view they were almost certainly mistaken. Rather, what had been at stake were two different views of the heroic tradition itself. What had been at stake also was rather the question of whether the Mbasi priest or the Lwembe would *extend* their influence to the other's area than any danger that representatives of the heroes would lose influence alto-gether. Mwanafungubo had lost his chance to command princes in Lwembe's area or, indeed, anywhere else, but the victory of Lwembe meant that his cult centre would become in future the focus of any attempt at combined action. This became clear in 1897 when a widely ranging group of princes met at Lubaga to consecrate their planned uprising against the Germans.

To understand the events which led to the uprising of 1897 we must turn to the question of Nyakyusa response to German rule. While the Mbasi contro-versy had been going on, Hermann von Wissman had arrived with the first contingent of German armed forces to lay claim to south-western Tanzania.

When von Wissmann demanded recognition of the German flag he met with only one prince who early realised the implication of the demand and refused it; but soon the presumptions of subsequent German officials aroused the Nyakyusa generally to a defence of their whole culture.

In this situation a complex range of choices was made by the princes. Some opted for alliance with the Germans; others moved towards combined defiance. In the case of two of the most important princes, Mwanjabala and Mwankenja, their long term decisions were in direct contrast to their initial responses to German demands.

Up to mid-1892 Mwanjabala had been the closest friend of the white men. Although critical of the missionary interference with the heroic cults, he nevertheless readily accepted the German flag in 1893. Mwankenja refused it. The reasons for this rejection had to do with the obvious intent of von Wissmann to assume jurisdiction in internal affairs within Mwankenja's polity, by requiring him to surrender a man accused of murder to whom he had granted sanctuary. The offices of Nauhaus as arbitrator helped the two parties to make a settlement, just as Nauhaus had succeeded earlier in reconciling the prince with recalcitrant youths of one of his villages.[58]

One of the reasons for Mwankenja's suspicion had been the belief that von Wissmann was the 'friend' of his rival Mwanjabala. As events matured, however, it became increasingly obvious that Mwankenja would be the chief collaborator with the Germans. From a pragmatic point of view, it was obvious that he would be most impressed with the kind of power the colonial pretenders could muster, for Rumbira (renamed Langenburg) became the centre of police and judicial activities for all Rungwe. Mwankenja was the closest major Nyakyusa prince to the German headquarters, and it is perhaps a truism that the more distant the princes, the less inclined they were to comply with administrative directives.

Mwanjabala, on the other hand, became the chief exponent of the classic Nyakyusa style as opposed to the kind of power and authority Langenburg claimed for itself. For continuing to grant sanctuary to alleged malefactors, refusing to supply porters, and explicitly denying the legitimacy of colonial overrule, he and other princes sustained severe police punishment in 1894. Mwakalukwa, a nephew of Mwanjabala, was among the most afflicted. Four people were killed during the burning of one of his villages and he lost seventy-three cattle through confiscation.[59] The Nyakyusa took these actions to be attacks by an external foe, and talked of concerted resistance, behind the renewed leadership of the central princes as military leaders. Wishing to avoid a major confrontation, the German official of the time, Baron von Eltz, took a conciliatory line, summoned the princes to Langenburg, and sought to instruct them more sympathetically about the implications of the new regime. Certain Nyakyusa who balked at 'talking things over' were persuaded by missionaries to do so.[60]

Although a *modus vivendi* appeared to be developing in 1895, based upon a degree of mutual accommodation, it should be remembered that the situation had altered significantly since 1891. Mwankenja was by 1895 positively cultivating the missionaries, on one occasion in September of that year turning out an estimated one thousand listeners to hear them preach.[61] The PaliKyala cult was passive politically and its priest was on fraternally warm terms with Nau-haus.[62] Mwanjabala and his nephews on the central plain, however, who had been active as supporters of the Mbasi Cult, continued to rely upon the system of traditional religion as essential to the Nyakyusa being and princely authority, and assumed a posture of resistance to Europeans who had so clearly super-seded the Ngoni and other African powers as the prime menace. An assessment of tactics was always a delicate matter for Nyakyusa princes, however, for they were compelled to balance public opinion against probabilities of success in a military confrontation. Especially on the central and eastern plain, the people had a record of military success and doubtless believed that they would succeed when it came to the showdown. Objectively, the Langenburg officials did not have a very impressive force to back up their claims to overrule. The regular police in 1894 numbered ten only. At the time of the Nyakyusa 'rising' of 1897, the entire colonial force available consisted of forty-five askaris and officers.[63]

The accommodation achieved in 1895 was subtle, and entailed some adapta-tion in the behaviour of rulers. Many princes, if faced with the conflict between their ideas of justice and those of the administration, withdrew from involve-ment in certain classes of cases, rather than risk losing the good opinion of their followers. Popular suspicion of Langenburg flourished because the alien askaris carrying out its orders were arrogant and very often symbolized a kind of justice biased in favour of the plaintiff. Being attuned to Nyakyusa values and promot-ing their image as independent from the officials, the missionaries were called upon increasingly to settle disputes. Von Eltz acquiesced in this development and in 1895 formally deputised the missionaries as courtholders. He further responded to African sensibilities by arranging for an official court circuit which would employ local assessors.[64]

The fragile political balance was rudely destroyed in mid-1896 when Captain von Elpons took over the district. On his first tour he decided that owing to their sympathy with local sentiment missionaries could not be trusted to administer 'German' justice. In returning to Langenburg he passed by way of Mwaya, to find the princes of the central plain and their people unwilling to offer supplies for his caravan or otherwise unready to defer to his authority. The tough, autocratic officer had never met such a rich but independent-minded people.[65]

The number of patrols and punitive actions in Rungwe increased sharply in 1897. Mwakiembe on the western plain was attacked because he refused food to askaris. The Lufilio area near Wangemannshöh was rocked by a fierce engagement in August, after which von Elpons began to accuse the Berlin missionaries of conspiring with the Nyakyusa against him. Other actions took place in Ukinga, where the people received quite clear indications that the Lutherans were on their side. Just a year after von Elpons arrived, the scene was set for a rising.

In early November of 1897, the princes were ordered to assemble at Mwan-kenja's, then to proceed to Langenburg, presumably to be lectured by the now hated von Elpons. On 22 November the princes sent word of their refusal. The next day, a hundred of Mwakalukwa's cattle were driven across the Mbasi river, away from Langenburg. This herd joined with the rest of the cattle which together with women and children were being sent to safer places. The resolve to fight it out with the German administration had crystallised. No missionary was permitted to arbitrate and deputations from Langenburg were rebuffed.[66] Mwankenja alone responded when Christian Bunk, the acting head of the Berlin Mission, called the princes to discuss matters. Mwankenja adhered to his pro-European policy and compelled his nephew Mwakabolofa also to stay out of the league of resisters.[67]

For their part the resistant princes now turned to the heroic tradition to legitimise and consecrate their resistance. For a prince like Mwanjabala, who had once supported the Mbasi priests, there was now no alternative but to support the Lwembe. The league of resistant princes met at the Lwembe shrine at Lubaga on 25 November, turning to the Lwembe because no other place and frame of reference for large-scale mobilisation existed. Ordinarily princes conducted ritual preparations for war in their own polity, but Lubaga was a ritual centre not only for the princes of Selya and of 'Nyakyusa proper', but also of the Kinga, who had likewise been goaded by the activities of the askari. It is unknown what role Lwembe himself played in the ceremony or whether anyone represented the German enemy as a pestilence, seizing cattle and disturbing the people. Reports heard by missionaries made it clear that all the anticipated booty had been apportioned in advance, true to custom. Whether just the officials were to be driven out, or all white men, remained in doubt even if it was known that missionary possessions had been claimed in the preliminaries.[68]

An important reason for consecrating the confrontation properly was that the princes were under great pressure of public opinion, and the whole style of religion and politics was in crisis. The young men, as usual, wanted to fight. The *waganga* and diviners, certain reports suggest, were also active agitators. These practitioners had apparently felt threatened by the activities of a German medical officer, whose death they claimed to be through the revenge of the spirits.[69] Just as von Elpons' summons was instrumental in causing the princes to coalesce and resolve to act, so spontaneous popular support and pressure had its specific impulses. Three hundred people from Mwakalinga's villages, for example, had been conscripted to work at Langenburg. Resolving not to tolerate the harsh treatment there any longer, they had decamped and returned home to spread the story of their experiences. At about the same time, a man named in a complaint was taken in chains to prison at Langenburg, where he became paralysed and was sent home to die.[70] So it was that the miscarriage of justice, resentment against labour levies and antagonism towards askari raids brought public outrage and pressure on the princes to a peak, at the very moment von Elpons decided to call them to order.

The Nyakyusa camped on the lakeshore, eagerly defensive. They sent a broken spear to von Elpons and kept watch day and night on the beach for the enemy to respond to the challenge. Time passed without response. Growing impatient, they sent a man to Langenburg to tell von Elpons that 'he need only come, they were ready'.[71] Where Nyakyusa taunts failed, the appearance of a Kinga force just an hour's march south of Langenburg succeeded. Fearing an attack from two sides, von Elpons made a pre-emptive strike at Mwaya. In the early hours of 2 December, 1897, the Maxim gun proved definitively that the era of traditional warfare was over. Mwakalinga died in the battle and was mourned as a good gentle man who had been forced by the pressure of his people into a fight he did not want.[72]

Eye witnesses estimated the fatalities at between thirty and fifty.[73] Later tradition puts the number at five hundred, a figure with no factual credibility, but a poetic justification if this battle at Mwaya is understood as the last stand of an integrated religious and political style.[74] The heroic tradition and political authority thereafter became increasingly dissociated.

During the last years of the century, the colonial regime pushed its effective control farther and farther into the uplands, not without spilling 'much innocent blood'.[75] Von Elpons reformed to the extent of employing more local men in the police, but his aim continued to be unquestioning subjugation. As indices of his progress, he took the volume of cases submitted to his court and the turn-out of labour. Under sustained colonial pressure, the peoples of Rungwe could not go back to their old ideas of a religious and economic order. Taxation confirmed the revolution. The Christian era began in Rungwe not because of a spiritual conversion but because, even while to European eyes the Nyakyusa and Kukwe remained unreconciled, certain leaders showed great initiative in starting schools to gain the new *ifingila*, literacy.[76] Mission stations provided a certain protection and the possibility of earning cash, another symbol of new times. Christian theology gradually took root in church communities, spread through missionary education and eventually coloured the vestiges of the heroic tradition.

To summarise briefly, it is evident that the heroic tradition was the major common mechanism for united action in an otherwise segmented society. The cults within the tradition were subject to change and did alter as a result of political and economic crises. Their elasticity provided for the continued integration of the Nyakyusa universe. Moreover, through the consolidation of the heroic tradition at Lubaga, there existed in 1897 a ritual centre at which to mobilise resistance on an enlarged scale. But the rising was a last stand. Thereafter pressures of colonialism and new sources of power shattered the traditional synthesis.

NOTES

[1] See George Park, 'Kinga Priests: the Politics of Pestilence', in M. J. Swartz, V. W. Turner and A. Tuden (eds.) *Political Anthropology* (Chicago 1966) pp. 229 ff.

[2] The Ngonde of northern Malawi and the Kukwe, to the north of the Nyakyusa, both honour the charter of Kyungu, whose descendents ruled the Ngonde. While the Kukwe acknowledged the Kyungu line to be superior ritually, they had their own local secluded prince-priest as well.

[3] Rungwe was called Kondeland by the early Scottish, Moravian and Lutheran missionaries. In British times it became Tukuyu.

[4] Nyakyusa, when unqualified, will refer to the rulers and people of the plain and Selya. For a useful ethnographic survey, see Monica Wilson *Peoples of the Nyasa-Tanganyika Corridor* (Capetown 1959).

[5] See, for example, L. Monteith Fotheringham *Adventures in Nyasaland* (London 1891) p. 285. This usage of the term 'prince' was introduced by S. R. Charsley in his useful discussion of Nyakyusa politics in the 1890s *The Princes of Nyakyusa* E.A.S. 32 (Nairobi 1969) pp. 45 ff.

[6] Monica Wilson *Communal Rituals of the Nyakyusa* (London 1959) Chapter 2 passim and

p. 154. I include Mbasi as one of the brothers because he was autonomous in the 1890s. Although Kyungu of Ngonde belongs to the same genre, he does not feature in the Nyakyusa versions of the heroic tradition.

[7] *Berliner Missionsberichte (BMB)* 1902, 48–9.

[8] *Idem.*

[9] Wilson *Communal Rituals* pp. 26–7, 30, 48.

[10] Priests at Lubaga claimed in 1935 that formerly, in addition to performing rituals when princes came to them in circumstances of misfortune, they had initiated rituals by means of prophecy. The question of initiative is important in terms both of religion and politics. There is no evidence available, however, to back up these claims by the priests. See Godfrey Wilson, 'An Introduction to Nyakyusa Society' *Bantu Studies* X (1936) p. 288.

[11] Monica Wilson *Divine Kings and the 'Breath of Men'* Frazer Lecture (Cambridge 1959) p. 22.

[12] Wilson *Communal Rituals* pp. 56 ff.; Charsley *op. cit.* p. 53.

[13] Monica Wilson *Good Company: A Study of Nyakyusa Age-Villages* (London 1951) chapter 5.

[14] Wilson *Communal Rituals* pp. 9, 57, 124.

[15] Wilson *Good Company* pp. 163 ff.

[16] Godfrey Wilson *op. cit.* p. 282.

[17] *Ibid.* pp. 287–8.

[18] *Ibid.* p. 288.

[19] Monica Wilson *Communal Rituals* p. 28.

[20] Godfrey Wilson *The Constitution of the Ngonde* Rhodes–Livingstone Institute Paper no. 1 (Livingstone 1939), p. 9.

[21] *Ibid.* p. 31.

[22] M. Wilson *Communal Rituals* p. 18.

[23] M. Wilson *Divine Kingship* p. 23.

[24] *BMB* 1902, p. 49.

[25] M. Wilson *Common Rituals* pp. 8–9.

[26] *Ibid.* p. 47.

[27] Alexander Merensky *Deutsche Arbeit am Njassa* (Berlin 1894) p. 212.

[28] *Ibid.* p. 112.

[29] M. Wilson *Communal Rituals* p. 47.

[30] Charsley *op. cit.* p. 34.

[31] Merensky *op. cit.* p. 112.

[32] *Ibid.* p. 112.

[33] Bain to Laws, 14 August, 1888 (National Library of Scotland 7890).

[34] See Lazarus Mwakalukwa's account in the Tanzanian National Archives, Southern Highlands Province Book,

[35] D. R. MacKenzie *The Spirit-Ridden Konde* (London 1925) chapter 13.

[36] Bain to Laws, 11 April, 1887 (N.L.S. 7890).

[37] Bain to Laws, 11 April, 1887 (N.L.S. 7890).

[38] Mwakalukwa's account (T.N.A. S.H.P. Book).

[39] See H. W. Macmillan, 'The Origins and Development of the African Lakes Company', unpublished Ph.D. thesis, Edinburgh University, 1970.

[40] Mwakalukwa's account (T.N.A. S.H.P. Book).

[41] Bain to Laws, 14 August, 1888 (N.L.S. 7890).

[42] See Marcia Wright *German Missions in Tanganyika, 1891–1941: Lutherans and Moravians in the Southern Highlands* (Oxford 1971) p. 39.

[43] Bain was able to patch up relations between the men, partly because of his neutrality, partly because both sides valued the support of the whites at this juncture. Murray to Laws, 27 October, 1888; Bain to Laws, 12 January, 1889 (N.L.S. 7890).

[44] *BMB* 1892, 360. See also Merensky *op. cit.* p. 290.

[45] On the score of economic complacency, see D. Kerr-Cross, 'Crater Lakes North of Lake Nyasa', in *The Geographical Journal* V (1895) p. 118.

[46] See Elmslie to Laws, 3 October, 1889 (N.L.S. 7890).

[47] Mwakalukwa's account (T.N.A. S.H.P. Book). See also Oscar Gemuseus, 'The Chronicle of Rungwe in German Times' *ibid.* 1938.

[48] The missionaries sent by the Berlin Mission Society (Lutheran) are frequently referred to collectively as the Berliners. For details of their history see Marcia Wright *op. cit.*

[49] Nauhaus to Committee of the Berlin Mission (Berlin Com.) 26 December, 1893 (Berlin IV 1 8b).

[50] *BMB* 1892, 359–360.

[51] *BMB* 1892, 357. See also Merensky *op. cit.*

[52] Charsley *op. cit.* chapter 2. See also Merensky *op. cit.* pp. 94, 123.

[53] Merensky *op. cit.* p. 214.

[54] Wright *op. cit.* p. 55.

[55] Nauhaus to Berlin Com. 26 December, 1893 (Berlin IV 1 8b.)

[56] Nauhaus to Berlin Com. 26 December, 1893 (Berlin IV 1 8b); *BMB* 1893, 546.

[57] Nauhaus to Berlin Com. 26 December, 1893 (Berlin IV 1 8b).

[58] *BMB* 1893, 463, 521.

[59] von Elpons to Governor, 31 October, 1898 (TNA G9/27).

[60] See reports in *Missionsblatt der Brüdergemeine* (*HMB*) 1894 and 1895.

[61] *BMB* 1896, 222.

[62] See Nauhaus, 'Description of Ikombe' (1897) (Berlin IV 1 8b).

[63] von Elpons to Governor, 31 October, 1898 (TNA G9/27); Zache to Governor, 30 January, 1901 (German Central Archives, Potsdam [DZAP] Bez. 1-19).

[64] AAKA to Berlin Com. 14 June, 1897 (TNA G9/27). See also *BMB* 1896, 220-221; *BMB* 1897, 219.

[65] von Elpons to Governor, 31 October, 1898 (TNA G9/27).

[66] von Elpons to Governor, 31 October, 1898 (TNA G9/27).

[67] Bunk to Berlin Com., 6 December, 1897 (Berlin IV 1 8b).

[68] *BMB* 1898, 195; *HMB* 1898, 182.

[69] von Elpons to Governor, 31 October, 1898 (TNA G9/27); Periodical Accounts (PA) 1898, 624 f.

[70] Bunk to Berlin Com., 6 December, 1897 (Berlin IV 1 8b).

[71] Bunk to Berlin Com., 6 December, 1897 (Berlin IV 1 8b).

[72] Gemuseus, 'Chronicle' (TNA SHP Book).

[73] Bunk to Berlin Com., 6 December, 1897 (Berlin IV 1 8b).

[74] Mwakalukwa's account (T.N.A. S.H.P. Book).

[75] Nauhaus to Berlin Com., 30 March, 1900 (Berlin IV 1 8b).

[76] Oskar Gemuseus *Sakalija Mwakasungula* (Hamburg 1953), p. 8.

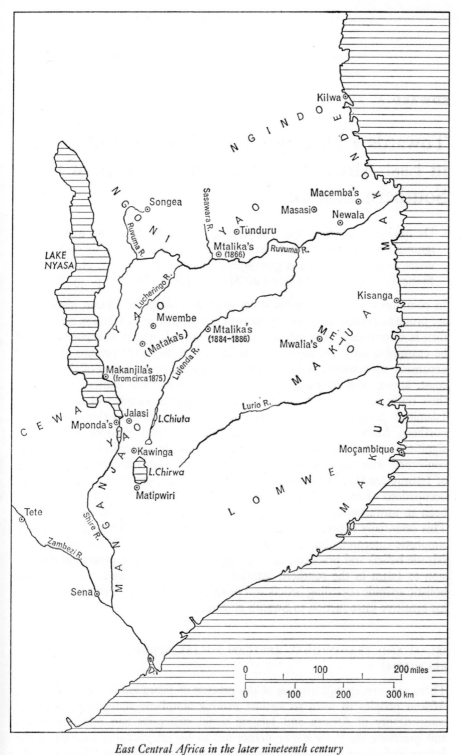

East Central Africa in the later nineteenth century

Adapted from E. A. Alpers, 'Trade, State and Society among the Yao in the Nineteenth Century' *Jl.Afr.Hist.*X, 3 (1969) p. 408.

EDWARD A. ALPERS

Towards a History of the Expansion of Islam in East Africa: the Matrilineal Peoples of the Southern Interior

De quelques questions que j'ai posées, j'ai tiré la conviction que ces Yao ignorent tout des origines de leur conversion. Ils savent qu'ils sont musul-mans, comme leur pères et grand-pères; ils ne cherchent pas plus loin.
François Balsan, *Terres Vierges au Mozambique* (Paris 1960) p. 49.

In common with a great many other neglected topics in African history, we are prone to assume considerably more about the history of Islam in East Africa than is warranted by the actual state of our knowledge. In this paper, I shall be examining only one aspect of that history, namely, the process of Islamic expansion up-country, away from the already Islamised towns of the Swahili coast, among various peoples who had previously been content to practise their traditional religions. More specifically, my discussion will focus on the Islamised peoples of the southern interior, including southern Tanzania, northern Mozambique and southern Malawi, which comprises the most significant area of Islamic penetration away from the coast. In this essay, I am concerned with the process of Islamic *expansion*, rather than with the nature of Islamic *practice*, in the southern interior. Indeed, one of the annoying pre-occupations of many scholarly discussions of Islam in Africa, in general, has been an unwarranted concern over the 'unorthodox' nature of African Islam. This essentially deprecating attitude has, it seems to me, frequently led to a simplistic interpretation of the dynamic interaction between pre-Islamic and Islamic beliefs and practices. Accordingly, in looking at the process of conver-sion to Islam in the southern interior of East Africa, I prefer to adopt the holistic attitude regarding beliefs and practices expressed by Peter Lienhardt in his sensitive introduction to Swahili culture.[1]

ISLAM AND TRADITIONAL AFRICAN SOCIAL STRUCTURE AND RELIGION

There are now enough studies of the process of Islamisation among different African peoples to warn us against making simplistic statements about the compatibility of African and Islamic social structures and religious beliefs and practices. As Peter Rigby points out in his enlightening analysis of the factors underlying the negative response of the Gogo to Islam, 'What must be demonstrated is the compatibility (or incompatibility) of specific structural relations and the accompanying religious and cosmological ideas within a society, with the basic elements of Islamic religion and its cultural correlates.'[2]

That the adaptability of Islam is not peculiar to Africa is made perfectly clear in G. E. von Grunebaum's brilliant essay on 'Islam: Its Inherent Power of Expansion and Adaptation'.[3]

> The gradual drifting away of canon law from operational effectiveness . . . fortified the catholicity of the Muslim institution . . . On the one hand, it facilitated the integration into the community of as yet alien communities by allowing them to carry over into their existence as Muslims much of their traditional way of life; on the other hand, it provided the community with a norm that was all the more readily acceptable because to a large extent there was no insistence on full compliance.

Thus, he remarks elsewhere, 'The acceptance into Islam of an individual or a group on the basis of declared intention to belong constitutes the premise of Islamic inclusiveness and hence its amazing cross-cultural absorptiveness.' At another point in his essay, von Grunebaum echoes this theme in his observation that: 'In the general consciousness, the intention to be and to remain a Muslim counts for more than the failings that are observable in its implementation.' In this respect, and of particular importance for Africa, where ritual observance is the foundation of religious practice, he emphasises: 'It is orthopraxy that matters most of all, not orthodoxy.'

Regarding Islam in Africa as a more particular phenomenon, we are admirably served by I. M. Lewis' comprehensive and stimulating introduction to *Islam in Tropical Africa*.[4] For Africa, Lewis suggests that in the

> process of the Islamization of traditional belief the most important aspect of Muslim religious phenomenology which has greatly facilitated its initial impact and appeal . . . is its truly catholic recognition of the multiplicity of mystical power . . . as long as God's lofty pre-eminence is not compromised, the Quran itself provides scriptural warrant for the existence of a host of subsidiary powers and spirits . . . Consequently, as long as traditional beliefs can be adjusted in such a way that they fall into place within a Muslim schema in which the absoluteness of Allah remains unquestioned, Islam does not ask its new adherents to abandon confidence in all their mystical forces.[5]

This capacity was very much a factor in the expansion of Islam in East Central Africa.[6]

All the matrilineal peoples of East Central Africa share a common belief in a supreme deity, a phenomenon which Fr Franz Schildknecht refers to as 'practical monotheism'.[7] Thus, at the most abstract cosmological plane there was a ubiquitous religious concept that could be readily identified with Allah.[8] But religious practice did not centre on the direct worship of this supreme deity, who was variously called *mulungu* (Yao and Ngindo), *muluku* (Makua) or *nnungu* (Makonde). Rather, it was 'ancestor veneration' which constituted the mainspring of traditional African religion in the southern interior.[9]

Unfortunately, we do not know as much as we should about the cosmological conceptions involved in 'ancestor veneration' among the several related peoples whose conversion to Islam is the focus of this essay. For the Yao, however, a beginning can be made with Alexander Hetherwick's description of *lisoka*, which he states was the Yao equivalent of the soul, shade or spirit of each human being, the 'inspiring agent' in his life.[10] The *lisoka* bore the same relationship to the body as did a picture (*ciwilili*) to reality. When Hetherwick first tried to photograph some Yao he was refused, as it was feared that he was stealing their *masoka*. (Unfortunately, Hetherwick does not indicate whether or not this conceit reflected unadulterated pre-Islamic Yao cosmology.) Dreams, madness and epileptic fits were all said to be '*wa masoka*' while *masoka* were also believed to be the 'inspiring agents' of the 'witch detective' who was called into a village to locate the source of trouble in particularly thorny disputes. Finally, *lisoka* was a specifically human phenomenon and was not transferable to animals or objects. At death a man's *lisoka* left the earth for all time and went to *mulungu*, i.e. entered the spirit world. There it had powers which it never had on earth, but the living prayed only to *mulungu* and never to *masoka*. For the Yao, Hetherwick writes, *mulungu* was a collective 'aggregate of the spirits of all the dead', but lacking personal identity. Nevertheless, he claims, Yao did imply belief in a personified God when they said that '*mulungu* did so and so'.[11] Hetherwick's interpretation of Yao religious cosmology, especially his understanding that the *masoka* of the dead elders acquired powers which they did not have while those elders were living, would appear at first sight to be in conflict with Igor Kopytoff's argument that it is the continuum in 'eldership' which is most significant, rather than the dichotomy between living elders and dead ancestors.[12] But Hetherwick was writing in 1902, and as an ordained missionary of the Church of Scotland Mission in Central Africa he cannot be said to have been exempt from precisely the sort of Western connotations which are the object of Kopytoff's revisionist essay. Nevertheless, Hetherwick's discussion opens the way for a less simplistic and more specific appreciation of Yao cosmology and its relationship to Yao 'ancestor veneration'.

Among the Yao there have been several different levels of 'ancestor veneration' co-existing over the past century, each corresponding to the scale of social and political organisation. At the most personal, microcosmic level, 'ancestor veneration' seems to have involved only members of the local matrilineage, especially those who formed a discrete residential unit, or village. According to Clyde Mitchell, 'the depth of a matrilineage within a village is seldom more than five or six generations from the founding ancestress to the newborn children . . . The ancestress is known as the *likolo* or *lipata*, words which also refer to the trunk of a tree.' Thus, Mitchell continues,

> the founding ancestress is seen as the stem or root from which all the members of the lineage have sprung, and the various sections of the matrilineage are seen as the branches (*nyambi*). This symbol of the lineage appears also during offerings to the ancestors. The chief, or headman, in making the oblation, pours the beer or sprinkles the flour at the root (*lipata*) of a shrine-tree (*nsolo*).[13]

At the same time, however, a Yao village represented a corporate structure which often included individuals who were not members of the core matrilineage which gave rise to it. Accordingly, as Duff MacDonald noted during his mission to the Mangoche Yao in the Shire Highlands of Malawi from 1878 to 1881, the village headman presents prayers and offerings on behalf of all that live in his village . . . It is his relatives that are the village gods. Everyone that lives in the village recognizes these gods but if anyone removes to another village he changes his gods. He now recognizes the gods of his new chief (i.e., headman).[14]

Clearly, then, 'ancestor veneration' among the Yao was intimately associated with local political and social structure and was not simply dictated by kinship relations.

Interestingly, and at first sight confusingly, when Hetherwick comes to his description of 'ancestor veneration' in the village, he makes absolutely no mention of the *nsolo* tree, which is central to Mitchell's description. Instead, he observes that the village shrine for 'ancestor veneration' was the grave-hut of the departed chief, or village headman. Such a shrine marked the grave of almost every important chief or headman, Hetherwick continues, and

> is regarded as the abode of his soul or the spot where his *mulungu* is most accessible. If his successor is about to undertake a long journey or enter on any warlike expedition against an enemy or neighbour, he must first *kutaga mbepesi*, place an offering here to secure the favour and assistance of the *mulungu* of the dead.

Chiefly shrines, in his day, were located in any village which had been inhabited for a long time and were regarded with awe. If the village had moved from its original site, as was not infrequent, the shrine was not forgotten and propitiatory and periodical visits were made to it by the appropriate authorities of the living community.[15]

Happily, Canon Lamburn's treatment of Yao society and religion in Tunduru resolves the apparent dichotomy between the 'ancestor veneration' at the *nsolo* and at the shrine of a chiefly grave-hut, and establishes that both practices could and did exist within the same religious system:

> The chief's first wife, the most important woman in the community, pounds and grinds fine flour. This is taken by her husband to the tree known as the 'msoro' tree, and here, all the adult members of the village congregate . . . All kneel and the chief addresses the spirits of his dead ancestors, usually by name, going back for some two or three generations, and he begs the blessings that are needed at the moment, rain or the prosperity of an initiation rite, or whatever the need may be. As he does this he sprinkles the flour so that it falls into tiny cones; meanwhile the people keep up a rhythmical handclapping with great reverence. At the end the remainder of the flour is poured out to unite the tiny cones into one big one, and at last they bring in the name of God—'Chonde Ambuje Mlungu Mtukolele chanasa' (We beseech Thee, o Lord God, have mercy upon us).[16]

At the same time, it is clear that the ancestral graves of both Sultans and chiefs (or chiefs and headmen, in Mitchell's terminology), were regarded with the same veneration in Tunduru during the 1940s as was observed at the beginning of the century by Hetherwick in southern Malawi. 'To take what is the headstone of a chief's grave would be an offense punishable by death.' Indeed,

Lamburn records: 'The late Sultan Mtalika is known to have killed a boy of whom he was extremely fond just because the boy had the audacity to take a roll of cloth off the grave of the deceased uncle of Mtalika.'[17]

With this evidence now before us, I think that we can not only begin to see the basic elements of Yao 'ancestor veneration' but that we can also infer a cosmological capacity for it to develop from a localised, kin-determined religious system, focused on worship at the *nsolo* tree, into a chiefly cult, focused on the chief's grave, extending over a large, territorially defined political unit. Furthermore, it is clear from the descriptions of Mitchell, Hetherwick and Lamburn that every manifestation of 'ancestor veneration' among the Yao emphasised communal, rather than individual, values, in common with virtually all traditional African religions. All of these factors—belief in *mulungu* and of his accessibility through the medium of the *masoka* of the dead elders, the emphasis on communal over individual religious values, and the development of broadly inclusive and politically significant chiefly 'ancestor cults' around the powerful Yao chiefs who dominated much of the nineteenth-century history of this region—seem to have favourably predisposed the Yao for the spread of Islam among them.

Although the sources are both less extensive and less satisfactory for the other matrilineal peoples of the southern interior, they point to an essential similarity in the basic nature of traditional 'ancestor veneration'. At the same time, it becomes evident that there are differences to be noted between the observances of the Yao and their neighbours, and that these differences are primarily a function of different political structures. Accordingly, in discussing the latter I will focus my attention on the relationship between political and religious organisation. First, there were never any centralised chiefdoms among the Makonde of Tanzania or the Maconde of Mozambique; the same was true for the Mwera, Machinga, Ndonde and Ngindo of southern Tanzania. The political authority of both the village headmen and the head of the clan, was clearly circumscribed. Nor were there any external stimuli which might have precipitated political centralisation among them in the pre-colonial period.[18] Second, the political structure of the various Makua-Lomwe peoples seems to stand mid-way between that of these peoples, with their ritually significant but politically weak clan organisation and their total absence of centralised territorial chiefship, and that of the Yao, with their ritually and politically powerful chiefship structure, which has all but obliterated any traces of significant clan organisation.[19]

In his paper on 'Missionary Adaptation of African Religious Institutions: The Masasi Case', T. O. Ranger's notes on the Makua focus on their clan structure, for there were no important Makua chiefs, or indeed clan heads, who migrated into Masasi from the south.[20] The picture in Mozambique itself, however, reflects more vividly the variety of political structures which abounded among the Makua-Lomwe. In the early 1880s, H. E. O'Neill, H. M. Consul at Mozambique, variously described their political organisation as 'a number of petty despotisms' or 'a number of confederations of petty chieftains', depending on where he was travelling. In the latter case, O'Neill noted, the subordinate chiefs were completely independent in their control of internal affairs. 'It appears to be only in regard to external matters affecting the general weal, such as difficulties with neighbouring tribes, or war, that the smaller chiefs are subject to the decision of their leader.'[21] Writing sixty years later on the Makua of Meto, which is located north of the Lúrio and east of the Lujenda Rivers, whence most of the Makua immigrants into Tanzania originated, Fr. Gerard noted the attrition of strong and extensive territorial chieftainship.[22] Only in the description of Makua religion provided by Abel dos Santos Baptista, who served as an administrator in their country, do we find evidence of the sort of chiefly cult which we have already noted among the Yao and which must surely have developed around powerful chieftainships like that of Mauruça, which dominated Itoculo and plagued the Portuguese at Mozambique Island from the late sixteenth until the end of the nineteenth century.[23]

According to Santos Baptista, Makua 'ancestor veneration' in the late 1940s was closely related to the clan structure, each clan (nihimo) having its own particular place of worship (nifulo). This could be a tree (capurene), or a cemetery (mahie), or simply a designated spot (nifuloni), where a deceased clansman had died. Each member of the living family (òlápa) participated in turn in the ceremonial invocation of the dead elders, which was accompanied by the hand clapping of the others. Matrilineal order was scrupulously maintained in the religious rites. The first to officiate in the ritual supplication was the great wife of the family, who called in order the founding ancestress (àcúlo; cf. Yao likolo), the great-aunts (ànaque), the great-uncles (àhálo), the grandparents (àpápa or âtîti) and the brothers (nulupaliaca and muàmuáca). Sorghum, flour, water and beer were offered to their spirits, but of these flour was the most significant and could under no circumstances be omitted. In fact, the name for the flour, èpépa, was given to the entire ceremony of 'ancestor veneration'.[24] The whole ceremony was concluded with feasting, drinking and dancing.[25]

The same basic ritual pattern of observance was maintained in the 'ancestor veneration' which focused on the chiefdom, rather than the family. Only here, as with the Yao, the congregation, so to speak, included everyone resident in the territory of the chiefdom who was subordinant to the political and ritual authority of the chief. In each chiefdom, Santos indicates, the chief's nifulo was located close to his village and served the needs of his own clan. 'But it also serves for the collective ritual practised by the tribe [sic], in cases of calamity which embrace the people in general. Only individuals of the nihimo of the chief officiate, however, as a rule preceded by his mother (puiamuene).' The names of all the deceased chiefs were invoked, and the ceremony, which was also known as òlápa (living family), was followed by feasting and dancing, 'in the most unrestrained delight, until the greatest ecstasy and rapture is attained'.[26] The similarity with Lamburn's description of Yao chiefly 'ancestor veneration' in Tunduru is striking. And when we consider the description of the already Islamised ndalanga dance for the chiefly 'ancestral' spirits of Mataka, the most important of all the Yao chiefs, we can begin to see more clearly that these practices could provide an important entry point for Islam.

The ndalanga, lasting three days,

is the dance of the chief—it is only organized by Chief Mataka and by Mwenye Gwaja with the consent of the Chief. The primary object is to 'piga sadaka', a propitiation of the departed spirits of the ancestors.[27]

Meredith Sanderson has pointed out that *sadaka* is derived from the Arabic word for alms, *sadaqa*, while Mitchell confirms more generally from Malawi 'that the ancestor cult survives as part of the practice of Islam'. The feasts associated with these observances are called *sadaka* and at them Islamic texts are chanted in Arabic.[28] With regard to the specific sociological significance of the development of more powerful institutions of chiefship to the spread of Islam, however, the question which is raised by this example of Afro-Islamic syncretism is what structural aspects of chiefly observances existed among the Yao which facilitated the absorption of Islamic practices. Here we move away from the realm of 'ancestor veneration' *per se* and turn to a consideration of chiefly installation ceremonies among the Yao and Makua.

Mwenye Gwaja not only had responsibility for organising Sultan Mataka's *ndalanga* dance, it was also his duty to officiate over the burial of a dead sultan and the installation of a new one.[29] Mitchell's research vividly shows the great importance of Yao installation ceremonies:

> First, there is the ritual death and rebirth of the village headman. The heir is 'killed' by a blow with the fist on the forehead, but is reborn the headman. The Yao do not believe that the spirit of the headman is inherited by the heir; he has only eaten the name.

Consonant with this idea, which also confirms Hetherwick's discussion of the fate of a man's *lisoka* at death, he inherited the wives and property of the deceased.

> But this structural reincarnation of the headman has the important implication that the headman is immortal. He shares this characteristic with the group of which he is the leader . . . In his rebirth he occupies the status that his predecessor held before he died, in both the kinship system and the political structure.[30]

What was true for headmen was equally true for chiefs or sultans, and the political ramifications were naturally more significant.

All of this has parallels in Makua installation ceremonies, as described by Santos Baptista. The death of a chief was signalled by beating upon the royal drum (*icavento*.) Chiefs were usually buried in hills and in private burial grounds, and access to them was limited to members of their own clan, led by 'the old *nihumo*—a sort of prime-minister of the chief'. A round hut with a single doorway was built over the grave. 'From the death of the chief until the nomination of his successor, the *nihumo* assumed the 'regency' of the chiefdom.' The period of mourning, which lasted about a month or more, was declared by the *nihumo* and marked by the killing of all cocks in the kingdom. No others might be acquired until after the nomination of a new chief. The successor was chosen by the *nihumo* in consultation first with the uncles (*mezulahuma*) and cousins (*muanahuma*) of the deceased chief, and then with his mother (*puiamuene*) or eldest living aunt. The announcement of the successor, who was seized forcibly in his hut and whisked off under cover to another, was marked by the beating of the *icavento*. There he spent two days in seclusion with two of his predecessor's wives, one of whom he chose to be his great wife. Finally, his installation ceremony involves a supplication by the *puiamuene* of the spirit of his predecessor at his grave.[31]

Although the descriptions are not exactly the same, it seems indisputable that Mwenye Gwaja was Mataka's equivalent of the Makua *nihumo*. And at least one other important Yao chief, Mtalika (in 1881), is said to have had a 'prime minister'.[32] Similarly, although Santos Baptista does not specifically use the terms 'ritual death and rebirth', such is implied in the communal killing of all cocks and in the new chief's choosing of a great wife from among the wives of the deceased chief. Finally, although Santos Baptista says nothing about it, structural reincarnation and perpetual kinship among the Makua chiefs are further attested to by the historical perseverance of titular names like Mauruça over three centuries, as recorded in Portuguese documentation.

The significance of these installation practices for religious change among the Yao and the Makua becomes apparent when we refer to the important theoretical work of Professor Victor W. Turner. Here, we are most interested in his discussion of rites of passage, especially life-crisis rituals, 'marking the transition from one phase of life or social status to another', and their relevance to chiefly installation ceremonies. 'These "crisis" ceremonies not only concern the individuals on whom they are centered,' Turner writes, 'but also mark changes in the relationships of all people connected with them by ties of blood, marriage, cash, political control, and in many other ways.'[33] Turner also emphasises the crucial importance in the transitional process of liminality, the period between phases when the subject is 'structurally, if not physically, "invisible" '. In this ambiguous state of being he includes 'a candidate undergoing initiation rites or a chief-designate before his installation'. Symbolically, 'neophytes are neither living nor dead from one aspect, and both living and dead from another. Their condition is one of ambiguity and paradox, a confusion of all customary categories.' Thus suspended from all constraints which normally operate in a society, the liminal period, Turner suggests, represents 'a realm of pure possibility whence novel configurations of ideas and relations may arise'.[34]

Turner is primarily concerned with the symbolic possibilities of all this, but if he is correct, the liminal period during the installation rites of a chief would seem to be a structurally ideal situation for the introduction of Islamic connotations and practices that would, perforce, permeate the entire society, however small or large. A specific illustration of this is the conversion of Monjesa, 'who adopted Islam as his official court religion just before becoming chief [of a Machinga Yao group] in about 1880, and who accordingly changed his name to Zuraf, or Jalasi, as it is rendered by the Yao'.[35] And perhaps the widespread assimilation of the concept of *sadaka* among Islamised Yao also owes its prominence to its early association with the chiefly *ndalanga* dance at the time of installation. Thus, although the significance of chiefs in the spread of Islam in Africa has long been recognised,[36] we now have a more specific idea of the African sociological configurations which might have affected the acceptance of Islam by both Yao and Makua chiefs in the southern interior of East Africa. And with a more thorough appreciation of their traditional political and ritual authority we can begin to see why their conversion would have greatly facilitated, encouraged and perhaps obligated their subjects to do likewise.

There remains one other social and religious institution to be discussed: initiation rites. Since Professor Ranger has so much to say on this subject in his paper on Masasi, I shall try to be brief and broadly interpretive.[37] Initiation ceremonies among the Yao have been very successfully Islamised, boys' and girls' alike. Unfortunately, there is almost nothing in the literature about the Islamisation of Makua initiation ceremonies, but among Muslim Makua this has almost certainly taken place. Following Turner again, these rites of passage clearly present an ideal opening for the spread of Islam in a particular society.[38]

Mitchell observes:

At the aggregation rites at the end of the period of seclusion, the star and crescent appears as one of the symbols along with the whale (*namungumi*), antelope (*mbalapi*), leopard (*cisuwi*), and other tribal effigies which are shown to the boys. Christianity in the south has had a similar effect.[39]

Similarly, the ritual bathing of the male neophytes which occurred at the end of their lengthy period of isolation admirably accommodated the entrance into Islam which was described by Amini bin Saidi as common among the Islamised Yao of Fort Johnston in about 1930:

In the morning [after the communal feast of the previous day which celebrated their return from the bush] the children go with the Mohammedan teacher to the river where they are baptized into the Mohammedan faith. They return at the third hour of the day [i.e. 9:00 a.m.] when each father pays the Mohammedan teacher 6d.

The ceremony then concluded along traditional lines back in the village.[40] Additionally, the fact that circumcision was an essential aspect of male initiation rites among the Yao and Makua surely facilitated their Islamisation. Islam made few demands on the form of traditional Yao, and presumably Makua, initiation rites; there were opportunities within the traditional rites for the introduction of specifically Islamic symbols and practices; and the very nature of such life-crisis rituals made them ideally susceptible to religious innovation.

In looking at the sources on Yao and Makua social and religious structure, however, I am much more impressed with initiation rites as a *vehicle*, rather than an agent, of Islamisation. Chiefly control of initiation ceremonies was a very important index and manifestation of political and ritual power. To have surrendered control of the initiation rites to an independent religious authority, in this case a local *mwalimu*, would have been to lose considerable prestige and a very real source of social control over one's people. Mitchell records that this was already taking place in Jalasi's area in the late 1940s.[41] But the very significance of control over the initiation rites to Yao headmen and chiefs suggests to me that however liable to Islamisation they proved to be, in the precolonial period the political strength of the chiefs was too much in need of constant ritual reinforcement and legitimisation to have allowed this to happen unchallenged. Any Muslim interloper who attempted it would surely have suffered the same fate as befell the favoured, though errant, boy who despoiled the grave of Mtalika's uncle. Instead, as I have already suggested and as I hope to document below, it was the conversion of the Yao and Makua chiefs which proved to be the crucial internal factor effecting the spread of Islam among their people. And although there is little hard substantiating evidence, I suggest that their control of initiation rites was probably the most effective way of extending the faith to all of their people.

There is little information relating to the religious beliefs of the other matrilineal peoples of the southern interior, except to note that all shared the practice of 'ancestor veneration'. The only evidence which I have been able to find clearly relating any of the traditional, pre-Islamic religious practices of these people more specifically to the Yao–Makua–Makonde group, comes from Eugène de Froberville, a remarkable mid-nineteenth century French ethnographer who conducted interviews with Africans of slave origin at Mauritius. Froberville learned that the Ngindo had both male and female initiation rites, called *anhiago* (cf. Yao *unyago*), which for the boys involved circumcision. In beseeching *mulungu* they used the flour-cone augury and they also used the word *mbopehu* or *mbopei* for that symbol of worship, which is generically the same as the Yao word, *mbepesi*, which is ubiquitous in Masasi.[42] There is, then, at least some evidence at hand for grouping the social and religious practices of these matrilineal peoples of the southern Tanzanian coastal hinterland together with the Yao, Makua-Lomwe, and Makonde/Maconde. But the absence of the emergence of strong territorial chiefship among them during the pre-colonial era should warn us that we must look for other explanations of their predisposition to accept Islam than those which I have suggested for the Yao and Makua.

I have spent most of my time on the Yao because they are the most significant example of an almost completely Islamised people in the far interior of East Africa. And although the literature is insufficient to warrant firm conclusions, it strikes me that there were few essential differences in religious beliefs and practices among the major ethnic groups of the southern interior which might have differentially affected their response to Islam as an abstracted belief system. Rather, given a whole range of very favourable political, social and religious pre-conditions, the most significant variable internal factor in operation before the imposition of colonial rule was the existence or absence of territorial chiefdoms. These were most prevalent among the Yao, for most of whom Islam is synonymous with being Yao;[43] they were significant, though not universally so, among the Makua, more than half of whom are today Muslims; and they were totally absent among all the remaining matrilineal peoples of the the southern interior belief system complex, among whom Islam made almost no headway during the pre-colonial period. For these related peoples nearer to the Kilwa coast who did not have significant territorial chiefdoms, but who are today overwhelmingly Islamised, such as the Ngindo, Mwera, Machinga, Ndonde and Makonde (but not the Maconde of Mozambique, as we shall see below), the key variable factors seem to have been the nature of their relationship with Swahili society and the crisis in their societies which was brought about by the imposition of colonial rule, especially by their involvement in the Maji Maji Rising of 1905–7.

HISTORICAL EVIDENCE FOR THE SPREAD OF ISLAM

Most of what we know about the spread of Islam in the southern interior also pertains to the Yao. I have argued elsewhere that the Yao were probably trading with the coast of East Africa early in the seventeenth century. I have also attempted to demonstrate the intimacy of the economic ties with the Kilwa and Mozambique coasts in the eighteenth century. But it is only in the nineteenth century, when a new generation of powerful Yao chiefs emerged to dominate the region to the east of Lake Nyasa, that Islam seems to have begun to take hold among them.[44]

The first dateable evidence bearing witness to the permeation of coastal influence in Yaoland comes from David Livingstone, who in 1866 was the first European to travel through their territory since Gaspar Bocarro had done so in 1616. When he reached Mwembe, the town of Chief Mataka I Nyambi, Livingstone noted: 'He is about sixty years of age, dressed as an Arab . . . He had never seen any but Arabs before. He gave me a square house to live in, and indeed most of the houses here are square, for the Arabs are imitated in everything.'[45] In fact, as Abdallah vividly shows us, Mwembe was specifically designed by Mataka as a replica of a coastal community.

> Che Mataka . . . moved and built a village at Mloi; there he planted mangoes from the coast which grew, sprouted, and flourished. He was delighted and said, 'Ah! now I have changed Yao so that it resembles the coast, and the sweet fruits of the coast now will I eat in my own home; this place is no longer Mloi but its name is Mwembe, where I have planted the mango of the coast!'[46]

But Mataka I Nyambi, who died sometime between 1876 and 1880, was not the first Yao chief to convert to Islam. In fact, he never converted, for reasons which we shall soon see.

Instead, the first Yao chief to adopt Islam as his personal and 'court' religion was Makanjila III Banali, who Rangeley suggests was converted in about 1870.[47] If he is correct, as seems likely, then it means that all the descriptions that we have concerning Makanjila are of an already Islamised chief. Thus, from the almost exclusively European sources that are available to us, it is only for the Mataka chiefship that we can hope to discern the specific reasons determining why a decision was made to convert to Islam. For while it may be perfectly true to say that the long contact of these chiefs with the coast and their deep involvement in the slave trade naturally inclined them towards Islam, rather than Christianity, it is not historical to state categorically that this was the only operative reason for their conversion and the subsequent conversion of their people.

No Europeans visited Mataka again until 1875 when, following in the wake of Livingstone's call for a sustained Christian missionary effort in this part of the continent, a party headed by Bishop Edward Steere of the Anglican Universities' Mission to Central Africa reached Mwembe. Steere's observations on the Yao, and other African peoples with whom he was familiar, and on the struggle for their souls which he saw shaping up between Christianity and Islam, are typically lucid:

It is only on the young men of the present generation that Mohammedanism is beginning to exert a powerful influence, and this is just in proportion as they are struggling into some kind of civilization. It is therefore much more felt by the principal Yao chiefs than by the smaller, or by the less advanced Mweras.

The more thoughtful [Shambaa, in this case, although the same standard clearly operated in Steere's mind for the Yao] have unavoidably looked hitherto to the coast Mohammedans as the only people who had a religion to give to them. The coast people baptize them by dipping in a river, give them Arab names, charge them not to drink palm wine, nor to eat pork or the meat of any animal not slaughtered with the invocation of God's name, teach them an Arabic formula or two, fix them in the professed belief of only one God, and leave them with all their old charms and superstitions . . .

It is especially acceptable to the natives as giving them a recognized civilization. One can see in a moment what an immense social advantage it is to be admitted into such a community . . .

It seems to me morally certain that the Yaos will be Christians or Mohammedans before very long, and I think the question will turn a good deal upon which is the first to write and read their language. The Mohammedans have the advantage now, and we must work hard to win it from them. [48]

Steere apparently did not fail to convince Mataka that Christianity might offer him these same 'civilising' benefits, for in 1877 Nyambi sent nine representatives off to Zanzibar to fetch a teacher.[49] By the time that the U.M.C.A. was able to dispatch anyone to Mwembe, however, Mataka I Nyambi was on his deathbed and matters were very much confused. Steere was sensitive to the possibility of a succession struggle, and was also anxious not to intrude too aggressively at a time when the first effects of Sultan Barghash's anti-slave trade treaties with the British were beginning to show their effect on exportations from the coast.[50]

Abdallah's account of the succession indicates that Steere's initial fears were unwarranted, however, and that power was transferred smoothly, according to traditional practice:

Now at the time of Che Mataka's death, his nephew Che Nyenje was at Chiwinja [Kilwa Kivinje] on the coast, and Kumtelela (the son of Bibi Kwikanga) sent messengers to fetch him. When he arrived at Mwembe they made ready the Beer of Succession and he was installed by the Chief Kumtelela. There were great rejoicings for six days, the *Mundalanga* being danced, oxen slaughtered, and beer drunk; guns were fired constantly, for, they said, 'Our king Che Mataka has arisen again'.[51]

Mataka II Nyenje apparently felt that his people had seen enough war during the reign of his illustrious uncle, Nyambi, and his rule was remembered by Abdallah's informants as being peaceful and harmonious. He was, it seems, much loved and respected, whereas his predecessor had been greatly feared. And he was apparently more amenable than was the late Nyambi to the presence of a U.M.C.A. missionary at Mwembe. 'Here is an improvement since old Mataka would not entertain the idea of having a European in his town.'[52] It was in these favourable circumstances that W. P. Johnson arrived at Mwembe to preach the gospel in 1880.

Things did not go so well once Johnson arrived there. Although Mataka proved willing to have a church built at Mwembe, actual construction was delayed as a result of the weakened state of the population after a severe famine.[53] Meanwhile, Johnson encountered a different sort of problem, opposition from those whom he typified as 'roughs from the coast', who apparently succeeded in linking him in Mataka's mind with the British seizure of a slave caravan at the coast which belonged to Mataka. Several years after he was forced to leave Mwembe as a result of this incident, Johnson wrote that

> at first they did not attempt open opposition but always insinuated that I was a spy, and that the Europeans at the coast paid highly to get leave to live, trade, interfere with slave trade etc. Capt. Foote of H.M.S. Ruby heard a caravan of slaves was near Lindi, and came up to meet it, and released some 50 slaves, who promptly ran into the bush, and so have not come under any good influence, yet considerable loss was entailed on the caravan leaders. It turned out that the caravan was one of Mataka's, and on its return with very exaggerated report, Mataka had from his view good cause for complaint, and seems to have fallen under the coast influence in consequence; he lulled my fears which were considerable when I heard of what had been done, and I even went off to the Lujenda preaching with four of his boys; and on my return I heard he had seized everything, and refused to see me. I had some difficulty in getting off, however, there was no lack of signs of good will, and I have left no one enemy there—the Seyid [of Zanzibar] has written to Mataka on my behalf . . .[54]

But the Sultan of Zanzibar was not so influential in Yaoland that his recommendation could erase the ultimately realistic connection which Mataka had become convinced did exist between British naval anti-slave trade patrols and British missionaries. Mataka's commitment to the slave trade as an essential economic prop for his ever-increasing political authority was too fundamental to be exchanged for the abstract spiritual rewards which the missionaries offered. Even their literacy skills were of no appeal to him as his needs were for more precise communications with the political and commercial elite of Zanzibar and its subordinate towns on the coast, notably Kilwa. Mataka II Nyenje rejected conversion to Christianity and became a Muslim. This is confirmed by Abdallah's testimony that on Nyenje's death

> He was buried there on Namisuwi hill in the verandah of the Mosque, and that is why the Mwembe people say in making an oath, 'By the Mataka of the Mosque,' . . . I also have seen the grave and it is indeed near to Mosque at Namisuwi.[55]

The accession of Mataka III Bonomali in the mid-1880s confirmed the commitment to Islam and it is presumably from then that the Islamisation of Mataka's people began to progress apace.[56]

For the Mataka dynasty, then, there does seem to be clear evidence that the final turning to Islam and the rejection of Christianity was inextricably related to its vital economic links with the Swahili coast. Or so it appeared to the disappointed members of the U.M.C.A. What we lack for Mwembe, however, is evidence that there was a positive Muslim response to Mataka II Nyenje's desire to modernise his realm by the development of literacy among his people. All that we have before us points to the older sort of interpretation that the turn to Islam was a reactionary and conservative measure, for which the Yao were to be eternally penalised because it cut them off from the benefits of Western education. This last point, of course, was by no means determined in the 1880s. Nevertheless, any chance of a glimpse beyond this point of view was demolished when Mataka III Bonomali executed and enslaved the vanguard of the new Portuguese imperialism at Mwembe late in 1889 or early in 1890.[57] For the next twenty-two years each Mataka was the sworn enemy of the Portuguese and represented the main obstacle to their occupation of what was to become the Niassa Province of Mozambique. The issue was not resolved until Mataka V Cisonga removed himself and his followers north across the Ruvuma River into Tunduru District. After 1890 there is simply no external evidence for developments in the Mataka dynasty, the most important among all the Yao. We must necessarily look elsewhere for illustrations of the progressive and positive side of Islamic proselytisation in the southern interior, if it is to be found at all.

The answer is, I think, to be found in the literature on the growing Islamic community at Makanjila's, on the southeastern shore of Lake Nyasa. According to Abdallah, Makanjila's people 'built dhows copied from those of the Arabs; also they planted coconuts with the object of making the lake shore resemble the coast'.[58] Distinctly unimpressed, E. D. Young felt obliged to say no more about his encounter in 1876 with Makanjila III Banali than that 'He must have a considerable mixture of Arab blood, I imagine, and affects Arab ways.'[59] But J. F. Elton, who was a particularly observant traveller through nineteenth-century East Africa, was singularly struck by the prosperity of Makanjila's court. Moreover, he remarked, 'There is a "mwalimu" established here, who teaches reading and the Koran. We passed the schoolhouse, and saw the row of slates in the verandah.'[60] Muslim education continued to flourish in 1885, when the British Consul for Nyasa reported that Makanjila's town had a 'large schoolhouse' where the children learned Swahili and were instructed in the Koran.[61] Even more impressive was the situation at Mponda's, which in 1891 boasted twelve Qu'ranic schools and apparently an equal number of *waalimu*.[62]

The U.M.C.A. missionaries saw matters differently. Yet writing in 1893 from Unangu, Chauncy Maples, by then Bishop of Likoma, sounds more frustrated than convincing when he observes:

One hears something of the so-called Mohammedan *mwalimu* or *waalimu*, as the case may be, at Yao towns like those of Makanjila, Mponda, Mataka, and it might be supposed that their business consists in an active Mohammedan propaganda . . . These gentlemen are for the most part in residence merely as the scribes or clerks of the chiefs in whose employ they are engaged; . . . One does not find that as a rule they reach even the rudiments of reading and writing, still less of their religion . . . to the Yao youths of the towns in which they dwell.[63]

Indeed, the desire to convince themselves that what they were seeing was not really true reveals itself in the official history of the U.M.C.A.:

Makanjila's people are an instance of Bishop Steere's saying, 'that it is a race with Islam which shall have the tribes'. The Mohammedans flattered themselves they had converted Makanjila, and the chief brought a Mohammedan teacher with him; but they all visited Mr. Johnson, and asked for brandy![64]

Nevertheless, the U.M.C.A. could not will away the fact that the Muslim teachers of whom they thought so little were apparently regarded with considerable respect by the Yao chiefs. Their literacy enabled important trading chiefs like Mataka and Makanjila to communicate accurately with their business partners on the coast, and would have helped to rationalise their foreign relations in general had not the Germans and the Portuguese decided to assume hegemony over their coastal outlets at precisely the same time. As was the case with the states of the ancient Western Sudan, 'Ruling classes also saw advantages for their wider relations through professing Islam.'[65]

But this is still to beg the question of *why* these Yao chiefs chose to become Muslims in the late nineteenth century, when Yao had been trading to the Muslim coast for perhaps three centuries.[66] Literacy for diplomacy and even firearms for political aggrandisment were not tied to profession of Islam, as is demonstrated by the important example of the revolutionary Shambaa chief of Mazinde, Semboja.[67] Therefore, it seems prudent to look for motivations for their conversion to Islam within the more specific context of Yao social and political history during this period. I have already suggested elsewhere that during the nineteenth century Yao political organisation experienced a major growth in scale. New leadership emerged, leadership which was at once bold, innovative and insecure. A factor underlying the early success of Mtalika, for example, was his defiant challenge to traditional rituals associated with 'ancestor veneration'.[68] All of these important Yao chiefs were engaged in a struggle for ritual, as well as political, control with the headmen over whom they were attempting to extend or maintain their control. A direct consequence of this struggle appears to have been the attempt to assert the primacy of invoking the supreme deity, *mulungu*, through the dead elders or 'ancestors' of the chief, rather than through those of the village headman. Seen in this context Islam clearly offered itself as an attractive supplementary source of ritual authority to this emerging generation of Yao paramount chiefs who were laying claim to unprecedented authority for themselves and their families. Here I am indebted to David Parkin's important statement of this process at work within a quite different East African society, the Giriama of Kenya. Parkin argues that ritual syncretism

facilitates a process of role change, in which persons or groups compete with each other in an attempt to legitimize or reinforce their social positions. Cultural borrowing thus becomes a technique in this process of role change, by which these competing parties draw upon more powerful and possible legitimizing resources outside their society. The spread of religious belief systems and practices is a possible result of this technique.[69]

For the Yao chiefs who converted to Islam in the last three decades of the nineteenth century this possibility very likely became a reality.

As usual, there is little evidence for this period that sheds much light on the growth of Islam in other parts of the southern interior. Elton, in his travels in the immediate hinterland of Mozambique, where he served as British Consul in the 1870s, found its petty rulers considerably Islamised. But when in 1876 he visited Itoculo, not more than twenty-five miles from the coast, Elton did not believe that Mauruça was a convinced Muslim. 'Maruha, better known and always addressed by his followers, when in the presence, as the Hakim,' he described as being 'garbed in a half-Arab attire . . . His chief qualification and recommendation to his people is the reputation he enjoys as a wizard and spiritualist.'[70] All that Maples could say in 1881 about Sultan Mwalia, the Makua chief of the Meto country whose town lay athwart the route from Makanjila's and Mataka's towns to the coast at Kisanga, was that he was a disappointed youth whom the Arabs used as their tool.[71]

North of the Ruvuma, in what is now Tanzania, members of the U.M.C.A. and occasional explorers like Joseph Thomson were too preoccupied with the effects of the slave trade and Ngoni raids, not to mention the struggle to establish a Christian community at Masasi, to take much notice of Islam. Canon Lamburn, on the other hand, was able to gather some interesting notes on early Islamic proselytisation in Tunduru before the three big Yao Sultans—Mataka, Mtalika and Kandulu—entered the country:

It would seem that it was just about 1885 that two men came from the coast where they had become Moslems, to tell the Yaos about the blessings of the faith of Islam. Their names were Mfaume son of Kaligambe and Mfaume son of Torro, together with two others Mtingala and Kombo. None of these men actually administered the 'baptism' that is the initiation of a circumcised man into Islam, but those who having heard their preaching, wished to become Moslems, went to the coast towns to be initiated. Later Moslem teachers from the coast came up country to Yaoland, and there 'baptized' converts.[72]

Here for the first time we have the introduction of a completely new element, the wandering, itinerant Muslim preacher. From what we know about the *waal-imu* at Makanjila's and Mponda's, they would appear to have been more or less resident in the towns themselves, attached to the courts of the great chiefs, where their functions were well defined and their means of support were no doubt provided by the chiefs themselves. According to W. P. Johnson, another institutionalised locus in which *waalimu* operated at this time were the caravans, which he believed to form together 'a great brotherhood that makes for Mohammedanism . . .'. 'No caravans travelled without teachers, with or without the boards which are the usual school apparatus. No business was done without a writer, and every writer was professedly a Mohammedan teacher.'[73] But it is not at all clear what conditions were at play in the initial appearance of this new agency of Islamic proselytisation.[74]

What does seem clear, though, is that after 1890 Islam rapidly spread downwards from the chiefs to all the Yao. There were several elements at play in this mass conversion, although there is no general agreement among contemporary observers of this phenomenon as to what they were. In Malawi, some attributed its success to the chiefs and slavers who were reacting against limitations imposed on them by British colonial rule; others claimed that it was the work of wandering Muslim missionaries; some felt that it just spread by itself, without help from anyone. According to W. P. Johnson,

> It was very noticeable how in these years (after 1891) there was a recrudescence of the craze for Mohammedanism. It seemed as if the slavers, checked by the government, were determined to extend their moral force. As always, they used the native attachment to the old Yao initiation dances, in order to introduce gradually another dance, which was regarded as an initiation into Mohammedanism, though there is no foundation in the Quran or in tradition for any such custom; its name was *jandu*. They used the native funeral ceremonies in the same way.[75]

In the same vein is the observation made by Codrington that the Yao

> has readily acquired Mohammedanism . . . The perpetuation of this faith, which is, however, distinctly antagonistic to British influence and control, is a matter which receives considerable attention from the chiefs and headmen of the tribe.[76]

Johnson also represents another point of view in the following tale of a boy who was seized in a raid in 1887 at Losefa, on the eastern shore of Lake Nyasa to the north of Makanjila's town:

> He had been a free boy, the son of one Chikoko. Makanjila's people sold him and in due course of time he was owned by an Arab in Zanzibar. At that time a slave who could read and write well was worth having, so his master sent him to one of the Mohammedan schools, where they all used to shout the alphabet together. In due course Isa, for that was the name given him in Zanzibar, came back through the German territory to the north end of the Lake . . . He begged a passage back home again and a year had not passed when we found him leading a Mohammedan revival south of Losefa.

About two decades later Bishop Fisher of the U.M.C.A. was alarmed by ' "a certain quickening of the forces of Islam" ' around the same area of the lakeshore, 'where itinerating Muslim teachers, "as a rule men of some importance, and more intelligent than the average teacher resident in the villages," were increasingly active'.[77]

Finally, and completely opposed to the previous two interpretations, is the impression recorded in 1910 by Sir Alfred Sharpe, that the conversion of the Yao was spontaneous:

> Twenty years ago, when I first knew Nyasaland, Mohammedanism was almost non-existent except at one or two spots where it had been brought in by the Arabs. Since then it has spread greatly, particularly during the last eight or ten years. The Yaos are the tribe who have taken to Moslem teaching

mostly . . . The movement has grown of itself, there has been nothing in the shape of propaganda. All through Yaoland . . . there is in almost every village a mosque and a Moslem trader.[78]

One of the reasons why Islam might have grown as the result of a popular movement after about 1890 was that social tensions were exacerbated by the immediate threat of European domination. The best evidence comes from Mponda's town during the eighteen months from the beginning of 1890 to the middle of 1891, when the Roman Catholics were unsuccessfully attempting to establish a mission there. Ian Linden writes that 'Continual raiding for slaves, and skirmishes with the enemy, induced a state of permanent anxiety in all the inhabitants of Mponda's town. Apart from the traditional *mwabvi* [poison ordeal] . . . an enormous proliferation of magical charms and talismans gave individuals a semblance of security.' Among these were included the *Alibadiri*, which had verses from the Qu'ran wrapped up in leather thongs.[79] It will take much careful research to resolve these different points of view.

The sources for the spread of Islam in northeastern Mozambique reveal the same ambiguity. 'If Christianity only vegetates like an exotic plant, Mohammedanism is spread out like dog's grass,' wrote António Enes, the Portuguese Royal High Commissioner in Mozambique in the early 1890s:

Without aid of civil powers and without arms, without riches, without authority, without prestigious examples, almost without ostensive cult, without professional priesthood, it is gaining by its proselytization all the northern districts of the province of Moçambique . . . Yet the foci of Mohammedan propaganda are but poorly known; what one can see are its effects . . . A Makua who served me for a long time and was himself a *monhé* [i.e. Islamized] did not call Mohammedanism a religion, he called it a fashion (*moda*), and it has the power of spreading like a fashion. Especially in the North the natives become Muslims by imitation, and the imitation is stimulated by their own enthusiasm, because the white *cabaia* [*kanzu*] carries with it (I do not know why) prestige (*artes*), privileges of distinction. But the fashion is not only an appearance, not only a costume; it also means accepting practices of a religious character, and it imposes on its adherents obligations of solidarity, rules of subjection, the spirit of doctrine (*seita*). If Islam in Moçambique does not approach forming well defined communities, it forms groupings which scorn other natives, react against Christian influences, and in certain hypothetical situations will be capable of a common action.[80]

Enes managed to resolve his own contradictions rather ably. Long exposed to coastal influence and mindful of its self-assured cultural superiority, and coming for the very first time up against a military strong Portuguese imperial threat, the Makua of the coastal hinterland which was known to him were ripe for conversion. But if the rapid expansion of Islam was partly a matter of fashion, something which was taking place spontaneously in the last decade of the nineteenth century, it was equally promoted by chiefly example.

This is abundantly clear from the account of E. J. de Vilhena, who was Governor of the territories of the Niassa Colony in the first years of the present century. Islam was then widespread along and behind the coast as far west as 40° E., in all the Yao chiefdoms of the northwest, around Mogabo, and at Sultan Mwalia's, where observances were particularly strict among the local elite. Most of the Makua beyond 40° E. and all of the Maconde were untouched. This confirms Maples' earlier observation that Islam was spreading in from the Mozambique coast along the trade route to Lake Nyasa:

> The influence of Islam is also manifested in the places where it has reached by the diffusion of instruction, limited to writing in their own language, or in Swahili, in Arabic characters, and to the reading of religious books. The diffusion and teaching of religious practices is strictly tied to the instruction furnished by the preachers, or as they are called, perhaps erroneously, the *xerifes*. One of the perceptible results of Islamic influence is precisely the spread of instruction and the necessity that all the chiefs have today of being themselves instructed and of causing their close advisors (*proximos*) to be instructed in writing and reading, for which purpose they frequently call in men of the coast. They commonly maintain relations among themselves, and with the authorities, in writing, which is not the case in the south of the province where the chiefs are completely illiterate.[81]

Vilhena, like Enes, was also alarmed by the prospects of future concerted action against the Portuguese by the Islamised chiefs of northern Mozambique. Among literate Muslim chiefs, he warned, any hostile act taken against the Portuguese was reported from one to another. 'The Mataca, being the most powerful and assuming, perhaps because of this fact, the manner of a religious chief, is today still the inspiration for all the other Islamised chiefs . . .'[82] In the Mozambique hinterland the Islamisation of chiefs may well have been partly the result of reasons not unlike those motivating the Yao chiefs, but after 1890 it was also apparently catalysed by their desire to mount an effective challenge to the Portuguese. For those who had only recently been forcibly subjugated by the Portuguese, the example of successive Muslim Matakas defiantly maintaining their independence from that very same rule until 1912 must have set a powerful example and given hope for the future.

The situation was very much different, at least on the face of it, in southern Tanzania. There, until the arrival of the big Yao chiefs in Tunduru, there were few powerful political authorities to be Islamised. Indeed, what information we possess at the present suggests that not much progress was being made among the decentralised agriculturalists in the Kilwa hinterland until Maji Maji. To be sure, there was ample opportunity within the German colonial structure for individual conversions to Islam, as is emphasised by Trimingham. The Germans utilised Swahili *askari*, clerks, and local administrators throughout their East African colony, so that the pre-existing cultural influence of Swahili society was more widely disseminated than it had ever been before. As John Iliffe argues,

> It is likely that many of the frustrations which were elsewhere expressed in direct confrontation between African and European were absorbed in Tanganyika into an alternative social structure—a social career open to talent—which did not involve direct competition with Europeans . . . Again,

the Swahili sub-culture offered an alternative source of skills . . . It is certainly true that Swahili society became the refuge of those who had reason to abandon tribal life.[83]

True, indeed; but my main preoccupation in this paper has been with the conversion of those Africans who chose to *remain* an integral part of tribal life. For them, as both Iliffe and B. G. Martin have tentatively suggested, the breaking point came with the universal disillusionment that beset the survivors of the crushing defeat of Maji Maji. The Ngindo are said to have converted *en masse* to Islam during the course of the Rising. According to A. R. W. Crosse-Upcott, 'The magician-apostles of the cult were anything but orthodox Muslims, but they had a Koranic reader in attendance and contrived to give an Islamic colouring to their campaign.' He was also informed ' "that everyone had both to receive the water and adopt the Muslim faith" '. Although Islam lapsed somewhat among the Ngindo after Maji Maji, the commitment to Islam was there to be built upon in succeeding years.[84]

Similarly, the crisis brought on by the first World War caused many Africans of the interior to embrace Islam. Not only is it true that there were generally severe demands made on the colonial subjects of the European combatants to supply support for the troops in a variety of ways, but it is also essential to remember that a great part of the East African campaign was played out in the southern interior.

> The war gave a strong impetus to the spread of Mohammedanism; a religion introduced by the Arabs many years ago, but which, though common in the coast, has not penetrated into the interior to any great extent. Since the war, it is amazing to see the number of unsophisticated and uneducated natives who profess Mohammedanism . . .

> Practically without exception the natives call themselves Mohammedans more from the desire to attain social standing, than any spiritual advantage.[85]

In addition to the well-established example of the prestige of Swahili society, it has been suggested that the use of Muslim Indian troops by the British may have reinforced people's impression that the adoption of Islam was something to be emulated. It has also been pointed out that the German removal of the British U.M.C.A., followed by the British ousting of the German Benedictines may have suggested to people that Christianity was destined to be something less than a permanent fixture in the southern interior after the war. And while I have found no evidence of Islamic missionary activity behind Kilwa in this period, it was noted from Songea, to the west of Tunduru, that 'two itinerant exponents of the religion have passed through the district during the year'.[86] It would be instructive to know the extent of Qadiriya activity during and immediately after the first World War, particularly in view of the fact that it is so well established at Kilwa now.[87]

CONCLUSIONS

At this point I think that there are a number of tentative general conclusions which can be drawn about the process of Islamic expansion in the southern interior of East Africa. First, it appears that we can distinguish between two different stages of Islamic expansion in these parts: one pre-colonial, and the other colonial. The former focuses on the most important Yao trading chiefs, whose motives for conversion to Islam were divided between the need for political and ritual legitimisation and the desire for the regularisation of their economic ties with Zanzibar and the advantages offered to this end by the attainment of literacy in Arabic script. The politics of ritual syncretism among the Yao we have already explored. With respect to the latter motivating factor, their move to Islam emphatically represents a step towards the modernisation of their societies. The same logic would seem to apply to the appropriate Makua chiefs, as well. That none could foretell the future and the situation in which Islam would prove to be an actual deterrant to modernisation, as it is commonly conceived in the Western context, is not sufficient reason to label their action retrograde. This initial stage of expansion and the dualistic form of Islam that developed from it corresponds well enough to J. S. Trimingham's pre-theocratic era in West Africa (which gave rise to what he calls 'Traditional African Islam'), to suggest that we are here dealing with comparable situations.[88]

Concerning the spread of Islam during the colonial period, Schildknecht astutely observes, 'The strongest inroads have been made by Islam in times of crisis, i.e. during the Ngoni uprisings in southern Tanganyika around 1880, and after the European impact between 1910 and 1920.'[89] His analysis is clearly borne out by the data at our disposal. As a more general postulation, von Grunebaum writes:

> Once internal or external experience creates intellectual, emotional, or organizational needs that cannot be met by the insights or hypotheses evolved within the particular closed system, this system, its basic values as well as its doctrinal, ethical, artistic, and intellectual solutions, will command less and less unquestioning adherence. The door will be open for its transformation or even displacement.[90]

This perfectly describes the situation being faced by virtually every African society during the colonial period, and is especially apt for the southern interior of East Africa. Indeed, von Grunebaum's formulation applies equally to the reasons underlying the conversion of the Yao chiefs, thus providing a theoretical bridge between two historically linked, though analytically differentiated, stages of Islamisation.

Trimingham would subscribe to the applicability of von Grunebaum's generalisation to the nineteenth-century situation, but he has different ideas about the colonial period. Islam, he suggests,

> could only make inroads under conditions of great change—conditions which were provided in the nineteenth century. Given this preparation of the ground, the religious and cultural values which Islam had to offer could make their appeal. This period of pacification and consolidation by European powers was the main period when Islam spread, especially between 1880 and 1930.[91]

What Trimingham seems to be implying here is that it was only during the nineteenth century that great, disruptive changes were taking place in East

Africa, and that once these had shaken the foundation of East African societies the principal condition for the great spread of Islam in the twentieth century was the absence of crisis and the establishment of the *pax colonica*. On the contrary, I believe that for the African people whose history has been the concern of this essay, the most critical period from their point of view came with the imposition of colonial rule which was effected or dangerously imminent after 1890. This is an interpretation which I think is borne out by the evidence presented above, and which I think will stand up under further scrutiny and the presentation of more ample documentation.

Second, the external agents of Islamic proselytisation were, successively, Swahili and Arab traders who had established firm commercial relations with the Yao and Makua chiefs of the hinterland; Muslim *waalimu* who were resident in the towns of those chiefs; itinerant Muslim missionaries, who appear to have been especially active in southern Tanzania and along the eastern shore of Lake Nyasa; and last, the Swahili *askari* and minor functionaries who were associated particularly with the Germans, but who also seem to have been used by the Portuguese. Of these, the most important seem to have been the teachers and the preachers, whose specific charge it was to proselytise their faith by persuasion, rather than the traders and *askari* who were there to be emulated, but whose worldly concerns were more completely secular. The internal agents were first and foremost the great Yao and Makua chiefs. The only other indigenous elements who emerge from the documentation are Johnson's 'coastal roughs', those young men who had been to the coast, who affected its way (and implicitly its religion, as Enes observed), and who were regarded, according to the disillusioned Bishop Maples as 'altogether superior people on account of their connection with the coast'.[92]

In making such distinctions, however, particularly with regard to external agents, we must not forget that Islam does not possess a formally differentiated priesthood. Thus, as T. W. Arnold argues in his classic study of the subject, the individual Muslim, whatever his means of livelihood, is

> more likely to become an exponent of the missionary character of his creed in the presence of the unbeliever. The would-be proselytizer has not to refer his convert to some authorized religious teacher of his creed who may formally receive the neophyte into the body of the church . . . Accordingly, however great an exaggeration it may be to say . . . that every Muhammadan is a missionary, still it is true that every Muhammadan may be one, and few truly devout Muslims, living in daily contact with unbelievers, neglect the precept of their prophet: 'Summon them to the ways of thy Lord with wisdom and with kindly warning.'[93]

Perhaps if we were better informed about the activities of individual Muslim traders at the towns of the big Yao and Makua chiefs, and among the peoples of the Kilwa hinterland, we would need to re-evaluate their role in the Islamisation of the southern interior.[94]

Third, what I have chosen to call the vehicles of Islamic expansion in the southern interior of East Africa are extensively described in the first part of this essay. By these I mean the African and Islamic social and religious institutions which enabled these societies to integrate Islam into their social structure with minimal disruption and maximal revitalisation of society. The most significant of these for emphasising that the political society was now Islamic were the chiefly installation ceremonies, which among the Yao and Makua bear every sign of having been in the process of development as powerfully integrative ritual institutions both before and after their Islamisation. For the general Islamisation of the mass of the people, male and female initiation ceremonies, which were historically controlled by the chiefs, appear to have been the most effective vehicles. This is, however, less clearly indicated for the Makua than it is for the Yao. Similarly, the Islamisation of funeral ceremonies constituted an important means of personally expressing one's adherence to Islam. All of these fall into the category of life-cycle rituals, or rites of passage. And although the evidence is spotty, at a more popular level Islamic magic was yet another factor in the Islamisation of the southern interior. It is essential to recognise, however, that conversion to Islam in Africa cannot be explained entirely in terms of 'fit' and syncretism. 'Non-fit', the arresting attraction of beliefs and practices that are wholly novel and fundamentally different from those of the traditional belief system may often be the key in examining the vehicles of Islamic expansion. To cite only one example, the thoroughly Islamised Zaramo of Eastern Tanzania had neither initiation rites nor circumcision before their conversion to Islam; today they practise both. All that I am saying is that in the southern interior of East Africa the predominant configurations were adoptive, rather than differential.[95]

Together these various factors brought about a massive process of rapid Islamic expansion in the southern interior of East Africa, one which contrasts strikingly with the difficulties which have dogged Christian missionary efforts in the same field. Why should this have been? Most obviously, Islam was here as elsewhere more easily assimilated than Christianity because of its inherent attributes, and because of those of Christianity. To quote von Grunebaum a last time,

> agreement on the minimum demands of Muslim theology and law would ensure acceptance as members in good standing of any community that would wish to be so accepted. In other words, in striking contrast to the Christian attitude, which makes full acceptance contingent on the receiving community's passing on the qualifications of the individual applicant or of the applicant community (through a missionary, a priest, or an otherwise qualified representative), the Muslim *umma* is willing to allow acceptance on the basis of a unilateral declared intention to belong to the people of the Prophet. This attitude has greatly facilitated the transcultural effectiveness of the Muslim mission.[96]

Through all of this, however, one other factor, deeply pervasive and absolutely crucial, was at work: the historical relationship between the long Islamised Swahili coast and those parts of the interior with which it had become intimately involved through either long-distance international or regional trade. Swahili society and its religion, Islam, provided an external standard to which people like the Yao, Makua, Ngindo, Mwera, Machinga and Makonde, could compare and contrast their own values. Through trade there developed a social and cultural context in which the applicability of Robert Redfield's notion of great tradition and little tradition serves to sharpen our appreciation of the forces at play.[97] But it would be presumptuous, not to mention patronising, for us to assume that Swahili society was always seen to be superior to those of the pre-Islamic and illiterate peoples of the interior. As the up-country peoples were *washenzi* to the Swahili, then it is certain that there was an appropriate reciprocal appellation in each of those societies for the Swahili. But eventually the one must have gained a dominant position with respect to the others. Elements probably contributing to this development were the rise of the Zanzibari state in the nineteenth century, the tangible advantages offered by the acquisition of literacy in Arabic and firearms from the coast, the social prestige of Muslim agents of German colonial rule and the countervailing social system which Islam offered to Africans suffering under colonial rule and the standards of Western society. Once this relationship of great to little tradition was indeed established, the tendency to be positively inclined towards Swahili society and Islam, rather than (and even in the absence of) European civilisation and Christianity, was firmly rooted as a pre-condition of whatever else might follow.

It is frustrating to admit, however, that in an essay dealing with the interaction of traditional African religious beliefs and Islam, it is the spiritual recommendations of Islam which remain the most difficult to assess and document of all the factors underlying conversion. But an enormously stimulating beginning has been made in a very recently published and seminal article by Robin Horton.[98] At the centre of Horton's argument is an abstract sociological model of what he calls the 'typical traditional cosmology'. He then goes on to what he calls a 'thought-experiment' in which he attempts to predict the likely responses of this cosmology to a set of hypothetical changes which incorporate features of 'the modern situation' in isolation from the introduction of Islam and Christianity. Essentially, he sets himself the task of gauging the response of 'typical traditional cosmologies' to enlargement of scale. His conclusions are five, four of which concern us here: (1) The traditional religious system has 'considerable adaptive potential' and is not abandoned when confronted by significant social change. Rather it is re-moulded until it provides as effective a system of 'explanation–prediction–control' as it did before change was introduced. (2) People who are moving beyond the microcosm of the local community into the macrocosm of the wider world can only interpret these changes as indicating that the supreme being, as 'underpinner of the macrocosm', is assuming a more direct role in daily affairs to the detriment of the lesser spirits who were 'underpinners of the microcosm'. (3) Accordingly, the supreme being becomes morally concerned in the development of the social life and new moral code that individuals are pursuing in the macrocosm. (4) The foregoing developments are matters of degree, not kind. 'Hence there is an infinite number of potential positions between traditional religious life and the full-blooded monolatric cult of morally concerned supreme being.'[99]

The problem with Horton's model for the historian is that it is totally devoid of any historical referents. I believe, however, that a number of his points are borne out by the material presented in this essay and that my conclusions are, reciprocally, brought into sharper focus by his 'thought-experiment'. For example, Horton's theoretical point that the 'individual cosmological adjustment' and 'particular position taken up by a given individual will depend largely on the degree to which, in his own personal life, the boundaries of the microcosm have ceased to confine him', are admirably illustrated by the situations of the Yao and Makua chiefs and by Johnson's 'coastal roughs', among others. Remember that Mataka II Nyenje received the news of Mataka I Nyambi's death while he was at the coast. Even for those people who never left the village it was impossible to avoid its impact, as Johnson seems to have recognised when he wrote in 1884 that 'We were to them part of the bad world that journeyed backwards and forwards constantly by them.'[100] Similarly, the Yao chiefs were certainly engaged in the process of 'extending and developing the existing cosmology in such a way as to account for the new social situation and to bring it under some sort of control', a point which also lies at the heart of Parkin's analysis of the Giriama. Most attractive about Horton's hypothesis is his belief 'that acceptance of Islam and Christianity is due as much to development of the traditional cosmology in response to *other* features of the modern situation as it is to the activities of the missionaries', a perspective which differs substantially from (while it enhances) that of von Grunebaum.[101] Related to this point is his conclusion that 'the actual story of Islam and Christianity in Africa . . . is one of highly conditional and selective acceptance'. Nowhere in Africa is this point more vividly illustrated than in the southern interior of East Africa, where the principle of matrilineality has been affected hardly at all by conversion to Islam. For our purposes Horton's thesis completes itself with his assertion that 'such a conclusion reduces Islam and Christianity to the role of catalysts—i.e. stimulators and accelerators of changes which were "in the air" anyway'.[102] Without reiterating evidence already presented, I think that the expansion of Islam in the southern interior of East Africa, from the attempt of Yao chiefs to assert the primacy of their dead elders in the worship of *mulungu* to the interplay between Islam and the cult of the *maji* among the Ngindo, can be understood in these terms.

NOTES

[1] Hasani bin Ismail *The Medicine Man: Swifa ya Nguvumali* edited and translated by Peter Lienhardt (Oxford 1968) p. 38: 'In general I think it is better to consider the various beliefs and practices, whether "orthodox" or "unorthodox", which exist in the same minds as being a loose system which has its own internal logic and coherence.'

[2] P. J. A. Rigby, 'Sociological Factors in the Contact of the Gogo of Central Tanzania with Islam', in I. M. Lewis (ed.) *Islam in Tropical Africa* (London 1966) p. 274. Sociological and cosmological convergences or differentiations between African and Islamic social structure and religious beliefs cannot, however, be assumed to explain either the reasons for or the way in which conversion to Islam actually took place. Such a perspective by itself ignores both the historical and human dimensions of religious conversion. To ignore the impact and roles of individual human beings, Muslim and non-Muslim alike, would be a fundamental error.

[3] In G. E. von Grunebaum *Modern Islam: The Search for Cultural Identity* (New York 1964) pp. 3–18. The quoted passages are to be found at p. 10, p. 13 and p. 17.

[4] I. M. Lewis (ed.) *Islam in Tropical Africa* (London 1966) especially pp. 58–75.

[5] *Ibid.* p. 60.

[6] For an amusing incident from the Kilwa coast which illustrates Lewis' point about

scriptural warrant, see P. Lienhardt, 'A Controversy over Islamic Custom in Kilwa Kivinje, Tanzania', in *ibid.* pp. 383-4.

[7] Franz Schildknecht, 'Tanzania', in James Kritzeck and William H. Lewis (eds.) *Islam in Africa* (New York 1969) p. 235. Although they are today considered to be a patrilineal people, I have included the Ngindo with the matrilineal peoples because of the obvious similarity of their traditional religious system. See below, p. 181. Indeed, matrilineality does not itself seem to be a factor of great significance for understanding the process of Islamisation in this region, but it does help to identify a large culture complex which does not include the intrusive Ngoni of Songea District, Tanzania. Cf. George Peter Murdock *Africa : Its Peoples and their Culture History* (New York 1959) p. 295, where he includes the Ngindo in his 'Yao Cluster' and p. 298, where he notes their patrilineality.

[8] Cf. I. M. Lewis *op. cit.* p. 61.

[9] At the conference there was general dissatisfaction expressed with the continued usage of the misleading term 'ancestor worship', but no serious thought was given to developing a more appropriate terminology, although there was no doubt as to the conceptual clarity which would be achieved by such a re-definition of categories. Since then, however, an excellent beginning towards a solution of this conundrum has been made by Igor Kopytoff, 'Ancestors as Elders in Africa' *Africa* XLI, 2 (1971) pp. 129-42. Following his argument I have chosen to abandon 'ancestor worship' and to replace it in this essay with 'ancestor veneration', which at least has the virtue of clarifying the way in which the ancestors (or dead elders, in Kopytoff's categorisation) were being approached by the living community. Where I quote from earlier writers who use terms relating to 'ancestorship' the reader will need to re-conceptualize these in terms of 'eldership', as I have had to do.

[10] Throughout this essay I attempt to avoid use of the ethnographic present, as it introduces a severe conceptual flaw for the historian, with its false assumption of permanence of both social form and content.

[11] Alexander Hetherwick, 'Some Animistic Beliefs among the Yaos of British Central Africa' *The Journal of the Anthropological Institute of Great Britain and Ireland* XXXII (1902) pp. 89-94. It is worth noting that Hetherwick uses *mulungu* in both a general and a particular sense in the passages that I have quoted.

[12] Kopytoff, 'Ancestors as Elders', pp. 140-1.

[13] J. C. Mitchell *The Yao Village—A Study in the Social Structure of a Nyasaland Tribe* (Manchester 1956) pp. 133-4.

[14] Duff MacDonald *Africana : or, the Heart of Heathen Africa* (London 1882) vol. I, p. 65.

[15] Hetherwick 'Some Animistic Beliefs' pp. 89-94'

[16] But cf. F. J. Peirone *A Tribo Ajaua do Alto Niassa (Moçambique) e Alguns Aspectos da sua Problemática Neo-Islâmica* (Lisboa 1967) p. 61, where he specifically comments that it is the chief's sister, and not his wife, who prepares the supplicatory flour for offering at the *nsolo* tree.

[17] R. G. P. Lamburn, 'The Yaos of Tunduru: an essay in missionary anthropology', unpublished typescript in the library of the Makerere University, Kampala, Uganda (n.d.), p. 127. R. E. S. Tanner, 'Some Southern Province Trees with their African Names and Uses' *Tanganyika Notes and Records* 31 (1951) p. 64, identifies the *msoro* tree of southern Tanzania as *Caesalpinia Crista*, a medium-sized, smooth barked tree with round, yellow fruits that are eaten by duiker and eland, and having a habitat extending from the coast to the border of Songea. Like other trees, it is used locally for medicinal purposes, specifically as a cure for severe stomach pains. See also Y. B. Abdallah *The Yaos* (Zomba 1919) pp. 22-3.

[18] See, e.g. Tanzania National Archives, Kilwa District Book, p. 186; Lindi District Book, pp. 191 and 199; Newala District Book, pp. 104-5; Jorge Dias *Os Macondes de Moçambique* (Lisboa 1964) Vol. I, p. 63; J. P. Moffet (ed.) *Handbook of Tanganyika* second edn. (Dar es Salaam 1958) p. 223, also pp. 294 and 296.

[19] On this point, see Mitchell *op. cit.* pp. 71-2; Lamburn, 'Some Notes on the Yao' *Tanganyika Notes and Records* 29 (1950) p. 74; and Tanzania National Archives, Tunduru District Book, 'Manners and Customs', while also noting Pierone *op. cit.* pp. 39-42.

[20] T. O. Ranger, below, pp. 225-226.

[21] H. E. O'Neill, 'A Three Months' Journey in the Makua and Lomwe Countries' *Proceedings of the Royal Geographical Society* IV (1882) p. 199, and 'Journey from Mozambique to Lakes Shirwa and Amaramba', *P.R.G.S.*, VI (1884) p. 635.

[22] Pe. Gerard, 'Costumes dos Macua do Medo, região de Namuno, circunscrição de Montepuez' *Moçambique* 28 (1941) pp. 18-19.

[23] For Mauruça and the other major chiefs in the Mossuril hinterland, see E. A. Alpers, 'The role of the Yao in the development of trade in East-Central Africa, 1698-c. 1850', University of London, Ph.D. thesis, 1966, *passim*.

[24] In an earlier draft of his paper on 'Missionary Adaptation', Professor Ranger remarks upon the dominance of the Yao word, *mbepesi*, to describe 'ancestor veneration' in Masasi; see also, Tanzania National Archives, Mikindani District Book, 'Laws, Manners, and Customs'.

[25] Abel dos Santos Baptista *Monografia Etnográfica sobre os Macuas* (Lisboa 1951) pp. 32-3.

[26] *Ibid.* p. 33.

[27] Tanzania National Archives, Tunduru District Book, 'Manners and Customs: Ndalanga Dance'. See below, p. 183.

[28] Mitchell *op, cit.* pp. 139-40, and citing Meredith Sanderson, 'Ceremonial Purification among the Wayao, Nyasaland' *Man* XXII, 55 (1922) pp. 91-3.

[29] Tanzania National Archives, Tunduru District Book, 'Manners and Customs: Ndalanga Dance'.

[30] Mitchell *op. cit.* pp. 121-2.

[31] Santos Baptista *op. cit.* pp. 56-8; cf. Mitchell *op. cit.* pp. 114-18.

[32] E. A. Alpers, 'Trade, State, and Society among the Yao in the Nineteenth Century *Journal of African History* X, 3 (1969) p. 415.

[33] Victor W. Turner *The Forest of Symbols: Aspects of Ndembu Ritual* (Ithaca, New York 1967) p. 7.

[34] *Ibid.* pp. 96-7.

[35] Alpers, 'Trade, State, and Society', p. 420, citing W. H. J. Rangeley, 'The AmaCinga Ayao' *Nyasaland Journal* XV, 2 (1962) p. 46.

[36] See, e.g. I. M. Lewis *op. cit.* pp. 32-8.

[37] Additional descriptive material on Yao and Makua initiation rites may be found in Peirone *op. cit.* pp. 149-54; Lucy Mair, 'A Yao girl's initiation' *Man* 51 (1951) pp. 60-3; H. S. Stannus and J. B. Davey, 'The initiation ceremony for boys among the Yao of Nyasaland' *Jl. Anth. Inst. Gt. Br. and Ireland* XLIII (1913) pp. 119-23; Santos Baptista *op. cit.* pp. 50-1; Eugène de Froberville, 'Notes sur les mœurs, coûtumes et traditions des amakoua, sur le commerce et la traite des esclaves dans l'Afrique Orientale' *Bulletin de la Société de Géographie* 3e Serie, VIII (1847) pp. 318-20; Diogo da Camara Reis, 'Os Macuas de Mogovolas' *Boletim da Sociedade de Estudos de Moçambique* 131 (1962) pp. 16-17.

[38] Although I do not discuss them in this paper, funeral rites are equally susceptible to religious innovation and have been extensively Islamised in this region.

[39] Mitchell *op. cit.* p. 82; for a complete description of the traditional aggregation rites and the symbols involved in them, see M. Sanderson, 'Inyago—The Picture-models of the Yao Initiation Ceremonies' *Nyasaland Jl.* VIII, 2 (1955) pp. 36-57.

[40] 'The Story of Amini Bin Saidi of the Yao Tribe of Nyasaland', recorded by D. W. Malcolm in Margery Perham (ed.) *Ten Africans* second ed. (London 1963) p. 142. The problem of Islamic 'baptism' is a thorny one which merits closer investigation. See C. H. Becker, 'Materials for the Understanding of Islam in German East Africa', ed. and trs.

by B. G. Martin *Tanzania Notes and Records* 68 (1968) pp. 39, 42 and 53; Martin Klamroth, 'Ostafrikanischer Islam' *Allgemeine Missions-Zeitschrift* XXXVII (1910) p. 536.

[41] Mitchell, *op. cit.* pp. 81–2. The effect of this development was that control of initiation rites became less significant as an index of political influence, but after half a century of colonial rule there were other forms of prestige for which headmen competed, such as government recognition.

[42] Froberville, 'Notes sur les Va-Ngindo' *Bull. Soc. Géog.* 4e Serie, III (1852) pp. 433 and 437. Cf. A. R. W. Crosse-Upcott, 'The Social Structure of the KiNgindo-speaking Peoples', University of Cape Town Ph.D. thesis, 1956, pp. 270–270a and 284–284a.

[43] Cf. the significance of Christianity in Buganda, for which see D. A. Low *Religion and Society in Buganda, 1875–1900* (Kampala 1956) and F. B. Welbourn *Religion and Politics in Uganda, 1952–62* (Nairobi 1965).

[44] See Alpers, 'The role of the Yao' and 'Trade, State, and Society'.

[45] David Livingstone *Last Journals* ed. H. Waller (London 1874) vol. I, p. 73. The traditional shape of a Yao hut was round.

[46] Abdallah *op. cit.* p. 51. A. H. J. Prins *The Swahili-Speaking Peoples of Zanzibar and the East African Coast* (London 1961) p. 58, reports that the mango tree (*mwembe*) was said to be able to belong only to noble owners.

[47] W. H. J. Rangeley, 'The Ayao' *Nyasaland Jl.* XVI, 1 (1963) p. 25.

[48] As quoted in R. M. Heanley *A Memoir of Edward Steere, D.D., LL.D., Third Missionary Bishop in Central Africa* (London 1888) p. 152, 318–19.

[49] U.S.P.G. Archives, London UMCA A/I/iv, May Allen to R. M. Heanley, Mkunazini, Zanzibar, 18 July 1877.

[50] *Ibid.* UMCA A/I/iii, envelope #2, Steere to Heanley, Zanzibar, 13 November, 1877, and Steere to Noys, Zanzibar, 8 February, 1878.

[51] Abdallah *op. cit.* p. 55. Kumtelela appears to have filled the same role for the first Mataka as did Gwaja for the fifth.

[52] USPG, UMCA A/I/iii, envelope #2, Steere to Slater, Zanzibar, 28 July, 1881. In view of the 1877 embassy to Zanzibar, it is not altogether clear why Steere should have felt this way about Nyambi.

[53] *Ibid.* UMCA A/I/iii, envelope #1, Steere to Penney, Zanzibar, 30 June, 1881; see also W. P. Johnson *My African Reminiscences, 1875–1895* (London 1924) pp. 59–60.

[54] USPG, UMCA A/I/iv, [Johnson] to Randolph, Mbweni, 26 November [1886]. C. A. Smithies *A Journey to Lake Nyasa, and Visit to the Magwangwara and the Source of the Rovuma, in the Year 1886* (Kiungani, Zanzibar, n.d.) p. 43, notes that the man who was specifically said to have planted the flea in Mataka's ear was named Isa.

[55] Abdallah *op. cit.* p. 56.

[56] By the end of 1887 there was a regular Islamic call to prayer at Mataka's town. See *Central Africa: A Monthly Record of the Work of the Universities' Mission* 60 (December 1887) p. 176.

[57] For details, such as they exist for an obliterated expedition, see José Justino Teixeira Botelho *História Militar e Política dos Portugueses em Moçambique de 1883 aos nossos dias* second edn. (Lisboa, 1936) pp. 563–4; Eric Axelson *Portugal and the Scramble for Africa, 1875–1891* (Johannesburg 1967) p. 255, where Mataka is misspelled as Mutaca.

[58] Abdallah *op. cit.* pp. 43–4.

[59] E. D. Young *Nyassa: A Journal of Adventure* (London 1877) p. 139.

[60] J. F. Elton *Travels and Researches among the Lakes and Mountains of Eastern and Central Africa*, ed. H. B. Cotterill (London 1879) p. 289.

[61] Quoted by George Shepperson, 'The Jumbe of Kota Kota and some Aspects of the History of Islam in British Central Africa', in I. M. Lewis *op. cit.* p. 195.

[62] Ian Linden, 'Roman Catholics in Protestant Nyasaland, 1889–1939', p. 17 of an unpublished manuscript.

[63] Ellen Maples (ed.) *Journals and Papers of Chauncy Maples* (London 1899) p. 247.

[64] A. E. M. Anderson-Morshead *The History of the Universities' Mission to Central Africa, 1859–1909* (London 1909) pp. 131–2.

[65] J. S. Trimingham, 'The Expansion of Islam', in Kritzeck and Lewis *Islam in Africa* p. 16. For evidence of the continued vitality of Muslim education in early colonial Malawi, see A. G. Blood *The History of the U.M.C.A.* II: 1907–32 (London 1957) p. 162, where he cites Father Russell's assessment in 1911 of the challenge involved in establishing a mission school near Malindi: ' "The work will be uphill and hard, for the Mohammedans are both rich and flourishing, and have there (a thing I saw for the first time) a boarding school for boys." ' For testimony to the widespread literacy in Arabic script among the Yao in Moçambique, see A. Sousa Lobato, 'Monográfia Etnográfica Original sobro o Povo Ajaua' *Bol. Soc. Est. da Colónia de Moç.* 63 (1949) p. 16; Peirone *op. cit.* pp. 97–101.

[66] Although a number of very helpful criticisms were made during the discussion of my paper at the conference, this one was not. I am indebted to my research assistant, Robert Papstein, for helping me to come to grips with this deficiency in that draft of this essay. See Robert Papstein, 'The Spread of Islam into East Africa', unpublished seminar paper, University of California, Los Angeles, Fall Quarter, 1970, especially pp. 13–14.

[67] *Central Africa* 66 (June 1888) p. 85. Semboja was literate in Swahili in Arabic script, but the ritual importance of wild pig-hunting for the Kilindi dynasty made it impossible for him to consider adopting a religion which forbade the eating of pork. See Steven Feierman, 'The Shambaa' in A. D. Roberts (ed.) *Tanzania before 1900: Seven Area Histories* (Nairobi 1968) pp. 4–5, 10–11; Abdallah bin Hemedi, lAjjemy *The Kilindi* ed. J. W. T. Allen and William Kimweri (Nairobi 1963) chapters 3 and 8.

[68] Alpers, 'Trade, State, and Society', especially p. 414, while noting that I have here re-interpreted Mtalika's motives in stealing the flour from the graves of his ancestors.

[69] David Parkin, 'Politics of Ritual Syncretism: Islam among the non-Muslim Giriama of Kenya' *Africa* XL, 3 (1970) pp. 217–33, especially at p. 218.

[70] Elton *op. cit.* pp. 197–8.

[71] Maples *op. cit.* pp. 37–8.

[72] Lamburn *op. cit.* p. 176.

[73] *Central Africa* 16 (April 1884) p. 58, and 339 (March 1911) p. 57.

[74] The possibility that the emergence of itinerant preachers in the southern interior was caused by the growing influence of the Qadiriya and Shadhiliya *tarigas* remains attractive but still unproved.

[75] Johnson *op. cit.* p. 202; see also *Central Africa* 208 (April 1900) p. 54.

[76] Robert Codrington, 'The Central Angoniland District of the British Central Africa Protectorate' *The Geographical Journal* XI (1898) p. 516.

[77] Johnson *op. cit.* p. 146; Blood *op. cit.* p. 62, citing Bishop Fisher.

[78] Cited from the *Inverness Courier* of 19 July 1910 by Trimingham *Islam in East Africa* (Oxford 1964) p. 28, who was evidently much influenced by Sharpe's point of view, for which see pp. 61–2. With respect to Muslim propaganda, it is well worth noting that B. G. Martin, 'Muslim Politics and Resistance to Colonial Rule: Shaykh Uways B. Muhammad Al-Barāwī and Qādirīya brotherhood in East Africa' *Journal of African History* X, 3 (1969) p. 474, reports that 'in 1901 and 1902, and again in 1908, the Qadiriya was making special efforts to make converts'.

[79] Linden, 'Roman Catholics', p. 15.

[80] António Enes, *Moçambique: Relatório Apresentado ao Governo* (Lisboa 1893) as quoted in José Júlio Gonçalves *O Mundo Árabo-Islâmico e o Ultramar Português* second ed. (Lisboa 1962) pp. 273–4.

[81] For evidence that Makanjila maintained a voluminous correspondence in both Arabic

and Swahili, see R. A. Oliver *Sir Harry Johnston and the Scramble for Africa* (London 1958) p. 209.

[82] Ernesto Jardim de Vilhena *Relatorios e Memorias sobre os Territorios [do] Companhia do Nyassa* (Lisboa 1905) pp. 55–6, 71.

[83] John Iliffe, *Tanganyika under German Rule, 1905–1912* (Cambridge 1969) pp. 187–200, at p. 189. Cf. George Shepperson and Thomas Price *Independent African: John Chilembwe and the Origins, setting and significance of the Nyasaland native uprising of 1915* (Edinburgh 1958) p. 407, where they note that 'in Central African history, Islam had first offered a way of advance beyond rigid tribalism, and still provided a possible alternative for the African who sought some status of dignity *vis-à-vis* the European'.

[84] Crosse-Upcott, 'Social Structure', pp. 472, 484 and 493. Iliffe *op. cit.* pp. 189 and 194, and Martin, 'Muslim Politics', p. 479 and 486, both citing the same notation by Governor Albrecht Freiherr von Rechenberg, suggesting that the Qadiriya may have been implicated in these developments.

[85] Tanzania National Archives, Annual Reports, Kilwa, 1924 and 1925.

[86] Tanzania National Archives, Annual Report, Songea, 1923. I am indebted to Dr Iliffe for these references from the T.N.A.

[87] See Lienhardt, 'A Controversy over Islamic Custom', pp. 378–9.

[88] 'Traditional African Islam, where Islam is fitted into the indigenous system and embraces many grades of allegiance. Religious dualism and tolerance are characteristic, with authority recognizing all religious usages.' Trimingham, 'The Expansion of Islam', p. 33.

[89] Schildkneckt *op. cit.* p. 235.

[90] von Grunebaum *op. cit.* p. 20.

[91] Trimingham *Islam in East Africa* p. 58.

[92] Maples *op. cit.* p. 247; cf. Abdallah *op. cit.* p. 28, and cited in Alpers, 'Trade, State, and Society', p. 407.

[93] T. W. Arnold *The Preaching of Islam: A History of the Propagation of the Muslim Faith* second ed. (New York 1913) p. 409. More generally, see chapters. 1, 2 and 13.

[94] See, e.g., J. M. Gray, 'Ahmed bin Ibrahim—the First Arab to Reach Buganda' *Uganda Journal* XI, 2 (1947) pp. 80–97; Becker, 'Materials', p. 41.

[95] I am grateful to Drs Michael Gilsenan and Marja-Liisa Swantz for their comments on this important point.

[96] von Grunebaum *op. cit.* p. 91. In East Africa an especially vivid example of the contrast between missionary control over access to Christianity and the absence of such restraints with regard to Islam concerns houses of worship. Professor Ranger has pointed out to me that in Masasi churches were the objects of great competition between Christian villages and headmen, while the U.M.C.A. maintained firm control over their distribution. This may be contrasted with the ubiquity of mosques in Yaoland. Becker *op. cit.* p. 42; Balsan *op. cit.* p. 48 and illustration facing p. 41.

[97] Robert Redfield *Peasant Society and Culture* (Chicago 1956). For an initial attempt to apply Redfield's ideas to this area, although in a somewhat different context, see John Iliffe, 'The Organization of the Maji Maji Rebellion' *Journal of African History* VIII, 3 (1967) pp. 501–2.

[98] Robin Horton, 'African Conversion' *Africa* XLI, 2 (1971) pp. 85–108, especially section III.

[99] *Ibid.* pp. 101–3. Horton's fifth conclusion concerns the contrasting definitions of lesser spirits and the supreme being, a conceptualisation which does not seem immediately relevant to the present discussion.

[100] *Ibid.* p. 103; *Cemtral Africa* 17 (May 1884) p. 82.

[101] Horton, 'African Conversion', p. 103; see above, p. 34.

[102] Horton, 'African Conversion', p. 104.

G. C. K. GWASSA

Kinjikitile and the Ideology of Maji Maji

INTRODUCTION: MAJI MAJI AND IDEOLOGY

Maji Maji was a mass movement waged by Africans against German colonial rule in what was then German East Africa. It lasted from July 1905 to August 1907 and covered over 100,000 square miles of the southern third of what is now mainland Tanzania. It involved over twenty differing ethnic groups. In its organisational scale and its ethnic variety Maji Maji was a movement both different from and more complex than earlier reactions and resistances to the imposition of colonial rule, for the latter had usually been confined within ethnic boundaries. By comparison with the past Maji Maji was a revolutionary movement creating fundamental changes in traditional organisational scale. The problem is to show how this revolutionary development came about when and where it did.

One explanation often advanced is to stress German brutality which gave the varying peoples involved in Maji Maji a common grievance. Another is to stress the realisation by these southern Tanzanian peoples that such brutality was the consequence of alien over-rule and so to stress their desire for independence. Maji Maji *was* a protest against German oppression and it was also in a real sense a war for independence. But these cannot be total explanations. Other parts of the country were oppressed; other parts of the country desired independence from the Germans. But they did not revolt. Thus we must ask not only *why* people wished to rise up against the Germans but *how* they were able to do so. How were so many people brought out in arms against the Germans in southern Tanzania?

The answer to this question must be sought mainly in terms of ideology. The peoples of southern Tanzania wished to rise up in arms but they did not believe that they could do so effectively: 'Thus they waited for a long time because there was no plan or knowledge. Truly his (the German's) practices were bad. But while there were no superior weapons should the people not fear? Everywhere elders were busy thinking, "What should we do?" '[1]

A crisis of resentment against German rule and of frustrated desire to rise up against it had become widespread by 1903-4. The crisis was resolved by the emergence of an ideology which offered solutions to the problems of unity and morale. This ideology was couched in religious terms. It was revolutionary and it was created at that specific time for a specific purpose. Yet it drew upon pre-existing religious beliefs, combining them into new patterns. In order to understand how it did this we must examine briefly the peoples of southern Tanzania.

THE PEOPLES OF SOUTHERN TANZANIA

Most of the peoples of the Maji Maji area were organised on a small scale, usually into clans which constituted political units. The Ngoni of Songea provide a rare example of a centralised political system but even they were divided into two sometimes conflicting kingdoms. Yet despite this apparent diversity and even extreme disunity, the effects of the slave trade and of the raids of the Ngoni and Yao and the constant movements of peoples had produced so complex an ethnic admixture that it became impossible to draw meaningful ethnic boundaries. Thus Crosse-Upcott in his study of the Ngindo, who played an important role in Maji Maji, urges that Ngindo were scattered over the whole area between the Rufiji and the Ruvuma rivers and between the coast and Lake Nyasa.[2] In 1875 Thomson, travelling among the Mbunga, found that 'their language is identical with that of the Wagindo . . . One of our porters who had been brought up in Gindo, spoke the M'henge (Mbunga) idiom quite easily although he had never been in the country before.'[3] In the Rufiji valley Beardall found Wamahoro and Wamamboka who spoke the same language 'as that spoken by the Wangindo and the Wamatumbi'.[4]

These wide linguistic and cultural connections help to explain the present feeling of common origin among Ngindo, Kichi, Ikemba and the peoples of the Rufiji valley. There is evidence, too, which shows intermarriage between Ngoni and Ngindo, and between the latter and the Mwera. In all this intermixture was the basis of a cultural affinity.

Thus the old view that the southern Tanzanian peoples had had little in common, that they were perpetually at each other's throats, that they were so divided and weak that it was impossible for them to combine, falls away. Instead it has been shown that a complex web of cultural inter-mixture, and of wide-ranging social and marital relationships had been woven by events taking place before and during the nineteenth century. By the time Maji Maji broke out, southern Tanzania possessed the potentiality for some semblance of unity because ideological communication was possible and could be made both meaningful and effective. In other words most or all the Maji prescriptions and practices could be understood and accepted by the majority of the peoples of the Maji Maji area because the Maji ideology drew upon their commonly shared beliefs.

THE MAJI MAJI IDEOLOGY AND THE GENERAL CONCEPT OF THE HIERARCHY OF FORCE

The essence of the Maji ideology, as it was pronounced by Kinjikitile Ngwale of Ngarambe, can be simply stated. For a people politically divided and used to fighting limited defensive wars it was necessary to unite and take the fullest advantage of numerical superiority if victory over the Germans was to be assured. The teachings of Kinjikitile Ngwale were that all Africans were one, that they were free men, and that those who partook of the *maji* (water) would be immune from European bullets. The dead ancestors would assist them in a war which had been commanded by God.

We can perhaps best understand what is involved in this message in its most general terms by transposing Father Tempel's concept of 'vital force' into the southern Tanzanian context. All southern Tanzanian peoples believed in a hierarchy of forces. At its head is the Creator, the Supreme Being, who is himself the source of all power and who can therefore increase it in men. Below the Creator come the ancestors, the first founders of clans or ethnic groups who are believed to have received 'vital force' from the Creator and who are held to powerfully influence posterity. Among the Matumbi, for instance, each clan performs the *Mbekia* ceremony to propitiate such ancestors every year in August after the harvest. This explains why in August and September some Maji Maji fighters were seen drunk. They had come to fight the Germans from the *Mbekia* ceremonies.[5] Next in this hierarchy of forces come the dead members of a particular family who have immediate influence on their off-spring. Lastly, it is believed that the oldest living members of society are endowed with more 'vital force' than the younger ones and the clan head is considered to have more 'vital force' than any other man.

This hierarchy of forces has relevance to the Maji ideology in two ways. In one sense Kinjikitile's message combined the 'vital force' of the Creator, who had commanded the war; of the ancestors, who were to return to assist the living warriors; and of the living war leaders who were accepted by their fol-lowers at the ceremonies at Kinjikitile's pool.

In another sense Kinjikitile's exercise of his own powers fits into this hierar-chial pattern. Kinjikitile as man could exercise influence on those below him in the hierarchy of force—on trees or animals. Thus he is said to have made lions and snakes tame. Then it is believed that a man can influence the *being* of other men if he can obtain recourse to a vital external power and particu-larly through the intervention of God. Kinjikitile was believed to be endowed with force by God, who had entered and possessed him, and through this force it was believed that he could strengthen Africans against Germans.

Thus Kinjikitile was acceptable to the societies among whom he worked be-cause his *being* and teaching conformed to known metaphysics. At Ngarambe pool, where he preached the message, he provided a unitary ideology which cut across clan and ethnic boundaries and which in fact discouraged these boundaries. *Maji* as a war medicine was not to be of or for any single group, clan or ethnic identity, but of and for all people; his was a universal medicine having a universal appeal. Therefore the *Maji* ideology became the basis of a revolutionary commitment to mass action against German colonial rule. In addition, Kinjikitile, based in Ngarambe, and later his ambassadors to the various areas, provided means of contact between potential leaders from various localities, and in so doing gave opportunity for establishing ties and inter-group communications which became increasingly necessary in the mass move-ment.

THE MAJI IDEOLOGY AND THE CULT OF POSSESSION

The idea of the hierarchy of 'vital force' only explains Kinjikitile's teaching and its acceptability in the most general way. In order to grasp more exactly the ways in which he was accepted and in which his ideology was effective it is necessary to examine in more detail other related but more precise religious ideas, and particularly the immediate antecedents to Kinjikitile's meteoric rise to charismatic leadership. First it is necessary to grasp the nature of the cult of possession extant among Kinjikitile's client societies.

Among the Matumbi-Ngindo group possession is believed to give a man access to certain supernatural powers. He is said to have *Lilungu* and to be the symbolic representation of the spirit of *Lilungu* that has possessed him. He is above society, for he can walk naked and not be punished. Although he is not a prophet, but a medium through which God or a given spirit operates, his 'vital force' is greater than the greatest possible force in normal human beings. And because of this the man with *Lilungu* is held to have powers over all other beings inferior to him, not only ordinary men but also man-eating lions as well, so that he can sleep in the open without being harmed by them. Ordinarily he does not eat and yet he cannot die from hunger. Above all, he is pure from sin. When in the company of witches he hunts them down until he kills them all for it is said they stink before him. All field authorities agree that Kinjikitile had *Lilungu* and it was therefore natural that he should order all his clients to renounce witchcraft, failing which death would attend them. One informant put the powers of a man with *Lilungu* quite clearly:

People who have *Lilungu* were feared very much since the days of old. They can do anything. And if a man with *Lilungu* killed a person where could you go to charge (him)? The *Lukumbi* (inter-clan court)? Never at all! His affairs are god-like. A man with Lilungu does not fear anything. He can even go naked. Those things that are forbidden or are too dangerous to eat, he eats.'[6]

But Kinjikitile was more powerful than an ordinary man who has an ordinary *Lilungu*. Kinjikitile was possessed by the Hongo spirit, which was in itself very powerful, and it was believed that the Hongo spirit had been sent to Kinjikitile by the superior divinity, Bokero. At Ngarambe, which was Kinjikitile's headquarters, one informant explained that 'Hongo was to Bokero as Jesus is to God, or as Prophet Mohamed is to God'.[7] This hierarchical relationship between Bokero, Hongo and Kinjikitile was later extended to define the relationship between Kinjikitile and his assistants and messengers. Particularly outside the outbreak area of Maji Maji the title of Bokero came to be applied to Kinjikitile himself while the title of Hongo was reserved for those who carried and dispensed the *maji* and supervised drilling in the various areas of the war zone.

KINJIKITILE AND THE BOKERO CULT AT KIBESA

What was the significance of this claimed relationship with Bokero? Clearly Kinjikitile used the Bokero/Hongo concept to innovate. But the concept of the influence and power of the Bokero spirit long pre-dated Maji Maji. So also did the idea of Bokero's close link with water as a medicine. One of the main centres of the Bokero cult was situated in the Rufiji valley, outside the outbreak area of Maji Maji, but well known to the peoples who initiated the uprising. This cult centre had been located, for very many years before Maji Maji, at a place called Kibesa, above the Mpanga Falls on the Rufiji river; the place was some-times known as Rufiji Ruhingo, i.e. the upper reaches of the Rufiji. The riverine ecology of the Rufiji made that river affect the lives of the people there as the Nile affects the Egyptian's, though on a much smaller scale. When the floods were too high the Rufiji people lived in houses raised several yards above the ground and all movement from place to place had to be done in canoes. When the waters were too low and rain scarce famine threatened the people of the valley. Thus too low or too high waters could cause disaster to the population.

The Bokero cult in Rufiji had developed out of this situation. The people of Rufiji addressed Bokero, and his fellow divinities, Ulilo and Nyamguni, seeking from them enough but not excessive rain, the fertility of their soil, and so on. Originally it seems that Bokero, Ulilo and Nyamguni were all three propiti-ated at the Kibesa centre. At some time in the past the propitiation of Ulilo shifted to Mgende, which is still today a famous centre of *Uganga*. At any rate at the time of Maji Maji Bokero was certainly still being propitiated at Kibesa.[8] The peoples of Rufiji travelled annually to his cult centre to pray for rain. The rock shrine of Bokero was controlled by one Kologelo, which may have been the hereditary clan name of the medium of the divinity.

It appears from oral authorities that 1904–5 was a period of drought. To-wards the end of 1904 people went to Kibesa to ask for rain. Jumbe Mbanga Mbite and another clan head, Mapende Mburu, went to consult the divinities at Kologelo's: 'All went with salt and *kaniki* cloth (blue calico). They went there, they prayed for rain and water. They were successful'.[9] The medium-priest Kologelo gave to these, as well as to other applicants, water from the Kibesa pool, telling them to sprinkle it on their land and to use it in general as a panacea.[10]

It seems plain that there were close connections between this long-established cult and the practices of the cult centre which Kinjikitile set up at Ngarambe immediately preceding Maji Maji. There seems no doubt that Kinjikitile borrowed the idea of water, *maji*, as the panacea from the Bokero cult centre at Kibesa, though he developed it into a war medicine by combining the possession cult with ancestor observances and immunity beliefs. Kinjikitile himself acknowledged the seniority of the Kibesa or Rufiji Ruhingo shrine. After he had addressed his clients at Ngarambe and given them his message in a manner resembling a political rally, he would say, 'If there be anybody amongst you who does not believe me, let him go to prove this from Bokero in Rufiji Ruh-ingo.'[11]

Moreover, there were striking similarities of ritual procedure. Kinjikitile lived near to the shrine of the divinity as did Kologelo. All oral authorities agree that both mediums went under the water to consult the spirits before they addressed their clients. Both Kologelo's clients and the Maji Maji people dressed in *kaniki*. And today people at Ngarambe, the site of Kinjikitile's cult centre, still speak of the Bokero centre on the Rufiji and of Bokero's great powers.

'There at Bokero's there is a huge rock,' says Mzee Nimewako. 'Up to now motor-boats have failed to go beyond that rock of Bokero. The rock of Bokero has four windows and it is there at Ruhingo. The Germans tried to use a powder magazine to break it. They failed. They wanted recently to close those windows in order to get hydro-electricity; they failed . . . You cannot cross the river there . . . If you try you fall off and die. But there is nearby a guardian (or medium) of the rock of Bokero. This is the propitiator and the spirits of Bokero have possessed him. If you want to go across the rock you must first call on him, whereupon he will propitiate the spirits on your behalf. The following day you can cross safely.'[12]

KINJIKITILE AND OTHER CENTRES OF THE BOKERO CULT

Obviously Kinjikitile borrowed a great deal from the Kibesa cult centre of Bokero. The question now arises whether he had any connections with other centres of Bokero observance. The Bokero cult—or as it is most often called in the evidence, the Kolelo cult, from a condensation of the name Kologelo—is widespread. It extends to the Ndengereko, the Zaramo and the Luguru peoples as well as to the Rufiji. In addition to the Kibesa shrine on the Rufiji there was at least one other major centre of the cult situated in Uluguru.

The earliest known written reference to this centre comes from Burton:

They (the Luguru) have a place visited even by distant Wazaramo Pilgrims. It is described as a cave where a P'hepo or the disembodied spirit of man, in fact a ghost, produces a terrible subterranean sound, called by the people Kurero or Bokero; it arises probably from the flow of water underground . . . men sacrifice sheep and goats to obtain fruitful seasons and success in war.[13]

The existence of this cult centre in the Luguru mountains was subsequently confirmed by Martin Klamroth, a missionary at Maneromango. According to him, Kolelo was a great snake god, a point that is reminiscent of Hongo at Ngarambe, since the Hongo spirit was also supposed to embody itself on occasions in a snake. Like Hongo also, Kolelo in Klamroth's version was said to have come as a messenger of the great Creator to remove corruption. Kolelo was said to have marital connections with the Mlali clan, whom he commanded: 'You people of the Mlali clan shall be my people and serve me here forever in this cave in the Luguru mountains'. The Mlali clan guarded an area called Kolelo in the Matombo district of Morogoro to which representatives from various areas of Uzaramo brought offerings. As at the Kibesa shrine on the Rufiji, Bokero/Kolelo of Uluguru had a medium who interpreted the message of the divinity to clients.

It seems certain that the cult centre of the Uluguru mountains was part of a common system of belief and practice with that on the Rufiji river. But the question is whether it was also connected to the Maji Maji rising. Klamroth certainly believed that it was. According to him, Kolelo/Bokero of Uluguru had customarily concerned himself only with problems of fertility and rain. But in 1905:

Kolelo also concerned himself with politics. Kolelo had forbidden the further payment of taxes to the white foreigners; in mid-July a great flood would come and destroy all whites and their followers. Later it was said the earth would open and swallow them, that no bullets but only water would come from the soldiers' guns, seven lions would come and destroy the enemy; 'be not afraid, Kolelo spares his black children'.[14]

According to Klamroth the power of Kolelo/Bokero proved inadequate, so 'God himself now appeared' and people began talking about the 'resurrection of the dead'. Klamroth maintains that Kibasila, leader of Maji Maji in southern Uzaramo, was won over to the movement by being shown the resurrected ancestors.

Klamroth's account, though admittedly garbled, seems at first sight to describe the same sort of deployment of the hierarchy of force that comes out of the oral descriptions of Kinjikitile's teaching at Ngarambe. It is tempting to see the Maji ideology as the product of a general development out of the Bokero cult. And yet there is no further sound evidence that Kolelo/Bokero of Uluguru contributed to the Maji Maji ideology. Lloyd Swantz, who has made an ethnographic study of the Zaramo, has found no connection between their participation in Maji Maji and the Kolelo cult centre in Uluguru.[15] Oral authorities in Uzaramo are adamant that no connection existed. 'This Kolelo is in Uluguru mountains and has *no* relationship whatever with the Maji Maji war. Since the days of our ancestors (Wahenga) there were always his (Kolelo's) special servants.'[16] Or again: 'As for Kolelo this is an established tradition . . . For in times of drought and illness—life and rain—people receive these from Kolelo . . . Kolelo had nothing to do with Maji Maji for the work of Kolelo is good, it is to ensure affluence.'[17]

The case seems clearer still with yet another centre of Kolelo/Bokero propitiation. This concerns the Wadoe people. According to Mtoto bin Mwenyi Bakari, the Wadoe address prayers for rain to Kolelo, as prayers are addressed to Bokero in Rufiji. Kolelo is said to be the name of a place in Nguu country and the spirit living there is said to be that of a headman of Ukami who, being a great *mganga* and invulnerable to weapons, met a miraculous death, for his body vanished. 'All the elders and *Pazi* and the headmen of Kingalu's family revere this spirit.'[18] But the Wadoe did not participate in Maji Maji and no authority, archival or oral, has sought to associate the Kolelo shrine in Nguu with the uprising.

In short it seems that Kinjikitile had been associated with the Bokero shrine at Kibesa on the upper Rufiji river and that when he went south to open his own shrine at Ngarambe he developed the Bokero ritual and teaching as one of the bases of the Maji ideology. But it also seems that the Bokero net-work as a whole did not participate in or give spiritual support to the uprising.

KINJIKITILE AND THE SPIRITS OF THE DEAD

We have seen, then, the importance of the idea of possession in general and of the Bokero cult in particular to the making and acceptibility of Kinjikitile's message. Further related beliefs were also very important. One of the commonest religious beliefs in the Maji Maji districts is the belief in the importance of *Mahoka* (singular *lihoka*), the spirits of the dead. The term is widespread in Mtwara, Ruvuma, Coast and perhaps Morogoro regions. In the outbreak area nearly every homestead has a *Kijumba-Nungu*, the House of God. Each head of a family makes offerings to the *Kijumba-Nungu* for his ancestors' *Mahoka* who are then seen as *Nungu* or *Mulungu*. Now, Kinjikitile built at Ngarambe a very large *Kijumba-Nungu* at which he insisted that all clients should make offerings of rice, millet, salt or money before even greeting him as the great *Mganga*. In yet another sense, then, Kinjikitile was creating a unitary ideology for his was a *Kijumba-Nungu* not for individual families but for all Africans— Pogoro, Matumbi, Ngindo and so on. In a sense, the offerings were directed to the ancestors of all blackmen.

In order to appreciate the force of this idea it is necessary to remind ourselves of what Bishop Komba has written of the place of *Mahoka* in Ngoni metaphysics:

> *Mahoka* . . . resembles *Mulungu* (God) in certain respects . . . According to Bantu thought that state of *Mahoka* resembling *Mulungu* makes *Mahoka* become the symbol of *Mulungu*. And the philosophy of Bantu symbolism identifies symbol with the object symbolised—*Mahoka* to become *Mulungu* or *Mulungu* to become *Mahoka*.[19]

Thus when Kinjikitile announced that all dead ancestors were at Ngarambe and that anybody who came there would see them, he was stressing not so much the idea of resurrection as the fact that *Mulungu* in the symbol of *Mahoka*, in the symbol of the totality of the ancestral spirits, was there to help Africans. So every morning the pilgrims to Ngarambe, astonished that their offerings to the *Kijumba-Nungu* had vanished, were told by Kinjikitile's assistant: 'Do you see? The gods are pleased. They have taken all your good offerings'.[20]

Further, it was customary for all the people of the Maji Maji area, from the Matumbi to the Ngoni, to pray to their *Mahoka* before going to war. Offering at a 'national' *Kijumba-Nungu* at Ngarambe before going to war with the Germans was therefore both consistent with tradition and with a 'national' commitment, for there it was done on a wider and unitary scale.

KINJIKITILE AS MGANGA

Kinjikitile had *Lilungu*. He was possessed by Hongo, emissary of Bokero. At his cult centre offerings were made to the totality of the ancestors. He also enjoyed the prestige of the *Mganga*. The Matumbi and Ngindo regard the *Mganga* as an expert (*Pundi*), who enjoys high respect. *Pundis* used to walk about the country holding large fly whisks. Kinjikitile did not walk about, but he had a fly whisk as did his ambassadors. One authority tells us: '*Pundis* used to be feared very much. They were also honoured and respected a lot . . . if a *Pundi* said something we agreed. Today if a Bwana Doctor says a thing do we not believe?'[21]

Evidence from the field does not suggest that ordinary *Pundis* or *Waganga* were also possessed. So having *Lilungu* Kinjikitile was regarded as more powerful than any of the *waganga*. 'Kinjikitile excelled them all (aliwapiku). He was too powerful and too full of wisdom for them. They (Waganga) did not know how to go about him'.[22] Yet in some ways Kinjikitile performed as a characteristic *Mganga*. 'He could tell matters secret to the people and yet he was a mere newcomer there at Ngarambe. His instructions were good. He had said,

'Adultery is bad for it puts the body out of joint and God does not want it. Witchcraft is also bad and God hates it.' Then people said, 'Ayi, this man is truly from God for he forbids even witchcraft.'[23]

There is evidence also that some of Kinjikitile's ambassadors to the peoples beyond Ngarambe's direct area of influence—the so-called *Hongo* or *Mpokosi*—had formerly been traditional *Waganga*. It is certain that the woman who administered the *maji* medicine to the warriors of Matumbi was an *Mganga*.

> In Nandete the *jemadar* of the war was Sikwato Mbonde. And his wife, Nantabila Naupunda, my aunt, administered *maji* to the warriors and she lay across their path and they stepped over her. And if you ask why a woman was selected, it is because women are extremely expert at *Uganga* and they were thereby weakening that one (the Germans) so that he becomes like a woman.[24]

KINJIKITILE AND THE MAJI AS WAR MEDICINE

It remains to examine one last element in the syncretist ideology created by Kinjikitile—the belief that the *maji* would bestow invulnerability to bullets. Once again the idea of a war medicine was not new. As an informant testified:

> The reason why many people believed that bullets would turn into water or that they would not enter the body, was simply because that was our established tradition. Since our ancestors . . . these matters were extant in Umatumbi. All hunters had *dawa* (medicine) and even today these still exist. They used amulets for their safety and so that they could be more accurate . . . First, there is *Kirughe*. If you use this medicine neither bullet nor spear . . . can enter your body.[25]

Each group had its own trusted war medicines. An informant at Kibata listed the most famous medicines of the Matumbi and Ngindo:

> There are war medicines as well. There are two types. First there is *ndyengu*, which if used causes weapons, spears, arrows or bullets to be deflected away from the man who is the target. On the other hand, another medicine, *Kalunde*, prevents bullets, spears, knives or arrows from entering the body of the person who has taken it.[26]

Kinjikitile did not introduce the idea of a medicine that would make a man weapon proof. What he did was to universalise the idea. Traditional medicines were used within clan boundaries. Kinjikitile's *maji* was a 'national' medicine, promising 'national' victory. Ironically, Africans who fought on the side of the Germans against the Maji Maji warriors often made use of their own particularistic medicines—and boasted that they were more efficient in giving protection than the *maji*!

A NARRATIVE OF THE CAREER OF KINJIKITILE

It is necessary now to turn to the career of the remarkable man who brought together all these traditional elements to create his revolutionary ideology.

Kinjikitile is known to have been a recent immigrant into Ngarambe, arriving some three years before 1905. As a man he was very eloquent, brave and wise— a born leader. (These qualities are quite apparent today in his brother who is now the Chairman of the Village Development Committee of Ngarambe.) An elderly lady who saw Kinjikitile, one Nambulyo Mwiru, described him as follows:

> He was a middle aged man, an *Mpindo* of wisdom. But he was very tall and very strong . . . He wore white robes (*Kanzu*) down to his feet . . . His hair was not long and not white.[27]

It may be that people in the Matumbi-Ngindo areas were waiting for the arrival of such a leader to resolve their frustrated desire to fight; 'since olden times if there was an impending war some person came out and taught something, as Nguvumali later did. And so Kinjikitile himself.'[28] But Kinjikitile the man still had to be legitimised as Kinjikitile the leader.

A man who now resides in Kinjikitile's former homestead, and who claims to have been fifteen when Maji Maji broke out, has given the following account of Kinjikitile's emergence as leader which has been well corroborated by other Ngarambe authorities. A huge snake of a size and type never seen before, and having the head of a small black monkey, paid a visit to the house of one Mzee Machuya Nnundu of Lihenga near Ngarambe. The occupants of the house moved out in favour of the visitor. The snake was too big for the house so that its coils overflowed outside while it kept its head above the coils at the entrance into the house. It had large red glowing eyes and looked at people, who came to see the unwelcome visitor over the next three days, in a fearsome manner. It was coloured like the rainbow—one of the commonest attributes of the divinity, Hongo. On the third day the huge snake disappeared miraculously. Two women who had been harvesting sorghum that afternoon suddenly beheld a man dressed in a dazzlingly white *kanzu*—it was too white to look at in the afternoon sun. Before they could run away in fear the man disappeared and he and the snake were never seen again. Subsequent examination by the villagers revealed that the trail of the snake disappeared at the point where the man in the white *kanzu* was seen and was renewed where he had disappeared. From there the trail led to the Ngarambe river into which the huge snake was believed to have vanished.

The day following this incident, Kinjikitile, who lived three hundred yards from the river, was taken:

> He was taken by a spirit one day in the morning at about nine o'clock. Everyone saw it, and his children and wives as well. They were basking outside when they saw him go on his belly, his hands stretched out before him. They tried to get hold of his legs and pull him but it was impossible, and he cried out that he did not want (to be pulled back), and that they were hurting him. Then he disappeared in the pool of water. He slept in there and his relatives slept by the pool overnight waiting for him. Those who knew how to swim dived down into the pool but they did not see anything. Then they said, 'If he is dead we will see his body; if he has been taken by a spirit of the waters we shall see him returned dead or alive.' So they waited and the

following morning, at about nine o'clock again, he emerged unhurt with his clothes dry and as he had tucked them the previous day. After returning from there he began talking of prophetic matters. He said, 'All dead ancestors will come back; they are at Bokero's in Rufiji Ruhingo. No lion or leopard will eat men.'[29]

Kinjikitile taught other things too. He claimed to possess a medicine which would give invulnerability against white weapons. He mocked the whites with names like *utupi nkere*, red potter's clay, or *liyomba lya masi*, ugly fish of the sea, and stressed their weakness. He taught a new song, derived from the days of the power of the Sultan of Zanzibar, Seyyid Said, and meaning that all Africans were freemen, not slaves.

> Twe mkina seyyid Said twate
> Twe mkina seyyid twenga.
> (We are all members of Seyyid Said's clan.
> We are all freemen, all by ourselves).[30]

Report of Kinjikitile's experience and of his teaching spread through a movement called variously *Njwiywila, Jujila, Njwito* or *Mtemela.* Literally *Njwiywila* was a whispering campaign spreading the message of Kinjikitile.

> *Njwiywila* meant a secret communication such as at a secret meeting. At the time if you listened to *Njwiywila* you paid one *pice*.[31]

Another authority put it more aptly:

> Then through the whole country it sprang. A man met another, stopped him and said, 'I have a message, a special word to tell you. But first you must give me one *pice*.' Then on receiving the *pice* he said, 'Bring your ear closer', and said he should not tell anybody, it was secret. We all continued whispering behind their (the German's) backs.[32]

Njwiywila was not meant to reach German ears or those of their representatives. It had started by the middle of 1904 for Kinjikitile must have been possessed by June/July of that year and pilgrimages to Ngarambe seem to have begun by July/August. The message was from the first specifically about war:

> The message in *Njwiywila* was like this: 'This year is a year of war, for there is a man at Ngarambe who has been possessed. He has *Lilungu*. Why? Because we are suffering like this and because . . . we are oppressed by the *akidas*. We work without payment. There is an expert at Ngarambe to help us. How? There is *Jumbe* Hongo . . .' In the message of *Njwiywila* was also the information that those who went to Ngarambe would see their dead ancestors. Then people began going to Ngarambe to see for themselves.[33]

The second phase of the movement, after *Njwiywila*, was the phase of the 'pilgrimages' to Ngarambe. These began in late July or early August 1904. Mzee Ambrose Ngombale tells us that 'it was about the month of July or August 1904 when people began going to partake of *maji*, for it all developed very gradually until 1905 when war broke out'.[34] Pilgrims went to Ngarambe in their respective clans led by their own military veterans. They described themselves not by religious but by military terms. Thus each clan group became a *litapo* (detachment). Merit was the criterion for the choice of *litapo* leaders:

> A leader of a *litapo* was chosen at home. He was the one who was extremely brave, a strongly built and fierce looking man, one with muscles bulging out. He was very well known. Then on arriving there he (Kinjikitile) asked, 'Where do you come from?' 'We come from such a place.' 'Who is your leader?' 'It is so and so.' Then Kinjikitile took that same leader and confirmed him leader of war in that area. He received very many and much ... better medicine so that he could secure himself better. He received a very large amulet.[35]

The *litapo* groups began to drill during the night they spent at Ngarambe:

> Every company came with its own leader chosen from their home. If asked, 'Where are you going?' 'To Kinjikitile's,' they answered. It was like a wedding ceremony, I tell you. People sang, danced and ululated throughout. On arriving they were asked, 'Who is your leader?' ... When they arrived at Ngarambe they slept there. They did *likinda* (military drilling) every one in his own *litapo*. The following morning they received *dawa* and returned home.[36]

According to a German military officer who conducted operations in Matumbiland and the Kichi hills, the pilgrims went in 'great crowds of people—some of as many as 300 adults'.[37] But as the rains increased it became more and more difficult to travel to Ngarambe and the third and last phase of Kinjikitile's movement began.

In the last phase Kinjikitile 'regionalised' the *maji* movement. He sent out his ambassadors to various centres in the outbreak area. The title of those posted in Kichi and Matumbiland, as well as Ngarambe itself, was *Mpokosi*. Elsewhere they went by their personal names or by the more common title of *jumbe Hongo*, which strictly speaking, belonged to Kinjikitile himself. An informant at Ngarambe outlined the place of these assistants:

> *Mpokosi* or *Wampokosi* were leaders chosen by him himself (Kinjikitile). His younger brother Njugwemaina was an *Mpokosi* here at Ngarambe and the other one was an Mpogoro called Ling'ang'a. These were not *Wapindo* (clan heads) necessarily.[38]

> 'These *Wampokosi* were his assistants,' says a Matumbiland authority, 'He despatched them in all directions to spread his teaching ...' He had said, 'But War is not yet. It will come from inland (*bara*) to the coast and from the coast to *bara*. The reason he said that was that he wanted his *Wampokosi* to teach everywhere about the coming war.'[39]

THE OUTBREAK OF THE MAJI MAJI WAR

Thus Kinjikitile had carefully prepared the peoples of the outbreak area for war. His syncretic cult had provided an ideology which met their problems of morale and organisation. But he ordered them not to declare war before he commanded it:

> 'The Germans will leave,' he said. 'There will definitely be war. But for the time being go and work for him. If he orders you to cultivate cotton or to dig his road or to carry his load do as he requires. Go and remain quiet. When I am ready I will declare the war.'[40]

Kinjikitile presumably hoped to be able to extend his message further afield. But at this point we can see the inadequacies of his movement as well as its strengths. The movement had brought together war bands and their leaders, thereby improving communication and co-ordination. But it had not been able to replace the existing very fragmented military structures with anything more coherent or more directly under Kinjikitile's control. Military initiative lay firmly with the secular war leaders. Moreover, Kinjikitile's movement had greatly improved morale—but in some ways it had improved it too much. The Matumbi were confident, and thus they were impatient. They said to themselves:

> This *Mganga* said he would declare war . . . Why then is he delaying? When will the Europeans go? After all we have already received the *dawa* and we are brave men. Why should we wait? And yet we continue to dig and clean his roads, carry his loads, grow his cotton and carry bales to Kilwa. And always he continues lashing at us with his *kiboko* on our behind . . . And yet he was not one of us . . . he was not our ruler.[41]

In Nandete itself the bitterness ran deep:

> We became full of bitterness. German rule was no rule. It was impossible to wait and live under such torturous rule.[42]

Thus the Matumbi mobilised and declared war against Kinjikitile's instructions. They decided to uproot cotton as a symbol of defiance. It is interesting to note that the three people who uprooted cotton were Ngulumbalyo Mandai and Lindimyo Machela, both celebrated local *maganga*, and the woman over whom each soldier jumped, Nantabila Naupunda. There is no evidence that they were appointed to office by Kinjikitile. In this way, in the last week of July 1905, Maji Maji broke out.

War having broken out, Kinjikitile became the first Maji Maji victim on the German gallows. He was hanged, together with his assistant, on 5 August, 1905. But before he died Kinjikitile declared that his teaching had already spread far. German sources are silent on the circumstances of his capture. From oral authorities we get the following picture. All Ngarambe informants say that Juma Ndembo and Athuman Ndete, both of Mohoro, went to steal offerings made at the *Kijumba-Nungu*. Having cleared the *Kijumba-Nungu* of everything, the two returned to Mohoro where they reported having gone to the residence of 'the man of troubles', the *mganga*. Then Juma Ndembo guided German agents to the unsuspecting Kinjikitile After his arrest and death, his brother, Njugwemaina, assumed command of the administration of *maji* under the title of *Nyamguni*, one of the three divinities at Kibesa.

It is evident that Kinjikitile was in no sense a leader of the war once it had broken out. The Nandete leaders acted independently even of his ambassador in their area. Thus there were two main patterns of leadership in Maji Maji. One pattern was ideological and the other military. Kinjikitile's contribution was to the ideological pattern. He was the source of inspiration for the great uprisings which raged for so many months after his death.

CONCLUSION

Kinjikitile's career was obviously as remarkable as it was short. We may close with an assessment of its essential significance. This did not lie, as we have seen, in an *invention* of the idea of the commands of the divinities mediated through a possessed man, or of the idea of the influence of the ancestors, or of the idea of a war medicine. It lay in his demonstration that these ideas could be combined and above all universalised. It has often been said that the weakness of African traditional religious systems in the face of European pressure was that each was so limited in its area of application. Kinjikitile's importance lies in the attempt he made to overcome this weakness.

This attempt depended in general upon the essential similarities which underlay the different religious systems of southern Tanzania—upon the common notions of 'vital force'. In particular it depended upon the interaction of the specific religious ideas of the outbreak area. Merely to describe Kinjikitile's movement as 'superstitious' misses altogether the significance of his 'universalisation' of these religious ideas.

In the end Kinjikitile's movement went down in the defeat of Maji Maji. The future did not lie with a universalised traditional religion. But his message could be re-interpreted in secular terms. The theme of his teaching was 'unity to regain independence'. The echoes of 'Unity and Freedom' in Tanzania's coat of arms were implicit in Kinjikitile's teaching, and perhaps therein lies the legacy of the *maji* ideology to Tanzanians.[43]

NOTES

[1] Cited in G. C. K. Gwassa and John Iliffe *Records of the Maji Maji Rising* (Nairobi 1968) pp. 8–9.

[2] A. R. W. Crosse-Upcott, 'The Social Structure of the Ki-Ngindo Speaking Peoples', unpublished Ph.D. Thesis for the University of Cape Town, 1955, p. 5.

[3] Joseph Thomson, 'Notes on the Route taken by the Royal Geographical Society's last East African Expedition from Dar es Salaam to Uhehe, May 19th to August 29th 1879' *Proceedings of the Royal Geographical Society* II (1880) pp. 102–22.

[4] William Beardell, 'Exploration of the Rufiji under the Orders of the Sultan of Zanzibar' *PRGS* III (1881) pp. 641–2.

[5] Senior-Lieutenant Paasche saw drunken warriors in an engagement at Kipo on the northern bank of the Rufiji. Telegram, Back to Admiral, Berlin, 25 August, 1905 (Deutsches Zentralarchiv, Potsdam: Reichskolonialamt 722/21).

[6] Interview with Mzee Ndundule Mangaya, 10 September, 1967, Kipatimu Mission, Matumbi, Kilwa District.

[7] Interview with Mzee Mohamed Nganoga Nimekwako, 31 August, 1968, Ngarambe, Kilwa/Utete boundary.

[8] Subsequent to Maji Maji, so it is said, the Bokero spirit moved downstream to Kibesa towards the estuary of the Rufiji, where he became Islamicised under the title of Mgambo,

and was accounted one of the coastal divinities. There is evidence that a Mgambo shrine was destroyed by a Muslim sheikh on the lower reaches of the Rufiji in 1954. Information from Mr R. A. J. Lwanda, University College, Dar es Salaam, October 1969.

[9] Interview with Mzee Omari bin Said Bumbo, 25 October, 1967, Kilingongo, Utete.

[10] Clients always declared that they were going to Kolelo's, *kwa Kolelo*, meaning that they were going to approach the divinities at Kibesa through their guardian and medium, Kologelo. In the same way people who went to Ngarambe to receive the message of the spirit Hongo spoke of going to Kinjikitile's. The Rufiji, Matumbi and Ngindo pronounced their 'g' rather faintly so that to an untutored ear it may be taken for a 'w'. Thus Kologelo may have become Kolowelo and eventually Kolelo.

[11] Interview with Mzee Mohamed Nganoga Nimekwako (see note 7).

[12] Interview with Mzee Mohamed Nganoga Nimekwako (see note 7).

[13] Richard Burton *The Lake Regions of Central Africa* (London 1860, reprinted New York 1961) vol. 1, pp. 88–9.

[14] Martin Klamroth, 'Beiträge zum Verstädnis der religiösen Vorstellungen der Saramo im Bezirk Dar es Salaam' *Zeitschrift für Kolonialsprachen* 1, 1910–11.

[15] L. Swantz, 'The Zaramo of Tanzania: An Ethnographic Study', M.A. Thesis, Syracuse University, 1956, p. 60.

[16] Interview with Mzee Juya Dyanhutu, 17 January, 1968, Ruvu, Kisarawe.

[17] Interview with Mzee Shuruti, 17 January, 1968, Ruvu, Kisarawe.

[18] Carl Velten (ed) *Safari za Wasuaheli* (Göttingen 1901) pp. 172–90; also German translation of above *Schilderungen der Suaheli* (Göttingen 1901) pp. 138–97.

[19] Bishop James Komba, 'Uisharisho wa Kingoni', paper presented to the Swahili Writers' History Workshop, Dar es Salaam, December 1969.

[20] Interview with Mzee Mohamed Nganoga Nimekwako.

[21] Interview with Mzee Ndundule Mangaya (see note 6).

[22] Interview with Mzee Mangaya.

[23] Interview with Mzee Mangaya.

[24] Interview with Mzee Elisei Simbanimoto Upunda, 4 September, 1967, Nandete, Matumbi.

[25] Interview with Abdulrahman Lipunjo Mandwanga, 19 August, 1967, Kibata, Matumbi.

[26] Interview with Mzee Ambrose Ngombale Mwiru, 8 August, 1967, Kipatimu Mission, Matumbi.

Mzee Mwiru fought on the German side in Maji Maji. He spent over six months in the German stockade at Kibata. He recalls seeing other African supporters of the Germans, who had applied traditional protective medicines, saved by them from death. 'When we were in Kibata I saw two people being shot at and bullets dropping down off their bodies. One of these was *Jumbe* Matenga of Kibata, at whom the Maji Maji soldiers shot twelve bullets but all dropped off him. Another was Nakauka. This one received eight bullets and they all dropped down'.

[27] Interview with Bi. Nabulyo Mwiru, 31 August, 1967, Ngarambe.

[28] Interview with Mzee Ndundule Mangaya.

[29] Cited in Gwassa and Iliffe *op. cit.* p. 9.

[30] Interview with Mzee Said Mwingi, 31 August, 1967, Kiboko, Kichi, Utete.

[31] Cited in Gwassa and Iliffe *op. cit.* p. 9.

[32] Interview with Mzee Nassoro Hassan Kipungo, 14 October, 1967, Makata, Liwale.

[33] Cited in Gwassa and Iliffe *op. cit.* pp. 9–10.

[34] Interview with Mzee Ambrose Ngombale. This view was confirmed by Mzee Ngapatu Mkupali, 21 September, 1967, Mipoto Chumo, Matumbi. This evidence shows that Bell and other authorities on Maji Maji are mistaken in thinking that people only began to go to Ngarambe in 1905.

[35] Interview with Mzee Ndundule Mangaya.

[36] Interview with Mzee Mohamed Nganoga Nimekwako.

[37] Moritz Werjer, 'Uber die Aufstandsbewegung in Deutsch-Ostafrika' *Militär-Wochen-blatt* 91 (1906) 1922–3.

[38] Interview with Mzee Nimekwako.

[39] Interview with Mzee Mangaya. Oral evidence tells us much of the activity of the *Mpokosi*. Bwana Sebastian Upundu, whose father fought in Maji Maji, tells how the *Mpokosi* at Kitumbi Hill taught military drill and strict discipline. In some areas these representatives of Kinjikitile came to enjoy much prestige on their own account. In Liwale, for instance, the *Mpokosi* Ngameya is often confused with Kinjikitile himself. Stories are told about Ngameya which involve a descent into a pool and other events based on Kinjikitile's career. But it is plain that Ngameya was an ambassador of Kinjikitile rather than a distinct religious leader.

[40] Cited in Gwassa and Iliffe *op. cit.* p. 12. This account shows that those authorities who argue that the Maji Maji revolt broke out more or less spontaneously in 1905 are incorrect. The rising had been carefully prepared for many months before the outbreak.

[41] Cited in Gwassa and Iliffe *op. cit.* p. 12.

[42] Interview with Mzee Kibilange Upundu, 22 October, 1968, Nandete, Matumbi. Also with Mzee Nduli Njimbwi, 23 October, 1967, Kipatimu, Matumbi.

[43] This study is based on four years of research on 'The Outbreak and Development of the Maji Maji War, 1905–1907', the results of which will be submitted in 1971 for the doctoral degree of the University of Dar es Salaam. Much of the information used comes from oral interviews in the outbreak area. There has been no attempt made here to present a narrative of Maji Maji or to discuss the many other issues raised by an examination of the rising. These matters are fully discussed in my doctoral dissertation. Meanwhile readers are recommended to consult: Graf von Götzen *Deutsch-Ostafrika in Aufstand 1905/06* (Berlin 1909); R. M. Bell, 'The Maji Maji Rebellion in Liwale District' *Tanganyika Notes and Records* 28 January, 1950; John Iliffe, 'The Organisation of the Maji Maji Rebellion' *Journal of African History* VIII, 3, 1967; and G. C. W. Gwassa and John Iliffe *op. cit.* The writer is deeply indebted to Bishop James Komba for a valuable discussion on Bantu symbolism.

PART SIX

INTERACTIONS BETWEEN AFRICAN
RELIGION AND CHRISTIANITY IN THE
TWENTIETH CENTURY

TERENCE RANGER

Missionary Adaptation of African Religious Institutions.
The Masasi Case

INTRODUCTION

The attempt made by the Anglican church in the Masasi district of southern Tanzania in the 1920s and 1930s to Christianise African religious belief and practice was famous in its day. It was highly praised by missiologists and by British officials committed to Indirect Rule. It was criticised as immoral by many missionaries—and as impossible by some anthropologists. All these commentators saw the adaptation policy as essentially the brain-child of one man, Vincent Lucas, the first bishop of Masasi. Sources of remarkable richness are now available for a retrospective assessment of this adaptation attempt which turns out to have been surprisingly successful, though not exactly in the ways anticipated by Lucas. And it turns out, also, to be quite misleading to approach the whole topic in terms of Lucas' philosophy and hopes alone. The adaptation experiment in Masasi would never have got off the ground and certainly would never have continued for so long had it not been for the commitment to it of very many Africans.[1]

In order to understand what was involved in the attempt to Christianise African religious belief and practice in Masasi, especially to Christianise indigenous rites of initiation, we must examine three things. First, obviously, we need to look at the nature and history of African religion in the area. Secondly, and equally obviously, we need to look at the assumptions and policies of the missionaries of the Universities Mission to Central Africa. But we shall not understand what happened if we merely grasp the essence of two 'opposing' religious systems. We need to look at the men who moved from the one to the other and the men who moved back and to between them. In doing so we shall perhaps discover that these men inhabited a whole series of intermediate 'systems' of belief and practice, each combining elements in different ways, and each to be seen not so much in terms of 'syncretism' as in terms of its ability to meet the religious, and social and political, needs of individuals.

HISTORY, POLITICS AND RELIGION IN MASASI

As a matter of fact, this is also a good way of looking at the pre-Christian religious history of the Masasi area. The various peoples of the Masasi area

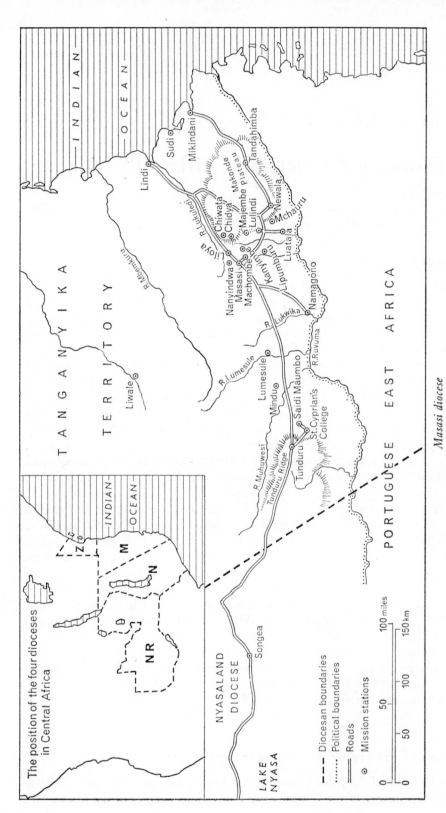

Masasi diocese

From *Maps of the Dioceses*, Universities' Mission to Central Africa, Westminster, 1939

combined a profound religious sense with a minimum of formal religious apparatus. So far as I can discover there were no cult systems influential over wide areas; no royal cults, and for that matter no kings; no formal priests or mediums. Everywhere there were the common notions of sacrifice at the *msolo* tree shrine, of approach to the God through the ancestors, of initiation of boys and girls. But as J. A. R. Wembah-Rashid writes, 'this religion could not have been universal because such a situation did not exist; a *Mwenye* and his people and their settlement were an independent political, ritualistic, economic unit. Religion had to be restricted to each *Mwenye's* area of effective power. Religion is meant to serve a particular community'.[2]

This was the situation described by one of the first African priests from the area, Kolumba Msigala, when he wrote of the time of his boyhood: 'At the time there was no *special* religion in the area between Masasi and Makonde. Everyone followed the traditional cults.' Thus each community made its own adaptations to its particular environment. Increasingly, moreover, these adaptations involved adapting to a mixed society, made up of groups from different 'tribes'. For as Msigala went on to say, in Masasi district the Makonde, the Makua and the Yao peoples all lived inter-mingled with each other 'in friendship and following the primitive religion'.[3]

The Masasi district and much of the rest of south-eastern Tanzania was a frontier zone into which immigrants from the south had been moving during the second half of the nineteenth century. First Makonde, then Makua, then Yao had crossed the Ruvuma river out of Mozambique and into Masasi and Newala. They had begun to clear the land for agriculture but by the time the missionaries arrived much of it was still uncleared bush, and even into the twentieth century the steady movement of southern peoples into the area went on. It is true that this movement resulted in some block settlements of one people. Thus most of the Makonde withdrew eastwards on to the in-accessible Makonde plateau; and later on in the Tunduru district to the west of Masasi massive Yao immigration created an overwhelming Yao dominance.

But in the areas around Masasi and Newala, where the U.M.C.A. was most active in the period under consideration, there had been a complex inter-mixture of peoples. By the 1870s there were Makua *mamwenye* or clanheads exercising authority over Yao settlers and Yao chiefs presiding over mixed populations of Yao, Makua, Makonde and fragments of yet other populations. There were chiefs like Nakaam who were the offspring of mixed Makua and Yao marriages and whose claim to authority was partly that of the Makua clan head and partly that of the successful Yao trader and warrior.

Moreover, recent though any large-scale settlement in the area had been, Masasi and Newala were on the cross-roads of trading and raiding in the late nineteenth century. Masasi was a salt-producing area and this attracted people to trade over long distances. It also attracted the powerful Ngoni of Songea, who demanded a tribute in salt and raided the area if the tribute was not paid. Trading caravans from the southern interior passed through Masasi and Newala on their way to the coast. The growth of trade in slaves led to an increase in internal slavery, and the Yao chiefs of the area assimilated Mwera and other slaves into their followings. Thus the relatively small-scale units of ritual and religious practice were nevertheless often units which had been brought together by a complex and recent process of movement and change. The arrival at Masasi in 1876 of the U.M.C.A. colony of Nyasa freed slaves did not seem anything very out of the ordinary, even though the white missionaries themselves at first caused great excitement.[4]

In short, this was a region of constant movement—the movement of individuals as hunters, traders, minstrels, diviners, military adventurers; the movement of raiding parties and caravans; the movement of villages; the movement of populations. This posed all sorts of problems for the U.M.C.A. in the twentieth century as mission stations were regularly left stranded by the movement away of villages or of chiefs and their followers. In the nineteenth century this mobility made for a very considerable intermixture of ideas.

It was, of course, easier for this intermixture to take place because the Makonde and the Makua and the Yao shared a common sub-stratum of notions and institutions. Still, there were significant differences between the rituals of these peoples as they entered the Masasi and Newala areas. Thus, for example, the sequence and the symbols—some said the whole atmosphere—of initiation ceremonies for boys and girls were very different from one group to another.[5]

But once in Masasi and Newala a complex process of borrowing and adaptation took place so that initiation ceremonies there became something new—or rather became a whole series of new things—as the result of the influence of the Yao on the Makua or *vice versa*. Moreover the interaction did not cease there. Yao influence in ritual and symbolic matters increased as Yao political power and prestige increased. Ritual experts from the neighbouring Mwera people were increasingly made use of—Mwera circumcisors were regularly employed in the boys' initiation rites. Yao and Makua men went to the coast to purchase the bangles and coloured cloth which had become a necessary part of the girls' initiation rites.[6]

Evidence of some of these interactions has been recorded by almost the only modern anthropological inquiry in the area. In 1951 Wilfred Whiteley, then Government sociologist, submitted a report on the Makua people of Masasi. He commented in particular on 'the propensity of the Tanganyika Makua to assimilate into the (initiation) ceremonies elements from other groups'. This was part of a much wider pattern of acculturation. The Makua of Mozambique, he wrote, said of the Tanganyika Makua that 'they have lived so long among the Yao that their customs are not like ours'. In the Masasi district, although Makua made up by the 1950s some 60 per cent of the population, Makua lineages had 'become widely dispersed (and) have been interpenetrated by members of several other tribal groups'.

> The Makua readily learned to speak Yao and Mwera, etc., and assimilated many elements from dances, initiation ceremonies and earlier, from agriculture . . . Because of the esteem in which the Yao are held when a Makua woman marries a Yao, the children may follow the father's clan and adopt Yao custom and language; follow the mother's clan and retain Yao custom and language; or, finally, follow the mother's clan and retain Makua custom. Thus, the Anivako clan has Yao, Matambwe and Makua elements.[7]

All this had produced great changes in the ritual context of initiation ceremonies. According to Whiteley these ceremonies had once constituted for the Makua 'the one occasion at which the members of a clan came together'. But in Tanganyika 'the clan has almost no functions at all'. 'So far as I can gather,' wrote Whiteley with reference to initiation, 'in Portuguese East Africa the Makua treat the ceremonies on a clan basis, an occasion on which clansfolk come together, but in Tanganyika it appears to have been based largely on locality,' It was little wonder, then, that he found numerous 'Yao assimilations' in the initiation rites of the Masasi Makua.[8]

It is true, of course, that the change to Christianised initiation ceremonies was different in kind as well as in degree from these earlier changes. Still, a process of adaptation of initiation to the needs of new social groupings had been going on before the U.M.C.A. proposed the Christianised *Jando* and in some ways popular experience of that *Jando* was a continuation of rather than a total breach with the experience of the past.[9]

Moreover there had been interactions between Yao and Makua in the sphere of the ritual observances connected with political authority as well as in the sphere of initiation, and these had important consequences for the U.M.C.A's relations with the Makua *mamwenye* and the Yao chiefs. A double process had been going on during the later nineteenth century. In the first place the Makua *mamwenye* had been modifying some of the ritual practices of their original home-land in accordance with local political realities. In the second place Yao adventurers who arrived on the scene later had initially been obliged to accept the ritual supremacy of the Makua *mamwenye* and subsequently sought to break away from it.

In central Makua country, south of the Ruvuma river, the clan-head had ritual authority over numbers of lineages and subordinate clan section leaders. This authority was symbolised in and expressed through his control of the clan's *mbepesi*, a word 'sometimes used to denote the symbol of worship (generally flour) and sometimes to describe the religious virtue or the material right which belongs to the holder'. The clan head would sacrifice through the ancestors on behalf of his people or use his *mbepesi* for divination; he would delegate the right of *mbepesi* to subordinate clan authorities.

Most of the Makua authorities of the Masasi district had originally been subordinates to the clan head, and often quite junior subordinates. The recognised senior heads of their clans had remained south of the Ruvuma and not migrated into Masasi and Newala districts. So in Masasi men who had been subordinates welcomed the chance to establish an autonomous authority. In Masasi the *mbepesi* was conferred on a man succeeding to authority not by the senior clan head but by the *mamwenye* of the Masasi district acting as a body.[10]

These Makua *mamwenye* greeted the U.M.C.A. with suspicion and reserve. Their position as authorities depended very largely on traditional ritual privileges and responsibilities; even their economic position depended to some extent on their control over initiation ceremonies. They jealously guarded the small-scale autonomy which they had won as the result of their migration and resented the influence of African teachers and catechists. They felt that they had nothing to gain from Christianity. Consequently there was a dogged passive resistance by most Makua *mamwenye* and consequently their suspicion and distrust was returned by the missionaries. The robust early chronicle of the U.M.C.A. described the Masasi Makua as 'a singularly dull, unreceptive race, believing in very little, and very tenacious of that little'.[11]

Very different was the relationship of the missions with those Yao adventurers who had become chiefs, like Matola I of Newala, or with men like Nakaam who had chosen the outward looking Yao part of their heritage. This difference sprang partly from the whole innovative attitude of Matola and Nakaam and their involvement in a wide network of trading and cultural contacts.[12] But it also sprang partly from the ambiguous ritual position that Matola occupied in 'traditional' Newala. Matola I had moved into the area of the Makua *mwenye* Mwawa and had accepted his ritual authority. Subsequently his success as a warrior, hunter and trader had enabled him to set up a chiefdom for himself. But the ritual subordination to Mwawa remained.

It was not surprising that Matola I should have been the leading patron of the U.M.C.A., 'a Clovis or Ethelbert to go before his people in Christianity as in war'. Matola wanted the prestige and wealth to be gained by 'modernisation'. He wanted a military alliance with the whites. And he wanted a way in which he could reverse his role of ritual subordinate to Mwawa. His successor, Matola II, found through his alliance with the missionaries the means to achieve this. 'Matola I lived formerly in P.E.A. under the then Yao chief Mtarika,' recorded a British official inquiry in 1928.

> In consequence of Ngoni attacks he fled with a few relatives and crossed the Rovuma into the Newala Division where he sought refuge under the Makua *Mweni* Mwawa I. By native law and custom Matola I had to remain Mwawa's follower and could not leave without payment and then only if Mwawa consented. By reason of his personality, courage, hunting prowess he acquired influence but his importance was much accentuated by his close contact with and keen support of the U.M.C.A . . . The Mission supported and advised him and on the establishment of the German administration and his cultivation of friendly relations with it his influence grew and all the more so because the Makua were suspicious of the Mission and the German government. Matola I was created a *Jumbe* by the German government. Matola II (nephew of Matola I) suceeded . . . and later was made *Akida* over the Newala Makua and Yao. Mwawa II and his followers were accused of killing a native in a case of witchcraft and were arrested by Matola II . . . Mwawa II was kept by Matola II at Newala but became so weak that he was released: he fled with followers to P.E.A. and died there a few days later. The Makuas attribute his death to Matola II and allege that the latter's intention was to usurp the power.[13]

Thus in the Masasi area both the life-crisis rituals central to the coherence of communities and the rituals which lent prestige to secular authority were in a constant process of interaction and change. Moreover, there was great opportunity for any ritual expert who could demonstrate the instrumentality of his cult. The peoples of Masasi were farmers and desired the fertility of their land and the plentiful supply of rain. Many of them were recent migrants in to the area and some of them had been hunters before they became farmers: they did not suppose that it made sense to rely only upon their 'own' rites of intercession. Instead they drew upon any ritual expert from near or far who had the reputation for being effective as a blesser of crops or maker of rain. Similarly they were interested in healing and in protection from witchcraft. Once again it is plain that they drew upon all sorts of different specialists —diviners employing a variety of different techniques, Muslim exorcisers of spirits, herbalists, experts in *chisango* witchcraft detection. Such specialists might come from the coast or from Mozambique or from the northern interior and they were applied to by Yao, Makua and Makonde alike. It seems plain that the first impact made by Islam in the Masasi area occurred in this context as men had recourse to 'Islamic' doctors and diviners. And if Christian missionaries proved effective as healers or as intercessors the peoples of Masasi would certainly apply to them also.[14]

THE ATTITUDES AND APPROACH OF THE U.M.C.A.

In many ways, then, the missionaries found themselves in a favourable situation in Masasi. There was not only a history of ritual change and adaptation but also a history of widening contacts which called for the development of a cosmology suitable to the situation of late nineteenth-century Masasi. How did they respond?

In answering this question it is important to realise that the leadership of the U.M.C.A. did not really confront the 'traditional' religious situation in Masasi until relatively late on. This was partly due to the particular history of the mission. It began in 1876 with an *enclave* settlement of freed slaves who showed no enthusiasm for sharing the Christian message with the indigenous peoples of Masasi. Then after the Ngoni raid on the freed slave settlement in 1882 and a general disillusionment with its progress, there followed a period in which the U.M.C.A. allied itself closely with the Yao chiefs, Nakaam and Matola II. In this period it was in some ways a 'court' church rather than a people's church, and it was content to take the word of Matola II that there was nothing very terrible about traditional initiation ceremonies, for example, if they were controlled by a Christian chief. It was only after Maji Maji that a movement of feeling set in away from the idea of dependence upon Matola II, who was seen to be exploiting his alliance with the U.M.C.A. in order to gain greater wealth and power, and towards the creation of a real church of the people. So it was only in the years immediately before the first World War, when Vincent Lucas was priest in charge at Masasi, that the missionaries confronted the religious realities of the district.[15]

Thus, despite the widespread and obvious character of initiation ceremonies, it seems clear that the U.M.C.A. did not realise the pastoral problems involved in initiation until the period of rebuilding which followed the Maji Maji rising of 1905. This late realisation became almost proverbial in missionary circles. In 1911 Bishop Thomas Spreiter instructed the Benedictines of Kwiro that 'even if the existence of puberty rites has been repeatedly denied up till now, that is no proof that they are not there just the same; it is sometimes decades before such things are discovered. A classical instance is the old missionaries from Masasi who worked there for nearly 40 years without knowing anything, or suspecting anything, just because in the first years they heard nothing.'[16]

By the time the U.M.C.A. *did* confront the situation two important developments had taken place. One, which I shall consider fully in the next section, was that there were already a number of African clergy and teachers whose ideas on the Christianisation of African religious ideas were to be of determining importance. The other was that white U.M.C.A. thinking on the subject of the Christian encounter with African religion had undergone a progressive development from an early disbelief in the possibility of adapting African institutions to a much more positive missiological policy.

This development can be seen plainly in the writings of Bishop Maples, perhaps the most important of Lucas' predecessors. In 1882 Maples had explicitly denied that Africans had any urge to 'know more about God than their own ignorance has taught them' or that it was possible in African religion, as in Asian, 'to search out all the elements of truth that lurk in it and show their true place in the religion which alone is The Truth'. In Africa there was nothing but 'a set of unconnected superstitions'. Africans were 'supremely and hopelessly indifferent to all religion whatever'. One could only impress them by emphasising the *power* of Christ, by conveying a 'sense that they *must* obey'. Notions of Justice and Love would have to come later.[17]

Returning to the same topic in 1891 Maples had come to believe that God was seen by African peoples as the 'Personal Giver and Sustainer of Life'; their reason told them that God was Creator and they instinctively responded to his Holiness. The problem as he now saw it was how to base a moral code upon this sense of God. 'With Africans,' he wrote, 'we feel that we have but to carry on their belief for them, to exhibit Him whom they already know their Creator as also the Author of the Moral Law.'[18]

By 1895 he was ready to go further still. 'Those of us who have been able in a measure to study the African character from close acquaintance with it are convinced that it possesses many traits and qualities that only await the consecrating touch of Christianity in order to bring out and exhibit new sides of Christian life such as our Western and European natures have not in them to develop.'[19]

Vincent Lucas stood in and carried on this argumentative progression. Lucas believed that Africans were quintessentially religious. 'Wheresoever tribes are encountered as pagans,' he wrote, 'they press into God's Church with a ready eagerness that hardly waits to be called but the translation of faith into conduct is the real difficulty.' He believed that the more African religions were studied the more 'they show that the light that lighteth every man that cometh into the world has not been without its witness in the darkest parts of the earth'.[20]

Lucas was fascinated by the possibility of leading African converts into an understanding of Christianity by an extension of the themes and symbols of their own religious belief. His emphasis was upon liturgy and symbol rather than upon the dogma and argument. Two examples will show how his mind worked. Writing of the sacrifices made by the Yao to the ancestral spirits, Lucas held that

> great good may be done by linking the points of the pagan sacrifice with the perfect Christian sacrifice, to the offering of which they have now come. Many African peoples tend to regard Christianity as a beautiful European religion into which certain specially kind Europeans are prepared to enrol them as associates, and anything that will show them that Christianity is the fulfillment for them of what had already been adumbrated in the immemorial customs of the past will perhaps do more than anything to help the church to become really indigenous. An African of intelligence— when it was pointed out to him that the flour and cup of pagan sacrifice were the way in which God prepared them for the offering of the true Flour and the true Cup, that the '*msoro*' tree corresponded to the tree of Calvary, and that although Africans offer flour as being the whitest, purest, cleanest, shiniest thing that they knew, there is that which is purer and whiter still, the Body of our Lord, while the thrice repeated petition to God is an address to the Holy Trinity—coming then to realise that Christianity is an African religion in a very real sense, and that God had been preparing his forefathers until the time of the full revelation . . . was so moved that he could not speak until he had first been into church to pour out his Thanksgiving to God.[21]

My second example is taken from an entry by Lucas in the Masasi cathedral log-book for March 1st 1922, Ash Wednesday.

> I explained the meaning of ashes which seemed most likely to be understood in the country following the four uses of ashes here:
> (1) On the path to avert witchcraft from the home. We are to contend with the Devil in Lent.
> (2) Smearing a child's arm when a dream has been dreamed that evil has befallen the child and we wake to find it still safe. We only believe the judgements of God as a dream. Let us wake and while our soul is still safe use the ashes and guard it more diligently in the future.
> (3) Ashes are used as a sign of joy when a traveller returns from a distant land in safety. Let us return like the Prodigal from the land of destruction.
> (4) Ashes are used in the '*Unyago*' (initiation ceremony) rejoicing over the passage of a child from childishness to manhood. Our ashes should mean the abandonment of the unworthy things of nature and the beginning once again of a new life of Grace, c.f. the burial service where the use of ashes is closely linked to the hope of resurrection.[22]

THE APPROACH OF AFRICAN CHRISTIANS

One of the preconditions for the attempt to establish an initiation ceremony of a Christian character was the existence of large enough Christian congregations. Initiation was a communal activity and a Christian initiation could not take place until there was a Christian community. In the 1920s and 1930s, in fact, the policy of the U.M.C.A. varied from parish to parish according to the strength of Christian numbers. Where a majority or a large proportion of the population were Christians they were prohibited from attending traditional initiation ceremonies and required to put their children in Christianised rites. Where Christians were in a small minority, however, they could not be prohibited from attending traditional ceremonies without cutting themselves off from the community in a dangerous way. The Christianisation of African rites in Masasi, therefore, was not undertaken in order to make it easier to convert by presenting a more indigenous church. It was undertaken in order to Christianise the lives of converts. Clearly, it could only be successful if it commanded some support, or at least acquiescence, from them. How were these converts likely to respond?

The log-books of the Masasi and Newala parishes provide us with remarkably detailed answers to this question. Broadly the picture emerges in this way. Despite clerical grumbling attendance at church and devotion to the liturgical life of the church seems generally to have been good. There is not much evidence in the log-books, or in oral material, that people found much difficulty with the 'foreign' character of the liturgy. Perhaps the adaptations made by Lucas and others helped here; perhaps the strongly liturgical character of the U.M.C.A. helped to give a sense of community; perhaps people were just content to accept the avenues of approach to God which came with the new religion. In short the log-books bear out Maples' generalisation that the Africans of Masasi had responded readily to a further definition of a personal God, or Lucas' comment that they had pressed into the church 'with a ready eagerness that hardly waits to be called'.[23]

At the same time the log-books show what Lucas meant when he added that 'the translation of faith into conduct is the real difficulty'. There were two areas of conflict between African converts and the church. One was in the whole sphere of marriage. The other arose over the question of the instrumentality of religion. African converts in Masasi continued to be concerned with the fertility of their fields, with supply of rain, with witchcraft, with health. In default of Christian solutions to these problems they continued to apply non-Christian solutions. They called in the *chisango* expert or the witchcraft eradicator; they sprinkled medicine on their fields; they turned in case of ill health to the *fundis* and to the Muslim doctors. For doing so they were perpetually faced with church discipline; with public penance and withdrawal from the sacrament. Their submission to this discipline can be interpreted in terms of their desire not to lose the advantages of mission schooling or other material assets of the missionary presence; but the evidence seems to suggest that to many people the sacraments were as desired as rain and health. They wanted both.[24]

In fact some of the most fascinating evidence in the log-books concerns the way in which Christian congregations in Masasi were able to put pressure upon the missionaries as well as having to submit to pressure from them. There is space for only one example. This concerns the way in which the Christians of the cathedral parish of Masasi itself managed to obtain Christian equivalents for some of the pre-Christian invocations of spirit. Sometimes they exercised this pressure by continuing to attend non-Christian ceremonies despite all attempts at prohibition. Thus in 1913 Lucas began to develop an elaborate series of rites for the dead in response to the persistence of Christians in attending Islamic and 'traditional' ceremonies for dead relatives and friends. 'After Vespers,' recorded Lucas, 'we went to the Grave Yard and censed and sprinkled the graves. The people sang Dies Irae in the meantime.' Again, the persistent desire for spiritual help in ensuring fertility led Lucas to agree to process through the fields of Masasi blessing and praying for them.[25]

Sometimes pressure was exercised through the congregation determining for itself which aspects of the liturgy it regarded as significant. So in the 1930s the Masasi clergy were astonished to find a very large attendance on 30 November, St Andrews Day. St Andrew was 'regarded as a rain bringer'. The clergy were worried for fear that if his feast day 'becomes regarded as a Great Festival Advent Sunday will inevitably take second place'. So in 1936, when St Andrews Day fell on the Monday after Advent Sunday the priest in charge deliberately did not announce it. Nevertheless many people deferred communion until the Monday Mass which was followed by 'a heavy storm, the first for months'. 'It really looks,' recorded the resigned diarist, 'as if the Almighty wishes to encourage the belief in St Andrew as a rain-giver.'[26]

This kind of re-interpretation was presumably usually less conspicuous, but there are indications in the records of cathedral sermons of the anxiety of the European clergy. 'I preached against the idea,' recorded the priest in charge in October 1935, 'that Baptism is a charm for curing ills for which people have neglected to seek medical aid, also to counter the idea that sick people can be baptised whatever their moral state.'[27]

What was going on, in short, was a vigorous process of adaptation or attempted adaptation 'from below' which helps us to understand reactions to the process of adaptation from above. The Newala and Masasi Christians were highly unlikely passively to accept forms of adaptation imposed on them by the missionaries. They were highly likely to operate within such forms to ensure that they became more practically effective.

But these attitudes on the part of the congregations of Masasi did not distinguish the area from many other parts of East and Central Africa. What *did* distinguish it was the fact that by the time the Christianised *Jandos* began there were more African teachers and clergy in Masasi and Newala than almost anywhere else in eastern Africa. These men were the key figures in the adaptation attempt.

From the beginning the U.M.C.A. employed Yao and Makua agents in Masasi. At first these were men like the Yao Cecil Majaliwa or the Makua Hugh Mtoka, who had been released from slaver ships as small boys and educated by the U.M.C.A. in Zanzibar. But fairly soon recruitment first of teachers and then of clergy began in Masasi and Newala districts themselves. Most of these early recruits were drawn from the families of Matola and Nakaam, the two great secular allies of the U.M.C.A. And then the U.M.C.A. began to draw upon a wider and more varied field as boys were sent to U.M.C.A. schools by Yao and Makua parents in many villages.

The influence and prestige of these African teachers, deacons and priests both in relationship to the whites and in relationship to the African societies of Masasi was a determining factor in the way in which the adaptation policy developed. It is important to realise that this prestige went through three phases. To begin with the freed slave clergy like Majaliwa and Mtoka were not really very influential either on white missionaries or on African societies in Masasi. Majaliwa had to relearn Yao which he had lost during his Zanzibar years; he knew nothing of the customs of the country and he felt a keen sense of isolation. 'I am left alone in the midst of the heathen like a cottage in the middle of a forest,' he wrote from Barnaba Nakaam's headquarters of Chitangali in 1886. Not surprisingly the missionaries did not use him as an authority or adviser on local customs and though he is remembered as an important pioneer figure he was glad to return to Zanzibar in 1897.[28]

Very different was the prestige of the group of clergy recruited from the families of Matola and Nakaam. These men *were* made much use of as experts on local beliefs. 'The missionaries made the new African priests and deacons their right hands in matters of policy and guiding the people,' wrote one of the early Yao clergy in his memory of this period. 'We began to progress with councils and holding meetings to do away with various native customs which were not compatible with our religion, bringing them to the condition in which they now are by ordinances and without any trouble . . . The church flourished increasingly.' During the first decade of the twentieth century the U.M.C.A. based itself upon an alliance with the Christian chiefs and this naturally involved a good deal of power for the African clergy who were their relatives and associates. For a brief period, especially immediately after the Maji Maji rising, these Yao clergy had a dream of a Yao hegemony in church and state; for a brief period they enjoyed what bishop Frank Weston later described as Home Rule.[29]

This period of Home Rule came to a decisive end in 1910. Both the Germans and the U.M.C.A. missionaries had become disillusioned with their chiefly allies. In 1910 the Germans arrested, imprisoned and exiled Barnaba Nakaam. In the same year the U.M.C.A. brought to an end the control of the parishes of Newala district by Matola I's priest son, Daudi Machina, putting a white missionary in above him. In 1913 Machina was suspended from the priesthood altogether; in 1915 Matola II was arrested by the Germans and deposed in his turn. A third period began for the African clergy. It was a period in which a new generation of white missionary priests exercised a somewhat paternal control; a period in which the new British administrators began to move towards their policies of Indirect Rule and the support of the 'traditional' Makua clan-heads. In short it was a period in which African clergy were in many ways insecure in their relationships both to modern white and to traditional African authority. African teachers were, of course, even more insecure. The old days when the first African teachers were the natural leaders of the new Christian congregations and respected advisers of the whites were gone. After the first World War African teachers found themselves much less important and much more controlled than they had been earlier.[30]

It is important to realise that the adaptation attempts of bishop Lucas fell into this third period. The Christian *Jando*, though commenced just before the first World War, did not really get under way until the 1920s. In order to understand the attitude of the African clergy and teachers towards it we must briefly explore a little further their dilemmas in the third period.

The sources of prestige of the African priest and the African teacher were most obviously 'modern' ones—literacy, a 'modern' style of living, rank in the new church. But it is arguable that they also rather badly needed some additional sources of prestige which would make sense in more communal terms. This for two reasons. In the first place, the white missionaries who had re-imposed paternal control could obviously outdo the African clergy and teachers in terms of literacy, life style, rank. But the whites could not compete with Africans when it came to playing 'traditional' roles. In the second place, the African clergy and teachers often found themselves contesting for influence within the community with the *mamwenye* and with other representatives of the 'traditional' ritual order.

The tensions here could be very considerable. Nearly all the African clergy and teachers believed in the efficacy of witchcraft, for example. The teaching of their church gave them no help in dealing with witchcraft belief and no protection against witchcraft attack. Sometimes African clergy or teachers were denounced as witches themselves; sometimes they fell victim to their own fear of the use of witchcraft against them. A dramatic example of this is recorded in the first log kept by Lucas at Masasi. It concerned Deacon Benedict Njewa, one of the first of the local Makua clergy; a man of energy who had led his congregation in Miesi parish in the building of an impressive church. Njewa imposed discipline on Miesi Christians for offences against church law. And in October 1912 he 'went mad' as the U.M.C.A. journal put it. He had rebuked a local Christian for 'bigamy'; been threatened with retaliation through witchcraft; and believed that this retaliation had been effective. The report of his collapse is a moving one, showing his desperate attempt to continue to act like a 'modern' man until he would no longer disgrace his church. 'He had gone in a state of great excitement to the government *Boma*, taken off his cassock and girdle, folded them up, and asked that they might be sent to the Mission, and then instantly became insane and violent.' Lucas found him shackled to prevent him from harming himself and being treated by a *mganga*. He died of exhaustion in Lindi in 1913. And his case was rapidly followed by another when in April 1914 it was reported that an African teacher in Luatala had 'gone mad' under very similar circumstances.[31]

Of course these are melodramatic examples of tensions which were usually less extreme. But they help us to understand, perhaps, why some at least of the African clergy supplemented their prestige as leaders of the new church with a prestige derived from their supposed access to more traditional spiritual power. Kolumba Msigala, nephew of Matola I, one of the early Yao clergy, and later Canon and apostle to the Yao of Tunduru, was proud of the fact that his father had been an *mganga*. He tells us in his autobiography that he had inherited his father's medical skills, and African informants in the Masasi area say that he was widely believed to have inherited his father's power to harm as well as to heal. Once again not many African clergy had this sort of double reputation. But many of them felt the need for a position of prestige defined in traditional ritual terms. And it was here that the adaptation process became relevant.[32]

David Parkin, in his suggestive work on the Giriama, has postulated that syncretism of ritual and symbol is interesting to the sociologist because of the light that the process throws on attempts at role definition. The adaptation of initiation ceremonies in Masasi—a form of 'syncretism'—can very usefully be seen in this way as far as African clergy and teachers are concerned.[33]

THE INITIATION CEREMONIES OF MASASI AND NEWALA

The ground has now been laid for an account of the attempt to Christianise the initiation rites of the Makua and Yao peoples of Masasi. One thing alone is still missing—some account of the rites themselves. To provide an adequate account would be very difficult and is here impossible. As we have seen the rites of the Makua and the Makonde and the Yao differed from each other— and each has been copiously described by European and African observers.[33] Moreover, as we have seen also, there had been so many modifications and interactions that the initiation rites of each community differed in some ways from those of quite close neighbours. I shall fall back, therefore, on the in- adequate but vivid device of citing one authority only—and that authority not a 'traditionalist' but the Yao priest, Father Petro Ligunda. I do this partly because the sympathy which comes out of Ligunda's account of the traditional ceremony makes an important point about the attitudes of the African clergy.

'In my young days,' recalls Ligunda, 'the ceremony was conducted by somebody called Che Kalumbo (God bless the man, he did such a tremendous job!), who was very famous and a good singer too . . . When a certain chief wanted to hold this ceremony in his area he would invite Che Kalumbo to come and lead it . . . Before the ceremony Che Kalumbo would hang his switch on a tree in the area where he wanted the ceremony performed. Then the people would build a fence-like thatch and divide it into sections, each section belonging to the boy, his family and his sponsor (*mlombwe*). In the evening the boys whose heads had been shaved would be put in the hut and were not allowed to be seen by outsiders . . . Then Che Kalumbo and his helpers would start singing . . . the people would clap their hands and reply at the end of each verse. When the singing and drums were in rhythm Che Kalumbo's attendants would start dancing in a frenzied manner but the leader himself just moved smoothly in a majestic manner around the dancers . . . This would go on throughout the night—the boys were not allowed to sleep.

'Next morning breakfast was prepared and this consisted of rice and a cock. It was compulsory for the boys to eat even if they had lost their appetites. After breakfast the boys would stand up . . . Then each sponsor would take his boy and run to the forest where a special hut was built for them to live for as long as they were required. Then the boys would be circumcised by a special person skilled in such a job. Che Kalumbo would be at the head of the running line. The people who remained behind would sit silent waiting apprehensively. When everything was over Che Kalumbo would come back and say everything is alright and everybody would start cheering and dancing and the parents would be smeared with yesterday's ash. This lasted for a short time and then the chief would call on everybody to be quiet and listen to the warnings. The chief would then warn the parents to lead a decent life while their children were in the forest; they were not to quarrel, commit adultery or do anything wrong since it would affect the children who would come to harm.

'The boys would remain in the forest for a very long time getting various instructions such as how to behave properly in front of their elders when they got back . . . There was much torturing at this period and the boys had to endure everything . . . The boys were obliged to hunt birds and animals . . . and for each bird they killed they had to hang one wing on a tree called 'Lupanda', of which I'll tell you later . . . The boys used to make their own clothes from the bark of trees.

'The name of the ceremony was called Lupanda. The name itself is taken from a tree known as Lupanda which has many branches. During the ceremony, just before the people started dancing on the first night, certain people with a chief used to go to where this tree was growing and the men would climb slowly up the tree accompanied by the rhythm of drums and they'd choose a special branch to cut . . . They would then come down carrying the branch and it was placed where the people were dancing and after this at the boy's hut where they would hang each tail of an animal or wing of a bird they had killed. The procedure of cutting a branch of the Lupanda was a very confidential process, since nobody, especially the witches, were allowed to see this, so that the witches might not take any part of the tree, bewitch it and bring harm to the boys and spoil the ceremony.

'When the time for the boys to get back drew near the parents started the first preparations. On the night before the sponsors would go to each parents' house and knock asking for fire or anything else. Once the parent came out he was splashed with water from a home-made pipe. Soon the whole village was noisy with people splashing water at each other and cheering. Then the hut where the boys had been living was burnt and the boys were led in a single file to another hut; during this walk none of the boys were allowed to look back at their burning hut since this would show that the boy had not changed into the new young man he was supposed to be.

'Near dawn the boys had to take a special bath at which a specially chosen lady would pour water on the back of each boy . . . after the bath the boy and the lady, who then becomes his 'sister' had to perform another ceremony in which both hold a pestle and pound together in a mortar. This indicated that the boy and his sister had been united together; the boy was to respect this sister much more than any of his relatives. If a quarrel arose and nobody could settle it, this sister would be called and would give the last word which the boy would never oppose.

'After the bath the boys were given new clothes and veiled and they all assembled at the chief's where they were given the last instructions, especially on good behaviour. At the chief's each boy had to swear in front of everybody that he would change his behaviour and behave as he had been taught. Then each with his sponsor went home amid celebration and dancing.'[35]

It is clear from this account, and even clearer from more detailed ethnographic descriptions, that the boys' initiation ceremony was a protracted liturgical process. It was this aspect of it that fascinated Lucas. But it is also clear that it was much more. It was an educational process primarily concerned with generational and sex relationships. It was also a source of prestige and profit for the chiefs and clan heads.

In considering the attempt to Christianise the rites, indeed, it is important to situate them in their political context. Quite apart from the intervention of the mission a political struggle over initiation was going on in Masasi in the early colonial period. 'Traditionally' control of initiation in Masasi district had been very decentralised in correspondence to political realities. Each *mwenye*, who was often little more than a village head, controlled the initiation ceremonies for his own community. This situation contrasted with the position elsewhere. Among the Makua south of the Ruvuma, so Whiteley tells us, the senior clan head retained control over initiation for all his clan. In Tunduru, to the west of Masasi, where the Yao were ruled by a few powerful sultans, control of initiation was vested in senior chiefs only, to whom the headmen of villages had to make requests and gifts when the community desired to hold a ceremony. But Makua *mamwenye* of Masasi cherished their autonomy in this as in all other ritual matters.[36]

Its importance to them comes out of the oral testimony of old *Mwenye* Mchawala concerning initiation in Masasi itself. Before the coming of the missionaries

> only *Mwenye* Namkumba and I had the power to conduct *Unyago* (initiation rites) . . . traditionally the people would come to ask me to conduct the ceremony when they found that their children were grown enough to be circumcised. I could refuse . . . If I consented I would announce the day for the ceremony, after having arranged for the *Wangariba*, circumcisors . . . For this trouble I took to prepare for the ceremony the parents of the children who had been circumcised paid me some amount, about five shillings, for each child. Of this amount I retained three shillings and the other two shillings I gave to the *Wangariba*.[37]

One of the tensions which arose from the emergence of Yao chiefs like Matola in the territory of Makua *mamwenye* like Mwawa was the question of who controlled initiation. Presumably Mwawa did so in the beginning. But as Matola became more powerful the situation changed. And it changed very radically indeed under German rule when Matola was *Akida* over a very large area. The question then was whether a centralisation of ritual power should follow a centralisation of political power. The Germans first paid very little attention to such questions but when the colonial administration came to consider them it was generally in favour of a tidy degree of central supervision and set up a system whereby the senior African political authority had licensing control over circumcision ceremonies. And this became one of the issues at stake in the constant in-fighting between the *mamwenye* and those *akidas* and chiefs who exercised authority over a wider area.[38]

Clearly the political implications of intervening in the question of initiations were as complex as the symbolic ones! Equally complex was the question of female initiation.

Some East African peoples, as for example the Tiriki of Kenya, adopted initiation for boys and not for girls. Among the Tiriki, indeed, the women were hardly ritual beings at all and were excluded as uninitiated and uncircumcised from the formal religious life of the tribe. The case was very different in Masasi. Makonde, Makua and Yao alike not only had a communal initiation rite—*Chiputu*—in which young girls were taught how to manipulate the *labia minora* and received other instruction in a forest camp, but also three further stages of female initiation. When a girl menstruated the woman who stood sponsor for her at the *Chiputu* ceremony, together with other women instructors, would come to the house and instruct her to the accompaniment of singing and dancing. In the fifth month of pregnancy a woman underwent the *Litiwo* rite, at which women from miles around gather to impress upon the husband that his wife must be protected against all anxiety and that adultery on his part would be fatal to the child. Finally there was a concluding rite at the birth of the first child. There was no doubt that women were fully ritual members of Masasi African societies.[39]

Female initiation posed a special problem for the U.M.C.A. Save in the case of *Chiputu* the rites were individual and very difficult indeed to supervise or control. Moreover, women's rites were much more 'obscene' than the male ceremony, and the missionaries did not see this obscenity as relating valuably to the definition of womanhood in Masasi society, as modern anthropologists do. In any case, the missionaries did not approve of the concept of womanhood in Masasi society, regarding Yao and Makua marriages as defective and matrilineal institutions as a hindrance to the establishment of the Christian family.[40]

It was difficult for the missionaries, perhaps especially for the white laywomen who had most to do with female initiation, to see the rites as Africans saw them. Once again I propose to cite an account from an African Christian, this time by a woman who has been a life-long Christian and a pillar of the Mothers' Union. Her sympathy for the traditional *Chiputu* will give some idea of the adaptation problem.

> The girls were prepared for their future lives as wives [she remembers] in extending their lower parts in preparation for sex during their married life. The instructors also made certain that the girls should know all sorts of manners . . . The girl's bodies were washed with wet husks to make their skins lighter and beautiful and it was lovely to see them coming out looking so beautiful. The girls were given a proper bath in the morning of the day of coming out; they were also given new clothes and their bodies oiled and veiled. At the end of the ceremony each girl with her helper would have to do a 'belly dance' and this was a great amusement, especially for the boys, who usually came and chose the best dancers to be their future wives . . . Today the missionaries have changed all this . . . what we are left with now is the memory of the good old days.[41]

THE ESTABLISHMENT OF THE CHRISTIAN JANDO

For a long time the missionaries took an optimistic line about initiation. In the late 1880s they had already concluded that 'these *Unyagos* are connected with a great deal that is bad' but noted with relief that 'Matola assures us that a good chief can do away with what is objectionable'. This optimism was maintained during that period of mission strategy which concentrated on collaboration with 'the good chiefs'. In 1908 a conference of African clergy at Masasi 'testified to the fact that some of the worst features which were freely practised in the old days are dying out, even among the heathen'. It might be hoped that the church would not have to confront the issue.[42]

But as the church moved into the third period, the period of the people's church and of the more detailed supervision of the African clergy, the problem of initiation soon became central, and it was brought to Lucas' attention by the African clergy, teachers and elders themselves. They informed him that they regarded the traditional rites as intolerable and irredeemable. It was thereupon decided to prohibit participation in any traditional rite to all Christians and to attempt to create Christianised ceremonies to take their place. In June 1913 Bishop Frank Weston acted on these recommendations and issued an ordinance prohibiting *unyago*. Later in the year the first Christian *Jando* took place.[43]

THE ATTITUDE OF VINCENT LUCAS TOWARDS THE CHRISTIANISATION OF INITIATION

In describing the character and history of the Christian *Jando* I propose to examine the role of each party in turn. First Vincent Lucas himself; then other European clergy; then the African priests and teachers; then the *mamwenye*; and finally the African congregations of Masasi and Newala.

Lucas knew that 'the first answer of almost all European missionaries would tend to be condemnatory' of any idea that initiation could or should be Christianised. 'The decisive period in the life of an African youth,' wrote the German Protestant missionary, Julius Richter, 'is the time of the initiation rites, the *khoma* or *unyago* . . . This period, however, is poisoned by so many excrescences of pagan superstition and unbridled sensuality that many friends of the Negro think that the abrupt break and arrest of the intellectual and moral development of many young boys and girls at the age of thirteen or fourteen is the outcome of such orgies.' Accordingly, most missionaries waged relentless war on the idea of initiation.[44]

Lucas did not believe that it was easily possible to suppress the rites. But more than that—he was eager to 'turn the elements connected with paganism to the ends of Christianity'. He was worried that Christian teaching would produce a destructive individualism, worried about the dangers of 'de-tribalisation'. He wished to retain those aspects of initiation which made for communal identity while eliminating 'obscene' and 'immoral' aspects. Moreover, he was fascinated by the challenge of replacing the traditional symbols and ritual sequences with Christian equivalents.[45]

This liturgical work was for Lucas the most absorbing part of the adaptation process and one can see him at work in his parish log-books, elaborating the fairly simple initial Christian *Jando* of 1913 into more effective forms. 'The whole ground on which the rite will take place,' he wrote of the developed *Jando* liturgy,

is blessed with litany and prayer and sprinkled with holy water, replacing the flour; the Cross takes the place of the '*lupanda*' tree and the invocation of the Saints of Christendom replaces the appealing to the great ones of the tribal past . . . as the period (of seclusion and instruction) draws to its end special efforts are made to move each boy to a true repentance for all sins and failures of the past, and on the day before the end each boy makes his confession, as he does also in the heathen rite. Heads are then shaved, new clothes brought and early in the morning of the last day all that belongs to the old life is set fire to and burnt and the boys come to the church for the solemn Mass of Thanksgiving with a real determination to lead a new life. In the heathen rite they would be given a new name; but their new name in Christianity belongs to their baptism.

A real effort was made, though, to link the transition through the *Jando* with a meaningful transition to a new state as a Christian. Thus in Masasi in 1927 'three boys received the cross and five were admitted to baptism on the last day'.[46]

There is moving evidence that Lucas' care in thinking through this adaptation and especially his wholehearted participation in the new *Jando* had real successes. Thus in September 1925 Lucas went to Machombe parish to assist at the first Christian *Jando* there. When the circumcision was over, the African priest in charge, Edward Abdallah, recorded in his log:

> We returned in great jubilation together with the elders and the relatives of the children, and the parents who were in the lead when they started to run in excitement. Canon Lucas also joined with all his heart in taking part in the happy occasion in a way that no other European that I had seen in all my life up to this year. I was very happy because he showed me and my friends, that is we Africans, what ideal community is supposed to be, and that community of spirit is superior to community of flesh . . . Therefore, I for one that was educated by the English priests, proceed to write here a few words from the Gospel of St John the Evangelist on love. Ref. John XIII, 34-5, he says, 'A new law I give unto you—love one another. As I have loved you love one another likewise. Thus all people will know that you are my followers if you have love towards each other.' Even the parents of the children were very pleased with what had happened.[47]

Niether Lucas, nor anyone else, had this sort of success with Christianising the women's rites. There was no adequate theology of sexuality available and the traditional rituals were replaced with innocuous homilies which impoverished the symbolic and liturgical as well as the practical content of the ceremonies. Lucas himself put most effort into the Christian equivalent for the initial *Chiputu* ceremony which was known as *Malango*. Manipulation was prohibited but in other ways the ceremony was run rather like a shorter *Jando*. But approach to the succeeding individual rites of *Litiwo* and the rest was mainly negative, more a matter of ensuring that certain things did not happen than of ensuring that certain things did.

For these reasons the Christianised womens' rites did not command any enthusiasm nor bring home the reality of 'community of spirit'. At Machombe parish, where Edward Abdallah had recorded in 1925 his joy over the first *Jando* he was obliged in 1926 to record his anxieties over *Litiwo*. In the traditional ceremony all the women in the village and the villages around would flock to the house of the pregnant wife; the Christian rules limited attendance only to a few instructors and immediate family and banned altogether the dances and songs. 'After Mass,' wrote Abdallah, 'I collected all the women and elders and together we made a court in church where we discussed matters concerning *Malango*, for even these present here today did not refrain from gathering around any *Malango* that were being given and in their oneness tend to invite each other for these happenings; they are not content with missing any.' In this instance Abdallah could not appeal to a more profound concept of 'oneness' and had to fall back on law. 'I warned them with strong words and scared them that they must choose either to have the Padre taken away and be left without a church or else agree to obey the Bishop's regulations.'[48]

THE ATTITUDES OF THE WHITE CLERGY TOWARDS THE CHRISTIANISED RITES

Lucas' contributions to the institution of the Christian *Jando* and *Malango*, first as priest in charge at Masasi parish and then as first bishop of the new diocese of Masasi, was obviously very important indeed. Yet the experiment could not have survived and expanded without the commitment of many other people. It is important to ask who these people were. It seems plain that on the whole they were not the European clergy. Of course the white priests faithfully followed regulations and devoted much of their time to the administration of Christian initiation. And especially to begin with there were enthusiastic supporters of Lucas' whole adaptation doctrine. But the log-books reveal that many if not most of the white clergy became fairly rapidly disillusioned with the Christian initiations.

This was not surprising. The whole business was an extremely time-consuming one and often an embarrassing one, especially when the priest had to sort out the 'hordes of little girls' who were presented as candidates for the *Malango*, most of them under the age prescribed by the church. Moreover, control of the Christian initiation gave the European priest nothing that he did not already possess; no additional prestige, merely added responsibility and anxiety.

By the end of Lucas' episcopate some of the white clergy had come to express their dislike of the adaptation experiment very forcefully. 'I am told that the whole business was nothing but an orgy,' wrote the priest-in-charge at Lulindi about a *Jando* run by Edward Abdallah; 'worse, if possible, than former years . . . The more one sees and hears of these so-called "Christianised rites" the more one realises the futility of it all . . . The sooner these so-called Christian rites are abolished the better it will be for all concerned.'[49] 'I personally want nothing more to do with the *Jando* as we understand it here,' wrote the priest-in-charge at Masasi. 'I have not yet met anybody except our bishop who believes that there is any teaching of value in the *Jando*. I have met many people who say that there is a great deal of un-Christian teaching given by way of song, dance, story and suggestion.' 'It will be very convenient,' wrote this priest, 'if we can get all this sort of heathenism dealt with by the African clergy.'[50]

THE ATTITUDES OF THE AFRICAN CLERGY AND TEACHERS TOWARDS THE CHRISTIANISED RITES

It had in fact been the Africans who from the very beginning had been the most convinced supporters of the Christian *Jando*. It was they who had raised the question of the initiation rites with Lucas. It was they, and especially Deacon Reuben Namalowe, Kolumba Msigala and a few more, who had worked out the details of the Christian *Jando*. And it was Reuben Namalowe, Lucas' closest African friend, who achieved the breakthrough which led to the holding of the first Christian *Jando* in 1913.

In July 1913 Lucas recorded in the Masasi log that *Mwenye* Mkwatia of Nanyindwa, which was Reuben Namalowe's parish, had determined to have a large boys' initiation ceremony and that he had called on the Christian parents to put their boys in his *Unyago*. 'But Reuben was able to prevent any single one of them being put in.' This left *Mwenye* Mkwatia with only 19 boys for his ceremony and he was compelled to approach the mission in August. 'Che Mkwatia with many Nanyindwa men brought their boys to enter *Jando* here,' recorded Lucas on August 25th, 'according to the Bishop's regulations. This, I hope and believe, marks a great step forward in the Christianising of this district.'[51]

Equally it marked a great step forward in Reuben Namalowe's influence in Nanyindwa. *Mwenye* Mkwatia was one of the most prestigious of the Makua *mamwenye*, being one of the few who had *mbepesi* bestowed on him before he crossed the Ruvuma river. Namalowe was a Makua commoner. But he now began a dominance in Nanyindwa which was to last for some 40 years as he became a priest and then a Canon and as his son Robert became priest and his father's assistant in turn.

We can understand how the institution of the Christian *Jando* helped men like Namalowe to define and increase their prestige. Where it had been the prerogative of the *Mwenye* to decide when an initiation should be held now it was the right of the priest—at least for the children of the Christians who formed the majority in Nanyindwa. Where the initiation fees had partly gone to the *Mwenye*, they now went to the African teachers who slept with the boys in the *Jando*. Where the *Mwenye* and the other elders had been responsible for what was taught in the *Unyago*, now the priest was in sole control of teaching. Here was a really effective way of dramatising, in 'traditional' terms, the shift of power from the *mwenye* to the African priest, from the elders to the African teacher.

We can see how this worked out if we take the example of the career of Reuben Namalowe after 1913. Namalowe was far from being the stooge of the European missionaries. His log-books are full of criticism of European supervisors. '*I* shall decide what is right for the people,' he wrote after a clash with a white school supervisor. 'She is saying this for the mere fact of being a European.'[52] 'You know,' remembers his brother, *Mwalimu* Francis Namalowe, 'he was very frank, he never used to fear telling anybody the truth, whether it was a European or an African, young or old. You would hear him say, "If I find anything wrong I don't say it is right." If a European administrator was a bad man or if the missionary was also a bad man he would immediately report that man to his senior. It used to happen that some deacons

who were to become priests were denied that office by the European missionaries, but the Canon was always fighting for them and he made sure they were
ordained.'[53]

In Nanyindwa it was Namalowe much more than any European missionary
who was thought of as founder of the church. And in Nanyindwa it was Namalowe who thundered against *chisango* witchcraft detection, who exercised Chris-
tain discipline over the commoners and the *mamwenye* alike, and who symbolised his fatherly care for his people by his unremitting concern for the Christian
Jando. It was his wife, Mary, who became the chief presiding officer for the
women's rites not only in Nanyindwa parish but in Masasi also.

Namalowe's logs are full of records of tussles with the *mamwenye* for control
of the intitiation ceremonies, from his first victory in 1913 right up to his
move to the new parish of Kamundi in the 1950s, where his *Malango* in August
1952 was disrupted by the attempt of the Christian *mwenye* to assume command
of it, with the result that two rival ceremonies were held, one in the church
and one in the school. 'It is difficult to know what he wants,' recorded Namalowe of the *mwenye* concerned in this episode. 'He is a careless man. He takes
women anyhow. He claims responsibility over *Malangos* and *Jandos* which
is against the law. These are the priest's responsibility everywhere in the
diocese.'[54]

Namalowe was almost always able to enforce his control even when the
mamwenye had themselves become Christian. He had a high notion of the
rights of the church to discipline the secular power. 'Edward has abdicated,'
he noted on 12 December, 1936, 'in favour of his brother . . . Edward has
refused to obey the rules and for this reason the Archbishop has refused to
crown him.' What the Church of England could do in the case 'of the
King Emperor it could certainly do with *Mwenye* Mkwatia or *Mwenye*
Chivinja.[55]

So Namalowe imposed penances on Christian *mamwenye* when occasion
arose; and he invaded the traditional prerogatives of Muslim and 'pagan'
mamwenye. After his move to Kamundi he began to press in upon *Mwenye*
Mchawala, for example, whose reactions have been recorded by a student
interviewer.

> Until the coming of the missionaries in Masasi [claims Mchawala] only
> *Mwenye* Namkumba and I had the power to conduct *Unyago*. I main-
> tained this authority until 1949 when I conducted my last *Nipanta* on purely
> traditional lines . . . The missionaries were interested in sharing the money
> (paid to the *mwenye* by parents). This, I believe, is the reason they began
> interfering with us . . . in my area they built schools . . . in these schools
> they converted the natives and their children. This was the beginning of
> missionary influence in the traditional *Unyago*. Having converted the un-
> circumcised boys in these schools they refused to allow me to circumcise
> their school boys in traditional *Nipanta* . . . Today the *Mwenyes*, then the
> sub-chiefs, have to beg the missionaries for a *Jando*.[56]

Mwenye Mchawala in this interview directs his anger against the white
missionaries. Others saw Namalowe himself as the direct threat. Thus Namalowe
recorded in 1945 that he was being attacked by *Mwenye* Mkuruwira. 'James

Mkuruwira is spreading destructive ideas because he wants to get the respect due to a *Mwenye*. They say that my work here is opposing their authority.'[57]

Namalowe's logs are full of reports that his *Jandos* were successful and joyous occasions long after the European clergy had come to criticise the Christian initiations bitterly. He regarded the initiation of his son and then his grandson in the *Jando* as an event of great importance, comparing his feelings to those of Joseph at the circumcision of Jesus. Clearly he was profoundly committed to the Christian *Jando* on a theological and missiological basis. But his control of the *Jandos* also defined his own status more precisely than any other symbol could have done.

I have taken Namalowe as an example but the careers of Kolumba Msigala or Edward Abdallah or many others would have made the point with equal force. As the European clergy withdrew from the tangled and complex business of managing the rites so the African clergy took the initiative in further adapting them. Msigala in Tunduru allowed non-Christian sponsors to attend the Christian *Jando*. Edward Abdallah—and Namalowe come to that— welcomed Muslim boys into his initiations. So far as the African clergy were concerned the point of the *Jando* was to bring the whole community into a rite held under Christian sponsorship. They wanted this because they valued 'community of flesh' as well as 'community of spirit'. They also wanted it because they stood in this way defined as leaders of the total community.[58]

In a less crucial way the Christian *Jandos* were important to African teachers as well. They were a source of additional income and in view of the meagre salaries of teachers that was always welcome. And it was the teachers who spent the time in the *Jandos* with the boys, thereby assuming the role of the elders.

THE COUNTER-ATTACK OF THE MAMWENYE

As may be readily imagined the Makua *mamwenye* regarded the institution of the Christian *Jando* and *Malango* as a most severe blow to their prestige. What was involved for them can be estimated in the oral testimony of an embittered traditionalist.

> Traditionally the chief was asked to conduct the ceremony by his people and because he controlled them he had the power of refusing to do it. Today this power is reserved for the missionaries. It is the chief who has to beg the missionary for a ceremony. Not only has the chief lost power over the missionaries but also over his people. The people realise that their chief is a slave of the missionary; therefore instead of their being slaves to the chief there is a tendency to take the short route of being a slave to the missionary only.[59]

Despite their bitter resentment the Makua *mamwenye* could do little at first to resist the institution of the Christian *Jando*. 'Although they were my children', says *Mwenye* Mchawala, 'I could not resist . . . because they were supported by the colonial government. One time they wanted to detain me when I resisted allowing my children to be sent to a Christian *Jando* at Nandete.' Even when the Biritish began to set up Indirect Rule machinery in Masasi and Newala things were no better for traditionalist or Muslim *mamwenye*. The British certainly reacted against the old Yao influence and tried to restore what they rather absurdly thought of as 'pure' Makua institutions, and this involved a frustrating period of trying to turn the numerous *mamwenye* into some sort of local authority. However, the British regarded the Christian *Jando* as a means of preserving traditional institutions rather than of undermining them and they gave Lucas warm support.

The only way in which a *mwenye* could regain power over the initiation ceremonies for Christian boys and girls was by becoming a Christian in good standing and then demanding his rights as the most influential of the elders of the church. Of course the timing varied very much and men like *Mwenye* Mchawala were still putting up an unsuccessful passive resistance as Muslims or traditionalists into the 1950s. The point was that they lived in areas where Christian penetration was still recent. In the core areas of the U.M.C.A. in Masasi the great majority of the people had become Christians by the 1940s. And in those core areas a fascinating struggle for control of the initiation ceremonies was waged *within the church* between the Christian *mamwenye* on the one hand and the clergy and teachers on the other.

We can see this struggle clearly illuminated in the log-books of the Masasi cathedral parish. There were many *mamwenye* in the area, some of whom were formally Christians, but until the late 1930s few of them were in good enough standing as church members to be able to make a claim to control the *Jandos* through the parish council of elders. An entry in the log for August 1929 is eloquent. Listing the *mamwenye* of the area one by one the log laconically records their current state of grace: 'Davis Namkumba (in sin); Machinga (lapsed catechumen with two wives)' and so on through the full number.[60]

Mwenye Davis Namkumba had once been a mission teacher himself and *Mwenye* Machinga had entered the catechumenate. In the 1930s they set themselves straight with the church. In March 1936 the log records that village preaching had been held at Namkumba's 'quite openly, in spite of the difficulties of the position', adding that '*Mwalimu* Barnaba told us afterwards that Namkumba now only has his lawful wife, so we hope that today's sermon may have come opportunely'. In June 1938 it was recorded that '*Mwenye* Machinga is prepared to leave his second wife as soon as he can get a baraza together to agree on the provision to be made for her'. Machinga was baptised in May 1939.[61]

Almost at once Namkumba and Machinga used their new position as elders in good standing to challenge the clerical handling of initiation. On 22 July, 1939, two months after his baptism, Machinga attacked the priest in charge during a meeting of the elders of the church. Machinga's grievance was that the priest in charge had decided to hold two separate *Jando* ceremonies because of the numbers of boys so that 'some people would have children or nephews in two different *Jandos*'.

On 7 July the outraged priest in charge noted that 'the *Jando* has now been taken over by *Mwenye* Machinga in agreement with the *wakuu* of the church under Edwin Kasembe. I am told that I am not wanted but will be told the arrangement in due course!' In fact Machinga backed down from this rather exposed position and a reconciliation took place. But the next year saw another controversy over the Masasi *Jando*. This time it was *Mwenye* Namkumba's turn to take the offensive.

> After Mass at the request of Namkumba [runs the entry for 29 September, 1940] the Bishop and the *Wakuu* assembled to hear Namkumba's complaints about our *Jandos;* the excuse was the failure of one of his grandsons to heal properly but he brought in all kinds of matters praising by implication the "good old days" when the *Mwenyes* ran them; "*walombwe wa-asili*" are preferable to hireling teachers . . . teachers sleep in comfort in the *Jandos*, which is undesirable . . . get money and do little for it; why couldn't they cook and fetch water?[62]

It was this sort of clash which hastened the already quoted conclusion of the European priest in charge at Masasi that the *Jandos* and *Malangos* should be left to the African clergy in future. Thus the struggle to control the Christian *Jando* became more and more an inter-African struggle and there were many instances such as that already cited in which Namalowe and *Mwenye* Chivinja contested over the *Malango* ceremonies in Kamundi in 1952.

THE ATTITUDE OF THE AFRICAN CONGREGATIONS TO THE CHRISTIAN ADAPTATION OF INITIATION

An institution which attracted so much competition to control it can hardly be thought of as insignificant or futile. Clearly the Christian *Jando* had succeeded to the extent that it had become an important part of Masasi social and political life. But what about its acceptability to the African Christians as a whole? Did they feel that the *Jando* was a meaningful, and instrumental ceremony?

I intend to summarise rather rapidly a great mass of evidence on this point. Briefly it is my impression that the boys' *Jando* came to have a wide degree of acceptability. The circumcision performed during the *Jando* was accepted by traditionalists and Moslems alike as a valid indication of full adult membership of the 'tribes' of Masasi. As for the rest two things seem to have happened. One was that African Christians came to feel that the influence over the *Jandos* of the African clergy was an appropriate reflection of the new social realities. Initiation came to be closely associated with the passage of boys through the mission school system, for example, and people accepted it as part of a substitute Christian system of education. The other thing that happened was that the African Christians of Masasi did not passively accept whatever it was they were offered by Lucas or by the African clergy. Lucas had written of the traditional *unyago* in the following terms: 'If we could justly regard the rites and customs of a people as an antiquary regards the uncovered ruins of some ancient temple the problem would be immeasurably simpler . . . But a living people cannot be treated as a dead ruin. They are dynamic not static.' Exactly the same was true of the Christian *Jandos* despite the Bishop's regulations.

In so far as the *Jandos* came to be accepted as the means of initiation for Christian boys so they came to be influenced by the wishes of Christian parents. Especially during the period in which the African clergy were more or less left in charge many changes in the *Jandos* took place from below. These changes did not make the *Jando* 'pagan' as some European priests supposed. They remained very different indeed from the traditional *unyago*. They were a new thing.

I need to defend this positive view of the Christian *Jando* against two main criticisms. One is the criticism made by Wilfred Whiteley. Whiteley held that the influence of the U.M.C.A. had been responsible for the breakdown of clan and lineage structures. Since 'Christianity does not imply the existence of any social group larger than an elementary family . . . the Missions have from time to time felt it necessary to interfere with the larger social groups, i.e. the clan, when their organisation has appeared to conflict with Christian ideas, sometimes passively . . . sometimes actively, by discouraging and interfering with initiation ceremonies and dances, which seem to have taken place on a clan basis.' As a result 'the lives of the people have no focus at all . . . It is true that men like Bishop Lucas realised the value of an institution like initiation ceremonies, but he failed to realise that the pieces from one jig-saw puzzle cannot be used to perfect another, even though they are perfectly adequate for their own puzzle's perfection.'[63]

It appears to me that Whiteley was here attributing all too much to the U.M.C.A. The breakdown of the Makua clan system seems, on his own evidence, to have been advanced before Christianisation. The impact on the situation of the U.M.C.A. is extraordinarily hard to assess but the tendencies towards disintegration and individualism which some aspects of the mission's activity encouraged were balanced and checked by the communal emphasis of other aspects. The U.M.C.A. did its best to make the parish church the new focus for Christian communities.

As for Whiteley's image of the jig-saw puzzles, the whole point is that we are not dealing in Masasi with just *two* jig-saw puzzles, two exclusive systems of thought and practice, the jig-saw of 'traditional' religion and the jig-saw of Christianity. The Christian *Jandos* were part of a third jig-saw, in which they were an important piece, and in which they made perfectly good sense.

The second criticism arises from contemporary oral testimony. Bitter criticisms of the *Jandos* comes from non-Christians; from Christians; and from clergy. They fail in their educational duty, it is said; the boys do not have a hard enough time; the Christian initiation is not a real test of manhood; above all, the boys go into the *Jandos* too young and are not ready to take their place as adults. On this my view is that only part of what is being criticised here arises from the inadequacy of the ritual quality of the Christian *Jandos* and most arises from a general crisis facing virtually all systems of African initiation in Tanzania—not excluding the modern Primary school system. The age of initiates has dropped in traditional and Moslem ceremonies in southern Tanzania as well as in Christian ones. The age of initiates, and consequently the rigour and relevance of initiation, has dropped in areas remote from any Christian influence at all, as Mrs Swantz demonstrates in her study of Uzaramo.[64]

The U.M.C.A. have striven hard over the decades to preserve the old image of initiation. European and African priests used to flog all the boys in the *Jandos* and to determine which traditional 'tortures' were permissible and which not; they fought a losing battle against the admittance of small boys, which after all made nonsense of their own hopes of making the experience into a meaningful initiation into Christianity. In fact the more pertinent criticism may very well be that which some Masasi 'progressives' bring against the U.M.C.A., namely that the Christianisation of the initiation rites has helped to preserve the idea of their importance and necessity at a time when the general crisis of initiation might have resulted in the dwindling away of initiation into the mere act of infant circumcision.

The degree of success of the *Jandos*—which of course was a success for the African clergy and the African congregations at least as much as a success for the ideas of Lucas—can be measured against the over-all failure of the Christian initiation rites for women. If the *Jandos* were adequately instrumental, the female rites were not. Boys were still circumcised but girls no longer were taught to elongate. There were many Christian women who did not feel that the *Malango* was a true initiation at all. 'It frequently happened that women, who were otherwise exemplary matrons, freely consented to their girls being put into the heathen rite so that they could be taught elongation.'[65]

I have written above about the symbolic poverty of the Christian substitutes for the later female rites. These were difficult to control, in any case, and the log-books show a constant evasion by Christian women of the church rules. Many things were at issue here. Women held no office in the church, had not been consulted about the adaptation process, and had no new roles to define by asserting control over new ceremonies as male African clergy did. Moreover, there was a constant tension between the mission view of the role of women in Masasi and the women's view of their own role. Sometimes this came sharply to the surface—as when the U.M.C.A. supported an official proposal to introduce bride-price into the area in order to stabilise marriage and the proposal was hastily dropped in the face of 'the weight of feminine opinion'. More often it was an implicit conflict between the patriarchal assumptions of the church and the matrilineal realities of Masasi.[66]

Adaptation, in short, worked in the one case, though in a very complex way, with all sorts of unpredicted social and political ramifications. In the other case it did not really work at all.

CONCLUSION

I have been trying to show that the Christianisation of male initiation was more than just the brain-child of Vincent Lucas; more than just a relatively superficial tinkering around with symbolic substitution. Lucas' tolerance of and enthusiasm for the idea of a Christian *Jando* were, indeed, extremely important since they ensured that the need for a man to be at once a Christian and a fully initiated member of his community could be met within the church rather than in revolt against it. But it was not Lucas' enthusiasm alone which turned the *Jando* into an institution with its own vitality and dynamics of development. This happened because the Christianised initiation turned out to be the focus of many different interests and aspirations. In this way the *Jando* came to be a key point of *interaction* between Christian and 'traditional' ideas, between modern and traditional roles, rather than merely an experiment in adaptation.

NOTES

[1] This paper is based on a wide range of published and unpublished sources. The most important of the unpublished sources are the log-books of the Masasi and Newala parishes which in 1967 Bishop Trevor Huddleston entrusted to the History Department of the University of Dar es Salaam. These log-books, which number some 200, are daily records of parish affairs, in some cases going back as early as 1906, in others going forward into the 1960s. The majority are in Swahili and were kept by African priests and teachers. A catalogue and guide to them exists in duplicated form in the library of the University of Dar es Salaam, where the log-books are now deposited. I am very grateful to Miss R. Ipopo, Miss S. Maira, Miss R. Maindi, Mr I. Kamugisha and Mr G. Mutahaba for their translations from the Swahili log-books. Where I quote from a Swahili log in this paper it will be in their translations. The logs are most numerous for the Makua area around Masasi and this to some extent accounts for the emphases in this paper.

In addition to the log-books I have made use of much material in the National Archives, Dar es Salaam, especially the administrative correspondence of the Masasi district and the District Books for Masasi and neighbouring areas.

Finally, I employed two students from the Masasi area to collect oral material for me in 1968 and 1969. They were Miss S. Maira and Mr M. Mchawala. Both students adopted the same technique. They did not possess a tape-recorder but wrote up a full statement as though it were a transcript from tape, checking it with their informants. Where I quote from Masasi oral informants I am quoting these statements.

[2] Mr J. A. R. Wembah-Rashid is working as Ethnographer at the National Museum of Tanzania. He is embarked on an ethnographic study of southern Tanzania. His quoted comments come from a letter to the author dated 8 September, 1970.

[3] 'Reminiscences of the Revd. Canon Kolumba Yohana Msigala of Chilonji, Namasakata, P. O. Tunduru, started in July 1955', transcribed and translated by A. G. Blood, S.P.G. Archives, London, now in the library of the University of Dar es Salaam in a photo-copied version, EAF.BV 3625.

[4] It is true, however, that the descendants of the Nyasa freed slaves continued to have their own separate headman and remained distinguished from the surrounding Makua and Yao. Miss S. Maira interviewed the headman of the community in 1969.

[5] The German ethnographer, Karl Weule, travelled in Masasi and Newala just after Maji Maji. His record of the journey was translated into English and published as, Karl Weule *Native Life in East Africa* translated Alice Werner (London 1909). Weule remarked that inquiry into the 'tribal affinities of the Masasi people should land one in a very chaos of tribes . . . Makua, Wayao, Wangindo, a few Makonde, and in addition a large percentage of Coast men: such are the voluntary migrants to this little centre of social evolution.' Later, however, he made sharp distinctions between the atmosphere of Yao and Makua initiations. 'Of all the tribes in the South of German East Africa, the Yao seem to be, not only the most progressive, but the most prosaic and unimaginative, and in fact their initiation ceremonies are very simple, compared to those of the Makonde and the Makua. Those of the latter have to a certain extent a dramatic character.' Weule's speculations on Makua and Makonde rites were also quite dramatic, since he believed that the Makua were following megalithic ritual practices and that the Makonde preserved an element of fire-worship! Weule, pp. 69–70, 300.

[6] Weule recorded the 'brightly coloured fantastic figures' of the girls, adorned in 'massive brass bangles . . . and calico of the brightest colours . . . just bought from the Indian traders at Lindi or Mrweka, at great expense, by the gallant husbands, who have recently made an expedition to the coast for the purpose'. Weule *op. cit.* p. 222.

[7] W. H. Whiteley, 'Sociological Research—Makua Tribe of the Southern Province' December 1951, Secretariat file 42186, National Archives, Dar es Salaam.

[8] W. H. Whiteley, 'Sociological Research'.

[9] Marja-Liisa Swantz in her study of ritual and symbolic change in Uzaramo writes: 'The introduction of Christianity provided a new creative opportunity within the framework of symbol formation. Christianity caused a change in the presentational symbolism but at the same time provided for its development into articulated forms of logical, discursive symbolism. Deficiencies may have been many in the manner of its introduction in relation to the existing system, yet the introduction of a new religion accompanied by meaningful education made the symbolic adjustment possible. At the same time as there was sufficient symbolic continuity the new religion gave security and a new mode of individual integration furthered the new orientation.' Marja-Liisa Swantz *Ritual and Symbol in transitional Zaramo society* (Uppsala 1970) p. 341.

[10] Masasi District Book, vol. 1, 'Mbepesi: Makua', on microfilm in the library of the University of Dar es Salaam, MIF 1/7.

[11] A. E. M. Anderson-Morshead *The History of the Universities' Mission to Central Africa*, vol. 1, *1859–1909* (London 1909) pp. 136–7.

[12] Travellers in Masasi and Newala remarked on the contrast between the handsome houses and cosmopolitan styles of dress of Nakaam and Matola, their experience of a wider society through travel and literacy, their network of trading and political connections and the limited horizons of the Makua *mamwenye*. It was a classic case of the difference between the man of the macrocosm and the man of the microcosm. J. A. R. Wembah-Rashid writes: 'Most of the Yao had had access to contact with non-African people for a long period, and for commercial purposes had found this useful. Very few Makua *mamwenye* did. I look at their negative attitude towards the U.M.C.A. as a protest against Yao, missionary or government sponsored leadership on the one hand and an attempt to preserve traditionalism on the other'.

[13] Mtwara-Lindi Provincial Book, 'Tribal Government. Yao Tribe', on microfilm in the University of Dar es Salaam library. This account of Matola II's dealings with Mwawa was written by Provincial Commissioner A. M. D. Turnbull on 2 February, 1928. It was a summary of 'an exhaustive inquiry' held in connection with setting up of Indirect Rule machinery in Newala. Matola II had claimed 'to be paramount chief of the Makua and Yao' but this claim had been denied by *Mzee* Amuri, heir of Mwawa, who together with 'all the Makua *mamweni* and *mzee* denied that Mwawa I had handed over his country to Matola I . . . the *mamwenye* adhered strongly to their declaration that they and Matola II were of equal status, that each was an independent *mwenye* and that Matola II was nothing more than the most influential *mwenye*.'

It is interesting to note that the U.M.C.A. journal, *Central Africa* reported in August 1899 that 'a small chief of a village' between Masasi and Newala 'was hung at Lindi recently for having a . . . person implicated in witchcraft killed by his order'. *Central Africa: A Monthly Record of the Work of the Universities Mission* no. 200 (August 1899) p. 140.

[14] One of the recognised duties of the *mamwenye* was to cleanse their communities of witchcraft by periodical recourse to *chisango*. In 1968 old *Mwenye* Mchawala described this duty, and also his conviction that Christianity had not turned out to be effective. 'Christianity and Islam are opposed to witchcraft but they have no power to influence it. They do not recognise the owners of *Chisango* who are the only people who can reduce it . . . Where *Chisango* is allowed witchcraft normally decreases. This was the case in Mchawala when I called Chikonda to do his *Chisango*. The deaths of children and young people decreased. The only people who died were people who were suspected to be practising witchcraft. This peace reigned for a very long time and when I suspected that the practice of witchcraft had started again I invited Matoroka from Mwera to conduct his *Chisango*, . . . In order to get rid of witchcraft completely I think religions should leave this problem to the local people . . . Witchcraft is a local problem; missionaries cannot believe it because

it does not affect them.' Interview with *Mwenye* Hassani Mchawala, 19 September, 1968.

[15] For a fuller account of the alliance of the U.M.C.A. with Matola and Nakaam see, T. O. Ranger, 'The Apostle: Kolumba Msigala', in John Iliffe (ed.) *Modern Tanzanians* (Nairobi, forthcoming).

[16] Bishop Thomas Spreiter, 'Kanonische Visitation in Kwiro von 18 dez. 1910 bis 11 Janvar 1911', Kwiro Archives, file KA-F. I am indebted to Mr Lorne Larson for this reference and for his translation from the original German.

[17] 'On the method of Evangelising Uncultured Races', 1882, in Ellen Maples (ed.) *Journals and Papers of Chauncy Maples Bishop of Likoma, Lake Nyasa* (London 1899) pp. 175–88.

[18] 'On the Power of the Conscience, the Sense of the Moral Law, and the Idea of God amongst certain Tribes in East Africa', 1891, Ellen Maples (ed.) *Journals and Papers of Chauncy Maples* pp. 189–202.

[19] 'Sermon preached on Anniversary Day', 1895, Ellen Maples (ed.) *Journals and Papers of Chauncy Maples* pp. 212–26.

[2] W. V. Lucas 'The Christian approach to non-Christian Customs', in *Christianity and Native Rites* (London 1950).

[21] W. V. Lucas *ibid*.

[22] Entry for 1 March, 1922, Masasi log-book, 1921–1925.

[23] W. V. Lucas *The Christian approach to non-Christian Customs*.

[24] Some of the most informative sections of the log-books of Masasi and Newala are the lists of cases of church discipline. These contain fairly full details of alleged offences and contain a wealth of material on marriage and family practice in Masasi as well as an accurate indication of the areas of tension between the church and its people.

[25] Entry for All Souls Day 1913, Masasi log-book, 1912–1915; entry for 14 December, 1921, Masasi log-book, 1921–1925.

[26] Entries for 30 November, 1925, and 30 November, 1936, Masasi log-book, 1934–1938.

[27] Entry for 20 October, 1935, Masasi log-book, 1934–1938.

[28] Majaliwa's letter is in *Central Africa* no. 47 (November 1886) p. 174.

[29] 'Reminiscences of the Revd. Canon Kolumba Yohana Msigala'; T. O. Ranger, 'The Apostle: Kolumba Msigala', in John Iliffe (ed.) *Modern Tanzanians* (Nairobi, forthcoming).

[30] T. O. Ranger *ibid*.

[31] Entries for 15 January, 1913, 21 January, 1913, 2 February, 1913, Masasi log-book, 1912–1915; *Central Africa* no. 374 (February 1914); *Central Africa* no. 376 (April 1914).

[32] 'Reminiscences of the Revd. Canon Kolumba Msigala'.

[33] David Parkin, 'Politics of Ritual Syncretism: Islam among the non-Muslim Giriama of Kenya', *Africa* vol. XL, no. 3 (1970) pp. 217–33.

[34] The initiation rites of the Masasi area have been described by: Karl Weule *Wissenschaftliche Ergebnisse Meiner Ethnographische Forschungsreise in den Südosten Deutsch-Ostafrikas* (Berlin 1908); R. G. P. Lamburn, 'The Yaos of Tunduru: an essay in missionary anthropology', unpublished typescript in the library of Makerere College, Kampala, Uganda and on microfilm in the library of the University of Dar es Salaam, MIF 40 part 2; and in the District Books for Masasi, Newala, Tunduru, etc.

[35] Interview with Father Petro Ligunda, 23 September, 1968.

[36] W. H. Whiteley, 'Sociological Research—Makua Tribe of the Southern Province', December 1951, Sec. 42186, National Archives, Dar es Salaam; R. G. P. Lamburn, 'The Yaos of Tunduru: an essay in missionary anthropology'.

[37] Interview with *Mwenye* Hassani Mchawala, 19 September, 1968.

[38] I draw this paragraph largely from the Masasi log-books where there is constant reference to the need to get permission for initiation ceremonies from African *Akidas*. There was often much resentment of this need. In July 1944, for example, *Mwenye* Magongo announced that he would not write to Nakaam to get permission. 'He did not think it necessary to

have such a letter and that he would hold a *Jando* in his own village in accordance with the ancient custom.' Entry for 18 July 1944, Masasi log-book, 1941–1944.

[39] W. H. Sangree *Age, Prayer and Politics in Tiriki, Kenya* (London 1966).

[40] Bishop Weston wrote that 'the homes of the tribe were founded on marriages that could not last'; Lucas held that 'the marriage of Yaos is no true union at all'.

[41] Interview with Mrs Janet Bora, 26 September, 1963.

[42] *Central Africa* no. 62 (February 1888); *Central Africa* no. 303 (March 1908).

[43] This sequence of events is based on entries in the Masasi log-book, 1912–1915.

[44] D. Julius Richter *Tanganyika and its Future* (London 1934) p. 59.

[45] W. V. Lucas *The Christian approach to non-Christian customs.*

[46] W. V. Lucas, *ibid.*: entries for 12 and 13 August, 11 September, 1921, Masasi log-book, 1918–1921.

[47] Entry for 15 September, 1925, Machombe log-book, 1925–1928, translated by Miss Regina Ipopo.

[48] Entry for 11 July, 1926, Machombe log-book, 1925–1928, translated by Miss Regina Ipopo.

[49] Entry for 11 September, 1945, Lulindi log-book, 1943–1948.

[50] Entry for 16 July, 1944, Masasi log-book, 1941–1944.

[51] Entries for 27 July and 25 August, 1913, Masasi log-book, 1912–1915.

[52] Entry for 15 February, 1951, Kamundi log-book, 1950–1954, translated by Miss R. Maindi.

[53] Interview with Francis Namalowe, May 1969.

[54] Entry for 26 August, 1952, Kamundi log-book, 1950–1954, translated by Miss R. Maindi.

[55] Entry for 12 December, 1936, Nanyindwa log-book, 1936–1939, translated by Miss R. Maindi.

[56] Interview with *Mwenye* Hassani Mchawala, 19 September, 1968.

[57] Entry for 30 August, 1945, Nanyindwa log-book, 1943–1950, translated by Miss R. Maindi.

[58] The priest-in-charge at Lulindi, already cited, who regarded the *Jando* as nothing but an orgy and desired to see it suppressed complained about Abdallah's management of it: 'Father Edward had accepted Moslems and put them in with the Christians! ! ! The place swam with *pombe* . . . The Moslems took off their children and began firing off guns outside the church at the beginning of Mass! ! !' Entry for 11 September, 1945, Lulindi log-book, 1943–1948.

[59] Interview with Maida Masanje, September 1968.

[60] List of *mamwenye*, August 1929, Masasi log-book, 1926–1934.

[61] Entries for 5 June, 1930, 18 March, 1936, 14 June, 1938, 26 May, 1939, Masasi log-books, 1934–1938, 1938–1941.

[62] Entries for 2 July, 4 July, 7 July, 1939, and for 29 September, 1940, Masasi log-books, 1938–1941.

[63] W. H. Whiteley, 'Essays on the Makua', Sec. 42186, National Archives, Dar es Salaam.

[64] For the decline in age of boys going into Uzaramo initiations, see M. L. Swantz *Ritual and Symbol in transitional Zaramo society* (Uppsala 1970).

[65] R. G. P. Lamburn, 'The Yaos of Tunduru: an essay in missionary anthropology'.

[66] For the attempt to introduce bride-price see, Annual Report, Masasi District, 1948, file 16/11/260, National Archives, Dar es Salaam.

MATTHEW SCHOFFELEERS and I. LINDEN

The Resistance of the Nyau Societies to the Roman Catholic Missions in Colonial Malawi

INTRODUCTION

Studies of the function of religion in resistance to colonial rule have concentrated largely on its inspirational and integrative role in armed uprisings. In Central Africa, opposition to colonialism has been articulated in the past in terms of traditional religion as in the Ndebele and Shona rebellions; in terms of the non-Christian millenarianism of the Maji Maji rising and of the Congolese Epikilipikili movement; in terms of politico-eschatological Christianity ranging from Watchtower to John Chilembwe's Providence Industrial Mission; and finally in the secular language of national congresses. Religious and messianic themes have played a progressively minor role; the rise of Westernised elites, increasingly divorced from the daily life and thought patterns of their people, has been accompanied by a pronounced secularisation of political discourse. On the other hand, religion has remained the backbone of traditional African society.

The struggle at village level to maintain a socio-cultural identity against pressures from planter, administration and mission, because it was less spectacular and asked from the historian detailed ethnographical knowledge that often he did not possess, has been rarely open to historical inspection. The role of traditional religion in this aspect of resistance has stayed constant and fundamental; although virtually unco-ordinated, it has proved remarkably effective in opposing European intrusion. It is the aim of this paper to describe the confrontation between the *Nyau* cult, an important element in the traditional religion of the Chewa-speaking peoples of Malawi, and the Catholic missions, among the most powerful and village-oriented of the European missionary bodies during the colonial period.[2]

The successive invasions undergone by the Chewa-speaking peoples of Malawi since the middle of the nineteenth century can be classified in three categories according to the numerical and military strength of the invaders: massive armed invasions such as those mounted by the Yao; massive non-armed invasions such as the migrations of the Lomwe and Sena from Mozambique; and small or medium-sized invasions that were openly military or relied on the threat of arms, such as those of the Ngoni, Kololo and Europeans. A brief review of the response of the Chewa-speaking peoples to the intruders at the political, social and cultural levels will help to focus on the type of resistance undertaken by the *Nyau* societies. This, of course, cannot follow a chronological order.

The Yao invasion of the southern end of Lake Malawi brought about an

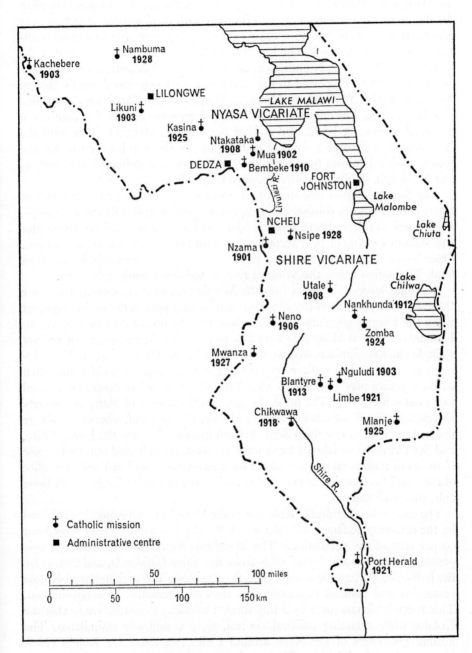

Distribution of Roman Catholic Missions in 1928

almost total collapse of the Chewa-speaking Nyanja and Mang'anja societies of the Zomba and Fort Johnston districts. There were not only successive waves of Mangoche, Machinga and Masininga Yao, well-armed with guns supplied by the Arabs, but the invaders also brought with them a social structure very similar to that of the Chewa-speaking peoples, and were able to oppose traditional religion with Islam. The last of the Maravi Kalonga, Sosola, died at the hands of the Yao chief, Ndindi, as a result of a personal dispute. Large numbers of captives were transported to the East Coast, or taken into domestic slavery by the powerful Yao such as Mponda, Matapwiri and Zarafi who controlled the slave routes. The only way to political power in the area of Yao dominance involved embracing Islam, and at least one Chewa, Makanjila, rose with the Yao system to become a slaver. For the majority the Yao invasion meant the loss of political control together with several important cultural losses such as the *Nyau* cult, doubtless under pressure from Islam.[3]

The Sena migration into the Lower Shire valley during the first quarter of the twentieth century consisted of waves of disparate patrilineal virilocal groups. Both a series of droughts in Mozambique territory and political pressures after the Makombe rising of 1917 account in part for this massive unarmed invasion. Once inside the country the Sena continued to push northwards in search of land. The region below the Mwanza river is today predominantly Sena.

A similar large-scale influx into the Mlanje area of groups given the name 'Lomwe' took place from the 1890s onwards with a peak in the period 1925–31 when the Lomwe population of Nyasaland rose by 90 per cent to 144,000. In both areas the local Mang'anja were able to maintain their political power. Not a single chieftainship was won by the Lomwe in the Mlanje district. The migrants were allowed to settle piecemeal under Mang'anja authorities and often used as 'guinea pigs' in relations with Administration and missions, being used to try out schools, etc.[4] The price, though, was the erosion of Mang'anja society and culture; the *Nyau* was lost around Mlanje. It seems that, whenever a village reached the level of one third Sena through immigration into the Lower Shire, and Sena virilocal social structures were imposed, the cult died out. Only those elements of traditional religion which were intimately associated with the office of the chief, his function as rain-maker and owner of the land, e.g. the M'Bona cult, were maintained.

The success of a handful of Kololo over the Mang'anja can be partly explained by the catastrophic famine of 1862 which Rowley estimated to have wiped out 90 per cent of the population.[5] The Mang'anja were also under considerable pressure from Yao and Ngoni raids from the Shire Highlands, and attacks by the half-caste Portuguese slavers from the Zambesi. The acceptance of Kololo protection and political hegemony was thus an alternative to extermination. This remarkable take-over by a tiny foreign minority is instructive in that the Kololo, while retaining political control, were completely assimilated. The leading promoters of the Nyau around Chikwawa today are Kololo chiefs Katunga, Kasisi, Makwira and Masseah.[6]

Since provision for assimilation of foreign groups was integral to Ngoni martial society, the Ngoni invasion provided a test case for Chewa resistance. From the 1860s the Fort Jameson and Maseko Ngoni of the Dedza district extended their control over the Mbo, Ntumba, Chewa and Maravi villages around them. The huge numbers of captives taken formed the lowest section of society employed in cultivation of the extensive Ngoni gardens. A well fortified hilltop might occasionally allow an individual Chewa group to withstand the well disciplined raiding parties; Odete on Chirenje Hill in the heart of the Ngoni raiding territory survived until dislodged by British cannon in 1898.[7]

While the Maseko Ngoni were vastly superior in numbers to the Kololo—considering the number of members of the highest aristocratic Swazi clans alone—the incorporation of large numbers of Chewa wives appears to have posed the Ngoni patrilineal society some difficulties. Reports in the 1870s of *mwabvi* ordeals, and later of magical gates used to stop the enemy and other 'medicines' in the area under the control of the Maseko Paramount, Chikusi, would suggest that the Chewa were, at the least, maintaining their cultural identity.[8] The contemptuous attitude, even today, of Ngoni towards Chewa child-rearing practices, sorcery and *Nyau* is perhaps a vestige of the defence put up by a numerically weak aristocracy to counteract the cultural onslaught from their captives.[9]

The 1898 census put the number of Europeans in Nyasaland at 340, a figure comparable to the number of Trans-Zambesi clan members among the Maseko in their heyday. European colonial society, like the former Ngoni society, rested ultimately on military strength and was faced with the dual problem of maintaining political control of a large population with few personnel and assimilating an indigenous people into alien institutions. The interaction of the Ngoni aristocracy with the Chewa anticipates this later European settlement and the analogous efforts of the missions to absorb the Chewa-speaking peoples into the socio-cultural structures of their churches. Because European settlement was so thin, never exceeding a few thousand, and Europeans remained aloof from the local population, the confrontation at the village level in socio-cultural terms was not the *fait accompli* of the Yao invasion, but took on the nature of a prolonged struggle. It is this struggle, exemplified by the confrontation between the *Nyau* and Catholicism, whose evolution will be traced here.

CATHOLIC MISSIONS AMONG THE CHEWA

After an initial failure of the U.M.C.A. to establish a mission in the 1860s, European penetration of the Shire Highlands gained momentum in the 1890s extending to most Chewa areas farther north. The Kirk Range was dotted with mission stations at Livelezi, Goa, Ntonda, Chuoli and Pantumba, staffed by Scots from Blantyre, Dutch from the Cape, American Baptists and Booth's Zambesi Industrial Mission. Sufficient Chewa were being attracted to these centres to pose a threat to the Maseko Paramount, Gomani I, and it was his attack on villages around these stations that led to his execution by the British on October 27th, 1896.[10]

The more institutional and socially organised Catholics had yet to gain a foothold. The White Fathers' Mission to Mponda's which arrived under Portuguese auspices on 28 December, 1889, were to sit helplessly through a succession of disputes between Mponda and his relatives along the Shire—the Chungwarungwaru war—without making a convert. The only contribution they were allowed to make to the strongly Islamic Machinga Yao was a gift of powder to Mponda in return for permission to build a house and a short-lived school.[11] After their withdrawal in 1891 ten years elapsed before the Montfort-Fathers founded a mission at Nzama, near Ncheu. The White Fathers began again at Kachebere, Mua and Likuni during 1902–3. With the exception of Likuni these stations were in areas under Ngoni control: Nzama under a sub-chief of Gomani II, Njobvualema; Mua under Kachindamoto and Kachebere under Mpezeni. By 1925 the Catholic missions had extended as far south as Chikwawa and Port Herald (now Nsanje), while the region North of Blantyre was being covered by missions at Utale, Neno, Nguludi (near Blantyre), Limbe, Ntaka-taka, Bembeke and Blantyre itself.

The first priests were mainly from farming areas of France and Holland, particularly Brittany and Limbourg. An intensive seminary training tended to produce a uniformity in intellectual outlook which contrasted with the variety of Protestant personalities. While their educational level was certainly higher than the lesser lights of the Protestant missions, it was an education structured around the niceties of theology and canon-law. Drawn from the low water mark of nineteenth-century Catholicism, their philosophical training was apologetic and narrow, suffering from that unfortunate combination of superficiality and dogmatism that characterised the seminary manuals of the day.

The attitudes of the early missionaries towards society grew out of Church–State controversies in the Europe of the half-century after Pius IX's flight to Gaeta in 1848. The last vestiges of liberalism had been left behind. The clerical *zeitgeist* was equally a product of French piety; life was divided into ecclesiastical and secular spheres. Lawfully constituted authority was always to be upheld provided it did not actively encroach on the Church's traditional preserve which included such issues as communal initiation ceremonies and divorce.

Morality centred on the individual; social issues such as conditions on plantations, tax collection, emigration and land were seen in terms of individual suffering but rarely confronted in holistic terms. The ideal of 'Work, labours and thoughts are but bent on what is heavenly to the exclusion of everything else'[12] was always tempered by a natural concern for the material welfare of the people around the missions. Leprosaria and dispensaries were not merely incidental to missionary endeavour. The attempt to develop a *corpus christianum* was always implicit in the work of each mission. Each station in the White Fathers' vicariate acted as a local focus, a large building staffed with three missionaries and, when available, lay brothers to look after the material needs of the house. Around this would grow up church and school, with, later, accommodation for nuns. From this focus radiated the indigenous catechists, and after 1930, an overlapping system of local Catholic groups. The 'Gurupa' in the Central Regions and the 'Kapitao' in the south were the established leaders in the villages whose primary occupation was the supervision of the local Catholic community. Similarly the 'Legion of Mary', while primarily a pious association, tended to strengthen the Catholics in the village through organisation, discipline and regular meetings. At the heart of this structure lay the liturgical celebration of the eucharist as the *terminus ad quem* and *terminus a quo* of the mission's life.

Rambling networks of schools spread out from each station staffed by catechists, who were often only a few steps ahead of their pupils. The three year training in the catechumenate among the White Fathers, two with the Mont-fort–Marists, included reading, writing and arithmetic. The lure of education brought thousands of villagers within the orbit of the mission. There was little pretence as to the role of the schools:

> At the S.C. de Propoganda Fide I was instructed to dwell everywhere on the importance of the school. It is the atrium or portal of the Church. Our missionaries should be urged to concentrate on the schools. If anywhere, I was told, it is a question of building a Church or building a school, the school should have preference, even if the building has also to be used as a Church.[13]

When it was not possible to erect wattle and daub huts for a classroom, catechists gave lessons on the 'bwalo'—the public square. Villages with well-built schools tended to become 'outstations' where a church might be built later.

Communications between the centre and periphery of this structure were two-way; priests travelled round the villages for periods up to three weeks, hearing confessions, teaching and celebrating the mass, while from each level of the hierarchy, church elders, catechists, Gurupa, Legion of Mary, Christians and catechumens, groups would come to the mission for retreats, refresher courses and instruction, lasting in the case of preparation for baptism up to six weeks. A minor seminary was begun in each vicariate and successful students were sent to the Major Seminary at Tabora for a ten-year course as candidates for the priesthood.

THE STRUCTURE AND FUNCTION OF THE NYAU

Like the Catholic Church the *Nyau* is not only a system of beliefs but a society with all embracing claims on its membership. The name 'Nyau' refers to the societies themselves, their masks and other apparel in which the dancers per-form. The cult is shared by the Mang'anja and the Chewa peoples north of the Shire Highlands extending into N.E. Zambia, although there are significant differences between the two forms. In the Chewa version there are a number of dancers, the *akapoli*, who appear practically naked and use various clays to coat their bodies. Women play a more active role in responding to the songs of the male dancers and the behaviour of the *akapoli* seems to be generally more overtly sexually provocative than in the Mang'anja version.

If the analogy with the Catholic Church can be pressed further the perform-ances of the dancers make up a liturgical celebration. In cosmic terms they may be interpreted as a re-enactment of the primal co-existence of the three cate-gories of men, animals and spirits in friendship, and their subsequent division by fire. Fundamental to the religious significance of the cult is the belief that underneath his mask the dancer has undergone what might be called a 'spiritual transubstantiation' to become a spirit. The spirits and animals come in from the bush and a temporary reconciliation with man is enacted as they associate with the people in the village around pots of beer, as in the Chewa creation myth they were first united around the waters which came with them from heaven.[14]

Initiation into the society takes the form, as in Christian baptism, of a symbolic death with the neophyte protected by a sponsor, the *phungu*, who is already a member. The neophyte is introduced to the *Nyau* secret vocabulary, songs and the meaning of the masks and enjoined under pain of death not to divulge the secrets. In the Lower Shire valley each branch of the *Nyau* is led by 'the elder of the forest' who, as senior member, receives applications for performances and is in charge of initiation. The second in command is the 'elder of the village' who is responsible for the performance itself. In Chewa areas, heads of villages have to make an application to an area head of the *Nyau*, the *mfumo dziko*, for a piece of ground set aside—'consecrated'—for the performance, called the *mzinda*, which can cost up to twenty goats. Finally there are senior women, *nankhungwi*, who are in charge of the women and female initiation.

Performance of the *Nyau* used to take place at the major transition rites of death and at female initiation ceremonies. In the puberty ceremonies *Nyau* members fulfilled the role of castigator of the initiates while in the mortuary rites, still common in Malawi, the *Nyau* can be classified with the 'funeral friend' and sons-in-law of the deceased who are traditionally set apart from the mourners proper. The characters portrayed by the *Nyau* are divided into diurnal and nocturnal representations; the former are mainly human figures in the form of masked persons while the nocturnal characters are all animals. In the course of the performance women are subjected to insults, obscenities and vituperative male behaviour. In the Chewa *Nyau* the initiate is required to run through the village of the matrilineage into which he has married to steal chickens from his mother-in-law. This pronounced sexual antagonism plays an important role in the resolution of social conflict within the traditional matrilineal society of the Chewa peoples.[15]

Active membership of the society requires that a person be either a leader, a drummer, a dancer or an assistant. Among the dancers and drummers there is further hierarchical distinction according to the degree of accomplishment; the more expert either play the major drums or wear the best masks. Initiates will spend a long period as assistants before rising in seniority. Nominal members of the society form a middle group between the active members and non-initiates. Formerly all villagers would be initiated, though this is, of course, no longer the case. By virtue of their initiation nominal members are allowed to go to the *mzinda* and watch the performances and they provide the clientele for the dances. It is an honour to have the *Nyau* performed at the funeral of one's kin and the lavishness of the performance serves as an indicator of social status; so the role of nominal members is not insignificant. However, there is considerable friction engendered between nominal and active members over finance. The charge for a performance, excluding the hire of drums, can range from 50p. to £3·00. plus a cow, unless the deceased is related to the leader of the cult.[16] Since the quality of the performance is largely a subjective judgement constant haggling can arise over the price, and on occasions the dances are broken off owing to disputes of this nature.

The exact historical relationship of the *Nyau* leadership to traditional village authorities is hard to ascertain. While the local chiefs are considered as the 'owners of the *Nyau*' in the Chewa areas, this role seems to have been lost among the Mang'anja. None the less the society claims jurisdiction over offences taking place during the course of the dances. 'Milandus' (litigation) involving dancers are tried at a special court presided over by the 'elder of the forest'. This is doubtless a consequence of the social function of *Nyau*; the normal judicial procedure would bring the member before a leader of his wife's matri-lineage and accentuate his uxorilocality and social predicament. A Kololo chief expressed the idea in these terms:

> You cannot arrest and punish an animal which has hurt you because what it did was pure accident. There is no case because there is no accused.[17]

Thus the *Nyau* member finds in the society a world in which all the normal rules of behaviour are reversed, a relative autonomy, financial benefits and an alternative structure in which to rise in social status.

THE ENCOUNTER BETWEEN CATHOLICISM AND NYAU

Inasmuch as the local Church was hierarchical from Father Superior to the applicant for entry to the catechumenate, with a regulated life, transition rites such as baptism, extreme unction, requiem mass and burial, a priesthood leading a liturgical celebration concerned with the primal event grounding the Christian community historically and spiritually, its idiom could hardly be considered as totally alien to the culture of the Chewa peoples. In its emphasis on liturgy it differed markedly from the Protestant missions. But inasmuch as it considered Western culture and standards not as optional but to be thought of as univer-sally valid, and set up parallel authoritarian structures to village headmen and *Nyau* leaders, it posed a serious threat to traditional patterns of life.

The conflict between *Nyau* and mission in the villages around each station was played out with the chain of civil authority running from the Governor at Zomba through the Provincial Commissioner, District Commissioner, to the local Native Authority, as arbiters. Within the Dedza district, where the aims of mission and Ngoni aristocracy often coincided, the interaction of the leading Maseko chiefs, Gomani and Kachindamoto, with their predominantly Chewa villages was a decisive factor. After being defeated by the British the Ngoni attempt to assimilate the Chewa was carried through into the colonial period, making them later the natural allies of the British administration before the rise of nationalism. The contrast between the conflict in the Likuni area, totally Chewa, and at Mua, controlled by Ngoni, highlights these contending forces.

Lacking training in anthropology, and with a rigid code of morality, it is not surprising that the first missionaries branded the *Nyau* as immoral without much understanding of its social and religious significance. Its immorality, for them, lay in the 'obscene' songs and the appearance of naked dancers in the presence of women. Christians and catechumens were forbidden to participate. This was not part of an indiscriminate campaign against local 'customs'; when-ever possible the missionaries went to watch the dances or used catechists to find out what went on in initiation rites. Dances that took place during the day-time without any mixing of the sexes were viewed favourably. This initial reaction of the priests should be seen therefore more in the context of a mild Jansenist prudery, rather than in the sinister sense of premeditated cultural imperialism, an attitude as typical of rural Irish clergy as of French and Dutch missionaries in Africa.

As early as 1909 an entry in the Mua diary reads:

This morning the Father Superior had to go to Makombe to 'excommunicate' two catechumens who have just joined the famous Zinyau society. He discovered they had just left for Blantyre.[18]

Christians and catechumens were also forbidden to take part in 'chinamwali', the communal female initiation rites, but this proved impossible to enforce. Bishop Auneau was reduced to suggesting that an alternative Christian rite should be presided over by older Christian matrons.[19]

The initial response to evangelisation in each area was strongly influenced by the balance of power between Ngoni, Chewa and colonial government. After five years at Nzama, 1901–6, a region under the control of Gomani's sub-chief Njobvualema, there were 120 'adult' baptisms, almost entirely children of school age.[20] Njobvulema had suffered no direct defeat at the hands of the British and stayed on the Mozambique border, an area with negligible Chewa influence, while Gomani escaped after his father's death. At Mua, under the other branch of the Maseko led by a princess regent, Nyathei, who had fled during the Maseko civil war in 1894 to a strongly Maravi area, there were 72 adult baptisms between 1902–7. Nyathei's dead brother, Kachindamoto, had enlisted the support of the British against Gomani and this branch of the Maseko was looked on favourably by the government. Kachebere, on the border with N.E. Zambia and under the Fort Jameson Ngoni, could only claim 22 adult baptisms for the period 1903–8. Mpezeni had barely recovered from a British attack in 1898. The area was mixed Chewa/Ngoni and the mission found itself badly placed away from the most important villages in the area.[21] Likuni, near an old Chewa fortification close to Lilongwe, was in a district unoccupied by the Ngoni and controlled by the Chewa chiefs, Matanda, Mkanda and Dzoole. And here the contrast is striking; between 1902–7 there was not a single baptism and only in 1909 were the first seven catechumens baptised.

In 1914 the estimated populations of the areas evangelised by each mission were as follows: Mua—50,000; Likuni—35,000; Kachebere—25,000; Nzama—c. 25,000.[22] The figures for baptisms cannot, therefore, be considered as a reflection of population density. Similarly the intensity of Protestant mission activity in the four areas, with perhaps the exception of Likuni where it was less than average, was equally great.

The first World War brought missionary pressures on the *Nyau* to a halt. By 1918 all catechists had been withdrawn for some form of government service, either 'tangata' work or as porters keeping open the armies' lines of supply.[23] Four Nyasaland White Fathers were involved in the East Africa campaign for the duration of the war, while from both orders one or two German priests were interned. No supplies were getting through from Rome or the mother houses in France and Holland; even if there had been catechists available there would have been no money to pay them. On Monday, 25 January, 1915 David Kaduya led a splinter-group from the Chilembwe rising to destroy the headquarters of the Montfort-Fathers at Nguludi in retaliation for the burning of a Providence Industrial Mission school at Namchengwa.[24]

It took five years after the war for the Catholic missions to regain their previous momentum. Between 1918–23 in the Shire Vicariate, from south of the Livelezi to Port-Herald, the number of baptised Catholics rose from 5,000 to 10,000. From 1923–9 it shot up to 39,800. During this same period the number of baptised Protestants merely doubled from 22,000–40,000. Although these statistics included baptised infants and were from documents prepared for the consumption of benefactors in the U.S.A. and Europe, they provide a crude indication of the degree of missionary penetration after the war.

From the early 1920s the *Nyau* began to respond to this pressure in two ways, both of which involved some degree of development and change in the traditional character and discipline of the society. In order to reduce the mystique of the Catholic cult costumes were invented for key Christian figures such as the Virgin Mary, Joseph and St Peter. 'Maliya' portrayed a white woman with pronounced breasts, made of 'magwebe' (fruit of a type of palm), an animal tail for hair and red complexion, carrying a baby. The figures 'Josephe' and 'Simon' also imitated Europeans with red faces.[25] The *Nyau* song 'Wagona, wagona, wagona, ndi gojo'—'She slept, slept, slept with an impotent one', which was formerly a reference to the test of manhood faced by a fiancé after a girl's final rites of initiation, came to be associated with 'Maliya' and 'Josephe'.[26] These 'Christian' masks stayed as request items requiring an additional payment to the dancers.

This ability of the *Nyau* to respond to foreign pressures by assimilation has historical precedents. The Mang'anja who were in contact with the Portuguese at Sena from the sixteenth century and had intermittent relations with Arabs along the Zambesi, now use masks with long garments attached, so that only hands and feet are visible.[27] These are not found in the Chewa areas. Similarly it is not uncommon to find the local tax-collector or District Commissioner included among the daytime masks in both districts.

The Catholic policy of widespread elementary education in the rural areas linked to the catechumenate proved more of a threat than the cultic aspects of missionary Catholicism. Each child coming to school was registered and the schools supervised by catechists backed up by the priests. A good missionary would know everyone in a village of sixty people by sight, have the names of school attenders, pagans and mass-goers, details on the state of the Christian marriages and on potential opponents in the area. The effect of the mission acting through schools and education was to bring into existence in the villages a third class of people, non-initiates, who rejected *Nyau* and were not permitted to attend the dances.

From the early 1920s an active campaign to enroll children of school age into the *Nyau* societies was mounted. Contrary to tradition the stipulation that boys to be initiated must have reached the age of puberty was waived. Within a few years Catholic schools were emptying. At the major *Nyau mzinda* in the Mua area, Madziatsatsi, Bwanali, Johni and Mlongoti, schools had to shut down entirely. A survey in the Nyasa Vicariate under the White Fathers' bishop, Guilleme, undertaken in 1930, illustrates the effectiveness of the *Nyau* opposition to education.

1. Ntaka-taka, an Ngoni centre. Total Christians and catechumens on the baptismal role; 5,400. 24 schools with 1,165 boys and 855 girls registered: Average school attendance 60%, 765 boys and 525 girls. Three villages with

Nyau, Chikaole, Kudoole and Falikire, served by one school: 124 boys and 70 girls registered; average attendance: 6 boys, 2 girls.

2. Mua, under Ngoni control. Mixed Chewa and Ngoni. Total Christians and catechumens, 2,600. 16 schools: Average school attendance 45%. Three villages with Nyau: Mtyanja, 80 boys and 26 girls registered: attendance 0; Bwanali, 80 boys and 28 girls: attendance 5; Madziatsatsi, 40 boys and 26 girls: attendance 8.

3. Bembeke, under Chewa and Ngoni control (Masasa and Kasumbu). Total Christians and catechumens, 3,300. Average school attendance 50%; in Nyau villages 35%. Attendance in non-Nyau villages, 70%. (In nineteen villages without Nyau, average of 49 pupils registered and attendance 70%; in 29 villages with Nyau, average of 25 registered and attendance average of 8, i.e. 35%.)

4. Likuni, under Chewa control. 48 villages served by 18 schools, average attendance 20%. 30% of the villages had no children at school. Average number registered, 26 boys and 9 girls.[28]

The Kasina mission, also under Chewa control, which was founded in 1925, was recording the shutting down of eleven schools four years later through lack of pupils. The Montfort-Fathers among the Mang'anja at Chikwawa and Port-Herald suffered similar difficulties, and as late as 1959 the *Nyau* from Bodza and Nyanthusi branches (near Chikwawa) successfully opposed the erection of school buildings in their respective areas.

This attempt to undermine the educational side of the mission work can be correlated with statistics from the Chikwawa area collected in 1966 showing the low level of literacy among *Nyau* members. While there are no comparable figures for the population at large it is a common observation that the educational level of participants in the *Nyau* is lower than average.

The response of the Catholic missions to this campaign against the village schools was now tempered by the realisation that the *Nyau* was more than an immoral dance to be condemned from the pulpit. After the war the White Fathers had begun to study the society with varying degrees of acumen and objectivity, and the notes of Frs Braire, Denis and Roy are an eloquent testimony to the missionaries' intimacy with village life.[29] By April 1923 the mission had turned to enlisting government support, doubtless encouraged by the total ban on *Nyau* that was in force in N.E. Rhodesia. The Likuni mission, which was, of course, under the most pressure, approached the Provincial Commissioner at Lilongwe to plead with Zomba for a general suppression of the society.

He does seem convinced at last that these dances are not only opposed to the work of the mission but also to all European influence.[30]

The territory of the Chewa paramount Undi was divided by the Mozambique frontier and the missionaries at Kachebere had also been complaining of whole villages moving into Nyasaland to avoid the ban across the border. The reply of the government was that the *Nyau* was too prevalent in Nyasaland and that, like Chinamwali, attempts at suppression would be ineffective and therefore ought to be avoided.

While government policy had its ideological side of preserving 'native culture', with all the political overtones of a compliant rural peasantry, it was equally based on expediency. The Chewa speaking areas were highly populated, highly mobile with movement to and from the mines, and very thinly administered by government personnel who were fully occupied in tax collection, stopping epidemics and encouraging agricultural development. If missionaries

TABLE I*

Membership of 12 Nyau societies according to literacy and religious affiliation.

Society	Member- ship	Literacy				Religion			
		Illiter- ate	%	Semi- literate	%	Traditional %		Christian %	
Dzuwazina	50	44	88	6	12.0	46	92.0	4	8.0
Kadzumba	64	56	87.5	8	12.5	62	97.0	2	3.0
Kafumula	67	58	86.5	9	13.5	64	95.0	3	4.7
Kapasule	78	72	92	6	7.7	78	100.0	—	—
Mwita	35	27	77	8	23.0	29	83.0	6	17.0
Malemia	34	30	88	4	12.0	25	73.0	9	26.5
Mdzachi	*7	7	100	—	—	6	85.0	1	14.0
Muonda	19	17	89.5	2	10.5	10	52.5	9	47.5
Tsapa	66	49	74	17	26.0	47	71.0	13	29.0
Jana	47	43	91.5	4	8.5	46	98.0	1	12.0
Makwira	38	31	81.5	7	18.5	25	66.0	13	34.0
Mwanayaya	92	82	89	10	11.0	83	90.0	9	10.0
Total	597	516	86.5%	81	13.5%	531	87%	76	13%

* Schoffeleers *Symbolic and Social Aspects* . . . p. 335.

living in the closest possible contact with the village had to listen to Nyau drums almost under the window, as at Mua even today, it was improbable that the constantly changing government officers could suppress a cult the activities of which took place at night in villages that they visited perhaps only four times a year.

Catholic missionaries hoped to by-pass the Protectorate Government by contacting the Phelps-Stokes commission of inquiry during its trip round Nyasaland but they were deliberately frustrated by Hetherwick.[31] He had arranged the itinerary of the commission to miss every Catholic mission and school; the Americans met their first priest, thrusting a letter of complaint at them, as their train moved out of Blantyre station. Exasperated, in May 1924 Guilleme was writing to Zomba in highly exaggerated terms:

Zinyau are a secret society, the first purpose of which is lubricity and robbery, by performing a dance ceremony for the dead.

There followed a list of calumnies and crimes committed by the society.[32]

With the 1924 District Administrative Ordinance and explicit indirect rule through Native Authorities, the government was able to avoid the issue by placing responsibility for the *Nyau* once again at the local level. For the next four years the mission was limited to the local struggle and attempted to get suppression district by district by bombarding the District Commissioners and chiefs with complaints.

The position of the *Nyau* in areas under Ngoni control was more perilous than in the Chikwawa district where the Kololo chiefs fully supported the dances. The missionaries were able to enlist the support of chiefs such as Kachindamoto who had an interest in keeping Chewa influence to a minimum. Two examples from this period illustrate the point. In November 1924 a Christian was almost throttled to death at Bwanali's near Mua mission; despite warnings he had been repeatedly caught by *Nyau* members singing the secret songs in public. The mission passed the case on to Kachindamoto at Ntakataka and the offending *Nyau* members were made to work in the chief's gardens for a week. More significant was that the headman, Bwanali, was then deposed and replaced by an older and more malleable appointee of the Ngoni chief.[33] The missionaries achieved their aim of having the *Nyau* banned in the village while the chief was able to use the incident to tighten his control over its Chewa inhabitants.

In the 'thirties the *Nyau* were suppressed under pressure from the Protestant missions in Gomani district, never to re-appear in some areas, e.g. Gania's at Kandeu.[34] Kachindamoto with less 'pure' Ngoni Swazi clan aristocracy, and far more diluted by Chewa villages, was never able to stop the *Nyau* in his area for longer than a couple of years despite his alliance with the mission at Mua.

In August 1925 Catholic catechists from Mahkhamba were sent to spy on the *mzinda* at Kafulama's near Mua. Chakumbira, a *kapito*, was later accused of public obscenity because of the *Nyau* songs and public indecency because of the naked *kapoli*. As a result of the trial Chakumbira was deposed by the District Commissioner but re-instated on an appeal by Kachindamoto, who in this instance wanted to remain on friendly terms with the powerful headman of the village.[35] This constant harrassment of the cult by bringing every possible infringement of the law during the performances to litigation remained the tactics of the mission throughout the 1920s and 1930s. It had the advantage of striking against the traditional immunity of the *Nyau* to public prosecution. However, it involved the British administration. The personnel of the Administrative centres were changing at the rate of three District Commissioners in five years in the Dedza district. No sooner had a heap of litigations and complaints convinced a District Commissioner that direct action against the society was needed, when he would be replaced, sometimes by a more liberal figure who attended the dances—albeit carefully censored versions—and was impervious to complaints from the mission.

The Catholic missionaries appear to have been at a loss to understand the apparent apathy of the government and local District Commissioners, seeing in it sometimes the fear of an uprising, other times a product of Protestant moral subjectivism. They wrote about the carefully engineered Chakumbira affair:

> There is enough filth to warrant a charge of public indecency. But Mr. Abraham's Protestant mentality will have to be taken into account. He has his own private religion and refuses to ban the *Nyau* as such.[36]

The Catholics held that the quality of the men in government service had dropped considerably after the war and that their degree of acquaintance with the villages in their district was often slight. Unable to manoeuvre the District Commissioners, this became a source of aggravation for the missionaries,

> Between you and I, the DC's are the most frightful nit-wits. As long as they have their *msonko* (taxes) and you don't kill yourself over much all they ask is to be left alone. And then they have no way of finding out what is going on. How can you expect them to know anything when they are changed so often?[37]

By the middle of 1928 the number of incidents between *Nyau* and Catholics was increasing. Zealous catechists were causing trouble over the admission of children to the dances and the increasing number of non-initiated villagers was an ever-present reminder to the society of their losses. Dissension was caused in families where one spouse was a *Nyau* member while the other was un-initiated. The *Nyau* created great tension in Christian families by allowing all women to watch the performance by the *mzinda*, while forcing the Christian husband to remain in his hut.[38] This sort of mild persecution had become common in the area of Chief Matanda near Likuni and had driven out several Christian families. A trap was set for Fr Denis, one of the missionaries who had been investigating the society. In May two Catholic prayer houses were burnt down in retaliation for the stealing of two *Nyau* masks by some Christians. These masks nearly resulted in the trial of the Father Superior of Likuni mission when the Provincial Commissioner at Lilongwe, Mr R. H. Murray, a man of liberal disposition who had reportedly once joined the dancing himself, threatened to prosecute for robbery.[39]

For the first time since their arrival in Nyasaland a Catholic missionary was prodded into a violent attack on the government. The fiery and eccentric Fr David Roy wrote:

> If it becomes a question of morality and civilization, we wonder to see such a sudden love of the 'native customs' by the people whom we thought did not care so much for these things. For example the Government have taken the property of the land from the natives—their most cherished possession; they have forbidden slave-trading, mwabvi-drinking, made game laws, reserved many trees, put the hut tax, given the country other principal headmen.[40]

By September school attendance had declined so steeply—partly due to famine—that the teachers, on the instigation of the missionaries, were writing to Zomba to complain to the Governor. Complaints had also been sent by the Dedza Planters Association who were worried about the effect of night dances on the availability and efficiency of labour.[41]

The issue entered the press in November in the guise of a bland article dwelling on the impossibility of banning the dances:

> Chinyawo, as now practiced seems to bear an extraordinary resemblance to something well-known in many lands as . . . carnival.[42]

However, behind the scenes the Governor was pressing the Apostolic Delegate, Msgr Hinsley, and Bishop Guilleme, to have Fr Roy removed for his unco-operative attitude towards the local administration. Their message—'correct the imprudence but do not quench the zeal'—resulted in Roy's removal to a part of the vicariate in N.E. Rhodesia, where the official ban had been effective in stopping the *Nyau*.

The 'carnival' article brought forth a reply from the education secretary of the White Fathers, a French Canadian, Fr Paradis, in an unsigned 'Plea for Prohibition' in the 29 January, 1929, *Nyasaland Times*. Paradis, twice decorated for bravery in the war, was a safe choice for chief Catholic protagonist. He altered the emphasis from education to the political dangers of a secret society which circumvented the normal channels of authority:

> The great privilege of Zinyao is that none of their cases are to be judged or debated at the village bwalo or in court. They have a court of their own where the headmen themselves have to report.

This approach was, of course, wide of the mark; the *Nyau* as a society stayed completely out of the principal proto-nationalist and nationalist movements in Malawi. A more emotive article from Paradis, 'The Devil Dancers of Terror' which had appeared in the periodical *East Africa* was reported in extract form in the *Nyasaland Times* of 16 April, 1928. Talks of appeals direct to London and Rome had been squashed by Hinsley who did not relish bad relations with the Colonial Office.

The Governor replied to these articles in a speech to the Legislative Council on April 29th. It contained a strong repudiation of the missionaries' accusations and reiterated the Government's position.

> The present position is that Government has not itself been able to obtain any evidence which would justify the suppression of Vinyau or the prosecution of any members of that society.

At a meeting of Chewa chiefs at Lilongwe,

> They said that they could see no reason why because they were not Christians they should be accused of doing things no decent native would think of.[43]

Once again the sentiments expressed in the public forum did not tally exactly with events behind the scenes. A far more cautious directive was sent to administrative officers on the same topic:

> Such allegations should constantly be borne in mind by administrative officers who should direct particular attention to their observation and study in order to ascertain to what extent they might be true and consequently indicative of a necessity for more drastic action.[44]

It was signed by the Acting Governor, W. B. Davidson-Houston, an Irish Protestant gentleman from Cork who doubtless felt competent at handling reactionary Catholic priests.

Recourse to the civil administration was not the prerogative of the clergy alone. On several occasions the *Nyau* leaders approached District Commissioners in the Dedza and Lilongwe districts in an attempt to obtain an official authorisation for the dances, and almost anything said by the District Commissioner was taken as approval. In late 1929 the Chewa chiefs of the Lilongwe area took the opportunity of the favourable climate after the Governor's speech to negotiate with the Provincial Commissioner and education officer in the hope of instituting reforms in the cult, and possibly to emphasise their 'ownership' over local and area leaders of the *Nyau*. Administrative demands and attempts at reform by the chiefs came together in a directive that reached villages before the end of 1929.

> To all owners of mzinda; We the chiefs of the Achewa tribe have heard that people are saying that the Vinyau is not being danced properly now, so we have written down instructions as to how it is to be controlled. No alterations are to be made without our permission.

The most significant of these regulations, in the light of the adaptations that had occurred in the *Nyau* society in response to missionary pressures, were the following:

> No boy is to be admitted until he has left his mother's house and then, only if his mother and father agree. No women except such as are past the age of childbirth may be admitted as members. Effigies may only be made to represent animals, not men. No compulsion must be allowed for the giving of presents to the dancers. Rules about abstention from sexual intercourse must be strictly observed.

The Administration demands can be clearly seen in the following two injunctions:

> Public roads and paths must never be closed because of the *Nyau*. Any fight or accident during the dance must be reported to the Boma.

Another result of the official stand was an attempt made by the Dutch Reformed missionaries and catechists to come to terms with the *Nyau* at a meeting in Lilongwe. In the course of the discussion the *Nyau* leaders described their discontent stating that the catechists were divulging the secrets of the society to the school children. The fact that any western education proved inimical to recruitment into the *Nyau* was hardly likely to be admitted in the presence of the education officer for the district. A headman, Njewa, expressed the attitude of the *Nyau* to teachers and catechists in the following terms:

> We Chewa, cannot allow our customs to disappear. They are the precious legacy of our ancestors. We hold to them as sacred things. If they hold their tongues and do not divulge our secrets, they will be left in peace.[45]

After a final attack in Chinyanja by Fr. Paradis in the newspaper *Zoona* in June,[46] followed by a visit by the Governor to Bishop Guilleme later in the year, the Catholic campaign at the national level was called off.

However, the missionaries were neither willing nor able in conscience to come to terms with the society and the confrontation continued at countless *milandus* between Christians and *Nyau* brought before the Native Authority, if he was Ngoni, or the District Commissioner if he was not. The Catholic belief that baptism *in articulo mortis*, provided there was adequate contrition, was sufficient for salvation, led to many disputes. After a life-time of mission influence it was rare to find *Nyau* members sufficiently courageous to turn away the cate-chist who appeared at their death-bed offering baptism. And once baptised the mission claimed the right to undertake a Christian burial. Since death and mortuary rites were the principal occasion for dancing *Nyau* this represented a serious threat to the society. The Christian and *Nyau* transition rites were in direct confrontation and the macabre squabbles over corpses that took place in the '30s and '40s,[47] both in the aptness of their symbolism and in their importance to both sides, were basic to the cultural struggle.

On some occasions active precautions were taken by the society to hide their members while catechists and priests were inquiring for them in the villages. Once the dying man was found no efforts were spared to bring about a quick conversion. It was the sincere belief of the priests that a man's eternal destiny lay in their hands in the last few moments before his death. The priest would usually speak of the merciful God whom the *Nyau* were said to have offended; there was also the occasional instance of a more Joycean method of inducing contrition.

The evolution of the confrontation with the Mang'anja around Chikwawa, where the mission was started in 1918, only reached its climax in 1935. Without any tradition of scholarly interest in indigenous peoples, as was insisted on by Lavigerie for his order of White Fathers, the Montfort-Fathers reacted pre-cipitously to the *Nyau*. Unlike their counterparts in the Dedza district there was no possibility of eliciting the support of the local Kololo chiefs for the suppression of Mang'anja customs. In 1966 there were 105 *Nyau* societies in the Lower Shire valley with an estimated active membership of 5,000. Of the eight chiefdoms around Chikwawa, seven had active societies. Ngabu's area had lost the Nyau through Sena influence. The average number of inhabitants per society was 400 in Masseah's area (Kololo), 721 in Makwira's (Kololo), 809 in Katunga's (Kololo), 1,072 in Lundu's (Mang'anja), 927 in Chapananga's (Mang'anja) and 1,241 in Kasisi's (Kololo).[48] The strength of *Nyau* in the same area in the 'thirties prior to thirty years of mission education can be imagined.

It is perhaps not insignificant that it was during one of the hottest months of the year, December 1935, that two priests, Kerrec and Heraud, set about a group of dancers with clubs near Chikwawa mission.[49] Despite complaints the case was dismissed by the Administration. During the next week there was a near-revolt at the mission with the catechists refusing to work. After persistent pressure from the missions based on the failure of the schools to attract pupils, the society was banned in the district by the Administration on 12 May, 1936.[50] As a result,

> General fury amongst even the Christians. A trip by Fr. Kerrec to Kavalo, an Ngoni from Ndalanda, made him realize that all this had made everyone very bitter.[51]

Three days later the corpse of a young Christian was snatched from a hut at Kasisi's and *Nyau* dances performed around it. Ignoring the ban, dances also started up at Ndalanda.

> All, both Christians and pagans have put up a solid front to save the *Nyau* and its leader Kasisi. Out of 60 Christians in the area only three put up any resistance whatsoever.[52]

In 1940, the education secretary of the Montfort-Fathers, one of the first English priests in Nyasaland, was again pressing the Administration. It was clear that the ban had been ineffective.

> Those who go to the *Nyau*, do not go to the army, produce nothing, and die of hunger the year around . . . having worked too hard during the night they can do nothing during the day. The few well-thinking natives in the said districts draw the conclusions that since the Government tolerated this state of affairs, it does not wish schools to be opened. The fact is that where there is Zinyau, schools empty themselves automatically.[53]

The situation in the Lower Shire in areas unaffected by the Sena immigration was strongly in favour of the *Nyau*. The intense heat and mosquitoes reduced European settlement to a minimum. Mang'anja religious and social structures had been largely maintained intact. Unlike the situation in the Ngoni-controlled Dedza district a large number of Christians were secretly initiated into the society. Baptised Catholics when faced with a choice generally opted for the traditional cults, and under normal circumstances kept the *Nyau* dances and the celebration of the eucharist in separate compartments of their minds. A case might be made that prolonged exposure to a very weak dose of Christianity emanating from the Portuguese at Sena, had over the centuries innoculated the Mang'anja against any total conversion into the western *corpus christianum*. The M'Bona cult undoubtedly shows a number of incorporated Christian themes which can only have come from contact with Catholic missions along the Zambesi.

The post-war interaction of *Nyau* and mission produced a virtual stalemate. Recruitment into the local churches kept the frequency of dancing and the number of *mzinda* at an almost constant level. In the Nyasa vicariate the system of Gurupa, and leaders of the Legion of Mary, consolidated Catholic gains. While they could solve minor marital difficulties and hand on more serious trouble in the Christian community to the priest, there was no way of stopping a small but constant percentage of drop-outs from the catechumenate and from among the baptised Christians. In both vicariates the standard for admission to baptism was maintained at a high level, and the majority of semi-literates in Table 1 clearly represent the few who scraped through their two-year catechumenate to baptism, only to join the *Nyau* afterwards.

The situation in Kachindamoto's area, where impressive gains might have been expected on the Catholic side because of Ngoni support, was also static. The chief lived in dread of poisoning if he exerted too much pressure and the Chewa influence, near the old capital of the Kalonga, Mankhamba, remained strong. As a whole the Maseko Ngoni seem to have suffered a decline in status during the 'thirties. Statistics for the Ncheu district of those claiming Ngoni origin gave 64,023 in 1926, 46,309 in 1931 and 14,243 in 1945. That this is not simply caused by emigration can be seen from comparable figures for the Mbelwa Ngoni at Mzimba, a 20,321 increase in the number of people claiming Ngoni origin between 1931–45. While in the north the Tumbuka for status reasons were claiming to be Ngoni, in the south the Chewa were doing the opposite. That this was caused by the different population densities of Tumbuka and Chewa can be seen by comparing the two branches of the Maseko, Gomani with a number of indunas from the Swazi clans, Kachindamoto, with almost none.[54] Gomani's prestige was sufficient to bring about a suppression of the *Nyau* with the help of his 'pure' Ngoni indunas. Although Kachindamoto was saying in 1946 that he would do 'like my brother Gomani'[55] it was only in 1950 that the combined meeting of chiefs of the Dedza district made the permission of the local Native Authority mandatory for the holding of dances at night, and so allowed Kachindamoto to stop all dancing for over two years.

By 1952 the *Nyau* leaders were pressing the Administration to countermand Kachindamoto's orders but the case was sent back to Ntakataka:

> Angoni and Achewa turned up at the chief's court with sticks and 'cibonga' to fight. The Angonis were saying, 'We do not want these dances' and the Achewa were saying that it was part of their 'makolo' (cibonga = clubs; makolo = ancestral customs). The Angonis warned them that they would fight if necessary. Hearing of the trouble the chief arrived in time just as sticks were being raised. But the nyau stay forbidden at Kachindamoto's and the people are a little cold towards us because of it.[56]

Dances were held sporadically in secret until independence when the *Nyau* openly performed on the church steps at Mua in a gesture of triumph. A number of old scores between Christians and *Nyau* were settled in the Dedza district. Since that date *Nyau* has been danced at Independence Day celebrations and a public performance given at Kwacha Cultural Centre, Blantyre, in 1969. The dance of triumph was warranted. Individual villages around Mua such as Kafulama's had kept the society alive for more than sixty years under continued pressure from missionaries allied with the Ngoni chiefs and against the intermittent opposition of the Administration.

But as a result of accommodation to the European presence, both missionary and settler, much of the religious significance of the cult had been lost in the Central Region and to a lesser degree in the Lower Shire. Financial interest had become an important factor alienating many non-active members from the dances. To this was added the influx of young children and a general slackening of discipline. The introduction of a financial element into the performances, with its disruptive effect on the membership of the society, can be correlated with the rise of the European cash economy. Villagers going to the mines and towns for paid employment, together with the growing numbers of people in white-collar jobs in government and schools, returned to the village with increased status. The high charges asked by the *Nyau* for performances may be seen as an attempt to keep up with this economic pressure, a partial acceptance of the western definition of value and status. This degeneration can only be placed at the missions' door inasmuch as elementary education equipped villagers with ambitions and goals within the western system, which they might otherwise not have had. The exodus to the towns and mines was opposed more or less vociferously by all the missions.

SUMMARY

None the less the *Nyau* cult has been of great religious and social significance to the Chewa-speaking peoples of Malawi. It has been both their greatest storehouse of religious ideas and their most elaborate religious ceremony. Neither has there been any institution among either the Chewa or Mang'anja which so faithfully reflects the fabric of their traditional society and the sentiments generated by it. The *Nyau* performance was not a

> savage expression of something sinister but a part of our training to instill discipline, good motherhood, fatherhood and citizenship.[57]

Its function in the small Chewa village societies was to reconcile conflicting loyalties and provide an alternative pathway to status within the framework of traditional values.

It is, and always has been, the opinion of the majority of missionaries, both Malawian and expatriate, that the *Nyau* is a great impediment to progress in Malawi. The growth of secondary education in the 1940s and the rise of a mission-trained and educated middle-class left the *Nyau* behind in the village. The Catholic church with its emphasis on widespread elementary education in rural areas produced an increasing volume of non-initiated villagers who considered the cult as incompatible with the new system of values that they had embraced. The mission, either through its own structures offered an alternative pathway to status within a western system of values as with the Gurupa, cate-chists and school teachers, or through primary education opened up jobs within the European economy. Once the western values of 'progress', 'individualism', 'education' and 'technology' were accepted, the *Nyau*, with its traditional value system offering status in traditional society, became redundant.

Prescinding from any judgement whether *Nyau* is 'reactionary', 'retrogressive' or represents a cultural 'good', the cult maintained itself for more than half a century against the most highly organised and 'cultic' of the Christian churches with its extensive system of village schools. The role of religious consciousness in maintaining the identity of the Chewa-speaking peoples of Malawi against the European cultural onslaught is apparent in this reaction to the Catholic missions. This is not to say that the Catholics were worse than the Protestant missions in imposing western values and thought patterns—attitudes to beer drinking and moral lapses would suggest the opposite. But the structured community set up round the mission was an alternative, and an enticing one in the very familiarity of many of its aspects, to traditional religion and society. It was above all, though, the educational impact of the Christian mission that drove home the European presence. Although for Catholics the emphasis was by and large on quantity rather than quality until after the second World War, it was enough to introduce countless villagers to different patterns of thought and concepts of status.

By undergoing a progressive secularisation the *Nyau* societies have survived to experience a virtual renaissance on the gaining of national independence. The assumption that traditional social institutions, with their religious core, must quickly disappear in the face of prolonged and intense pressure from churches is clearly false. The resistance of the *Nyau* to Catholic missions during the colonial period in Malawi provides an eloquent testimony to the conservative strength of traditional religious institutions in Chewa society.

NOTES

¹ Data on the *Nyau* were collected by Rev. Dr J. M. Schoffeleers in the course of field work in the Lower Shire Valley, 1966–7. Mission material, with the exception of correspondence between government and missions, has been translated from the French. Catholic documents are to be found at the White Fathers Archives, Via Aurelia, Rome, the Montfort Archives in Blantyre, and at the Catholic Secretariat in Limbe. In none of these places are the materials fully sorted and catalogued, therefore citations by name, place and date only can be given. During the period discussed in the paper Guilleme was bishop in the Nyasa Vicariate (White Fathers), and Auneau bishop in the Shire Vicariate (Montfort-Marist Fathers). Some diaries may still be found at mission stations, although many have been sent to the archives. The extensive government papers on the Nyau/mission conflict were unavailable to the authors, owing to the closure of the national archives to research workers from 1967–1971.

² The choice of the Roman Catholic missions for this study is partly due to the availability of documentary sources, and partly motivated by the special liturgical and institutional aspects of Catholicism, with their interesting parallels in *Nyau*. The similar struggle with the Dutch Reformed Mission and to a lesser degree with other Protestant missions has unfortunately proved beyond the authors' scope due to lack of documentary material.

³ Yohanna B. Abdallah *The Yaos* edited and translated by M. Sanderson, (Zomba 1919).

⁴ Oral testimonies: Collected August/September 1969 by Valens Koryo, seminarian. Antonio Katole, Mang'anja born Bondo Village, Mlanje; Matteo Manyamba, Lomwe, born Chilimba village, Portuguese East Africa; Pio Samikwa, Lomwe, born Mtendereni village, Portuguese East Africa. Interview with Marko Reid, Mang'anja, Mlanje, catechist, July 1969.

⁵ H. Rowley *The Story of the Universities' Mission to Central Africa* (London 1866).

⁶ J. M. Schoffeleers *Symbolic and Social Aspects of Spirit Worship Among the Mang'anja* (Doctoral dissertation, Oxford 1968) p. 320.

⁷ Pearce to Manning, 15 May, 1898; Brogden to Manning, 17 May, 1898. F.O. 2. 147.

⁸ *British Central Africa Gazette* 1 November, 1896, Genthe; and *ibid.*, 28 June, 1894, Nicholl.

⁹ M. Read *Children of their Fathers* (London 1959).

¹⁰ *British Central Africa Gazette* 1 November, 1896, Genthe.

¹¹ Mponda Mission Diary 1889–1891. White Fathers Archives, Via Aurelia, Rome.

¹² 'Ad Exteros', S.C. de Propaganda Fide, Rome, 1659.

¹³ 'Recommendations of the Apostolic Visitor', 10 August, 1928, Dar es Salaam.

¹⁴ Schoffeleers *op. cit.* pp. 412–14.

¹⁵ Schoffeleers *op. cit.* pp. 395–402.

¹⁶ Schoffeleers *op. cit.* p. 332.

¹⁷ *Ibid.* p. 341.

¹⁸ Mua Mission Diary, 19 April, 1909. Mua, Dedza.

¹⁹ Auneau to heads of missions, 6 November, 1939. Bishop's Archives, Blantyre.

²⁰ Baptismal Register. Nzama Mission, Ncheu.

²¹ Annual Reports of the White Fathers, 1905–1909. Kachebere, Mchinji.

²² Annual Reports of the White Fathers, 1914–1915. Kachebere, Mchinji.

²³ Oral Testimony: Interview with Louis François Villy, W.F., December 1969, Kasina, Lilongwe.

²⁴ Oral testimonies: Interviews with Valentino Mwasika, Ngoni, Ntonya village, Chiradzulu, cook; Augusto Liboti, Lomwe, George village, Chiradzulu, houseservant. July 1969.

²⁵ J. Jackson *Description of the Chinyau Dance, Central Province, Nyasaland*. Rhodes House Library MSS., Afr. s. 556, Oxford; J. Hovington *Notes on Chewa Customs* MSS., Kache-

bere, Mchinji; and, Braire to Paradis, 26 March, 1929 (White Fathers Archives, Via Aurelia, Rome).

[26] Schoffeleers *op. cit*, p. 362.

[27] J. M. Schoffeleers, *M'bona the Guardian Spirit of the Mang'anja* (B. Litt. Thesis, Oxford, 1966).

[28] Reports on Nyau, February 1930. (White Fathers Archives, Via Aurelia, Rome).

[29] J. Hovington, MSS., Kachebere, Mchinji; for Braire, Roy and Denis; White Fathers Archives, Via Aurelia, Rome.

[30] Villy to Guilleme, 19 April, 1924, White Fathers Archives, Via Aurelia, Rome.

[31] Alexander Hetherwick, Church of Scotland missionary in Nyasaland 1883–1928, was arranging the itinerary on behalf of the Federated (Protestant) Missions. A prominent Mason, he was a strong opponent of the 'Roman' missionaries.

[32] Guilleme to Governor, 15 May, 1924 in Hovington *op. cit.*

[33] Mua Mission Diary, November 1924. Mua, Dedza.

[34] Oral testimony: Interview with Henry Vernooy W.F., Kandeu, Ncheu, December 1969.

[35] Mua Mission Diary, 25 August, 1925. Mua, Dedza.

[36] *Ibid.*

[37] Paradis to Eken, 28 December, 1928. White Fathers Archives, Via Aurelia, Rome.

[38] Braire to Guilleme, 10 May, 1924. White Fathers Archives, Via Aurelia, Rome.

[39] J. Hovington, MSS.; Roy to DC Lilongwe, 10 May, 1928. White Fathers Archives, Via Aurelia, Rome.

[40] Roy to DC Lilongwe, 29 June, 1928. White Fathers Archives, Via Aurelia, Rome.

[41] Paradis to Editor, *Nyasaland Times* 28 December, 1928. Paradis to Eken, 28 December, 1928. Likuni Mission Teachers to Governor, 4 September, 1928. White Fathers Archives, Via Aurelia, Rome.

[42] *Nyasaland Times*, 27 November, 1928.

[43] *Nyasaland Times* 3 May, 1929.

[44] Davidson-Houston to administrative officers, 30 April, 1929. White Fathers Archives, Via Aurelia, Rome.

[45] Roy to Paradis, 27 September, 1929. White Fathers Archives, Via Aurelia, Rome.

[46] *Zoona*, 30 June, 1929.

[47] Mua and Bembeke Mission Diaries. Mua, Bembeke, Dedza.

[48] Schoffeleers *Symbolic and Social Aspects*, p. 324.

[49] Chikwawa Mission Diary, 8 December, 1935. Chikwawa.

[50] Heraud to Auneau, 14 August, 1937. Bishop's Archives, Blantyre.

[51] Chikwawa Mission Diary, 12 May, 1936. Chikwawa.

[52] *Ibid.* 28 May, 1936. Chikwawa.

[53] Hardman to Director of Education, Education Report 1940. Education Archives, Catholic Secretariat, Limbe.

[54] I. Linden, 'The Maseko Ngoni at Domwe, 1870–1900' *The Early History of Malawi*, (London 1972) pp. 237–252.

[55] Mua Mission Diary, 20 May, 1946. Mua, Dedza.

[56] Mua Mission Diary, 10 October, 1952. Mua Dedza.

[57] *Malawi Times* 23 July, 1963. Speech of His Excellency, Dr H. K. Banda, to Legislative Assembly.

INDEX

Index

A

Abdallah, Edward, on Christian *Jando*, 239, 243; his anxiety over *Litiwo*, 239–40

Abdallah, Y. B., on Mwembe, 182; on succession of Mataka II Nyenje, 183; on grave of Mataka II Nyenje, 184

Abraham, Donald, 24, 35

Achewa, 270

Adultery, Kinjikitile's pronouncement on, 210

Affliction, cults of, 11, 16, 24 n. 21

African Lakes Company, 160, 161, 162

Agriculture, and cults, 7, 91; agricultural revolution and specialists in ritual, 34; and increase of material culture, 40; Chief Molin Tengani and reform of, 86; reform following 1949 famine, 88; and cattle owners, 90; seed sowing, 98; Pare, 111; good spirits and, 125; rituals at sowing and harvesting, 125; collective farming, 148; in Nyakyusa country, 153; Mwakinyasa and, 159

Akure, and *Bura* cult, 127, 128; Liyong's *Bura Leb Bari*, 130

Allah, 16

Alpers, Edward, and spread of Islam, 16, 17; and Shona chiefs, 35

Altars, at Zimbabwe Acropolis, 34, 35; to Nyambe, 96

Amini bin Saidi, on Yao baptism into Islamic faith, 180

Ancestors, in settled societies, 40; and *kubandwa* cult, 65; ancestor cult in Lozi religion, 96–7; mediators between God and men, 113; ancestor worship, 113; their place in Pare worship, 114, 115, 116; ancestor veneration, 173–6, 181, 186; and Maji ideology, 203; in hierarchy of forces, 204; offerings to, 209

Ancestor-spirits, linguistic evidence on, 46; *balimu* in Lozi religion, 95, 97; Lozi ancestor-spirit cult, 96–7, 103; and Luvale beliefs, 97; and prayers for rain, 98–9; and Nyambe, 100; no evidence for cult in Bulozi, 100; ceremonial sacrifice to, 100

Ancient Ruins Company, 36

Andrew, St, rain bringer, 231

Angoni, 270

Animal husbandry, Pare herdsmen, 111

Animals, spirit possession by, 11; interment of bones, 36; associated with royalty, 36, 38; appearing in Benin art, 39; symbolic representation in the Nyau, 257, 258

Anthropologists and history of religions, 51

Anthropology, process anthropology, 12; direction of social, 50; myths and, 58

Arabs, Livingstone on Mataka I Nyambi, 182; baptismal names, 183; Young on Makanjila III Banali, 185; and Sultan Mwalia, 187; literacy in Arabic, 192, 195; and introduction of Islam, 188, 193; supply guns, 254

Archaeology, and sites of religious practice, 30; and Stone Age religion, 30–4; and Iron Age religion, 34–40

Arnold, T. W., on Muslim proselytisers, 193

Artefacts, bowls, 34, 35, 36, 37; and dating of religious developments, 49

Arts, graphic and plastic, 40

Ashes, 229, 234

Asu, *see* Pare

Anneau, Bishop, 260

B

Bacwezi, 37, 61 (*see also* Cwezi *and* Swezi)

Baganda, 129–30, 131

Bakari, Mtoto bin Mwenyi, and Kolelo cult, 208

Balsan, François, on Yao attitude to their religious background, 172

Bantu, word borrowing from, 46; population of Rwanda, 64; *Mahoka* and *Mulunga*, 209

Banyole, 127, 129

Banyoro, 61

Baptism, into Mohammedan faith, 180, 182; anxiety of European clergy over, 231; in colonial Malawi, 260; numbers of baptised Catholics and Protestants, 261; *in articulo mortis*, 267; standard for admission to Christian, 269

Barghash, Sultan, 183

Barotseland, religious history of, 7–8

Basoga, 127

Froberville, Eugène de, and Ngindo initiation rites, 181
Fulani, and Tassili paintings, 32, 33
Funerals, funerary rituals, 141; *uxwala* and, 146; Islamisation of funeral ceremonies, 194; performance of the Nyau at, 258

G

Gambia, circles of stones, 37
Gardens, 88, 89
Gardner, G. A., and Bambandyanalo burials, 36
Garlake, P. S., dates of Zimbabwe periods III and IV, 35
Genealogies, 66–7
Gerard, Fr, and Makua chieftainship, 177
Germany and Germans, colonial rule in S.W. Tanzania, 165–8, 232, 236; Maji Maji and, 202, 204; and rock of Bokero, 206–7; Matumbi and, 214
Ghana, excavations at Ahinsan, 38; study of Krachi shrines, 42
Gilsenan, Michael, 4, 7
Gluckman, Max, 51
God, and alien possessing spirits, 16; and millenium, 20; Padhola's concept of, 124; and Yao *mulungu*, 174
Gomani I, 255
Gomani II, 256, 260, 269, 270
Gongs, 33
Gonja, *ngaghe*, 115, 118
Goodall, A., and rock art, 32
Goody, Jack, and religion and the symbolic function, 50
Grave goods, 30, 40
Grave mounds, 7, 37, 38
Graves, royal, 8, 96–7, 100, 101, 102, 104; prehistoric, 38; furniture, 38; Iron Age, 40; and the ancestor cult in Lozi religion, 96–7; of Mboo, 100; keepers of royal, 104; Yao grave-hut shrine, 175; of Makua chiefs, 178; of Mataka II Nyenji, 184
Gravestones, Stone Age painted, 30
Grunebaum, G. E. von, 196; on Islam in Africa, 173, 194; on situations in which replacement of existing system is likely, 192
Guilleme, Bishop, 265, 267; on Zinyau, 263
Gwaja, *Mwenye*, and *ndalanga* dance, 177, 178; and death and installation ceremonies, 178
Gwassa, Gilbert, 6, 16, 20; and resistance against colonial rule, 18; and Maji Maji ideology, 19

H

Hall, R. N., 34
Halle, M., Lévi-Strauss and, 56
Hampate Ba, A., and Tassili paintings, 33
Headman, effect of immigrants on Mang' anja, 87; non-Mang'anja, 87–8; *infingila* for Nyakyusa, 156; ritual death and rebirth, 178; Yao chiefs and, 186
Healing, in spirit possession cults, 11; attitude of Africans to, 16
Health, and theology of monarchy, 9; African Christians and, 230
Heraud, Fr, 268
Heroic cults, 16; Nyakyusa, 154–6; history of, 156–8; context for re-interpretation of development of heroic tradition, 156–68
Hetherwick, Alexander, 176, 178; his interpretation of Yao religious cosmology, 173–4; on grave-hut shrine, 175; and Catholic missionaries, 263
Heusch, Luc de, his studies on Kingdom of Rwanda, 64–5; and historical study of myth, 65–6
High Gods, Mwari, 5, 6, 8, 9; Nyambe, 7; health and fertility, 9; in microcosmic society, 15; and macrocosmic challenge, 16; elaboration of idea of, 20; Lesa, 20; and ancestor-spirits, 46; shrines to, 76; worship at Kaphirintiwa directed to, 77; High God shrine of Msinja, 85
Himi-Tusa cattle cults, 36
Hinsley, Msgr., 265, 266
Historiography, and traditional African religious systems, 1–2
Holub, Emil, on power of magic, 102; on Sipopa's fall from power, 102
Hongo, Kinjikitile possessed by, 205, 209; embodied as a snake, 207, 211
Horton, Robin, 19; on development of cosmological beliefs, 10; and water spirit cults, 14; and effects of movement from microcosm to macrocosm, 15–17; and phenomenon of conversion, 22; on religion and the symbolic function, 50; his work on traditional religious system and monolatric cult, 195–6; on acceptance of Islam and Christianity, 196
Hunting, rock art and, 31, 34; ritual specialists in hunting groups, 34
Hutu, 64

I

Ideologies, of protest, 19, 20; Maji Maji, 203
Ikemba, 203
Iliffe, John, on Swahili sub-culture, 190–1

and take-over of cults, 7, 8; dead and living, 8; theology of monarchy, 9; the *Oba*, 39; special position of Lozi, 96; balance between bureaucracy and, 101

Kings, dead, spiritual power of, 5; sacrifice to, 5–6, 96, 98; spirits of, 6; and living monarch, 8; spirit possession, 11; spirit mediums, 13; special position of dead Lozi kings, 96–7; prayers for rain, 98–9

Kingship, Kololo and image of, 8; prehistoric regalia and ritual of, 30; sacred kingship in Rwanda, 64; and Lozi state, 96; eligibility for Lozi, 101; dual, 101; medicine men and magic, 102; Coillard on, 104; heroic cults and 'divine Kingship', 156, 157, 159

Kingship, cults of, *see* Royal cults

Kinjikitile Ngwale, and Maji ideology, 20, 203; his 'vital force', 204–5; spirit possession, 205; and Bokero cult at Kibesa, 205–7, 208; and spirits of the dead, 208–9; and *Mganga*, 209–10; career of, 210–13; and impending war, 213–14; hanged, 214; ideological leader, 215; significance of his career, 215

Kinjorobo, 163, 164

Kinship, declining strength of ties of, 9; Lévi-Strauss and, 56, 57; Mang'anja chiefs and Lundu, 75; among mediums of royal cults, 76; kin loyalty and political loyalty, 87; M'Bona cult and perpetual, 91; Pare kin groupings, 111; unity of segmented kin groups, 117–18; unity of several kingroups in same area, 118–19; rituals and, 157; Makua perpetual, 179

Kiriamagi, myth of, 113

Kirk, Dr John, and M'Bona's village at Khulubvi, 84

Kitto, H. D. F., on good spirits, 125

Kiumbi, myth of, 113; worship of, 113

Kivia, 119

Klamroth, Martin, and cult of Kolelo, 207–8

Kolelo, cult of, 6, 7, 207–8; and Maji Maji, 208

Kologelo, 206

Kololo, and Lozi royal cult, 8; descendents of Livingstone's servants, 75; Mankhokwe and, 83; Livingstone and, 84; and Mang'-anja, 89–90; and Lozi religious institutions, 106 n. 39; invasion by, 252; and Mang'-anja, 254, 268; and *Nyau*, 264, 268

Komba, Bishop James, on *Mahoka*, 209

Kopytoff, Igor, and Yao 'eldership', 174

Kubandwa, and cult of Ryangombe, 65; sickness and possession, 65; and Swezi

spirit possession guild, 147

Kukwe, 154, 160, 161

Kumoga, 162

Kyala, 154; Kinga and cult of, 155; restructure of cult, 159; survival of cult, 159; Lutheran missionaries and, 160

Kyunga, 157, 159, 160

L

Labour levies, 167

Lajoux, J. D., and Tassili paintings, 32

Lamburn, Canon, 176; and Yao ancestor veneration, 175; on early Islamic proselytisation of Yao, 187

Lampert, E., on spiritual ruthlessness, 134

Language, usefulness of word-reconstruction, 45; as evidence of trends of thinking, 45–6; religious loan-words, 46–7; as evidence of continuity of belief, 47; evidence from religious metaphors, 48; linguistics and social anthropology, 50; Lévi-Strauss's work on linguistics, 56–7; figurative language of Lozi kings, 96; of founder-groups of Lozi people, 99; Bantu, 111; Luganda, 131, 132; Dhupadhola, 131; symbolism and, 139; vernacular words for God, 160, 173

Lavigerie, Abp. Charles, 268

Leach, Edmund R., 50, 64; and myths of Solomon, 60, 61–2; and Oedipus myth, 61; of Pfeiffer's treatment of Solomon myth, 62; on his work on 3rd century Jewry, 63

Lesa, 20

Lévi-Strauss, Claude, 61; and structuralism, 51, 55–6; on Man, 53; his work on linguistics, 56–7; and history and anthropology, 57; and myths, 57–8, 62–3; methodology of myths, 58–9; on purpose of myths, 60; de Heusch and, 66; and symbolism, 139

Lewanika, Lubosi, and re-establishment of royal cult, 101, 104; uses Mbunda witchfinders, 102; and divination and witchcraft, 103; appeals to Coillard, 103; attitude to Christianity, 103–4

Lewis, I. M., 11; on Islam and traditional belief, 173

Lhote, Henri, and interpretation of Tassili paintings, 32, 33

Lichtheim, George 54

Lienhardt, Godfrey, *Divinity and Experience*, 50

Lienhardt, Peter, 16, 172

Life hereafter, 124–5

Ligunda, Fr Petro, on Yao initiation rites, 234–5

180, 181, 189; in Masasi district, 223; effect of mobility on ritual and religious practice, 224, 225; ritual supremacy of, 225; attitude to Christianity, 225; U.M.C.A.'s description of, 226; attitude to U.M.C.A., 226; control over initiation rites, 236

Makwira, Chief, 254

Mala, 85

Malango, Christian equivalent for *Chiputu*, 239; Abdallah on, 240; attitude of white clergy to, 240; at Kamundi, 242; Makua *mamwenye* and, 243–5; a failure, 247

Malawi, M'Bona cult, 5, 6; 'democratic' spirit possession, 13; *Nyau*, 23; shrines of, 42; M'Bona shrine at Khulubvi, 73; Mang'anja, 73, 75; shrines to High God, 76; heroic cult in Ngonde, 157; resistance of *Nyau* societies to R.C. missions in, 252–71

Malemia, 86

Malinga, Rev. Asanasiyo N., 132

Mandai, Ngulumbalyo, 214

Mamwenye of Makua, attitude to Christian *Jando* and *Malango*, 243–4

Mang'anja, 268; M'Bona cult and, 5, 73–92; spirit possession, 13; territory of, 73, 75; Chipeta and, 75; Phiri and, 75, 89; Lolo and, 81; effect of Sena immigration on society, 87–8; Sena and, 89, 254; Kololo and, 89–90, 254; and establishment of subsidiary shrines, 91; Yao invasion, 254; the *Nyau* among, 257, 258; 'Portuguese' and 'Arab' masks, 261; attitude to Christianity, 269

Mankhokwe, murder of, 79; founds Cholo shrine, 81; and the Chikunda, 81–2; and Khulubvi shrine, 82, 90; and the Portuguese, 82; and Europeans, 82–3; and new wife for M'Bona, 83; and U.M.C.A. missionaries, 83–4; political intrigues, 83–4; loses his chiefdom, 85; Lundu and, 90

Mantis, 31

Maples, Chauncy, Bishop of Likoma, 190; on Muslim *mwalimu*, 185–6; and Sultan Mwalia, 187; on Johnson's 'coastal roughs', 193; and African attitude to religion, 228, 230

Maquet, J. J., and cult of Ryangombe, 65

Maravi, 73, 77

Mariano, Paul, *alias* Matenkenya, 84

Martin, B. G., 191; and Islam, 17

Martinet, André, 56

Maruha, Elton on, 187

Marxism, historical process and conscious

thought, 57

Masiga, Rev. Erisa L., 132

Masks, masked figures in rock art, 32; the Nyau, 257, 258, 261; 'Christian', 261; of Portuguese and Arabs, 261; stolen, 265

Masseah, Chief, 254, 268

Mataka, Chief, and the *ndalanga* dance, 177, 178; and Islam, 190

Mataka I Nyambe, 195; Livingstone on, 182; Abdallah on, 182; and Christianity, 183; death of, 183

Mataka II Nyenje, 185, 195; accession of, 183; attitude to Christianity, 183–4; becomes Moslem, 184

Mataka III Bonomali, accession of, 184; and the Portuguese, 185

Mataka V Cisonga, 185

Matanda, Chief, 260, 265

Matapwiri, 254

Matekenya, *see* Mariano, Paul

Matola I, 226, 233

Matola II, history, 226, U.M.C.A. and, 227; recruits from family of, 231, 232; deposed, 232

Matopos, rock art, 31

Matrilineage, Mang'anja, 87; Yao, 174; Makua, 177; Islam and, 196; missionary disapproval of, 237

Matumbi, *Mbekia* ceremony, 204; spirit possession, 205; and *Mganga*, 209; war medicines of, 210; declare war, 211

Mauss, Marcel, 50, 57

Mazrui, Ali A., *Protest and Power in Black Africa*, 18

Mbaga, rain-making, 119–20; expansion of political influence of, 120; and conflict in North Pare, 120

Mbasi, 154; Kinga and, 155; Lwembe and, 158; missionaries and, 158; Mwanafungubo, 159; former seat of, 159; movement of priest, 162; influence of priest, 163; Mwanjabala and, 163, 166; priest of, 163–4

Mbeta, Group Village Headman, 76

Mbite, Jumbe Mbanga, 206

Mbiti, John, *African Religions and Philosophy*, 2

M'Bona, successive representations of, 77; changing image of, 77; and the 'Chipeta tattoos', 77; birthplaces of, 77; and Chief Kaphwiti, 78; and Lundu, 78–80; murder of, 79, 91; 'god of the river', 80; new wife sought for, 83; and death of U.M.C.A. missionaries, 84; and victory over Matekenya, 84; and virgin birth, 86; his

Yao installation ceremonies, 178; and control of initiation rites, 180

Mjema, 119

Mkanda, Chief, 260

Mkuruwira, *Mwenye* James, and Namalowe, 242–3

Mkwatia, *Mwenye*, 241

Mkwawa, 144

Mlali, 207

Mlolo, 85, 86

Mnduwambele, 119

Monarchy, 'sudanic', 4; cults and, 6, 7, 8; theology of, 9

Monemtera, Chief, 161

Monjesa, Chief (Jalasi), 179, 180

Morambala, Mt, 84

Mother Goddess, in rock art, 32

Mozambique, M'Bona cult and cult centres of, 5; Mang'anja, 73; Makua, 176, 177, 178, 187, 189; Yao, 185, 193; Mwembe, 182, 183, 184, 185; spread of Islam in, 189–90

Mpezeni, 256

Mponda, 254

Mranga, Chief, 120, 145

Mrungu wa Gu, symbol of fellowship with God, 114; and unity of lineages, 117–18

Msigala, Kolumba, on religion in Masasi, 223; Christian and *mganga*, 233; and Christian *Jando*, 241, 243

Mtalika, Sultan, 176, 179

Mtoka, Hugh, 231, 232

Mtoko rock art, 32

Mulambwa, King, and medicine and magic, 102; tradition about, 106 n. 45

Mulimu, *see* Nyambe

Mundu, Mwene, 102

Murray, R. H., 265

Mutapa, Mwene, and Dzivaguru cult, 5, 6, 8; religion of, 35

Mwabvi ordeal, 78

Mwachiluwi, Chief, 143

Mwaihojo, and German missionaries, 162, 163; and Merensky, 162; and Mwanafungubo, 163; Mwanjabala and, 163; and jealous Mbasi priest, 164

Mwaipopo, 164

Mwakabolofa, 167

Mwakalinga, 161; his people conscripted, 167; death in battle, 167–8

Mwakalukwa, 161; punished by Germans, 165; his cattle, 167

Mwakapesile, 161

Mwakatungile, feud with Kinga chief, 161; quarrels with priest, 163–4

Mwakinyasa, 159

Mwakyusa, 160, 161

Mwalia, Sultan, Maples's opinion of, 187; and Islam, 189

Mwamakula, 160, 161

Mwana Lesa movement, 20

Mwanafungubo, priest of Mbasi, 159; appearance, 159; Mwaihojo and, 163; missionaries snub, 163; and the Kinjorobo affair, 163–4; downfall of, 164

Mwanambinyi, traditions about, 101; employs medicine-men, 102

Mwandangara, 160

Mwandemere, 161

Mwanjabala, attempts to secure frontiers, 161; and Mbasi cult, 163; attitude to German rule, 165

Mwankenja, 161; and Kyala cult, 159; and pact with ALC, 161; attitude to German rule, 165, 167; and the missionaries, 165

Mwari, Daneel on, 24 n. 11

Mwari cult, M'Bona cult and, 5, 6, 73; effect of its involvement with political systems, 7; Ndebele and, 8, 24 n. 12; and Rozvi, 8–9, 76; spirit possession, 13; cult of the supreme being, 16; Zimbabwe, 35

Mwaseba, 161

Mwawa I, 226

Mwawa II, 226

Mwaya, battle at, 167, 168

Mwera, 203, 224

Mwevo, 119

Myths, martyr-, 7; of redemption through defeat and death, 7; and Bushman folklore, 31; and rock art, 32, 33; value as historical evidence, 51–2; Vico on, 52; in Vico's philosophy, 52–4; Lévi-Strauss and 56, 57–8, 60, 62–3; Lévi-Strauss's methodology of, 58–9; Lévi-Strauss on purpose of, 60; Leach and Solomon, 60, 61–2; and historical development, 62; cult of Ryangombe, 65; de Heusch and historical study of, 65–6; and cults of salvation, 66; Vico on Cadmus, 67–8; Vico on Orpheus, 68; of Kamunu and Nyambe, 95, 99–100, 102; gradual creation of Lozi, 100; of creation, 113, 120, 124, 257; Mount Olympus, 126; of origin of chiefly dynasty, 144; Nyau and creation myth, 257

Mzilikazi, 8

N

Nabaguzi, Baya, and the Balubaale shrines, 42

R

Radcliffe-Brown, A. R., 50; and concept of structure, 55

Rain, 6; in rock art, 31, 34; raincows, 31; accusations of rain-withholding, 78, 79; rain-caller, 81; ritual prayers for, 98–9, 208, 227; rain-doctors, 99; rainfall in Nyakyusa country, 153; and invocation of heroic cults, 155; rituals at PaliKyala, 159; whites blamed for failure of, 163; and Bokero cult at Kibesa, 206; African Christians and, 230; St Andrew the rain-giver, 231

Rain-making, spears and, 40; M'Bona's power of, 86; rituals, 119–20; Mbwekes and, 128; Mwakinyasa a rainmaker, 159

Rangeley, W. H. J., and conversion of Makanjila III Banali, 182

Ranger, Terence, 180; and Masasi initiation and Christianity, 23; and liminality, 146; on social movements, 147; and social structure of Makua, 176

Redfield, Robert, 194

Regalia, problems presented by, 30; Zimbabwe spears, 36; found at Mapungubwe, 36; iron models of cows, 36; cattle, 37; study of, 41; political function of, 100; conus-shells, 143, 145

Reincarnation, structural, 179, 180

Religion, and political history, 9, 10; and maintenance of unity, 10; Lucy Quimby on, 23 n. 5; definition of, 29–30; archaeology and Stone Age, 30–4; and rock art, 32; archaeology and Iron Age, 34–40

Religion, African, Dar es Salaam conference on, 1, 4; and historiography, 1–2; philosophical systems of, 2; nineteenth-century speculations on, 3; religious change, 10; millenarianism in, 19; in twentieth century, 21; Christianity and 22; Padholan adherents to traditional, 131; Manjubala relies on traditional, 166; adaptive potential of, 195; Islam and traditional, 254

Rhinoceros, Mapungubwe, 36

Rhodesia, M'Bona cult and cult centres of, 5; Mwari cult and, 6, 7, 8, 16; Ndebele invasion, 8; 1896 risings in, 19; rock art, 31, 32; figurines, 34, 40; Zimbabwe, 34–6; Khami findings, 36; Mapungubwe, 36

Richter, Julius, on initiation rites, 238

Rigby, Peter, 172–3

Rites (see also Jando and Malango), of initiation, 11, 12, 33, 119, 120, 145–6, 180–1, 194, 224, 225, 234–47; development after borrowing of, 12; purification of Lozi

princes, 96; symbolism and female puberty, 139; chiefly installation, 178–9, 183; *Mbekia* ancestor propitiation, 204; Christianity and, 227, 229–31, 237–41, 260; for the dead, 231; fertility, 231; female initiation, 236–7, 239–40, 247, 260; prohibition of, 238; performance of the Nyau at life crisis rites, 258, 268; Christian and Nyau transition, 268; Nyau dances and the eucharist, 269

Ritual, sacrifice, 6; to unite the people, 9, 10; *cha-njeku*, 10; life-crisis, 11, 12, 141, 145–6, 148, 179, 226; 'redressive' (ritual of affliction), 11, 141, 142, 143–5, 148; and symbolic action, 30; specialists, 34; bowl fragments and, 36; at burial sites, 38; significance of numbers, 41; ancient belief about Tenganis and, 89; non-Mang'anja and, 89, 90; hereditary positions at Khulubvi, 90; elevation of Lozi kings, 97; rain-making, 98–9, 119–20; in Pare worship, 115, 117, 118–20; Padhola, at sowing and harvest, 125; symbolism, history and, 139–48; Turner on, 140; and history-critique of Turner, 141–3; liminal, 141–2, 146–8; of the Kinga, 153; Wilson on ritual of Lwembe cult, 157; communal, 157; ancestor veneration, 175, 177; death and rebirth, 178, 179; bathing, 180; life-cycle rituals and Islam, 194; effect of mobility of ethnic groups on, 224–7

Ritual meals, 234

Ritual objects, general definition, 29–30; defined for purpose of Posnansky's paper, 30; terracotta figure from Entebbe, 32; Iron Age increase of, 34; figurines, 34; from Zimbabwe Acropolis, 35; fetishes, 41; conus-shells, 143, 144, 145

Ritual offerings, beer, 113, 115, 129, 159, 174, 175, 177; chickens, 129; bulls, 129; iron hoes, 155; grain, 159; elephant tusk, 163; flour, 174, 175, 177, 229, 238; water, 177, 238; sorghum, 177; salt, 206, 209; *kaniki* cloth, 206; rice, 209; millet, 209; money, 209

Rock art, dates and location, 31; interpretations of, 31, 32–3; supernatural depicted in, 31–2

Rockshelters, 35

Rocks, as shrines, 126; *Bura* shrines, 128, 129

Rotberg, R. I. *Protest and Power in Black Africa*, 18

Rowley, H., and the Cholo shrine, 82; and Khulubvi drought, 83; and 1862 famine, 254

Roy, Fr, 262, 265–6; his attack on government, 265
Royal cults, 4–9; M'Bona, 5–8; Dzivaguru, 5, 6; Mwari, 5, 6, 7, 8, 9; Lozi, 7–8, 96, 100, 101, 103; mediums, 11; and chiefdoms, 76
Royalty, animals associated with, 38; and territorial spirits, 76; and invocation of High God, 76; worship at shrines directed to, 77; divine ancestry of Lozi, 96; eligibility for Lozi kingship, 101
Rozvi, Mwari cult and, 5, 6, 8, 9, 16, 76; soapstone birds, 35, 106
Rudiki, myth of, 61
Rundo, 82
Rwanda, myths of redemption through death, 7; regalia, 37; system of power in, 64–5
Ryangombe, cult of, 65

S

Sacrifice, in M'Bona cult, 5–6; human, 39; rain, 91; by reigning to dead Lozi king, 96–7; by new Lozi rulers, 97; in time of drought, 98; to ancestor spirits, 100; in Pare worship, 115, 118–19; to *Were*, 124; in Padhola religion, 125; to *Bura*, 128; Kinga, 153; in Lwembe cult, 157–8; Lucas links pagan with Christian, 229
Sadaka, 177, 178, 179
Sahara, rock art, 31, 32
Sakhonja, and murder of Lundu chief, 79
Saku, Kyunga princes of, 159, 160
Saliva, in Pare worship, 113
Salvation, cults of, 66
Sanctuaries, at Lolui island, 33; natural, 40; man-made, 40; 'universal', 119; to *Were*, 124; spirit-huts for *God of the Courtyard*, 124, 125, 126; of *Kuni*, 126; foreign, in West Budama, 131–2
Sanderson, Meredith, and *sadaka*, 178
Sangree, Walter, his work on the Tiriki, 13
Sangu, 160, 161
Santos Baptista, Abel dos, and Makua ancestor veneration, 177; and Makua chiefly installation ceremony, 178–9
Sao culture, figurines of, 34
Saussure, Ferdinand de, and semiology, 50; and linguistics, 57
Schebesta, P., and M'Bona cult, 80
Schildknecht, Fr Franz, and African religious belief, 173; on spread of Islam, 192
Schmidt, Fr W., on worship of God, 122
Schoffeleers, Matthew, and the M'Bona cult, 5–6, 7; and 'democratic' spirit possession, 13; possession cult in Lower Shire

Valley, 14; and *Nyau* societies and Christianity, 23; and shrines of Malawi, 42
Schools, establishment of mission, 85; plethora of ill-run, 86; *uxwala* and, 146; and start of Christian era in Rungwe, 168; at Makanjila's, 185; advantage of mission schooling, 230; U.M.C.A. and, 231; White Fathers', 256–7; Catholic mission, 261; effect of Nyau on mission schools, 262, 265, 268, 269
Scott, R., on *Jok*, 124
Secret society, *uxwala*, 146
Semboja, Chief, 186, 200 n. 67
Sena, 89; migrations, 73, 75, 252, 254; effect on Mang'anja society, 87; and Nyau, 268, 269
Senegal, circles of stones, 37
Serpents, depicted in rock art, 31–2, 33
Seruti, 127
Shambaa, 117
Shambwe, 145
Sharpe, Sir Alfred, on conversion of Yao to Islam, 188–9
Shona, spirit mediums, 13; origin of spirit possession cults, 13; power of chiefs, 35; rebellion, 252
Shorter, Aylward, 11, 12
Shrine-keepers, *Buru*, 129
Shrines, python shrine at Zimbwe, 9; destroyed, 37; Luzira, 37; antiquity of, 37; Ife figures, 38; Iron Age, 40; jaw-bone, 41; need for research into, 41–2; M'Bona, 73, 76, 77–89, 91; Pare, 114–15, 116–17, 118, 119; rain-making, 119; Padhola, 126; *Bura*, 128, 129, 133, 134; Greek, 128; Christian, 131, 133; PaliKyala, 159; Lwembe, 167; Yao, 174, 175–6; Makua, 177; rock of Bokero, 206, 207
Shrubs, ritual, 118
Sickness, in *kubwanda* cult, 65
Sivira, 113
Skulls, of ancestors, 115; of sacrificial animals, 129
Sky, linguistic evidence of identification of God with, 46; conus-shells associated with, 144
Slavery, slave raids, 75, 84, 85, 160, 254; cargoes head for the Zambezi, 84; Mataka chiefs and, 182, 184; anti-slave trade treaties, 183; slave trade, 187, 223; slavers and Islam, 188; the literate Makanjila slave boy, 188; U.M.C.A. colony of freed slaves, 224, 227; freed slaves as clergy, 231, 232; Chewa taken into, 254

INDEX OF THEMES

Index of Themes

Agriculture and African religion: (see also Cattle, drought, fertility, plagues, rain water) the agricultural revolution and support of religious specialists, 34; greater material complexity and awareness of the ancestors in agricultural societies, 40; common symbolic patterns among early agriculturalists, 7; agricultural rituals in African societies: ritual billhooks and lacustrine monarchs, 41; chiefs of the earth and chiefs of the herd in Rwanda, 64; the High God and the sowing of seeds in Barotseland, 98; rituals of planting among the Padhola, 125; offerings to Nyakyusa heroes at planting time, 155; the hero, Mwakinyasa, and the introduction of new crops, 159; the *Bokero* cult on the Rufiji river and the supplications of farmers, 206; Masasi farmers and agricultural rites, 226; agriculture and religion during the modern period: *waganga* uproot German cotton before Maji Maji, 214; Masasi Christians apply pressure for the blessing of fields, 231; the Mang'anja oppose enforced ridging through the idiom of the M'Bona cult, 88; the M'Bona medium speaks for agriculturalists against cattle owners, 89

Ancestors and Ancestral spirits: (*see also,* Burial, clans, Kingship, kinship) ancestor veneration a more accurate term than ancestor worship, 197; linguistic evidence of the antiquity of the idea of ancestral spirits, 46; ancestors more influential in agricultural communities, 40; the authority of the ancestors legitimises change in Uzaramo, 14; ancestor and other spirits and the religion of the microcosm, 15; ancestral spirits in African societies: malevolent ancestors in Rwanda and the creation of a fictive ancestry in the Ryangombe cult, 65; spirits of non-royal ancestors in Barotseland contrasted to those of royal, 97; ancestors not the source of moral code in Luvale, 98; ancestors as

mediators with God in Upare, 113; the extension of scale in veneration of ancestors in Upare, 114-6; Padhola beliefs on the after-life, 124-5; Padhola Christians make offerings to the dead, 133; Nyungu ya Mawe monopolises sacrifices to the ancestors after conquest of Ukimbu, 144; ancestor veneration in southern interior, 173; ancestor veneration, among the Yao, 174; extension of scale in Yao ancestor veneration, 175-6; Makua ancestor veneration, 177; Ngindo ancestor veneration, 181; Yao chiefs attempt to undercut ancestor rites by headmen, 186; Matumbi propitiation of the ancestors, 204, 208; Kinjikitile's extension of scale in ancestor veneration during Maji Maji, 209, 212; African pressures on church in Masasi for a developed liturgy of the dead, 231

Animals in African religion: (*see also* Cattle snakes) animals and the religion of hunting groups, 31, 32, 34; animals and initiation, 180, 235; animals as symbols of royal power, 36, 38, 39; animals and the prophetic shrine, 204, 205, 208; animals and secret societies—the *Nyau* re-enacts the myth of union of men and animals, 257, 258, 259; animals as possessing spirits in peripheral cults, 11

Anthropology: Anthropological interest in liminality and cults of affliction, 11; process anthropology, 11-12; historical confrontations with anthropology, 18, 21; acculturation anthropology, 22; collaboration with archaeology, 42; treatment of myth, 50-68; Luc de Heusch and the synthesis of anthropological and historical method, 64-6; collaboration with history, 66, 67; the work of Victor Turner, micro-history and history, 139-48; the work of Godfrey and Monica Wilson and interpretations of Nyakyusa heroic cults, 156-8

Archaeology: use and abuse in reconstructing African religious history, 4, 29-42;

299